# Table of Contents

# The Classic Hikes Sampler

## The Classic Hikes Sampler

| Classic Hike | Page number | Day-hike or overnight | Length | Sidetrips or variations? | Elevation Trailhead | Elevation High point |
|---|---|---|---|---|---|---|
| 1. Aylmer Pass/Aylmer Lookout | 18 | day-hike/overnight | up to 30.4 km return | Y | 1480 m | 2288 m |
| 2. C-Level Cirque | 21 | day-hike | 4.0 km | N | 1461 m | 1920 m |
| 3. Cascade Amphitheatre | 24 | day-hike | 7.7 km | N | 1701 m | 2195 m |
| 4. Cory Pass | 26 | day-hike | 13.6 km loop | Y | 1415 m | 2363 m |
| 5. Elk Pass | 29 | day-hike/overnight | up to 35.8 km loop | Y | 1701 m | 2055 m |
| 6. Sawback | 33 | overnight | 73.5 km | Y | 1701 m | 2365 m |
| 7. Mt. Assiniboine | 41 | overnight | 59.5 km | Y | 1690 m | 2395 m |
| 8. Simpson Pass/Healy Pass | 48 | day-hike/overnight | up to 21.2 km loop | Y | 1690 m | 2330 m |
| 9. Lakes and Larches | 52 | overnight | 40.8 km | Y | 1690 m | 2330 m |
| 10. Bourgeau Lake | 58 | day-hike | 7.4 km | Y | 1410 m | 2175 m |
| 11. Johnston Canyon and the Ink Pots | 60 | day-hike | 5.9 km | N | 1430 m | 1760 m |
| 12. Rockbound Lake | 63 | day-hike | 8.4 km | Y | 1450 m | 2210 m |
| 13. Boom Lake | 65 | day-hike | 5.1 km | N | 1723 m | 1894 m |
| 14. The Beehives and the Plain of the Six Glaciers | 67 | day-hike | 21.2 km loop | Y | 1735 m | 2270 m |
| 15. Saddleback Pass | 72 | day-hike | 14.9 km loop | Y | 1735 m | 2330 m |
| 16. Paradise Valley | 74 | day-hike/overnight | 19.3 km loop | Y | 1729 m | 2119 m |
| 17. Sentinel Pass | 77 | day-hike/overnight | 5.8 km up to 20.0 km loop | Y | 1888 m | 2611 m |
| 18. Wenkchemna Pass | 80 | day-hike | 9.7 km | Y | 1888 m | 2600m |
| 19. Skoki | 82 | day-hike/overnight | up to 36.9 km loop | Y | 1698 m | 2485 m |
| 20. Mosquito Creek | 89 | day-hike/overnight | up to 31.6 km return | Y | 1828 m | 2593 m |
| 21. Dolomite Pass | 93 | day-hike/overnight | 8.9 km | Y | 1944 m | 2500 m |
| 22. Bow Glacier Falls | 96 | day-hike | 5.0 km | N | 1940 m | 2103 m |
| 23. Chephren Lake/Cirque Lake | 99 | day-hike | up to 13.4 km return | Y | 1684 m | 1791 m |
| 24. Sarbach Lookout | 104 | day-hike | 5.3 km | N | 1520 m | 2043 m |
| 25. Glacier Lake | 107 | day-hike/overnight | 9.1 km or 18.6 km | Y | 1443 m | 1493 m |
| 26. Sunset Pass/Sunset Lookout | 110 | day-hike/overnight | 4.5 km to 19.6 km return | Y | 1438 m | 2165 m |
| 27. Saskatchewan Glacier | 113 | day-hike | 5.6 km | Y | 1599 m | 1768 m |
| 28. Parker Ridge | 118 | day-hike | 2.4 km | N | 1997 m | 2285 m |
| 29. Brazeau | 122 | day-hike/overnight | up to 80.0 km loop | Y | 1864 m | 2490 m |
| 30. Wilcox Pass | 129 | day-hike | 4.5 km to 12.0 km | Y | 2040 m | 2355 m |
| 31. Maligne Pass | 132 | day-hike/overnight | 15.2 km | Y | 1540 m | 2260 m |
| 32. Fryatt Valley | 137 | overnight | 23.2 km | N | 1215 m | 2035 m |

# Classic Hikes
## in the
# Canadian Rockies

by Graeme Pole
Altitude Publishing
Canadian Rockies/Vancouver

# Altitude Publishing Canada Ltd.

The Canadian Rockies/Vancouver
Head Office:
1500 Railway Avenue
Canmore, Alberta T1W 1P6
1-800-957-6888
**www.altitudepublishing.com**
First edition 1994
Second edition 2003 © Graeme Pole

## Canadian Cataloguing in Publication Data

Pole, Graeme, 1956-
Classic Hikes in the Canadian Rockies
(Superguide)
Includes index
ISBN 1-55153-709-5
ISBN 1-55153-710-9 (Binder edition)

1.Rocky Mountains, Canadian (B.C. and Alta.)--Guidebooks. 2. Hiking--Rocky Mountains, Canadian (B.C. and Alta.)--Guidebooks. I. Title. II. Series.
FC219.P64 1995  917.1104'4  C95-910842-4
F1090.P64 1995

## Altitude GreenTree Program

Altitude Publishing will plant twice as many trees as were used in the manufacturing of this product.

*Front cover: Lake O'Hara Alpine Circuit,*
*Yoho National Park*
*Frontispiece: Saskatchewan Glacier from Parker Ridge*
*Banff National Park*
*Back cover: Skyline hikers of the Canadian Rockies,*
*Paradise Valley, Banff National Park, 1933*

## Project Development

| | |
|---|---|
| Layout | Scott Manktelow |
| Maps | Scott Manktelow |
| | Virginia Boulay |
| Editor | Frances Purslow |

Made in Western Canada
Printed and bound in Canada by Friesen Printers

We acknowledge the financial support of the Government of Canada through the Book Publishing Industry Development Program (BPIDP) for our publishing activities.

## A Note from the Publisher

The world described in Altitude SuperGuides is a unique and fascinating place. It is a world filled with surprise and discovery, beauty and enjoyment, questions and answers. It is a world of people, cities, landscapes, animals and wilderness as seen through the eyes of those who live in, work with, and care for this world. The process of describing this world is also a means of defining ourselves.

It is also a world of relationship, where people derive their meaning from a deep and abiding contact with the land—as well as from each other. And it is this sense of relationship that guides all of us at Altitude to ensure that these places continue to survive and evolve in the decades ahead.

Altitude SuperGuides are books intended to be used, as much as read. Like the world they describe, Altitude SuperGuides are evolving, adapting and growing. Please write to us with your comments and observations, and we will do our best to incorporate your ideas into future editions of these books.

Stephen Hutchings
Publisher

*For Charlotte and for Natalie,*
*my favourite little hikers;*
*and for Marnie, who shares the trail.*

## The Classic Hikes Sampler

| Classic Hike | Page number | Day-hike or overnight | Length | Sidetrips or variations? | Elevation Trailhead | High point |
|---|---|---|---|---|---|---|
| 33. Tonquin Valley | 141 | 🚶/⛺ | 43.7 km | Y | 1738 m | 2210 m |
| 34. Cavell Meadows | 147 | 🚶 | 8.0 km loop | N | 1753 m | 2160 m |
| 35. Maligne Canyon | 150 | 🚶 | 3.7 km | N | 1015 m | 1145 m |
| 36. Opal Hills | 153 | 🚶 | 8.2 km loop | N | 1700 m | 2160 m |
| 37. Bald Hills | 156 | 🚶 | 5.2 km to 7.1 km | Y | 1697 m | 2170m, 2280m or 2320 m |
| 38. Skyline | 158 | 🚶/⛺ | 44.1 km | Y | 1690 m | 2530 m |
| 39. Sulphur Skyline | 164 | 🚶 | 4.6 km | N | 1372 m | 2060 m |
| 40. Berg Lake | 166 | 🚶/⛺ | 20.2 to 22.6 km | Y | 862 m | up to 2425 m |
| 41. Paget Lookout | 175 | 🚶 | 3.5 km | Y | 1616 m | 2134 m |
| 42. Sherbrooke Valley | 178 | 🚶 | 9.8 km | Y | 1616 m | 2317 m |
| 43. Lake O'Hara Alpine Circuit | 180 | 🚶 | 12.4 km loop | Y | 2015 m | 2538 m |
| 44. Lake McArthur | 185 | 🚶 | 6.3 km loop | Y | 2015 m | 2375 m |
| 45. Iceline | 189 | 🚶/⛺ | 21.1 km loop | Y | 1509 m | 2230 m |
| 46. Yoho/Little Yoho | 193 | 🚶/⛺ | 29.4 km loop | Y | 1509 m | up to 2454 m |
| 47. Wapta Highline | 198 | 🚶/⛺ | 19.9 km loop | Y | 1302 m | 2195 m |
| 48. Hamilton Lake | 201 | 🚶 | 5.3 km | N | 1302 m | 2149 m |
| 49. Mt. Hunter | 203 | 🚶 | 7.0 km return or 13.0 km return | Y | 1125 m | 1532 m or 1966 m |
| 50. Stanley Glacier | 207 | 🚶 | 4.2 km | N | 1593 m | 1921 m |
| 51. Kaufmann Lake | 209 | 🚶/⛺ | 15.1 km | N | 1479 m | 2057 m |
| 52. Rockwall | 211 | 🚶/⛺ | 55.0 km | Y | 1338 m | 2370 m |
| 53. Kindersley/Sinclair | 219 | 🚶 | 20.2 km return or 17.4 km loop | Y | 1335 m | 2393 m |
| 54. Burstall Pass | 223 | 🚶 | 7.6 km | Y | 1910 m | 2380 m |
| 55. Chester Lake | 227 | 🚶 | 4.0 km | Y | 1920 m | 2220 m |
| 56. Mt. Indefatigable | 229 | 🚶 | 2.5 km or 4.0 km | Y | 1722 m | 2222 m or 2484 m |
| 57. South Kananaskis Pass | 233 | 🚶/⛺ | 13.5 km | Y | 1722 m | 2285 m |
| 58. Ptarmigan Cirque | 238 | 🚶 | 4.4 km loop | Y | 2200 m | 2408 m |
| 59. Bertha Lake | 243 | 🚶/⛺ | 5.7 km | Y | 1295 m | 1767 m |
| 60. Carthew/Alderson | 246 | 🚶/⛺ | 19.9 km | Y | 1661 m | 2311 m |
| 61. Crypt Lake | 250 | 🚶 | 8.7 km | Y | 1279 m | 1945 m |
| 62. Tamarack | 254 | 🚶/⛺ | 36.1 km | Y | 1600 m | 2560 m |
| 63. Forum Lake/Wall Lake | 262 | 🚶/⛺ | 8.8 km return to 20.4 km return | Y | 1670 m | 2220 m |

🚶 Day-hike          ⛺ Overnight

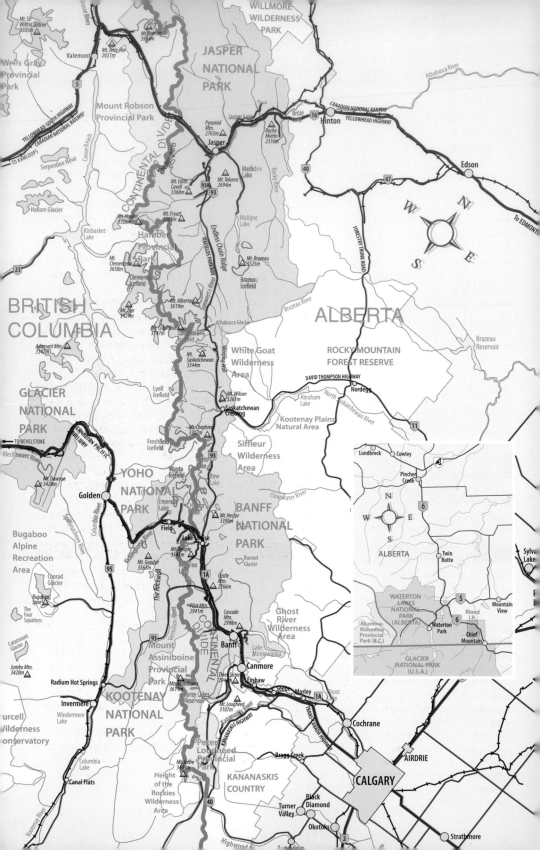

# Introduction

## Acknowledgements

Many people assisted me in identifying the decade's worth of changes that have affected these trails.

Don Gorrie, Backcountry Facilities Manager, reviewed text for Banff National Park. Kim Baines, Backcountry Facilities Manager, and Jenny Klafki, Warden Service Communication Specialist, reviewed text for Yoho, Kootenay, and northern Banff national parks. The Jasper material was vetted, in part or in whole, by a host of willing reviewers: Gord Antoniuk, Karen Beyers, Shawn Cardiff, Kim Forster, Ben Gadd, Cia Gadd, Greg Horne, Wayne Kennedy, Loni Klettle, Wendy Niven, Jim Suttill, Bert Wade, Vicki Wallace, and Kim Weir. Park wardens Edwin Knox and Bill Thorpe reviewed text for Waterton Lakes National Park. Wayne Van Velzen commented on the Mt. Robson text. Kim Winter, Senior Park Ranger, and Edwin Knox reviewed the Forum Lake/Wall Lake hike. Duane Fizor fielded questions and reviewed the hikes in Peter Lougheed Provincial Park. Joel Christensen clarified some details concerning the Mt. Indefatigable trail.

When I couldn't find the answer in his *Handbook of the Canadian Rockies*, Ben Gadd fielded queries and proofed passages on geology. Text describing emergency preparedness and first-aid was reviewed by Dr. Jeff Boyd, Medical Director, Emergency Department, Mineral Springs Hospital, and by Tim Auger, Public Safety Supervisor for Banff National Park. Dr. Desmond Collins, Curator in Charge of Invertebrate Paleontology at the Royal Ontario Museum, reviewed the text on the Burgess Shale. George Mercer, Wildlife Biologist with Jasper National Park, reviewed material on the mountain caribou. Andy MacKinnon reviewed portions of the text that describe vegetation. Jim Pojar added comments. Ian Pengelly, Vegetation Specialist, reviewed relevant text for Banff National Park. Park wardens, Derek Petersen, Alan Dibb, Terry Damm, and John Niddrie fielded questions for Kootenay and Yoho. Diane and Mike McIvor brought decades of experience as naturalists to bear on a few passages of text. Donna Nelson helped with maps. David Richard Boyd provided an expert opinion on environmental legislation in Canada. Professor Dave Cruden, Department of Civil Engineering, University of Alberta, ferreted out a paper that describes the Palliser Slide, and proofed my subsequent attempt to paraphrase it. Dr. David Schindler, Killiam Memorial Professor of Ecology, Department of Biological Sciences at the University of Alberta, explained the process behind atmospheric pollution of glacial lakes. Scott Manktelow was helpful

## Notice of Assumption of Risk

**Hiking, backpacking,** backcountry travel, and backcountry camping may expose you to dangers. These include, but are not limited to: getting lost; encountering black bears and grizzly bears, aggressive wildlife, insect bites and diseases, rough trails, unbridged streams, slippery footing, suspension bridges, hunters, inclement weather, lightning, forest fires, falling trees, contaminated drinking water, avalanches, late-lying snow, rockfalls, mudslides, and flash-floods. Perhaps the greatest danger of all is highway travel on your way to and from trailheads. Summer traffic in the Canadian Rockies is often heavy and chaotic. Drive with caution.

The author has hiked every trail in this book at least once, and has endeavoured to render trail descriptions with accuracy and with safety in mind. However, conditions in the backcountry are not static. Bridges and trail signs may or may not be present as described in the text, and the locations of stream crossings, avalanche deposits, snow patches, and ice-cored moraines may change from year to year.

*Classic Hikes* contains ample information to assist you in preparing for safe backcountry travel. However, you are responsible for your well-being in the backcountry of the Rockies. Neither the author nor the publisher can be held responsible for any difficulties, injuries, disabilities, misfortune, or loss of property or income that arises from using the information presented.

In this book, the term *backpacking* means to hike and to camp self-sufficiently in the backcountry. It does not imply that any of the services associated with low-budget travel (also called backpacking in Europe and Australasia) will be present.

during the production. Peggy and Phil Muir provided space where I could sort slides and work on maps without my research assistants covering the proceedings with Lego.

With all this expert help, I should have everything right. The embarrassments that remain are mine alone. Please send corrections in care of the publisher, or visit mountainvision.ca and send me an e-mail.

The maps in this book are based on digital copies of the National Topographic System, and are used with the permission of the digital copyright holder, Spectrum Digital Imaging, which holds a licence from Natural Resources Canada.

Permission to quote from *The American Geographies*, by Barry Holstun Lopez, was granted by his literary agent, Sterling Lord Literistic Inc.

I was blessed with the generosity and the company of friends who opened their homes during the fieldwork for this edition: Cia and Ben Gadd, Diane and Mike McIvor, Nadine Delorme and Mike Henderson, Ann and John Henderson, Alice Wagenaar and Edwin Knox, Nadine Fletcher and Joel Hagan, Jill and Basil Seaton, and Alex Taylor.

Most of all, I thank Marnie, Charlotte, and Natalie for their help and for accommodating my absence when the harvest was on.

## Preface to the First Edition

Authors of guidebooks take a great risk, and have a tremendous obligation. Guidebooks to natural areas include landscapes that are unique or special. The risk lies in advertising these landscapes to a broader public, so that destinations subsequently become overrun and tarnished. Bears, wolves, wolverines and caribou require places where there are no people. Although it is an unintended effect, the unrestrained enthusiasm of a guidebook author can contribute to the many pressures confronting natural areas and species, and accelerate their declines.

Thus, *Classic Hikes* does not include descriptions of unbeaten paths leading to backcountry secrets. You will only find 1070 km of trails that comprise the established hikes and backpacking trips for which the Canadian Rockies are renowned.

Some of the hikes have quotas that limit the number of overnight users allowed on the trail at any given time. Quotas and other management tools should ensure these hikes do not become spoiled. However, the onus is on you, the hiker, to

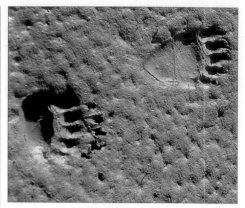

*Grizzly bear tracks*

travel and camp responsibly, and thereby guarantee that the special qualities of these trails, and the species that dwell in the areas they traverse, are not lost.

The information provided in this work reflects more than a decade of experience, observation and research, involving more than 11,000 km of travel in the backcountry of the Canadian Rockies. It is the author's sincere hope that many decades hence, these mountains will continue to be a haven for resident species, and offer visitors as vital a wilderness touchstone as they do today.

## Preface to the Second Edition

For the fabric of any guidebook to survive to a second edition, three elusive threads must be part of the weave: the publisher must remain committed to the project, the readership must remain interested, and the author must once again be willing to attempt to describe a moving target. Economies change, readers come and go, and trails are subject to natural processes of change and — to a much greater extent — to unnatural bureaucratic ones. Fortunately, two of the threads necessary to this project have never threatened to unravel — the Canadian Rockies endure as a place of inspiration, and publisher Stephen Hutchings has remained committed to *Classic Hikes*, making incremental corrections with each printing. This new edition culminates that commitment to provide readers with the most complete information on the best hikes in the Canadian Rockies.

As for my contribution, this project continues to be a pleasure. I have completely re-written the text, and added new hikes and new photographs. Those familiar with the first edition can rest assured that the benchmark for what qualifies as a "Classic Hike" has not been lowered. The addition of fourteen hikes simply reflects the extra time available for fieldwork for this edition, my broader acquaintance with the Canadian Rockies, and the publisher's desire to expand the scope of this work.

A major part of the rewriting is the text on bear safety. I urge you to read this material. Your safety and — at least in part — the future of bears in the Rockies depends on it.

To avoid including information that is perpetually in a state of change, I have deleted some specifics from the text. Instead, for such things as fees, quotas, and permits, I recommend that you consult a park information centre at the time of your visit. For readers so inclined, Internet links are included to Web sites that will enrich appreciation of the Canadian Rockies.

The wilderness touchstone described in the first edition endures, but the pressures that would tarnish it mount unabated. Perhaps as a reflection of the accelerated pace of life, use of the deep backcountry has decreased in the past decade, while most of the day-hikes are far busier — some are overrun. In the frontcountry, in townsites, and just outside the park boundaries, development has proliferated. As backcountry hikers and campers we can win small victories for the land by treating it with reverence and with respect.

## Wild Places, Wild Hearts

*If a society forgets or no longer cares where it lives, then anyone with the political power and the will to do so can manipulate the landscape to conform to certain social ideals or nostalgic visions. People may hardly notice that anything has happened, or assume that whatever happens – a mountain stripped of its timber and eroding into its creeks – is for the common good. The more superficial a society's knowledge of the real dimensions of the land it occupies becomes, the more vulnerable the land is to exploitation, to manipulation for short-term gain. The land, virtually powerless before political and commercial entities, finds itself finally with no defenders. It finds itself bereft of intimates with indispensable, concrete knowledge.*

Barry Lopez, *The American Geographies*
(Copyright 1989 by Barry Holstun Lopez. Reprinted with the permission of Sterling Lord Literistic Inc.)

Personal experiences of wilderness are as diverse as the places we call wild. Hikers whose boots have trundled enough trails describe a fascination — wilderness is restorative; wilderness is a challenge; wilderness is an echo, a reminder, a tugging that embodies celebration and lament.

What we connect with in wilderness is a story that is greater in scope and time than our own. When we hike a backcountry trail in the Canadian Rockies, we walk through an essentially unaltered place and can see the handiwork of glaciers long departed, can feel the presence of predatory animals that invokes a time when humankind did not dominate the earth. We may be humbled — caught unprepared on a high ridge in a snowstorm – or we may bask away a blissful afternoon beside a tumbling stream with not a care except when to get up and pitch the tent. We may see a glacier lily poking through an ice-encrusted snowpatch and marvel at the cycle of life that repeats in environments benevolent and harsh. These things, and many others, are gifts – gifts of the land, of the day, of the moment.

Somewhere between a season and a lifetime of hiking, those gifts amass into a knowledge. That knowledge brings with it a familiarity and necessitates a caring. Some people share their knowledge with words or through other artistic expression; others simply hold it within. But if you study these silent ones closely you cannot miss it. Passionate caring shines from their eyes – mountain blues, whites, grays, browns, and greens.

Whether that knowledge is held or imparted, it is, as Barry Lopez describes, indispensable to the continuation of wild places. If you have a favourite Classic Hike or two, you may want to keep a journal or scrapbook. Record your experiences, photographs, wildlife sightings, the array of wildflowers; your impressions of how the trail and the landscape it traverses change from visit to visit, from season to season, from year to year. You might want to make your own map of the trail, cataloguing places of personal interest – a waterfall, a patch of orchids, an osprey nest, an aspen trunk scarred by bear claws. These observations and activities will move you closer to association with the land. You will never own the place but, eventually, you will earn the right to speak for it. The land will have become part of your story and you, in a small way, will have become part of its story. And that simple exchange, it appears, if repeated often enough by caring people in many places around the world, is the only way by which the greater, wilder story of life on earth will continue to be told.

## Hiking in the Rockies

Be prepared and self-reliant when hiking in the Rockies, as help is seldom close at hand. Even experienced hikers encounter difficult situations from time to time. In the Rockies, these might include a bear encounter, a squirrel or jay eating your food, a lost backpack, a fall into a river, a fall on a patch of late-lying snow, a mid-summer blizzard, and

*Be prepared for the unexpected.*

injury or illness. In addition, you might create hazards by attempting an outing that is beyond your ability or by venturing off-trail into hazardous terrain.

The principal wildlife hazards are bears, elk, moose, and wood ticks. You will find a thorough discussion of bear safety on p. 277-81. Avoid elk and moose during the autumn rut and in spring when calves are born. Keep at least 50 m away from any large mammal, especially if it is with young. Check yourself for tick bites after hiking in May and June, as wood tick bites can cause complications. Wolves may take a curious look at you or your camp but, at press time, they had not attacked people. However, please note that wolves in the Rockies are becoming less wary. Coyotes and cougars have attacked people, so be especially cautious of these animals if you encounter them when you are hiking with children. If any large mammal other than a bear approaches, group together and scare it off by making loud noises and by waving your arms over your head.

### Gridlock and Rush Hours

**Solitude is hard** to find on some of the day-hikes. The peak hours are between 10 am and 3 pm, with fair weather days being the busiest. Parking lots at Moraine Lake, Lake Louise, and Mt. Edith Cavell are jammed during these times, so avoid nearby trails — Classic Hikes #14 – 18, and #34. The other trails that experience a mid-day crush are Johnston Canyon, Bow Glacier Falls, Parker Ridge, Wilcox Pass, Maligne Canyon, Bald Hills, Mt. Indefatigable, Chester Lake, and Ptarmigan Cirque.

Porcupines, red squirrels, ground squirrels, chipmunks, marmots, martens, wolverines, jays, and ravens can raid your food supply and damage unattended equipment around camp. There are no poisonous spiders, venomous snakes, or scorpions in the Rockies, but bees, wasps, and hornets are present.

In an emergency, preparedness will be your best ally. In general, your first option in the face of

### Park Regulations

**The list below covers** most park regulations pertinent to backcountry users.

- Vehicles stopping in national parks must pay the appropriate fee at a park gate or information centre. Call 800-748-7275 for details.
- Firearms are not permitted, unless securely locked or dismantled.
- Hunting and trapping of wildlife (other than certain fish species) is not permitted.
- Anglers must obtain a national park fishing permit or a provincial fishing licence, and be aware of restrictions and catch limits for the waterbodies they intend to fish.
- It is illegal to disturb, remove, or deface any natural, cultural, or historic object or artifact.
- It is illegal to approach, feed, entice, or harass wildlife.
- It is illegal to enter a closed area.
- Fees apply to overnight backcountry use.
- Mountain biking is permitted only on certain trails. Check at a park information centre.
- There are restrictions on taking dogs into the backcountry in most parks. Check at a park information centre.

backcountry calamity should be to consider retreat. If you must spend another night out, pitch camp quickly in order to stay warm and dry. Don't worry about using a designated campground in a true emergency; no one will ticket you. Carry reliable, lightweight equipment. Ensure that each person in the party knows how to operate the stove, and is aware of the hiking route, potential escape routes, and the locations of campgrounds and park warden cabins. Although there is no guarantee of finding help at these locations, they are the best initial destinations in an emergency

## Minimum Impact Travel

**When backpacking became popular** in the 1970s, "no-trace" camping and hiking was the buzz. The idealism was short-lived, butting against the harsh edge of human reality. It is not possible to move without leaving a trace in the landscape, but it is possible to minimize impacts. The "how-to" is easily listed; putting the list into practice is a challenge. Read the following before each hike. At trail's end, review these items to see if you can make improvements on your next outing.
• Inform yourself about where you are going and what to expect. Plan ahead, prepare, and equip yourself appropriately.
• Keep to maintained trails.
• Concentrate your impacts in high-use areas.
• Spread your impacts in pristine areas.
• Avoid places where human impacts are beginning to show, and places recovering from impacts.
• Walk through snow, muck, and puddles to stay on the trail.
• Keep off sections of trail that are closed for rehabilitation.
• Keep to the trail on switchbacks.
• Pack out all your trash, and pick up any left by others. Make the effort to recycle what you can.
• Cigarette butts and spent matches are litter, too. Pack them out.
• Protect watercourses. Be responsible with human waste. Use the facilities provided. If none is available, do your business properly — 100 m away from streams, lakes, and ponds.
• Use a campstove for cooking.
• Use fires responsibly, only where permitted, and only when necessary. Gather firewood carefully.
• Do not remove or disturb natural objects.
• Respect wildlife. Do not feed them. Keep at least 50 m away from large mammals, especially when they are with young. Leave your dog at home.

when you are more than a day's hike from the trailhead.

### First-Aid
Each member of your party should carry a first-aid kit and be knowledgeable about treatment for shock, management of fractures and sprains using improvised splints, and hemorrhage control. See p. 274 for a more detailed discussion.

### Leaving Word
Whether you are going on a day-hike or a multi-day backpacking trip, write down your itinerary and leave it with a responsible person. Specify the number in your party, your route, where you intend to camp, and when you will be completing your trip. Describe your vehicle, its licence plate number, and where it will be parked. Tell your contact person when to report you overdue, and where to make the report.

If you are a visitor to the Rockies, you may use the voluntary registration system to ensure that someone will be looking for you if you are overdue. Contact a park information centre or a warden office for details.

Whichever of these two safety plans you choose, always carry an extra night's rations with you in the event that your trip takes longer than planned. Even on a day-hike close to the highway, you should be equipped for extremes of weather and for the possibility of having to stay out overnight. You don't have to carry sleeping gear on day-hikes. However, warm clothing, rain gear, extra food, a space blanket, and any essential daily medications should be in your pack.

## Hiking Etiquette

**While travelling** in the backcountry, it's important to recognize the intangible spiritual value of the Canadian Rockies, and to act in a manner that does not tarnish the experience or the safety of others.
• Respect other visitors' requirements for solitude. Hike and camp in small groups. Do not use cell-phones or portable music devices.
• Share the facilities provided.
• Those hiking downhill have the right of way. Yield to them.
• Step to the downhill side of the trail to allow horse parties to pass. Do not speak or make any movement that might startle the horses.
• Fish odours attract bears. Do not fish on overnight trips. Anglers should dispose of fish viscera properly.

### The Wilderness Pass

You require a "wilderness pass" for overnight trips in national parks. You may purchase a wilderness pass for an individual outing, or a season pass for a twelve-month period. If you will be camping seven nights or more in the coming year, purchase the season pass. If you are not sure how much camping you will be doing, save your permits. If you tally seven nights, turn the permits in at an information centre and you will be issued a season pass at no charge. You must still obtain a camping permit for each outing even if you have purchased the season pass. Refunds are not given for bad weather. Parks Canada has not yet instituted a fee for day-hikes, but has considered it.

Purchase your wilderness pass immediately prior to your hike, at a park information centre in the park where your hike is located. Groups of more than six persons are discouraged. Larger groups require the permission of the park superintendent.

Camping in the other parks is also subject to fees. You may reserve campsites on the South Kananaskis Pass trail by phoning the Peter Lougheed Provincial Park information centre, 403-591-6322. Pick up and pay for your permit on the way to the trailhead. For Berg Lake, purchase your trail permit at the visitor centre at Mt. Robson Junction on Highway 16. A portion of the trail quota can be reserved in advance. Phone 250-566-4325 or 800-689-9025 for details. To reserve space and find out about fees at Og Lake and Lake Magog campgrounds, and at Naiset Cabins, phone Mt. Assiniboine Lodge, 403-678-2883. A fee applies to camping in Akamina-Kishenina Provincial Park. Phone BC Parks at 250-422-4200 for details; phone 800-689-9025 to make a reservation. Place your fee in the drop box at the Forum Lake junction.

### Quotas

All backcountry campgrounds have quotas. When the quota is filled, wilderness passes and camping permits will not be issued.

In national parks, a portion of backcountry campground quotas can be reserved up to three months in advance. A portion of the quota is also set aside for issue on the day of use, so early risers can *usually* get onto their desired trail on the desired day. However, be flexible when scheduling a hike on a popular trail — particularly Berg Lake, Skyline, Tonquin Valley, Brazeau, and those in Yoho.

## Rained Out?

**There are real summers,** and then there are those that masquerade. If you find yourself in the Rockies during a not-so summer, or otherwise beset by a stretch of inclement weather, here are some diversions to having squeegee feet.

- **Public libraries:** Banff, Canmore, Jasper, Hinton, Golden
- **Museums and archives:** Banff (2), Canmore, Jasper, Golden, Waterton
- **Indoor swimming:** The Banff Centre, Canmore, Jasper, Golden, Waterton
- **Hot springs:** Banff, Radium, Miette
- **Park information centres:** Banff, Lake Louise, Field, Columbia Icefield, Jasper, Waterton.
- The Altitude SuperGuide, *Walks and Easy Hikes in the Canadian Rockies* is packed with shorter outings, ideal for capitalizing on breaks during spells of fickle weather.

## Setting Out, Gearing Down

We live in such a hurried society that it takes a conscious effort to leave behind the trappings of home and work — the scheduled world — when we step onto a trail. If you are hiking with children or with a group of adults, the logistics of getting to a trailhead and setting out can make the morning of departure even busier. Allow some time for a transition. Walk down the trail until the sound of the highway, railway, or nearby town fades. Take off your pack and pull up a rock or a stump. Sit down. Do nothing. De-focus. Listen. Let go. When your head has cleared, pick up your pack and carry on.

## Observe, Record, Report

If you see someone committing what you consider to be an illegal act in the backcountry — poaching, illegal fishing, arson, theft, or destruction of natural objects — you can gather information and make a report to the appropriate authority. In no case should you put yourself or members of your party in danger. Do not confront the perpetrators yourself. Observe the act, then write down details — descriptions of those involved, the time, the location, the vehicle description and licence plate number, and any conversation overheard. Make a report at the end of your hike. In the national parks, call 800-WARDENS. In K-Country, call 800-642-3800. In BC, call the 800-663-WILD.

*Strive to leave a minimal trace of your stay.*

Backcountry use has not increased during the last decade, but some day-hikes are overrun. Parks Canada may close some trails and campgrounds permanently or seasonally to protect wildlife such as grizzly bears, wolves, and caribou. Other trails will be closed during snowmelt to protect vegetation and to reduce trail damage.

I have endeavoured to exclude trails that may be subject to outright closure. However, please abide by any new regulations that supersede the information here.

## Climate

Hiking trails in the Rockies are generally clear of snow from late May to early October at low elevations, and from mid-June to mid-September higher up. At treeline, the average annual temperature is -4°C, and more than 75 percent of the annual precipitation falls as snow. In the high country you will frequently encounter snow, whether freshly fallen or lingering from last winter. After a few outings you may agree with some locals, who describe the climate of the Rockies as "nine months of winter, and three months of poor skiing." There is a pattern to summer snowstorms. Significant snowfalls often occur in the middle of July, in the first week of

## Average Daytime Temperature in °C

| Station | May High | May Low | June High | June Low | July High | July Low | August High | August Low | September High | September Low | October High | October Low |
|---|---|---|---|---|---|---|---|---|---|---|---|---|
| Banff | 14.2 | 1.5 | 18.7 | 5.4 | 22.1 | 7.4 | 21.6 | 6.8 | 16.1 | 2.7 | 10.1 | -1.1 |
| Lake Louise | 12.8 | -1.7 | 17.2 | 2.1 | 20.4 | 3.6 | 20.1 | 3.1 | 14.3 | -0.8 | 7.9 | -5.3 |
| Columbia Icefield | 9.1 | -3.5 | 12.1 | 0.2 | 15.2 | 2.9 | 14.3 | 2.7 | 10.3 | -0.5 | 3.5 | -5.9 |
| Jasper | 15.6 | 1.7 | 19.2 | 5.6 | 22.5 | 7.6 | 21.4 | 7.0 | 16.4 | 3.2 | 10.3 | -1.0 |
| Yoho | 14.8 | 1.7 | 19.0 | 5.3 | 21.8 | 7.3 | 21.3 | 6.8 | 15.9 | 2.6 | 8.2 | -1.8 |
| Kootenay Crossing | 16.4 | 0.2 | 19.6 | 3.5 | 23.1 | 5.3 | 22.8 | 4.2 | 17.1 | 0.1 | 9.0 | -3.9 |
| Waterton | 15.0 | 2.0 | 19.0 | 6.0 | 23.0 | 7.0 | 22.0 | 7.0 | 17.0 | 3.0 | 12.0 | 0.0 |

## Average Precipitation: Rain in mm; Snow in cm

| Station | May Rain | May Snow | June Rain | June Snow | July Rain | July Snow | August Rain | August Snow | September Rain | September Snow | October Rain | October Snow |
|---|---|---|---|---|---|---|---|---|---|---|---|---|
| Banff | 42.4 | 17.1 | 58.4 | 1.7 | 51.1 | 0 | 51.2 | 0 | 37.7 | 7.0 | 15.4 | 18.9 |
| Lake Louise | 34.4 | 7.4 | 54.5 | 0.1 | 61.2 | 0 | 54.0 | 0 | 41.1 | 3.4 | 13.6 | 24.4 |
| Columbia Icefield | 7.1 | 35.0 | 58.5 | 10.0 | 49.9 | 1.4 | 55.4 | 2.1 | 39.5 | 13.8 | 17.8 | 64.1 |
| Jasper | 30.3 | 3.1 | 54.8 | tr. | 49.7 | 0 | 48.4 | 0.1 | 36.8 | 1.1 | 24.2 | 5.4 |
| Yoho | 55.3 | 1.4 | 69.4 | 0.1 | 81.2 | 0 | 66.6 | 0 | 45.2 | 1.5 | 27.2 | 11.5 |
| Kootenay Crossing | 55.2 | 1.7 | 65.8 | 0.2 | 55.6 | 0 | 54.6 | 0 | 40.9 | 1.0 | 26.2 | 6.5 |
| Waterton * | 70.0 | | 116.0 | | 44.0 | | 61.0 | | 64.0 | | 51.0 | |

* Precipitation for Waterton is combined rain and snow, in mm.

August, in the third week of August, and in the first week of September.

The prevailing weather systems arrive from the southwest. The trend is for more precipitation on the western side of the continental divide — Yoho, northern Kootenay, and Mt. Robson. In May and June, "upslope" storms, which arrive from the east, can plague Banff and Jasper. During these times, the weather may improve if you travel west to Yoho, Kootenay or Mt. Robson. On days when the weather is mixed, marked changes often occur a short distance away. For example, if it is raining at Lake Louise, it might be partly cloudy with the odd shower north of Bow Summit, or in Yoho or Kootenay. Alternatively, it could be worse.

One of the more enjoyable times for backpacking in the Rockies is between mid-September and late October. The fair weather spells during this time are characterized by cool nights, sunny days, colourful larch trees, and an absence of bugs.

*To reduce trail braiding, stay in the muck.*

## The Hike Descriptions

The introductory information summarizes the hike by:
• identifying the outing as a day-hike or as an overnight trip;
• giving the best time of day (when relevant) for viewing the destination;
• giving landmarks along the route and providing distances;
• indicating relevant maps;
• describing possible variations;
• indicating any quotas or access restrictions.

Some of the shorter overnight hikes can be completed in a day by fit hikers. Some of the longer day-hikes can be turned into overnight hikes by using campgrounds along the route.

Distances are given between the trailhead and landmarks — passes, lakes, bridges, trail junctions, and campgrounds (CG). The elevations of these landmarks are shown. By comparing elevations, you can estimate the elevation gain or loss for different sections of the hike. When a parking lot is not immediately adjacent to a trailhead, I have included the intervening distance to more accurately represent the total for the outing. On some of the longer backpacking trips, you can use campgrounds that are a short distance from the described route, on adjoining trails. These campgrounds appear in the route information summary with a "+" in the distance column. Add that distance to and from the main trail if you camp

### Sidetrips

**The day-hiker** symbol indicates convenient sidetrips that you can make from the route of overnight trips. The distance of a sidetrip is not included in the overall distance of the outing.

### Variations

**Variations include** day-hiking the first leg or the last leg of a longer outing, hiking a longer outing in reverse, using a backcountry campground as a basecamp to explore adjacent trails, linking trails, and alternate beginnings and endings for longer outings.

### Novice Backpacks

**These campgrounds** are a short distance from their respective trailheads, and are recommended to novice backpackers. You can camp at any of these, and day-hike beyond with lighter packs.

• Aylmer Pass Junction (#1)
• Healy Creek (#8, #9)
• Paradise Valley (#16)
• Hidden Lake (#19)
• Mosquito Creek (#20)
• Norman Lake (#26)
• Evelyn Creek (#38)
• Kinney Lake (#40)
• Yoho Lake (#45, #46, #47)
• Laughing Falls (#46)
• Twin Falls (#46)
• Forks (#57)
• Akamina Creek (#63)

*August 15th in the Dolomite Creek valley*

there. I use the same method for indicating the distances to sidetrail destinations on day-hikes. Some of the longer overnight trips incorporate sections of different trails. The important junctions are noted. If, while on one of these outings, the weather deteriorates or you are beset by an emergency, you can curtail your trip by exiting from one of the junctions.

In the descriptions, "trail" refers to designated and maintained trails. You will find that maintenance standards vary between parks, and between heavily used and remote areas within each park. "Path" and "track" refer to unmaintained routes where travel will likely be slower and more difficult. "Rooted" means that a trail contains many tree roots. All river, creek, and stream crossings should be bridged unless stated.

Read the entire text for a hike before you decide if it is appropriate for your ability and fitness level, the trail conditions, and the time of year. Before each hike, consult a park information centre for current conditions, warnings, restrictions, and closure information. You can obtain a weather forecast, purchase maps, and participate in the voluntary safety registration program. You will also be able to purchase your camping permit and vehicle permit, and pay any other necessary park use fees.

### Distances and Times

All measurements in the text are metric. Read the route information summary to find out the length of a particular hike or variation. A minimum and a maximum number of days are suggested for each overnight trip. The minimum infers that no sidetrips are undertaken and that you spend longer days backpacking. The maximum infers that all the sidetrips are completed, and that you

spend shorter days backpacking. The distance for an overnight trip does not include any sidetrips. Refer to the description of each sidetrip to find out its length. Once you have determined your plans, adjust your estimated time and the food and fuel that you carry.

Most trailheads and junctions have signs. Those without are referred to as "unsigned." The trail distances given in the text are usually those provided by the parks. These have been checked against the Gem Trek maps, on which trails were plotted from global positioning system (GPS) waypoints. If you find that a distance given is at variance with a sign or a map, it is because field-checking revealed an error that has been corrected. Trail sign vandalism is a problem in all parks. Please report damaged or missing signs.

Hiking times are not given, because they are dependent on your experience, pace, ability, and the conditions of the day. As a rule, if you are accustomed to backpacking in mountains you will average 2.5 km/h, including all manner of stops during the day. Novices will average 1.5 km/h. Those of intermediate ability will cover somewhere between these two figures. On day-hikes, strong hikers with light packs can cover 4 to 5 km/h. However, most people average 2.5 to 3.5 km/h.

Take note of trails that are shared with horses and mountain bikers. Some trails have horse barriers, designed to keep horses from sections of trail intended only for use by hikers.

### Maps

The maps in this book will get you to the trailhead and to your destination and back, but most of us are curious about the surrounding landscape. Although the 1:50,000 map sheets of the National Topographic Survey (NTS) do a good job with landscape features, they show most trails in the Canadian Rockies inaccurately or incompletely. The best maps for hikers are by Gem Trek. Trail positions and campgrounds on the Gem Trek maps have been accurately plotted from GPS coordinates. Some of the maps are available on waterproof paper. All but six of the Classic Hikes are covered by a selection of nine Gem Trek maps. A Waterton map was in the works at press time.

Yoho National Park is covered on a single sheet at 1:50,000, published by Natural Resources Canada, and available at the Friends of Yoho store at the Field information centre. Chrismar Mapping markets two products under the brand name, The Adventure Map — Lake O'Hara,

1:20,000; and The Rockwall, 1:50,000. Although the following maps are out of print, you might still be able to find them: Environment Canada, Waterton Lakes National Park, 1:50,000; Environment Canada, Banff National Park, 1:200,000; Environment Canada, Jasper National Park, 1:200,000; Inland Waters Directorate, Columbia Icefield, 1:50,000; BC Ministry of Environment, Lands and Parks, Mount Robson Park, 1:125,000.

When you see the name of a landscape feature in quotation marks, it means that the name is unofficial.

## Hiking Map Elevation

**Altitude is indicated** on all hiking maps by the following colour guide:

| | |
|---|---|
| | Greater than 2600m |
| | 2200m – 2600m |
| | 1800m – 2200m |
| | 1400m – 1800m |
| | Less than 1400m |

## Weather Lore

**Signs of Storm:**
- The *rapid* movement of high cirrus clouds (mare's tails) across an otherwise clear sky
- A lunar halo, especially in late summer and autumn
- Clouds massing on the windward sides of mountains
- Small, puffy clouds developing on the leeward side of summits

*Some skies are easy to "read;" others are more subtle.*

- A "roll cloud" that plumes from the windward side of a peak, over the summit and partway down the leeward side
- Two layers of cloud that develop during the day
- A "buttermilk sky" (alto-cumulus perlucidus) that develops after a period of good weather (You will often see a buttermilk sky at dawn. Even if the sky clears, look for thunder by the afternoon.)
- Masses of "listless" alto-cumulus clouds in the early morning (These are probably the remains of yesterday's thunderstorms in the BC interior. The air is unstable.)
- Limestone cliffs appear detailed and darkly-streaked when viewed from a distance.
- A chill east or northeast wind in the front ranges foretells an "upslope" storm. Expect snow.
- A rapid clearing during a storm is often false.
- A "veering wind" — one that shifts from north or west quadrants to south or east quadrants
- If the surface wind is blowing from southerly quadrants at a right-angle to the upper wind (the direction of cloud movement), a low pressure system is on the way.

**Signs of Improvement:**
- A "buttermilk sky" (alto-cumulus perlucidus) that develops after a period of poor weather
- If a valley bottom fog appears dark where it meets the mountainsides, it is sunny above. The fog is an inversion cloud that will burn off.
- Banner clouds that plume from summits and that gradually dissipate during the day
- If the day's weather has been improving gradually, take note of the sky about 5 pm. If there is only one layer of cloud and it doesn't appear threatening, then the clearing will continue overnight.
- A lingering, vividly-coloured twilight foretells good weather next day.
- A gradual clearing indicates the arrival of a high-pressure system.
- A "backing wind" — one that moves from east or south quadrants to west or north quadrants
- If the surface wind is blowing from northerly quadrants at a right-angle to the upper wind (the direction of cloud movement), the low pressure system has passed.

# Banff National Park

*The view from Pulsatilla Pass at the apex of the Sawback trail*

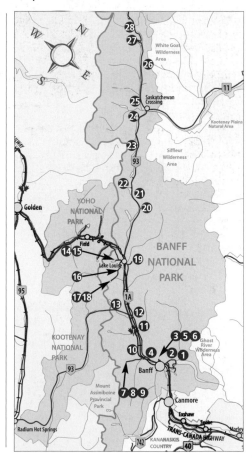

Established in 1885, Banff is Canada's oldest national park. Today it includes 6641 km² of the front ranges and eastern main ranges. The park has approximately 1500 km of maintained hiking trails. Some are among the more heavily used trails in the country. Others are remote outings completed by only a few hundred backpackers a year. The park features tremendous scenic diversity, including many of the trademark Rocky Mountain backcountry views.

The major centres are Banff townsite (129 km west of Calgary) and Lake Louise Village (187 km west of Calgary). Access is by car or by passenger bus along the Trans-Canada Highway (Highway 1). A full range of services, supplies, and accommodation is available at these centres, and at Canmore 22 km east of Banff. Basic groceries and fuel are available at Castle Mountain Village and at Saskatchewan River Crossing.

There are six hostels. The 13 frontcountry campgrounds have 1958 tenting sites. The park information centres are in Banff townsite and at Lake Louise Village. The park warden offices are in the industrial compounds at Banff and at Lake Louise.

17

*From Aylmer Pass, you look north to the limestone peaks of the Ghost River Wilderness.*

# 1. Aylmer Pass/ Aylmer Lookout

## Route

**Day-hike or overnight**

| Route | Elevation (m) | Distance (km) |
|---|---|---|
| Trailhead gate | 1480 | 0 |
| Trailhead sign | 1480 | 0.5 |
| Stewart Canyon | 1486 | 1.7 |
| Aylmer Pass Jct and CG | 1488 | 7.8 |
| Aylmer Lookout Jct | 1982 | 10.1 |
| Aylmer Lookout | 2134 | +1.7 |
| Aylmer Pass | 2288 | 13.5 |

**Maps**
NTS: 82 O/3 and 82 O/6
Gem Trek: Banff and Mt. Assiniboine

## Trailhead

**Follow Banff Avenue** 3 km from Banff townsite to the Trans-Canada Highway (Highway 1) interchange. Continue straight ahead (northeast) on the Lake Minnewanka Road for 5.9 km to the Lake Minnewanka parking area. Park on the north side of the road. Walk east from the parking lot to the gate. The trail begins as a road through the picnic area.

The Aylmer Pass trail takes you from shoreline to timberline in a landscape typical of Banff's front ranges. The trail features views of the largest body of water in Banff National Park. You walk through forest burned in the 1980s and 1990s as part of the park's prescribed burn program. Bighorn sheep frequent the pass and the slopes of Mt. Aylmer. Because the front ranges are in a snow shadow and this trail traverses south-facing slopes, Aylmer Pass is often Banff's first high-country destination to become snow-free. You share the trail with mountain bikers as far as Aylmer Pass Junction.

### Trailhead to Aylmer Pass Junction

The trail skirts the shore of Lake Minnewanka for 1.7 km to Stewart Canyon, which is named for George Stewart, first Superintendent of Banff National Park. Here, the Cascade River flows along a seam in the bedrock of the Etherington Formation. The axis of the canyon is along the strike of the Rockies, southeast to northwest. Cross the bridge and take the trail angling uphill to the north (left). Turn east (right) at the next junction.

The steep, south-facing slope traversed by the trail is typical of the montane ecoregion in the

## Variations

- Day-hike to Aylmer Lookout, 23.6 km return
- Day-hike to Aylmer Pass, 27.0 km return
- Day-hike both destinations, 30.4 km return
- Camp at Aylmer Pass Junction and day-hike to the pass and lookout

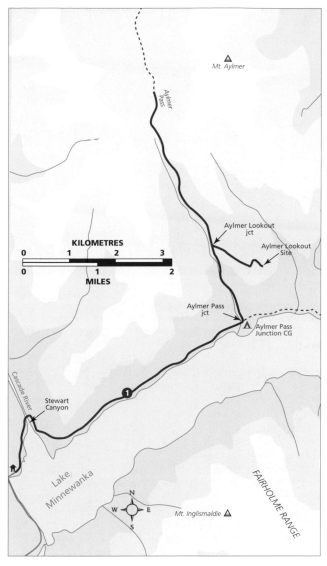

lake, this stream is the only water source on the hike. You reach the Aylmer Pass junction 100 m later. The campground is 200 m to the south (right). Aylmer Pass and Aylmer Lookout are to the north (left).

## Aylmer Pass Junction to Aylmer Lookout Junction

Until now, this outing has involved little elevation gain. Ahead, the trail climbs 800 m to Aylmer Pass. You reach the Aylmer Lookout junction in 2.3 km, from where a 1.7 km sidetrail leads southeast to the site of Aylmer Lookout.

## Aylmer Lookout

Constructed in 1948, Aylmer Lookout was one of seven fire lookouts in Banff. It saw use until 1978. Parks Canada removed the buildings in 1985. The site provides an excellent view of Lake Minnewanka, 654 m below. Bighorn sheep frequent the site – the lookout knoll reeks of their urine. The area is a haven for wood ticks in late spring and early summer. The 1990 prescribed burn consumed most of the trees nearby – an irony that underscores the change in outlook toward forest fires.

## Aylmer Lookout Junction to Aylmer Pass

Back on the trail to Aylmer Pass, the forest soon becomes upper subalpine in character. The trail crosses several avalanche slopes, where crimson coloured paintbrush, white globeflower, and western springbeauty thrive. Keep alert, for this is grizzly country. The trail cuts through a shale ravine and drops to the creek just before the pass. Rock-hop to the west side. From here, the track is sometimes sketchy as it crosses the tundra of scree, rockslide, sedges, and snow patches for the remaining 700 m to the pass.

Aylmer Pass marks the boundary between Banff National Park and the Ghost River Wilderness, a 153 km² provincial wilderness area. Self-reliant backpackers, competent at route finding, may explore north. Random camping is allowed;

front ranges. The principal trees in the forest are lodgepole pine, trembling aspen, Douglas-fir, and limber pine. Colourful wildflowers grace these dry soils in late spring; including blue clematis, northern blue columbine, and scorpionweed. The blue and purple pigmentation of the petals assists in blocking harsh ultraviolet radiation, enabling these plants to better survive on sun-baked slopes. The forest nearby was burned in a prescribed burn in the spring of 1994.

After the trail crosses a series of flash-flood stream courses, a bridge takes you across the stream that drains Aylmer Pass. Apart from the

*Although the buildings at Aylmer Lookout are removed, the grand prospect over Lake Minnewanka endures.*

## Working with Fire

**Fire helps regulate** the vitality of forest and grassland ecosystems. Forest fires were actively suppressed in the Rocky Mountain parks until the late 1980s. Fire suppression was so effective in the 1960s and 1970s, wildfires burned less than 6 km² of Banff National Park.

Park managers have inventoried the forests — mapping tree stands and determining the locations, dates, frequency, extent, and intensity of past fires. It is principally the frequency and the intensity of fires that control vegetation patterns and the vitality of the forest ecosystem. Research determined that near Lake Minnewanka, large, moderately intense fires should occur every 20 to 50 years. Since the most recent significant wildfires took place in 1884, park managers decided to "prescribe" a series of burns to reintroduce fire into the ecosystem.

Fire guards were prepared in the autumn of 1987, and the forest was ignited April 17, 1988. This first burn affected 750 ha. Park wardens studied the burn to appraise its success in terms of duplicating a natural fire. More burning was needed, so the forest was re-ignited in September 1990, affecting another 400 ha. In total, 36 percent of the forested area was burned with an intensity that killed all vegetation — a "crown fire." The area just east of Stewart Canyon was subsequently burned in 1994.

As you hike through the area, notice the patchwork of burned and unburned forest that resulted from the prescribed burns. You will see some trees that candled or "crowned." The thick bark of many

*The 1988 prescribed burn*

older Douglas-fir trees enabled them to survive, while smaller trees nearby were consumed. The resulting mosaic of new and old growth has enhanced the forest's vitality. Elk, which were absent before the burns, rediscovered the area, attracted by the new growth of aspens.

From a public relations point of view, the prescribed burn program has been something of an uphill effort. Some critics see fire as destructive and as a source of pollution. What they fail to acknowledge is that, because of a relative absence of fires in the past century, many forest stands in the Rockies have stagnated and are now marginal as habitat. These forests also beg the hazard of Yellowstone-scale conflagrations. By using prescribed burns and by letting wildfires burn in remote areas, park managers may be able to simulate the vital, natural process of forest succession.

**Lake Minnewanka** is the largest of the 480 mapped lakes and ponds in Banff National Park. The lake we see today is a hydro-electric reservoir, the only one in a Canadian national park. The lake's outlet has been dammed three times, raising the water level a total of 25 m and lengthening the body of water 8 km. The most recent dam was constructed in 1941 under the War Measures Act. The lake now has an area of just over 2217 hectares, and is slightly more than 97 m deep.

Sir George Simpson, governor of the Hudson's Bay Company, and his entourage were probably the first Europeans to see the lake. In 1841, Simpson followed its north shore on his way across Canada and around the world. The lake was known to Natives long before Simpson's visit. It fills a massive breach in the eastern wall of the Rockies, and offers an obvious travel route. Archaeologists have excavated a campsite on the north shore near the mouth of the Cascade River, where they unearthed a 10,000-year-old arrow point.

"Minnewanka" is a rendition of the Stoney name, *Minne-waki*, which has been translated as "lake of the water spirit," "spirit water," or "water of the spirits." A Stoney legend tells of a creature, half-human and half-fish, that could move the waters at will. In the late 1800s and early 1900s, the lake was called Devil's Lake in reference to this legend. Lake trout is the only native fish species, and a 15 kg specimen was caught in 1987. At least eight other fish species have been introduced.

Lake Minnewanka is in the montane ecoregion, which comprises only 2.95 percent, or 196 square kilometres, of Banff National Park. Highways, roads, townsites, and the railway have severely impacted this ecoregion, disrupting wildlife habitat and severing travel corridors. Banff's montane ecoregion would be significantly larger today if Lake Minnewanka's area had not been doubled by the dams.

The upper Ghost River at the east end of the lake was diverted westward from its natural course to help fill the reservoir in 1941. The rising waters inundated the village of Minnewanka Landing. Today, scuba divers explore the submerged ruins. Adding to Lake Minnewanka's unusual character is the fact that it is the only lake in Banff open to powerboats.

permits are not required. Looking south, Mt. Inglismaldie (2964 m) forms the backdrop to Lake Minnewanka. Inglisdmaldie castle was the Scottish home of the Earl of Kintore, who visited Banff in 1887. Mt. Aylmer (3163 m), the highest mountain in this part of Banff National Park, towers above the east side of the pass. The mountain, first climbed in 1889 by surveyor J.J. McArthur, remains a popular ascent today. Aylmer was McArthur's hometown in Quebec.

# 2. C-Level Cirque

**Day-hike**

| Route | Elevation (m) | Distance (km) |
| --- | --- | --- |
| Trailhead | 1461 | 0 |
| C-Level buildings | 1646 | 1.0 |
| C-Level Cirque | 1920 | 4.0 |

**Maps**
NTS: 82 O/4
Gem Trek: Banff and Mt. Assiniboine, or Banff Up-Close

**Best lighting:** morning

**Follow Banff Avenue** 3 km east from town to the Trans-Canada Highway. Continue straight ahead (northeast) on the Lake Minnewanka Road for 3.7 km. Turn north (left) into the Upper Bankhead picnic area. There are two trailheads here; the one for C-Level Cirque is on the west (left) side of the parking area.

In the short outing to C-Level Cirque, you climb from aspen parkland to avalanche swept, alpine slopes. The coupling of ecological diversity with interesting human history makes the trail one of the more popular excursions near Banff townsite. It's also a stiff climb, offering a solid piece of exercise. Although the cirque itself is snowbound well into summer, the trail is often clear early in the hiking season.

### Trailhead to Mine Ruins
The trail climbs steadily for 1 km through montane forest to the remains of two mine buildings. This was the uppermost of three workings of the

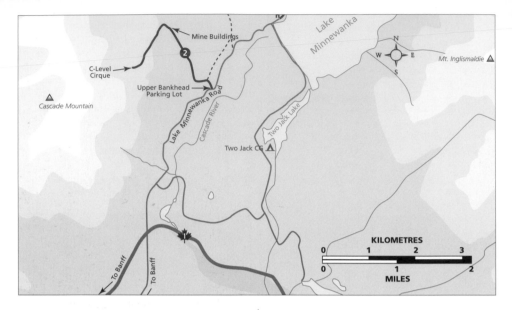

Bankhead mine in Cascade Mountain — the "C-Level" mine. Fenced-off ventilation shafts are nearby. You can walk east from the buildings onto a coal tailings pile, which grants fine views — east to Lake Minnewanka, south into the Bow Valley, and north into the Cascade Valley. Look for the charred forest of a 1992 prescribed burn in the distance, on the east side of the Cascade Valley.

## Bankhead

The Canadian Pacific Railway developed the Bankhead coal mine in 1903 to supply coal for the railway's locomotives. However, the coal shortage of 1906–07 created a national demand for coal. The CPR quickly expanded its mining operations and built a town nearby.

Mine production peaked in 1911, when more than 250,000 tonnes were extracted. The population of Bankhead reached maximum the same year, with estimates varying from 900 to 2000 people. Most of the miners were immigrants from Europe and China. The mine featured a coal-burning power plant that also supplied electricity to Banff.

Bankhead's semi-anthracite coal was extracted in an unusual fashion. Instead of removing the coal through vertical shafts, miners excavated tunnels, known as raises, slightly upward into the mountainside. The coal was knocked down into railcars that gravity propelled back to the portals. In all, more than 300 km of mining, transportation, and ventilation tunnels were excavated in the flanks of Cascade Mountain.

Labour unrest and failing economics put an end to the Bankhead mine in 1922. Total production was 2.6 million tonnes of coal. Most of the buildings were soon demolished or moved, many to Banff. Bankhead became a ghost town. New mining claims in national parks have not been allowed since the National Parks Act was proclaimed in 1930. However, a few mining titles — including some held by Canadian Pacific — have yet to be surrendered.

## To C-Level Cirque

About 500 m beyond the mine buildings, the trail narrows and angles sharply west (left). The forest at trailside becomes subalpine in character. Between here and the entrance to the cirque, the trail cuts through several coal seams — exposures of the Early Cretaceous, Kootenay group of sedimentary formations.

If you are hiking in June, you will be greeted by glacier lilies and calypso orchids along the last

### Cliff Builder

**The cliffs that flank** C-Level Cirque display a sequence of sedimentary rock formations common in the front ranges. The lower cliffs are Palliser Formation limestone (Late Devonian), the middle ledge is Banff Formation shale (Early Mississippian), and the cliffs above are Rundle Formation limestone (Middle Mississippian). This vertical world is home to mountain goats and bighorn sheep, and offers nesting sites for ravens.

# C-Level Cirque

C-Level Cirque is backed by Cascade Mountain.

The tipple at the Bankhead mine

## Noisy Leaf

The trailhead is in a stand of trembling aspen, the most common and widely distributed tree species in North America. A member of the willow family, aspen is abundant in the montane ecoregion of the front ranges, where it grows on the calcium-rich soils of glacial and alluvial rubble, often close to streams. Aspens propagate principally by root suckering, forming dense clonal stands of uniform age, where each tree leafs-out at the same time in the spring, and sheds its leaves at the same time in late summer. Some aspen stands may have originated at the end of the Wisconsin Glaciation, making them among the older and larger organisms on Earth.

The whitish-green trunks of mature aspens are often scarred to several metres in height, where elk or deer have stripped the protective outer bark to gain access to the sugary cambium layer beneath. These animals may also use small aspens as "rub trees," to remove the velvet from their antlers before the autumn rut. Where aspens grow near wetlands there will be beavers. The tree is the animal's staple food and building material. From the point of

view of birdlife, aspen forests are the most productive in Canada. Look and listen for woodpeckers, vireos, and warblers.

Fire is essential to the regeneration of aspen forests. In the absence of forest fires, browsing by ungulates has put severe pressure on the aspen stands of the Bow Valley. New suckers don't have a chance to become established, while the older trees are dying as they reach maximum age — approximately 120 years.

Natives knew the aspen as "noisy leaf" — an appropriate name when a breeze is blowing. The flat leaf stems readily catch the slightest wind, causing the leaves to flutter. The trait is recognized in the common name, "trembling," and in the Latin species name, *tremuloides*. One folk tale predicts impending bad weather if aspen leaves tremble when there is *no* breeze. This belief probably reflects the fact that aspen leaves tremble before the leaves of other trees. The tree bark is coated in a silvery dust that helps block UV radiation. Natives reportedly used the dust as a sunscreen and as a cure for headaches — ASA, the medicinal compound in aspirin, comes from the willow family.

*Cascade Amphitheatre is a glacier-carved hollow on the southwest slopes of Cascade Mountain.*

few hundred metres of trail. Although the elevation here is 300 m below normal for treeline in this area, the cirque is a treeless, alpine environment. The northeast facing slope, with its rocky soils and perennial snow patches, is swept by avalanches in winter. It is too chilly here for a forest to grow. Many of the trees along the eastern edge of the cirque are in kruppelholz form, stunted by the cold, and damaged by avalanches.

## C-Level Cirque

C-Level Cirque is not a classic, deeply eroded glacial cirque. Much of the cirque's shape is the result of mechanical weathering, erosion by water, and avalanches. The hummock at the end of the maintained trail is moraine debris known as a kame. The lakelet is a kettle pond. Both indicate that the area was once covered in glacial ice. The hummock is frequented by pikas, hoary marmots, and golden-mantled ground squirrels. The reddish tinge in snowpatches is watermelon snow — coloured by algae with a red pigment.

An unmaintained path heads north along the eastern edge of the cirque, to a larch-covered knoll. From the knoll you may enjoy a fine prospect south over the Bow Valley. The limestone boulders on the knoll exhibit *rillenkarren* — furrows eroded over centuries by naturally acidic rainwater and by snowmelt, in a process called solution.

# 3. Cascade Amphitheatre

## Route

**Day-hike**

| Route | Elevation (m) | Distance (km) |
|---|---|---|
| Trailhead | 1701 | 0 |
| Forty Mile Creek jct | 1680 | 0.8 |
| Forty Mile Creek bridge | 1560 | 3.1 |
| Cascade Amphitheatre jct | 1799 | 4.3 |
| Cascade Amphitheatre | 2195 | 7.7 |

**Maps**
NTS: 82 0/4
Gem Trek: Banff and Mt. Assiniboine, or Banff Up-Close

**Best lighting:** afternoon

## Trailhead

**Follow Gopher Street** north out of Banff. Cross the Trans-Canada Highway and follow the Mt. Norquay Road 6 km to the first parking lot on the north (right) at the ski area. The trailhead kiosk is at the north end of the parking lot.

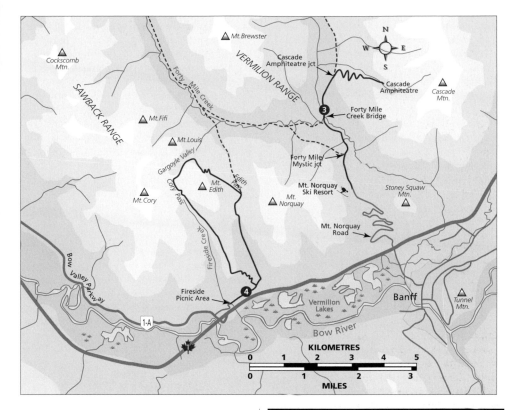

A Banff landmark, Cascade Mountain forms the northern skyline in the view from town. The Cascade Amphitheatre trail ascends into a steeply walled cirque on the southwest flank of the mountain. The approach trail is generally snow-free by mid-May. You share the trail with horses as far as the Amphitheatre junction.

## Trailhead to Forty Mile Creek

Walk on asphalt between the ski area ticket office and the day lodge to pick up the trail, which begins as a bulldozed track. Just past the Mystic chairlift, the trail begins a steady descent north through open lodgepole pine forest. (It is nice to start a hike with a downhill, but remember, this will be an uphill poke at the end of the day.) Keep straight ahead at the Mystic Pass-Forty Mile Summit junction at 0.8 km. At 3.0 km, you reach a "T" junction on the banks of Forty Mile Creek. Turn east (right), and continue 150 metres, where you will cross a bridge over Forty Mile Creek.

## Forty Mile Creek to Cascade Amphitheatre

Across the bridge, the uphill begins in earnest — 640 m of gain in the remaining 4.6 km. The dogtooth spire of Mt. Louis (LOO-eee) (2682 m) in the

## Forty Miles from Somewhere

**The first Europeans** in the Rockies often named a feature for its distance from a known location. Forty Mile Creek is not 40 miles long, so it was probably named because it is 40 miles from somewhere. The creek crossed the route of the Canadian Pacific Railway approximately 40 miles away from two points: the old railway siding of Padmore to the east, which was a major resupply point during the railway survey of 1881–82; and the crest of Kicking Horse Pass to the west.

In the spring and summer of 1982, Banff endured an outbreak of "beaver fever" (giardiasis), caused by contamination of drinking water with the parasite, *Giardia lamblia*. Beavers living in the town water reservoir on lower Forty Mile Creek were deemed the carriers. They were trapped and destroyed as a short-term solution to the problem. In July, 1983, the town of Banff completed the switch to three groundwater wells. This was good news for townsfolk and for the beavers, for whom the meanders of Forty Mile Creek provide excellent habitat.

25

Sawback Range dominates the views west. At the Cascade Amphitheatre junction, turn east (right) to continue the steady ascent to the cirque.

During the climb from Forty Mile Creek, you pass from the montane ecoregion into the subalpine ecoregion, although the forest of lodgepole pines changes little. These trees seeded after a large forest fire in 1894. The trail levels at the entrance to the amphitheatre, where there is a marked transition from pine forest to a mix of Engelmann spruce and subalpine fir, typical of the upper subalpine ecoregion. The paths that branch south (right) join the approach to the regular mountaineering route on Cascade Mountain. Continue straight ahead.

## Cascade Amphitheatre

Cirque valleys, such as Cascade Amphitheatre, were created and enlarged by glacial erosion

## Cascade Mountain

**The summit** of Cascade Mountain (2998 m) is east of trail's end. The mountain's name, given by James Hector in 1858, is a rendition of the Stoney word, *Minnehappa* — "the mountain where the water falls." Cascade is a miniature mountain range — a massif — 12.5 km long, with half a dozen summits. The most northerly summit is slightly higher than the one you see here.

Cascade is an overthrust mountain. Its tilted, southwest-facing slope (the ridge south of the amphitheatre), ends on a northeast-facing cliff (seen from C-Level Cirque, Classic Hike #2). Approximately 80 million years ago, the sedimentary rock layers that comprise the mountain were fractured along faults, and then thrust upward and northeastward over underlying layers. Overthrust mountains are common in the front ranges.

The rock layers of Cascade Mountain exhibit much folding. When deep within Earth's crust, the layers were made pliable by heat and were subsequently warped into folds by the forces of mountain building. U-shaped folds are known as synclines (SIN-clines). Arch-shaped folds are called anticlines. You can see a prominent syncline from the end of trail. A tremendous assortment of folds decorates Cascade Mountain's eastern flank, visible from the Lake Minnewanka Road.

The upper slopes of Cascade Mountain are Rundle Formation limestone and dolomite, containing sediments deposited during the Middle Mississippian period. Although it appears inhospitable, this terrain is excellent habitat for bighorn sheep.

during the various ice ages of the last 2 million years. Glaciologists speculate that there have been 20 to 30 glacial advances in this time. The trail undulates over a series of low recessional moraines as it enters the amphitheatre. These moraines mark places of brief pause during the most recent glacial retreat.

Although the glacial ice is now gone, a chill remains on the floor of the amphitheatre. Cold air flows downhill and collects in depressions, creating frost hollows where full-sized trees cannot develop. The many small mounds are earth hummocks, relict formations produced when permafrost existed under the soil. The meadows support the typical array of moisture-loving, alpine wildflowers, along with sedges and willows.

The trail is vague in places but keeps to the western edge of the meadows, where it crosses rockslide debris from which several springs issue. About 1 km after entering the amphitheatre, you climb through a small stand of trees to trail's end on a knoll of rockslide debris. You may see white-tailed ptarmigan, pikas, and hoary marmots nearby.

# 4. Cory Pass

## Route

**Day-hike**

| Route | Elevation (m) | Distance (km) |
|---|---|---|
| Trailhead | 1415 | 0 |
| Cory Pass jct | 1470 | 1.1 |
| Cory Pass | 2363 | 5.8 |
| Mouth of Gargoyle Valley | 2134 | 7.4 |
| Edith Pass jct | 1860 | 9.6 |
| Cory Pass jct | 1470 | 12.5 |
| Trailhead | 1415 | 13.6 |

**Maps**
NTS: 82 O/4
Gem Trek: Banff and Mt. Assiniboine, or Banff Up-Close
**See map on p.25**

## Trailhead

**Follow the Trans-Canada** Highway west from the Mt. Norquay (Banff) interchange for 5.6 km to the Bow Valley Parkway exit (Highway 1A). Follow the Bow Valley Parkway 500 m west and turn east (right) onto the Fireside picnic area access road. Follow this narrow road 600 m to its end.

*The Gargoyle Valley from Cory Pass*

The Cory Pass outing is the most spectacular and strenuous day-hike near Banff. Set among the rugged limestone peaks of the Sawback Range, the trail displays tremendous ecological diversity as it ventures from montane valley bottom to well above treeline. You may see bighorn sheep, white-tailed deer, mule deer, and elk. In early summer, lingering snow covers the north slope of the pass and the steep sideslopes of the Gargoyle Valley. Locals are split on the preferred direction for hiking this loop, but the direction described has at least three advantages. 1. You ascend the steepest parts of the trail — although you may huff and puff, your knees won't take such a pounding on the way down. 2. From Cory Pass, you can assess the snow cover before descending northeast. If it still looks like winter in the Gargoyle Valley, you can turn around and go home. 3. The homestretch is in shaded forest — perfect on a hot afternoon.

## Trailhead to Cory Pass

From the trailhead, cross the footbridge over "Fireside Creek" and turn south (right) onto a broad trail. After 200 m, you will come to a junction; turn north (left). This part of the trail is in a forest typical of south-facing slopes in the montane ecoregion of the front ranges. Lodgepole pine is the most common tree, but there are homogenous stands of trembling aspen. The understory contains buffaloberry, prickly wild rose, common juniper, paintbrush, showy aster, and groundsel.

You reach the Cory Pass junction at km 1.1. Turn north (left), and get ready to burn up your breakfast as you climb 350 m in the next 1.5 km. The initial part of the grind is on a grassy, flower-

## Blowout!

**In August 1999,** a debris flow — or blowout — transformed seemingly innocuous "Fireside Creek" into a torrent. The deluge destroyed part of the picnic area and piled debris — including a picnic table — on the Trans-Canada, forcing its closure for two days. Debris flows occur when a heavy rain or a sudden snowmelt mixes with the surface layer of soil and rock on a steep slope, transforming that material into a slurry. In this case, 50 mm of rain fell in one evening. The debris surged downward into the confines of the stream course, the funnelling action producing a flow of tremendous power. Debris flows are commonplace in the front ranges of the Rockies. They build many of the alluvial fans that spread into valley bottoms. Lesser flows occurred along the creek in 2000 and 2001. Parks Canada plans to create new berms in the creek bed to divert far-reaching flows out of the main channel, dispersing them on the lower mountain slope. The agency hopes that this will help protect the highway and the railway, while reinstating some of the natural process of the alluvial fan formation.

## Variations

- Hike to Cory Pass, 11.6 km return
- Hike the loop in reverse

filled slope, dotted with aspens. Elk, deer, and bighorn sheep frequent this area. Pause at the knoll about halfway into the climb; the steepest part is just ahead. The grade backs off as you gain the thinly-forested south ridge of Mt. Edith at km 2.6. About 1 km along the ridge, you encounter a short step. Ignore the path that heads east (right). Descend north (left). It's not really downclimbing, but take care. After this awkward bit, the trail breaks through treeline to traverse a steep sideslope as it completes the climb to the pass. Use caution if snow lingers in the gullies. The open slopes feature wildflowers with yellow blooms: stonecrop, alpine bladder pod, golden fleabane, yellow beardtongue, and yellow mountain saxifrage. Look back for fine views of Mt. Assiniboine (3618 m) and the many meanders of the Bow River.

## Cory Pass

Cory Pass is a narrow, rocky, and often windswept breach. Set in the alpine ecoregion, the thin soils of the pass support only scattered mats of hardy wildflowers, such as white mountain avens and moss campion. Views south include the Bow Valley, Mt. Rundle, Sulphur Mountain, and the Sundance Range. West of this range, the Fatigue Thrust Fault separates the gray limestone peaks of the front ranges from the eastern main ranges. The "gargoyles" flanking Cory Pass are shattered pinnacles of Eldon Formation limestone. The weathering of the ages has eroded an opening, or "window" into one of them. Cory Pass and Mt. Cory (2802 m) commemorate William Cory, Deputy Minister of the Interior from 1905 to 1930.

## Gargoyle Valley

Mt. Louis (LOO-eee) (2682 m) beckons you northeast into the Gargoyle Valley. Use care if portions of the route are snow-covered. The trail is vague at first as you make a sidehill descent on the south flank of the valley in the shade of Mt. Edith (2554 m). Edith Cox accompanied Prime Minister John A. Macdonald when he visited Banff in 1886 following completion of the CPR. The mountain has three summits; the most northerly is the highest. But it won't be Mt. Edith's shaded slabs that grab your attention — your eyes will be glued to Mt. Louis, the scenic focal point of this hike. Its dogtooth spire of vertically thrust Palliser Formation limestone makes it one of the more striking peaks in the Canadian Rockies. First climbed in 1916, the south ridge is popular with rock climbers today. Louis Stewart was a companion of explorer A.P. Coleman on two of his travels to the Rockies, in 1892 and 1903.

## Douglas-fir

A few majestic Douglas-fir trees grace the grassy slopes near the trailhead. Douglas-fir is the climax tree species of the montane ecoregion. Not a true fir, the Latin genus name, *Pseudotsuga*, means "false hemlock." The thick, grooved, corky bark of the mature tree allows it to withstand moderate ground fires and infestation by many insects, although in places in the Rockies, entire stands are succumbing to beetles. Forest fires remove competing vegetation in older Douglas-fir forests, creating open parkland dotted with stately trees. Douglas-firs in such settings in the Rockies may live 600 years. The last wildfire on these slopes was in 1910, although prescribed burns in the 1990s touched spots nearby. The oldest known Douglas-fir in Alberta, estimated at about 690 years, grows just east of Banff on a terrace above the Bow River. The age record for the species, from BC's Elaho (EE-la-hoe) Valley, is greater than 2000 years.

*Douglas-fir*

There are two varieties of Douglas-fir: coastal and interior. Although they hybridize, the interior or "blue Douglas-fir" is the variety in the Rockies. Large specimens are 30 m to 40 m tall and 1 m in diameter, often with a gracefully curving trunk. In Pacific rainforests, the coastal variety commonly attains heights of 80 m (record approximately 100 m), diameters in excess of 4 m, and ages of more than 1000 years.

The common name of the tree commemorates David Douglas, a Scottish botanist who collected in the Rockies in 1826 and 1827. The species name, *menziesia*, celebrates another Scot — Archibald Menzies, surgeon and naturalist on George Vancouver's 1792 voyage. Menzies was the first botanist to describe the huge conifer species of the North American Pacific coast.

*The limestone spire of Mt. Louis*

# 5. Elk Pass

## Route

Day-hike or overnight

| Route | Elevation (m) | Distance (km) |
|---|---|---|
| Trailhead | 1701 | 0 |
| Forty Mile/Mystic jct | 1680 | 0.8 |
| Forty Mile Creek bridge | 1560 | 3.1 |
| Cascade Amphitheatre jct | 1799 | 4.3 |
| Elk Pass CG | 2055 | 11.5 |
| Elk Lake jct | 2055 | 11.6 |
| Elk Pass | 2055 | 12.8 |
| Cascade River bridge | 1631 | 20.2 |
| Stony Creek bridge | 1631 | 20.4 |
| Stony Creek CG | 1635 | +0.3 |
| Cascade trail jct | 1640 | 21.0 |
| Cascade Bridge CG | 1545 | 29.2 |
| Upper Bankhead parking | 1461 | 35.8 |

**Maps**
NTS: 82 O/4 and 82 O/5
Gem Trek: Banff and Mt. Assiniboine

## Trailhead

**Follow Gopher Street** north out of Banff. Cross the Trans-Canada Highway and follow the Mt. Norquay Road 6 km to the first parking lot on the north (right) at the ski area. The trailhead kiosk is at the north end of the parking lot.

## Variations

- Hike the described loop in 2–3 days, 35.8 km
- Day-hike to Elk Lake in a long day, 27.4 km return
- For an easy two-day backpack, camp at Elk Pass, day-hike to the lake, return the same way, 27.4 km return
- Hike the loop in reverse

Although close to town, the loop over Elk Pass provides a taste of Banff's front range hinterland of rugged limestone peaks, an area that is home to grizzly bears, wolves, coyotes, cougars, elk, deer, mountain goats, and bighorn sheep. The entire loop is used by commercial horse parties. Mountain bikes are allowed on the Cascade fireroad.

Don't become so rapt in the view that you miss an important turn in the trail, 1.6 km from the pass. More than a few hikers have inadvertently followed the drainage all the way down to Forty Mile Creek. Here, the trail heads east (right). The trail cuts right onto a scree slope, ascending this before branching left into the trees. Having turned the north end of Mt. Edith, you then make a descending traverse beneath the mountain's northeast face, with fine views into Forty Mile Creek and down onto the forested saddle of Edith Pass. Mt. Norquay (NOR-kway) (2522 m) is east across the pass. John Norquay was Premier of Manitoba when he climbed this peak in 1888. The mountain to the north, across Forty Mile Creek, is Mt. Brewster (2859 m), named for Jim Brewster, trail guide, outfitter, and Banff businessman. A huge limestone block sits on its southwest slope. After about 1.5 km, the trail descends steeply on an avalanche slope to gain the Edith Pass trail. Turn south (right).

**Edith Pass Trail to Trailhead**
The trail drops into the shady ravine that drains Edith Pass. The forest is markedly different on this part of the hike — a mix of lodgepole pine, Douglas-fir, and white spruce. Fire studies show that this forest has not seen a wildfire since 1850. The rocky soils are home to feathermosses and shade-tolerant wildflowers, including several species of orchids. Continue straight ahead at the Cory Pass junction — you don't want to go up that hill again! — to complete the loop.

## Trailhead to Elk Pass

Walk on asphalt between the ski area ticket office and the day lodge to pick up the trail, which begins as a bulldozed track. Just past the Mystic chairlift, the trail begins a steady descent north through open lodgepole pine forest. Continue straight ahead at the Mystic Pass-Forty Mile Summit junction at 0.8 km. At km 3.0, you reach a "T" junction on the banks of Forty Mile Creek. Turn east (right), and continue 150 m, where you will cross a bridge over Forty Mile Creek.

The trail ascends for 1.2 km through lodgepole pine forest to the Cascade Amphitheatre junction. Most of the pines here seeded after a large forest fire in 1894. The resin-sealed cone of the lodge-pole cracks open at 45°C, scattering the seeds and producing a dog-hair forest of pines. At this elevation, most of the pines would normally have been replaced within 60 years by Engelmann spruce and subalpine fir — the climax species of the subalpine forest. However, these steep, well-drained, sun-exposed slopes offer a perfect niche for pines. A few small spruce are taking hold beneath the canopy, where buffaloberry, bearberry, and wolf willow also grow. Views west through the forest feature the dogtooth spire of Mt. Louis (LOO-eee) (2682 m) in the Sawback Range.

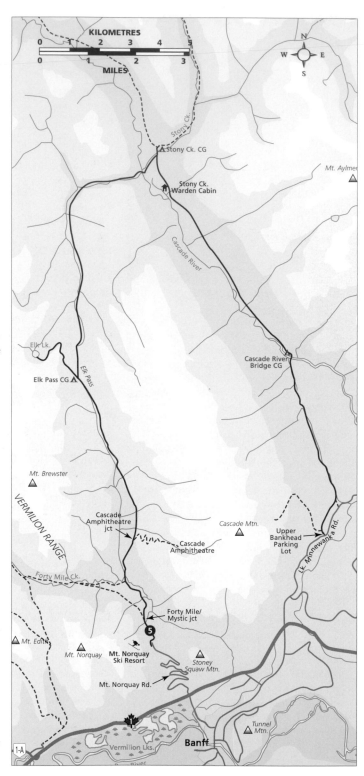

*Elk Lake is a short sidetrip from Elk Pass campground.*

## Elk Lake, 2.2 km

**An early morning visit** to Elk Lake is the highlight of this outing. From the junction on the main trail just north of the campground, a wide and sometimes muddy trail climbs northwest (left) into treeline forest. After crossing a spur of Mt. Brewster, the trail descends west to Elk Lake. Lyall's larch is common in the forest. If you are hiking in early summer you will see white globeflowers and glacier lilies among the tufts of heather at trailside. On the north side of the trail, you may see moose and elk in a nearby slough. The trail fades at the lakeshore, which is buggy, boggy, and fringed with alpine buttercup.

Elk Lake is a classic cirque lake, nestled in a glacial depression beneath Mt. Brewster (2859 m). The mountain's cliffs are the leading edge of the Sulphur Mountain Thrust Fault. They display the cliff-building sequence of the front ranges: Palliser Formation limestone, Banff Formation shale, with a topping of Rundle Formation limestone.

Cutthroat trout are present in the lake. As there is no record of stocking at Elk Lake, these fish may be endemic — a rarity among accessible lakes in the Rockies.

Continue straight ahead at the Cascade Amphitheatre junction. The wide and sometimes rocky horse trail continues north, crossing several flash-flood stream courses. As you climb toward Elk Pass, note the subtle transition to upper subalpine forest. Through openings in the trees, you have views south to Cascade Mountain (2997 m), Mt. Norquay (2525 m), Sulphur Mountain (2770 m), and the Sundance Range. The purple bloom of silky scorpionweed graces some of the shale banks at trailside. Open glades of willow mark the final approach to the pass. The slopes to the east are covered in silver spar trees from a 1914 forest fire.

At km 11.5, follow a trail 100 m northwest (left) from the main trail to Elk Pass campground, a pleasant camping place set in a grove of spruce. The water source is questionable — a small stream rich with organic material and frequented by deer and elk. Boil or filter the water before consumption.

While camped here we were visited by a mule deer doe and buck, who approached within 5 m. While drifting off to sleep, I was awakened by the unmistakable snarl of a big cat near the tent — probably a cougar. In the morning, we woke to the yelping and commotion from a coyote den on the opposite side of the valley. We found the skin of a goat in the willow meadows near the campground junction. The goat may have been killed by a cougar or by wolves.

### Elk Pass to Cascade Fireroad

The willow meadow stretches for 1.5 km across Elk Pass. As this is ideal habitat for snowshoe hares, mice, voles, least chipmunks, and Columbian ground squirrels; predators — wolves, coyotes, lynx, and cougars — frequent this area. You may see tracks and scats at trailside. From the north edge of the pass, the trail descends parallel to the stream course. During wet weather, there is some awful muck, churned by horse traffic.

## Space for Grizzlies and Wolves

**Since May 1993,** Banff National Park has seasonally closed the Cascade Valley above Stony Creek to recreational use. The closure protects resident populations of grizzly bears and wolves. Previously, park areas had only been closed because of avalanche hazard or following wildlife incidents. The Cascade seasonal closure was the first proactive measure intended to protect wide-ranging carnivores from human disturbance.

However, fine views west to Mt. Brewster compensate for the difficult travel.

Roughly 5 km north of Elk Pass, the trail crosses a bridge over the stream to its north bank and turns east toward Cascade Valley. The bridge is built from railway ties, soaked in creosote. In the 1960s and 1970s, many backcountry structures were built from this weatherproof wood. Unfortunately, creosote is toxic and readily leaches into streams. When you also consider that these timbers were flown here by helicopter, this bridge is anything but "environmentally friendly."

The final 2.2 km to the Cascade River is through a montane valley typical of the front ranges. Bright wildflowers dot the slopes: common dandelion — transported here in horse feed and dung — orange-flowered false dandelion,

goatsbeard, yellow columbine, prairie groundsel, paintbrush, yellow penstemon, blue penstemon, and yellow hedysarum.

The steep, grassy slopes to the north of the trail are ideal habitat for mountain goats and bighorn sheep. The shaded avalanche slopes to the south provide enticing food sources for bears. Toward the mouth of the creek, the trail passes through several groves of trembling aspen. Visibility is limited and the creek is noisy. Make plenty of noise in this area to alert bears to your presence.

The trail cuts through a limestone bluff that marks the Rundle Thrust Fault, to emerge onto the west bank of the Cascade River near its junction with Stony Creek. Cross the river on two footbridges located 50 m to the south (right). Turn north (left) 20 m beyond the second bridge, and

## A Road in the Backcountry?

**The headwaters** of the Cascade River are the wilderness heartland of Banff National Park, an area important to wolves and grizzly bears. It may seem unthinkable today that a road was built here. The existence of the Cascade fireroad epitomizes the change in attitudes toward resource management in the Rocky Mountain parks.

The most extensive wildfires in Banff National Park took place in 1936. Three major burns consumed about 70 km² of park forests. Almost 90 percent of this total resulted from a single fire at Flints Park in the upper Cascade Valley. Park managers of the day were obsessed with protecting timber. They quickly mobilized to extinguish the fire.

*The upper Cascade Valley*

As part of the firefighting effort, crews bulldozed a road north to Flints Park. In the years following the fire, the road was upgraded and lengthened north over Wigmore and Snow Creek summits to the Red Deer River, and then east to the park boundary — a distance of almost 70 km.

By the 1950s, fireroads ran the lengths of most major backcountry valleys in the Rocky Mountain parks. Warden cabins sprang up along the roads. Park maintenance crews and wardens routinely drove into the heart of prime wildlife habitat. In 1971, Parks Canada announced plans to pave

many of the fireroads and open them to traffic. Fortunately, the public strongly opposed the proposals, so the agency dropped the idea.

The fireroads have been obsolete since the 1980s, usurped by the use of helicopters for smoke patrols and initial attack on fires. Road deactivation has been achieved by installing "tank traps" near trailheads, by removing bridges, or — as on the Cascade fireroad — by downscaling bridges to pedestrian width. Park managers now refer to the Cascade fireroad as a "trail," but it will be decades before vegetation reclaims the tread to trail width.

follow this trail for 30 m. Angle northeast (right) onto a well-beaten trail that parallels the north bank of Stony Creek. A series of split-log bridges cross this creek. There is a maze of horse trails, paths, and fireroads on the south bank of the creek. Disregard them and, instead, follow Stony Creek upstream for 600 m to the concrete bridge on the Cascade fireroad. If you want to camp nearby, hike east 300 m from the trail junction just north of the bridge, to Stony Creek campground.

### Stony Creek to Upper Bankhead Parking Lot

The outing concludes with an enjoyable walk south along the Cascade fireroad. The Stony Creek warden cabin is on a sideroad, approximately 1.3 km south of Stony Creek. The Cascade River Bridge campground is located on the west side of the fireroad, just before it crosses the Cascade River. Beyond the bridge, the trail climbs into lower subalpine forest that features a number of sloughs created by beavers. With views of Bow Valley ahead, the trail descends to the Upper Bankhead parking lot on the Lake Minnewanka Road. If you have not pre-arranged transportation, plan to arrive early enough to hitchhike. The

### Mountains On Strike

**The topographic maps** show that Elk Lake occupies one of more than a dozen east-facing cirques along the 21 km length of Mt. Brewster. With its numerous summits, Mt. Brewster is a fine example of a *massif* — a miniature mountain range. The front range landscape of Banff and Jasper national parks is dominated by a series of parallel massifs, oriented along the northwest-southeast strike of the Rockies. Cascade Mountain is another example. Major streams and rivers erode their courses parallel to the massifs. Secondary streams enter the major streams at right angles, producing a pattern known as trellis drainage. A few antecedent streams have managed to bisect the massifs, eroding downward as the mountains were thrust upward.

Mt. Brewster was named for Jim Brewster, who rose from humble beginnings in Banff to gain control of a transportation empire in the early 1900s. The summits immediately above Elk Lake are 2805 m. Elsewhere north and south, the summits are slightly higher. The southernmost peak of the Brewster massif, to which the name Mt. Brewster is formally applied, is visible from places in Banff townsite.

6.7 km of road into town is a real heel-burner.

You should remain alert for grizzly bears while hiking the Cascade fireroad. The valley offers good habitat. Grizzly bears are more commonly observed here than anywhere else in Banff National Park.

# 6. Sawback

## Route

**Overnight, 4–7 days**

| Route | Elevation (m) | Distance (km) |
|---|---|---|
| Trailhead | 1701 | 0 |
| Forty Mile/Mystic jct | 1707 | 0.8 |
| Forty Mile Creek bridge | 1631 | 4.0 |
| Cockscomb Mountain CG | 1723 | 8.2 |
| Mystic Pass jct | 1838 | 15.9 |
| Mystic Junction CG | 1840 | +0.5 |
| Mystic Valley CG | 1921 | 18.6 |
| Mystic Lake jct | 1951 | 19.1 |
| Mystic Pass | 2285 | 22.7 |
| Johnston Creek jct | 1692 | 29.3 |
| Larry's Camp CG | 1692 | +0.1 |
| Luellen Lake jct | 1890 | 37.8 |
| Johnston Creek CG | 1875 | +0.2 |
| Luellen Lake CG | 1970 | +0.8 |
| Badger Pass jct | 2027 | 43.7 |
| Badger Pass Junction CG | 2043 | 44.2 |
| Pulsatilla Pass | 2365 | 47.6 |
| Baker Creek jct | 1814 | 54.0 |
| Wildflower Creek CG | 1814 | 54.0 |
| Red Deer Lakes jct | 2133 | 59.2 |
| Baker Lake CG | 2210 | 60.0 |
| Boulder Pass | 2345 | 64.9 |
| Hidden Lake CG jct | 2195 | 7.2 |
| Hidden Lake CG | 2198 | +0.1 |
| Fish Creek parking area | 1698 | 73.5 |

**Maps**
NTS: 82 O/4, and 82 O/5, and 82 N/8
Gem Trek: Banff and Mt. Assiniboine

## Trailhead

**Parks Canada is considering** restricting access in the Skoki area at trail's end. Check at a park information centre. Follow Gopher Street north out of Banff. Cross the Trans-Canada Highway and follow the Mt. Norquay Road 6 km to the first parking lot on the north (right) at the ski area. The trailhead kiosk is at the north end of the parking lot.

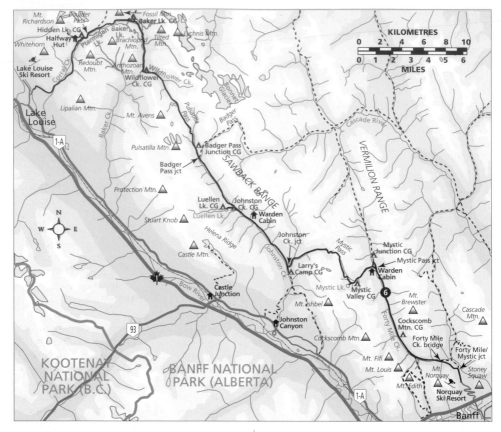

The Sawback trail connects a series of spectacular passes as it winds over the crest of its namesake range from Banff to Lake Louise. This outing includes sections of the following trails: Forty Mile Creek, Mystic Pass, Johnston Creek, Wildflower Creek, Baker Creek, Baker Lake, and Boulder Pass. The spacing of campgrounds allows for short days on the trail and time for exploration. This outing traverses prime grizzly habitat. You share the tread with horse traffic, so during poor weather much of the trail is quagmire.

**Trailhead to Mystic Valley Campground**

Walk on asphalt between the ski area ticket office and the day lodge to pick up the trail, which begins as a bulldozed track. At the junction in 0.8 km, just past the Spirit chairlift, branch left, following signs for Mystic Pass. The trail ascends over a spur of Mt. Norquay, gaining 70 m of elevation, before descending to a bridge over Forty Mile Creek at km 4.0.

For the next 12 km, the trail climbs gradually through open coniferous forest along the east bank of Forty Mile Creek. In places, the tread has been hardened with gravel and crowned to withstand the impact of horse travel. Views are limited, except where the trail crosses avalanche paths or draws alongside the creek. The dogtooth spires of Mt. Louis (LOO-eee) (2682 m) and Mt. Fifi (2621 m) dominate the west side of the valley. The Edith Pass junction is 6.0 km from the trailhead. Continue straight ahead. If you use the Cockscomb Mountain campground at km 8.2, treat all drinking water from Forty Mile Creek.

The unmarked trails that branch west prior to the Mystic Pass junction lead to a horse outfitter's

## Variations

- The most popular variation is a traverse of Mystic Pass, with exit or approach along Johnston Creek, 37.2 km, 2–4 days
- At the north end of the hike, you can add portions of the Skoki loop. See Classic Hike #19.
- Hike the trail in reverse. An alternate exit, bypassing Mystic Pass, is along Johnston Creek, 51.8 km

*On Mystic Pass, you cross the Sawback Range.*

junction just beyond, where the cutoff trail from Mystic Junction campground joins. After climbing and traversing a forested sideslope for 2 km, the trail descends avalanche paths to a bridge across Mystic Creek. The Mystic Valley campground is just beyond, situated on a bench between the creeks that drain Mystic Pass and Mystic Lake. Upstream, both creeks are forded by horses Treat all drinking water.

camp. Continue straight ahead until the junction. The trail is very poor in this area. (If you want to camp at Mystic Junction campground, hike north [straight ahead] from the junction for 500 m. To rejoin the Mystic Pass trail when you leave camp, travel 800 m along the cutoff trail that heads southwest from the campground.)

Turn west (left) at the Mystic Pass junction, and descend to a bridge over Forty Mile Creek. The trail skirts the north side of the Mystic warden cabin. Continue straight ahead (west) at the

## Mystic Valley Campground to Johnston Creek

At the junction 500 m west of the campground, turn north (right). The trail climbs moderately, with one bridged stream crossing and one rock-hop, to reach treeline at the southern entrance to Mystic Pass.

Aptly named, Mystic Pass is a narrow cleft between two parallel ridges of the Sawback Range. Larches dot the pass, adding to the allure in late summer. The axis of the pass lies directly on the

## Mystic Lake, 1.1 km

*Mystic Lake is bordered by ancient forest.*

**Mystic Lake is nestled** in a glacial cirque under the eastern ramparts of Mt. Ishbel (2908 m). The trail to the lake heads west from the campground, crosses the lake's

outlet stream and ascends to a junction in 500 m. Continue straight ahead. The muddy and rocky trail improves dramatically after the horse-hiker barrier about 300 m beyond the junction.

Mystic Lake has an area of 8 hectares and is 15 m deep. It is fringed by an ancient forest of spruce and fir that last burned in 1645. Arnica, fleabane, and leather-leaved saxifrage grow on the damp shoreline, along with the sedge, cotton-grass. Cutthroat trout and bull trout are the fish species in the lake.

The first recorded visits to Mystic Lake took place in 1891, when Jim Brewster was led here by William Twin of the Stoney band, and when surveyor J.J. McArthur stopped by. Ishbel was the daughter of Ramsay MacDonald, British prime minister in the 1920s and 1930s. Although you can make a rough circuit of this enchanting body of water, most visitors are content to gaze at the lake and Mt. Ishbel from near trail's end on the east shore.

Sawback Thrust Fault, which separates the drab, gray Devonian-aged, Palliser Formation limestone on the east side of the pass, from the more varied and older Cambrian-aged rocks to the west. These include the purple shales of the Arctomys (ARK-toe-miss) Formation at trailside. Bighorn sheep and mountain goats frequent the kilometre-long tundra of the pass. Their trails crisscross the surrounding slopes.

Leaving Mystic Pass, the trail swings west and plunges toward Johnston Creek. This sidevalley can be a scorching place on a hot afternoon. Sedimentary formations in the mountain to the north display extensive folding and small solution caves. As it levels, the trail alternates between rockslides and willow plains. Some sections are routed along a flash-flood stream course. Look for cairns that mark the way where the trail becomes faint.

The stream that drains Mystic Pass emerges from the base of a rockslide about 2.5 km below the pass. This rockslide may be the pika capital of

*Horsetail*

the Rockies. In dry weather, this will be your last water source for 3 km. Cross another flash-flood stream course and rock-hop the creek to its north bank. Continue the descent on a delightful section of trail. You cross an unnamed tributary stream about a kilometre before the Johnston Creek junction. A multitude of colourful montane

## Finding Faults

Although the ragged peaks of the front ranges seem chaotic, there is geologic order in this landscape. Front range valleys are oriented along weaknesses in the underlying bedrock. These weaknesses can be a fold, where the rock formations have been stretched or compressed; or, more often, a fault, where they have been shorn.

Pulsatilla Pass, Wildflower Creek, and upper Johnston Creek lie on the Castle Mountain Thrust Fault. As with most faults in the front ranges, this

*White boulders of the Gog Formation rest atop shales of the Survey Peak Formation on the crest of Pulsatilla Pass.*

fault is oriented along the strike of the Rockies — southeast to northwest. This creates a symmetrical landscape — each strike valley is walled by parallel mountain ranges composed of the leading edges of

a thrust sheet. The effect is repeated many times farther east in the front ranges.

On the crest of Pulsatilla Pass, you can see the contact surfaces of the Castle Mountain Thrust Fault. The trail follows the dividing line between whitish Gog Formation quartzite (Early Cambrian) to the west, and Survey Peak Formation shale (Late Cambrian) to the east. The quartzite is the leading edge of the thrust fault, brought from near the sedimentary basement of the Rockies to rest atop the younger shales. This rocky seam also separates two of the geological provinces of the Rockies — the main ranges to the west, from the younger front ranges to the east.

wildflowers blooms in July on the steep, dry slopes north of the trail. You have views south along Johnston Creek to Copper Mountain (2795 m). Johnston Creek was named for a prospector who frequented the area near Silver City, nearby in the Bow Valley in 1882.

## Johnston Creek to Luellen Lake

At the Johnston Creek junction, turn south (left) if you would like to stay at nearby Larry's Camp campground. You can also make an emergency exit from this point to the Bow Valley Parkway, 7.9 km south.

The Sawback trail continues northwest (right) from the junction, as a mucky, rooted horse trail along Johnston Creek. The walking is tiresome; the 8.5 km to the Luellen lake junction seems half that far again. Views south include the spire-like summit of Mt. Ishbel. In places, the trail is enclosed by ancient spruce forest. Listen for golden-crowned kinglets and for the drumming of woodpeckers. Look for trout in the creek at undercut banks. A wooden fence and gate mark the horse pasture at the Johnston Creek warden cabin. Please close the gate behind you.

Horsetails grow at trailside in this area. The genus they belong to — *Equisetum* — is among the more primitive and ancient group of vascular plants on Earth. Nine species in this genus occur in the Rockies. Those with prominent side-branches are known as horsetails; those without are called scouring rushes — most people know these plants as "snake grass" because of their segmented, hollow stems. When dinosaurs roamed, forests in many areas were dominated by tree-sized horsetails. Horsetails reproduce by shedding spores. They prefer damp habitats and are a favourite early summer food of bears.

The upper Johnston Creek valley is oriented along the Castle Mountain Thrust Fault. Bedrock in the lower slopes on the west side of the valley is purple and brown Miette (mee-YETT) Formation gritstone and shale. Miette rocks underlie much of the eastern main ranges, and are the oldest rocks visible in this part of the Rockies. Miette sediments accumulated to a maximum thickness of 9 km.

There are two camping options near the Luellen Lake junction. Johnston Creek campground is 200 m west (left) of the junction, on the near bank of the creek. This pleasant campground is an excellent choice for those wishing more

### Luellen Lake, 750 m

*Luellen Lake*

**The route to Luellen Lake** crosses Johnston Creek and climbs a rough track for 750 m to the campground. Luellen Lake is an attractive ribbon of water, 1.75 km long, with an area of 47 ha. The peculiar, blocky summit to the west is Stuart Knob (2850 m), named for Benjamin Stuart, son of Charles Walcott. Walcott is best known for his discovery of the Burgess Shale in 1909. The 500 m high quartzite cliffs of Helena Ridge form the backdrop for the lake. Walcott climbed the ridge in 1910, and named it for his second wife.

You may hear the call of common loons at Luellen Lake: "who-EEE-ooo." Many backcountry lakes in the Rockies are home to a pair of loons in summer. Loons eat fish and aquatic insects. They nest near water and are unable to take off from land. Loons in the Rockies migrate to the Pacific coast during winter.

### Fishing

**Luellen Lake** (named for the daughter of a fish hatchery superintendent) is one of the more popular backcountry fishing destinations in Banff National Park. Cutthroat trout are native. Luellen Lake and many other lakes were formerly stocked with non-native species to promote angling. As a result, few backcountry lakes in the Rockies now host a natural complement of species.

Sport fishing is the only extractive activity still permitted in the Rocky Mountain parks. Park managers are contemplating various measures to re-establish natural regimes in backcountry lakes. These may include increasing catch limits for introduced species until they are "fished out," and then closing the lakes to angling; or managing the lakes as "catch and release" fisheries only. Stocking of fish is now only considered to assist the recovery of native species.

solitude and fewer bugs than at nearby Luellen Lake campground.

## Luellen Lake to Badger Pass Junction

The Sawback trail continues northwest (straight ahead) from the Luellen Lake junction, along the east bank of Johnston Creek. This section of trail is narrower and much less travelled. The trail crosses to the west bank 500 m north of the junction, where the forest becomes more open and views improve. The trail descends to the creek and crosses it again. For the next 3 km, the route is through willow and shrub thickets near the creek. Keep to the hiker trail at the horse-hiker barrier or you may be obliged to ford and re-ford numerous braids of the creek. Cross Badger Creek to the Badger Pass trail junction. The Sawback trail continues north, reaching the Badger Pass Junction campground in 500 m. In late summer, the water source at this campground may dry up, requiring a 500 m walk to Johnston Creek. Bring a water billy.

## Badger Pass Junction to Baker Creek

For 2 km beyond Badger Pass Junction campground, the Sawback trail works its way through shrub thickets in the valley bottom. Boulder-hop Johnston Creek to its west bank. Wet meadows here feature an astounding array of wildflowers, including elephant head, fleabane, bracted lousewort, yellow hedysarum, and yellow paintbrush.

Pulsatilla Mountain (3035 m) dominates the west side of the valley. The east face of the mountain is a cliff, 6 km long and riddled with cirques. One of these cirques is still home to a sizeable glacier, which formed part of the mountain's first ascent route in 1930. From bottom to top, the cliffs display the main range, "castle-building"

sequence of Cathedral Formation limestone, Stephen Formation shale, and Eldon Formation limestone. This sequence is most commonly recognized at Castle Mountain, 10 km to the south.

The shrub thickets give way to larch forest as the trail nears Pulsatilla Pass. Look for the Z-shaped cascade in the creek. Rock-hop the creek to its east bank, take the northwest (left) trail fork, and begin the final climb to the pass, which is steeper and farther than it looks. Impressive wildflower displays make the climb enjoyable. *Pulsatilla* is an old genus name for the western anemone (*Anemone occidentalis*) (See photo on p. 82). This showy member of the buttercup family grows here in profusion. Anemone means "wind flower." Along with other typical upper subalpine wildflowers, these meadows contain two species normally found at lower elevations — mountain death-camas and cow parsnip. Contorted lousewort is also abundant.

Look back for a fine view of the upper Johnston Creek valley. The unnamed peak on the east

### Badger Pass (2545 m), 5.0 km

*Badger Pass*

## No Badgers Here

**Badger Pass is named** for the American badger, a nocturnal member of the weasel family. The alpine terrain of Badger Pass is not badger habitat, as the animal prefers low elevation grasslands and shrub meadows where it seeks the small rodents that comprise most of its diet. Southeast of the pass in the Cascade River valley, badgers are sighted more frequently than in any other watershed in Banff National Park, which is nonetheless not very often. Some people think that the name of the pass records a case of mistaken identity, that the "badger" was really a hoary marmot. The American badger is on the Alberta "blue list" of species at risk.

**You are fortunate** if you can visit the exquisite alpine realms of Badger Pass and Pulsatilla Pass on successive days. The trail to Badger Pass follows an idyllic stream through forest and meadows to the craggy divide between Johnston Creek and the upper Cascade River. The prospect east into the headwaters of the Cascade is one of the wilder views in Banff National Park. Ridge upon ridge of sawtooth mountains rear up like rocky waves in an ocean of sky. Badger Pass can be snowbound until mid-July. The horn mountains northwest of Badger Pass feature extensive grassy slopes that are excellent habitat for bighorn sheep, grizzly bears, and mountain goats.

*Baker Lake is the last stopping place for most hikers on the Sawback trail.*

side of the valley, just south of Badger Creek, features a summit formation known as a *klippe*. The horn-like, summit formation stands alone atop the bedding plane of the less-resistant, underlying formation.

The view north from Pulsatilla Pass (see photo, p.17)reveals one of the more exquisite alpine landscapes in Banff National Park. The centrepiece is Pulsatilla Lake, framed perfectly between the wild crags that border upper Wildflower Creek. In the distance, with its perennial snowpatch, Fossil Mountain (2946 m) keeps watch over the scene. While you stop to take in

## The Sawback Range

**James Hector merely** commented on the obvious when he named the "Saw-back" Range in 1858. The limestone slabs, capped by weak shales, were thrust vertically during mountain building. This created steep, southwest facing slopes that are oriented perpendicular to the prevailing weather systems. The shales atop the slabs are readily eroded through mechanical weathering, solution, and abrasion, creating the sawtooth ridges with hourglass-shaped gullies set in the slopes below. The gullies collect runoff and debris from vast areas near the ridgetops, funneling the water through slots of resistant limestone onto the lower slopes. Not surprisingly, flash-floods are common along the base of the Sawback Range.

the view, keep an eye on your packs. The pass is inhabited by particularly bold hoary marmots, high country highwaymen who will quickly depart with any loose object they find. I've heard of one that stole a T-shirt and took it down its burrow.

Descend steeply north from the pass on a good trail that hugs the east side of the valley to avoid wet meadows. About 500 m from the pass, the trail forks. The left path descends to the shore of Pulsatilla Lake. The path on the right traverses the sideslope above the lake. Take your pick; the routes converge a kilometre north.

Pulsatilla Lake is a sink lake. It has no visible outlet, indicating subterranean drainage in the limestone bedrock, known as karst. The lake is impounded behind an upturned edge of glacier-worn rock — a riegel (RYE-gull). The front ranges of Banff feature many sink lakes impounded in a similar fashion, but few are as large as Pulsatilla Lake.

From the cliff edge beyond the lake, you begin a steep descent into the valley of Wildflower Creek. The trail passes an unnamed pond, dammed by rockslide debris. It was near this pond that Mary Vaux Walcott, third wife of Charles Walcott, and a gifted botanist and artist, collected 82 species of flora during a visit in July 1921. In his diary, Charles Walcott recorded that Mary found "50 species in bloom within 200 feet of our tent." Accordingly, Mary called the valley

"Wild Flower Canyon," the origin of today's name. One August, we found the pond dry.

The forest in the confined valley bottom contains ancient Engelmann spruce and lodgepole pine. Some of the spruce trees are 45 m tall. The trail is vague where you rock-hop a tributary stream coming in from the east. About 5.5 km from Pulsatilla Pass, ford Wildflower Creek (straightforward) to its west bank. The steep descent continues to the Wildflower Creek campground and Baker Creek junction, skirting ancient moraines on the way.

## Wildflower Creek to Baker Lake

Turn north (right) to continue the Sawback trail. You may have to ford Wildflower Creek (straightforward) if the artful, felled-tree bridge has collapsed. On the climb north, you cross several avalanche slopes that offer views southwest to the Wenkchemna Peaks. Vegetation here is incredibly lush. The trail drops into a clearing where the route can be lost — a taste of things to come. There is an outfitter's camp at the north edge of this meadow. The trail descends to an extensive wet meadow along Baker Creek. Keep to the east of this boggy area, and try to keep your feet dry.

North of the wet meadow, the trail crosses the alluvial rubble of a flash-flood stream course — the handiwork of Lychnis Creek. The bridge here is routinely knocked out by flash-floods. *Lychnis* is an old genus name for various species of campion — showy wildflowers of the upper subalpine and alpine — now classified in the genus, *Silene*. If you lose the trail here, don't look for it in the forest; it keeps to the open willow plain. On the west side of the valley, two waterfalls on Anthozoan

Mountain (2695 m) emerge from underground. They drain a series of lakes concealed on the bench above. *Anthozoans* are reef-like deposits of coral found in the dolomite bedrock of this and other mountains nearby.

The steep ascent to the meadows south of Baker Lake demonstrates the full range of ills resulting from horse use — braiding, muck holes, damaged drainage control, churned up rocks, and trampled tree roots. Thankfully, this section lasts but a kilometre. Delightful upper subalpine meadows greet you at the top of the climb, silencing any curses that may have been about to spring forth.

Rock-hop Baker Creek to its west side just above a shale canyon. You reach an important junction 800 m beyond. Turn northwest (left) for the final 800 m to Baker Lake campground, a welcome sight at the end of this long day. The lake is impounded by a series of upturned rock benches that mark the edge of the Castle Mountain Thrust Fault. The outlet stream has eroded an interesting channel through these formations. Look for dippers here.

Baker Lake is another popular backcountry fishing destination — home to rainbow trout and cutthroat trout. Besides a multitude of campers, you will probably share this campground with mosquitoes, porcupines, and snowshoe hares.

## Baker Lake to Fish Creek

The Sawback trail concludes by heading west along the north shore of Baker Lake before climbing to Ptarmigan Lake and Boulder Pass. On the pass, the mountains of the Slate Range are close at hand. Mt. Temple (3543 m) looms to the southwest. Halfway Hut and Hidden Lake campground are 1.5 km beyond the pass. The hut, built as a stopover for packers supplying Skoki Lodge, is located halfway between the Lake Louise train station and the lodge. See Classic Hike #19 for more information on this area.

Beyond the hut, the trail re-enters subalpine forest. From here to trail's end, keep alert for grizzly bears. After 3 km, the trail emerges onto a ski run at the Lake Louise ski area. It is 3.5 km of steady downhill on a gravel road to the Fish Creek parking lot, with occasional views of Mt. Victoria en route. If you need a telephone to arrange transportation, follow a track north from the parking lot for 1 km to Whiskeyjack Lodge at the Lake Louise ski area. Otherwise, it's a downhill walk — 1 km to Whitehorn Drive, where you turn left for another 2 km to Lake Louise village.

### Little Baker Lake, 1.2 km

**Little Baker Lake** is one of three lakes tucked under the east flank of Brachiopod Mountain. Rock-hop the outlet of Baker Lake and follow beaten paths through larch forest to the southeast. Look back at Fossil Mountain to see the incredible Z-shaped, overturned fold in the upper part of the south face.

The maze of paths here defies sensible description. Pass a small unnamed pond (not shown on the topographic map) along its east shore, and continue to Little Baker Lake. You have views to Tilted Lake en route. Brachiopod Lake is farther south. This seasonal pond usually dries up by late summer.

*Mt. Assiniboine is sometimes called "the Canadian Matterhorn."*

# 7. Mt. Assiniboine

## Route

**Overnight, 3–6 days**

| Route | Elevation (m) | Distance (km) |
|---|---|---|
| Parking lot | 1690 | 0 |
| Trailhead | 1692 | 0.2 |
| Healy Pass jct | 1706 | 0.9 |
| Sunshine Village | 2195 | 6.2 |
| Rock Isle Lake jct | 2285 | 7.6 |
| Quartz Ridge | 2385 | 11.5 |
| Howard Douglas Lake CG | 2286 | 12.3 |
| Citadel Pass | 2362 | 15.9 |
| Porcupine CG jct | 1829 | 20.4 |
| Porcupine CG | 1800 | +0.2 |
| Simpson River jct | 1996 | 22.5 |
| Og Lake CG | 2060 | 28.0 |
| Lake Magog jct | 2165 | 33.9 |
| Lake Magog CG | 2165 | +1.6 |
| Naiset Cabins | 2175 | 34.4 |
| Wonder Pass | 2395 | 37.0 |
| Marvel Pass jct | 1950 | 40.1 |
| Marvel Lake connector jct | 1795 | 44.6 |
| Marvel Lake | 1785 | 45.1 |
| Marvel Lake CG | 1753 | 46.2 |
| Bryant Creek jct | 1750 | 46.8 |
| Big Springs CG | 1740 | 50.1 |
| Trail Centre jct | 1737 | 53.0 |
| Palliser Pass jct | 1725 | 53.7 |
| Mt. Shark trailhead | 1768 | 59.5 |

**Maps**
NTS: 82 0/4, and 82 J/13, and 82 J/14
Gem Trek: Banff and Mt. Assiniboine

## Trailhead

**Follow the Trans-Canada** Highway 8.3 km west from Banff to the Sunshine Interchange. Follow the Sunshine road 9 km to its end at the ski area parking lot. The trailhead kiosk is west of (behind) the gondola terminal, 200 m from the parking lot.

Mt. Assiniboine (a-SIN-ni-boyne) (3618 m) is the sixth highest mountain in the Canadian Rockies. Straddling the continental divide, "The Matterhorn of the Rockies" is the highest mountain in both Banff National Park and in adjoining Mt. Assiniboine Provincial Park. Ever since the mountain was noted and named by surveyor G.M. Dawson in 1884, it has been an irresistible backcountry icon, attracting travellers from around the world. The mountain was named for a Native band of the Sioux Confederation. Known elsewhere as the Nakoda or Dakota peoples, they were known locally as Stoney in Dawson's time. *Assiniboine* means "those who cook by placing hot rocks in water."

Half a dozen backpacking routes lead to Lake Magog at the base of Mt. Assiniboine. This outing describes a traverse of Mt. Assiniboine Provincial Park using Citadel Pass and Wonder Pass. This traverse, combined with the day-hiking options, provides the most complete experience of Mt. Assiniboine's spectacular scenery. Do not expect solitude. You will be sharing the area with hikers, mountain bikers, helicopters, and horse traffic. The Lake Magog campground is frequently crowded, and the Naiset cabins are overrun during poor weather. To reserve space at either, phone Mt. Assiniboine Lodge, 403-678-2883.

**41**

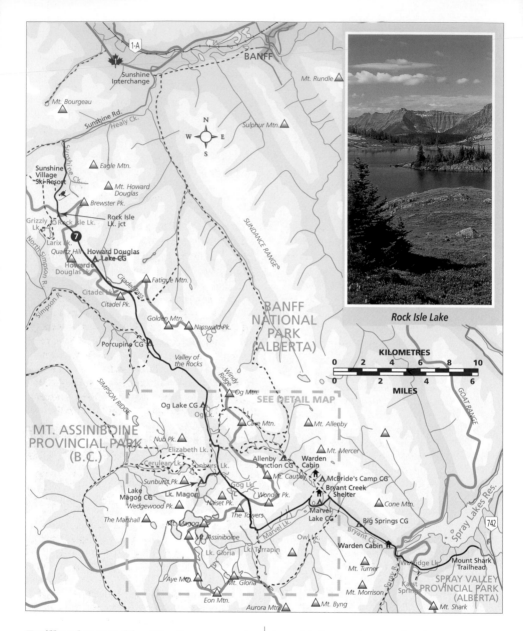

Rock Isle Lake

## Trailhead to Sunshine Meadows

From the trailhead behind the gondola terminal, follow the Healy Creek trail 700 m to a junction.

The Sunshine ski area originated with a cabin built by the Canadian Pacific Railway in 1928. Between 1929 and 1932, several ski parties from Banff visited the area. They were delighted with the winter snow. Jim Brewster, then owner of Brewster Transportation, was one of these skiers. In 1934, he leased the cabin for the winter, buying it outright in 1936. Brewster hired mountain guides to teach skiing, and the area's popularity grew rapidly.

Development at Sunshine has long been a thorny issue. As with most commercial enterprises in the national parks, the various owners of Sunshine Village have sought to expand their facilities and lease area. Environmentalists have questioned the appropriateness of private, commercial enterprise on national park land, due to the negative effects caused by expansion. Skiers and Banff business people note that the area has excellent snow. Many of them would like Sunshine to be allowed to expand further to cater to a larger market. By increments, they have been successful — new ski runs, new lifts, new buildings — the "footprint" of the ski area is forever expanding.

Sunshine Village is at road's end. Follow the crushed stone path south, through the sprawl of buildings. Fifteen metres past the avalanche station turn east (left) onto a gravelled trail and ascend south through open larch forest to the Sunshine Meadows — a spectacular hiking environment. Open vistas grace all directions. The towering horn of Mt. Assiniboine beckons from the south. After 1.1 km, the trail crests the Continental Divide and crosses the boundary from Banff National Park, Alberta, into Mt. Assiniboine Provincial Park, BC. The trail forks. The wider trail on the right leads to Rock Isle Lake. If you do not want to make this sidetrip, continue on the left-hand trail.

## Sunshine and Snow

**The Sunshine Meadows** occupy a 14 km arc along the Continental Divide, at an average elevation of 2225 m. Together with the meadows at Simpson Pass, Healy Pass, and above Lost Horse Creek, they form one of the larger mountain meadow systems in the world. The vegetation here is a heath tundra. Mountain heather, woolly everlasting, fleabane, valerian, arctic willow, western anemone, and sedges are the characteristic plants. In addition, 340 other plants have been recorded. This represents more than a third of the plant species of Banff and Jasper national parks. Some of the species are rare, and many are at the extreme northern or southern limits of their ranges.

The average temperature on the meadows is -4°C, and more than 7 m of snow falls each year. Snowbanks linger well into July. Vegetation is specially adapted, storing nutrients from summer's sunshine to release in a burst that promotes rapid growth the following year. Still, with a growing season so short, it may take many decades before some plants mature enough to carry blooms — 20 years is typical for moss campion. The thin soils are saturated with snowmelt for much of the summer. Travel off-trail causes immediate and sometimes permanent damage to the ground cover. Please keep to maintained trails.

### Sunshine Meadows to Citadel Pass

For 2.5 km beyond the Rock Isle Lake junction, the Assiniboine trail rambles through Sunshine Meadows and re-enters Banff National Park. The meadows are dotted with limestone erratics — boulders deposited by retreating glaciers. After descending into a hollow northeast of Quartz Hill (2579 m), the trail climbs over Quartz Ridge, with unimpeded views south to Mt. Assiniboine. Here, the trail improvements end, and a heavily braided, often slippery trail descends to the campground on the east shore of Howard Douglas Lake (incorrectly called "Sundown Lake" on older topographic maps). Howard Douglas was the second superintendent of Banff National Park. Mountaineers may readily ascend Quartz Hill from either the campground or from the trail's high point on Quartz Ridge. Eastern brook trout inhabit Howard Douglas Lake.

A classic alpland dotted with lakelets lies beyond Howard Douglas Lake. Near here, in August 1933, three hikers watched two wolves attack and kill a grizzly bear. After crossing Citadel Pass, you re-enter Mt. Assiniboine Provincial Park. A sign optimistically informs you that Lake Magog is 17 km and 5.5 hours distant. It is 18 km to the Magog Lake junction on a tough trail. Most mortals with backpacks should add three hours to the

## Rock Isle/Grizzly Lake/Larix Lake 5.7 km loop

 **This loop visits** three lakes in the northern part of Mt. Assiniboine Provincial Park. Some of the BC Parks trail signs call this outing The Garden Path. You reach the Rock Isle Lake viewpoint in 500 m. Turn southwest (left) at the next junction in 200 m. The trail descends through a delightful, flower-filled larch forest. Turn southwest (right) at the next junction, to pass along the east shore of Grizzly Lake. The trail curves south to a viewpoint that overlooks the upper Simpson Valley. After circling around Larix Lake, with impressive views west to The Monarch (2904 m), the trail climbs back to the loop junction below Rock Isle Lake.

Rock Isle Lake is dammed by an upturned lip of Outram Formation limestone. Another bedrock exposure creates the "isle." The lake drains underground. Grizzly Lake is shallow and filling with vegetation, while Larix Lake is deep with underwater ledges visible. *Larix* is the genus name of the Lyall's larch. You must carry your backpacks on this loop hike, as there is no place to cache them.

suggested hiking time.

## Citadel Pass to Og Lake

A kilometre south of the pass, the trail drops below treeline into larch forest, passes beside a small tarn — the last reliable water source for 13 km — and then begins a steep, switchbacking descent through avalanche paths. This is excellent bear habitat. Grizzly bears in Mt. Assiniboine Provincial Park are subjected to an annual spring hunt. After traversing south onto a sideslope, you reach the Porcupine campground junction. If you make the very steep descent to this campground, you don't have to climb back up to continue next day. Follow a faint track south from the campground for 2.1 km, to rejoin the main trail at the Simpson River junction.

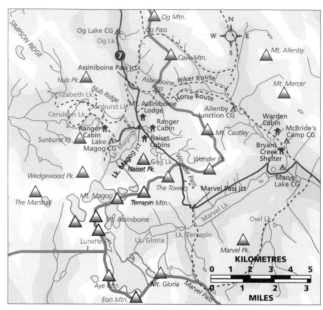

From the Porcupine campground junction, the high trail continues its southward traverse of the sideslope of Golden Mountain (2902 m). I counted more than 25 species of wildflowers in bloom here in early July. At the south end of this traverse, the trail contours around a rockslide that heralds the entrance to the Valley of the Rocks.

The Valley of the Rocks is not a valley, but a depression in the debris of an enormous landslide in the mountains to the east. This landslide is estimated to contain more than a billion cubic metres of material, making it the largest known rockslide in the Rockies, and one of the twenty largest in the world. The winding trail through the Valley of the Rocks seems double its 6 km length, and is virtually devoid of water. At the Simpson River junction, turn southeast (left). The small rockslide depression lake nearby is the only source of water before Og Lake. You should treat this water before consumption.

You will know that the travail through the Valley of the Rocks is over when Mt. Assiniboine again becomes visible, directly ahead. The trail descends to Og Lake and its campground. Og Lake is a sink lake; its waters drain underground. Many of the lakes near Mt. Assiniboine empty in a similar fashion. Although the karst system fed by the lakes is unstudied, a century ago Walter

## Windy Ridge (2635 m), 8.7 km

**Follow the Assiniboine Pass** trail northeast from the campground. At all junctions follow signs for Og Pass/Windy Ridge. The trail climbs toward Og Pass, and levels in meadows at a final junction at km 6.5. Og Pass is 300 m east. The Windy Ridge trail veers north (left) from the junction, and climbs 2.2 km to the barren ridgecrest north of Og Mountain. The ridge provides a splendid panorama of this part of the Rockies. Especially alluring is an unnamed lake, immediately northeast, in the upper reaches of Brewster Creek.

## Variations

- Hike the route in reverse
- Backpack from Sunshine to Lake Magog campground and return the same way, 71.0 km
- Exit from Lake Magog jct via Assiniboine Pass, to reach the Bryant Creek trail at the Wonder Pass jct. Carry on to Mt. Shark trailhead, 58.6 km
- Make a loop using Bryant Creek. Approach from Mt. Shark trailhead over Assiniboine Pass to Lake Magog (24.7 km). Exit via Wonder Pass (25.6 km), 3–5 days
- Camp at Howard Douglas Lake (12.3 km) and explore Citadel Pass and Sunshine Meadows
- Hike the route in reverse and combine it with Lakes and Larches (Classic Hike #9) to create an outing of 98.9 km, 6-10 days

Wilcox speculated that the disappearing water emerges as the source of the Simpson River, 6 km northwest.

## Og Lake to Lake Magog

From Og Lake, it is 5.9 km to the Lake Magog campground junction. Half of this distance is across a flat subalpine meadow, the probable location of an ancient lake. Trails proliferate as you approach Lake Magog. Any attempt to describe the lefts and rights will only confuse. If you are destined for the campground or for the Naiset Cabins, follow trail signs accordingly. The campground is set on a glacial terrace on the northwest shore of Lake Magog. It offers a commanding view of Mt. Assiniboine, whose graceful summit towers more than 1400 m above. As with most isolated and lofty peaks, Mt. Assiniboine creates local weather. Clouds frequently adorn the summit, and precipitation is common nearby — usually on your tent.

After the energy you've invested in reaching Mt. Assiniboine, you will probably want to spend several days in the area. The best day-hiking options are described in the sidebars. The distances are measured from Lake Magog campground.

## Mt. Assiniboine Lodge and Naiset Cabins

Mt. Assiniboine's popularity assures that you will have lots of company during your visit. Many stay at the Naiset Cabins or at Mt. Assiniboine Lodge. The five original Naiset Cabins were built in 1925 by A.O. Wheeler, founder of the Alpine Club of Canada (ACC). The cabins accommodated clients on "Wheeler's Walking Tours" of the Rockies. The enterprise soon went bankrupt, and the cabins were leased to various interests until 1944, when the ACC took them over. In 1971, ownership of the

## Sunburst Circuit/Chuck's Ridge, 9.1 km loop

*Cerulean Lake*

**Follow the trail** north past Sunburst Lake to Cerulean (seh-ROO-lee-an) Lake. *Cerulean* means "resembling the blue colour of the sky." At the junction on the far side of the lake, turn west (left) and follow the north shore. There are fine views of Sunburst Peak (2820 m) across the lake. At the west end of the lake, the trail descends to the north (right). After 200 m, angle east (right) at a junction, and climb 1.4 km to Elizabeth Lake. I saw a bald eagle here in 1992. The aquamarine lake was named for Lizzie Rummel, who operated Sunburst cabin as a tourist lodge from 1951 to 1970. The cabin has since been moved from its original location.

At the outlet of Elizabeth Lake, the 800 m side-trail to Chuck's Ridge veers north. Chuck's Ridge (2347 m) provides an excellent overview of this area, and of the meadows and lakes at the head of Nestor Creek. The glacier-draped form of The Marshall (3190 m) dominates the view southwest. You can also see Wedgewood Lake. This ridge was a favourite haunt of Chuck Millar, a packer for Mt. Assiniboine Lodge.

Return to Elizabeth Lake and follow the trail along the west shore for 400 metres until you come to a junction. If you would like to ascend to The Nub, turn east (left). Otherwise, continue straight ahead and descend to Cerulean Lake. Return via Sunburst Lake to the campground.

*The view from the Nub features the glaciated horn of Mt. Assiniboine.*

decrepit cabins passed to BC Parks, which refurbished them for use by hikers. The capacity is 31. Mt. Assiniboine Lodge now operates the cabins. *Naiset*, from the Sioux language, means "sunset."

Mt. Assiniboine Lodge was built by the Canadian Pacific Railway in the summer of 1928, at the behest of Italian sportsman Marquis delgi Albizzi and Norwegian skier Erling Strom. The two had visited Assiniboine the previous spring and were delighted with the skiing terrain. Strom subsequently operated the lodge for more than four decades. The lodge is now owned by the BC government, and is operated privately under lease. The park ranger station is located southeast of the lodge and cabins.

## Lake Magog to Marvel Lake

Because it is difficult to arrange transportation at the Mt. Shark trailhead at trail's end, some backpackers exit from Mt. Assiniboine via Sunshine. If you choose to backtrack, include Wonder Pass (4.4 km) as a half-day hike before you go.

The trail to Wonder Pass skirts the shore of Lake Magog to Naiset Cabins. Half a kilometre south of the cabins, the trail crosses the outlet of Gog Lake. Great blue herons nested at this lake in 1983 — the highest nesting elevation yet recorded for this species. The names Gog, Og, and Magog refer to legendary giants of Biblical times. The cliffs south and west of Gog Lake are the "type locality" for the Gog Group of sedimentary formations. This is where these rocks — quartzite, sandstone, and siltstone — were first studied in detail. Gog Formation quartzite is a metamorphic, quartz-rich sandstone. It is the hardest rock

## The Nub, 6.7 km loop

**Follow the trail** north past Sunburst Lake to Cerulean Lake. At the junction on the far shore of Cerulean Lake, turn northeast (right) for Elizabeth Lake. After a short climb, you reach The Nub junction. Turn east (right) and climb steadily to Nub Ridge (2390 m). If you would like to ascend higher onto Nub Peak, watch for a faint track that angles sharply to the north where the trail levels. By following this rough path to the prominent high point, you obtain superb views of the soaring fang of Mt. Assiniboine. You can see six lakes — Gog, Magog, Sunburst, Cerulean, Elizabeth, and Wedgewood. For those inclined, a beaten track leads north for 2 km along a shattered limestone ridge to the summit slopes of Nub Peak (2748 m). The view from this modest mountain is without equal in the vicinity.

From Nub Ridge you can return to the campground via your route of ascent (more direct), or make a loop by following the trail south from the end of the ridge to the Assiniboine Pass trail. At this junction, turn southwest (right) to reach the campground in 1.5 km.

exposed in the central Rockies.

Continuing south from Gog Lake, the trail climbs through wildflower meadows and larch forest to a viewpoint that overlooks a small waterfall and canyon. This canyon is cut in Miette (mee-YETT) Formation shale. You reach treeline about 500 m before Wonder Pass. From the crest of the pass, located on the Banff National Park boundary, there are inspiring views south to the overthrust limestone peaks of the Blue Range. On a clear day, the view north will include the mountains that flank Sunshine Meadows. Look for mountain goats on the cliffs of The Towers (2846 m), west of the pass.

Cross Wonder Pass. After 700 m, a faint track branches southeast (left); follow it 600 m to a viewpoint that overlooks Marvel Lake. This is an excellent extension for day-hikers. At treeline, the main trail cuts southwest across a gully. From this sideslope you have a spectacular vista of Marvel Lake, 550 m below. The lake is the sixth largest in Banff National Park, and is 67 m deep.

The next 1.8 km involves a steady descent. Initially the trail heads west, providing views of the extensive glacier beneath Mt. Gloria (2908 m), Mt. Eon (3310 m), and Mt. Aye (3243 m). You can now see two more lakes in the valley above Marvel Lake — Lake Gloria and Lake Terrapin. The colour of these lakes is caused by concentrations of glacial rock flour in their waters. These lakes act as

## "The Canadian Matterhorn"

**Surveyor, G.M. Dawson,** was the first explorer to describe Mt. Assiniboine, in 1884. The mountain was the object of several mountaineering attempts in the 1890s. The mountain's remote location and difficult approach thwarted all comers, but competition was keen. In 1901, Edward Whymper, of Matterhorn fame, visited the Rockies at the behest of the Canadian Pacific Railway. Railway executives hoped that he would make Mt. Assiniboine's first ascent. However, Whymper was past his mountaineering prime and could not even be enticed to make the approach. The first ascent was made in September that year by James Outram (OOT-rum) and guides. They ascended the southwest face, and descended the northeast arête, toward Lake Magog. This arête is the "regular" ascent route today. Although the climb is not difficult by contemporary standards, unpredictable weather, poor rock, and the presence of snow or ice make any attempt on Mt. Assiniboine a serious undertaking.

settling ponds, preventing much of the rock flour from entering Marvel Lake. Hence the water of Marvel Lake is a richer blue. A waterfall marks the outflow of Lake Terrapin.

Continue straight ahead (southeast) at the Marvel Pass junction. Although the trail is well travelled, the Marvel Lake valley is a wild corner of Banff National Park. As you begin the 4.5 km traverse above the north shore of the lake, watch for grizzly bears. A variety of wildflowers decorates the south-facing avalanche slopes.

### Marvel Lake to Mt. Shark Trailhead

The trail re-enters forest at the east end of Marvel Lake. Continue straight ahead at the first junction. At the second junction, turn south (right) to reach the outlet of Marvel Lake in 500 m. Head east from the outlet to Marvel Lake campground in 1 km. From the campground, it is 800 m to the Bryant Creek trail. Turn southeast (right), and follow this rolling backcountry artery through lodgepole pine forest, 6.4 km to the mouth of the Bryant Creek valley, passing the Big Springs campground in 3.6 km. The trail is fireroad width and is shared with horses. The valley was named for Henry Bryant, who made the first attempt to climb Mt. Assiniboine in 1899.

The trail junction at the Banff National Park boundary is known as Trail Centre. Take the south (right) trail for the Mt. Shark trailhead. Cross Bryant Creek on a footbridge and continue south for 500 m. This is part of the historic trail travelled by the Palliser Expedition in 1858. Spray Lakes Reservoir is to the north. The Spray Lakes area was removed from Banff National Park in 1930 for a hydroelectric development, completed in 1951.

Turn east (left) at the Palliser Pass junction, and cross the Spray River at a small canyon. The remaining 5.8 km to the Mt. Shark trailhead is along old logging roads. Watridge Lake and the nearby Karst Spring — one of the larger by volume in North America — make interesting sidetrips.

The hike to the Mt. Shark trailhead is a very long day from Lake Magog campground. Many backpackers use Marvel Lake or Big Springs campgrounds to break the journey into two days. If you do not have transportation prearranged, plan to arrive at the Mt. Shark trailhead early. The trailhead is 4.6 km along a gravel road from the Smith Dorrien-Spray Road. The junction of these two roads is 37 km south of Canmore. Traffic is light in the evening.

# 8. Simpson Pass/ Healy Pass

## Route

Day-hike or overnight

| Route | Elevation (m) | Distance (km) |
|---|---|---|
| Parking lot | 1690 | 0 |
| Trailhead | 1692 | 0.2 |
| Healy Creek CG | 1973 | 5.7 |
| Simpson Pass jct | 1981 | 6.1 |
| Simpson Pass | 2107 | 7.7 |
| Healy Meadows jct | 2095 | 10.3 |
| Healy Pass | 2330 | 11.8 |
| Healy Meadows jct | 2095 | 13.3 |
| Trailhead | 1692 | 21.0 |
| Parking lot | 1690 | 21.2 |

**Maps**

NTS: 82 O/4
Gem Trek: Banff and Mt. Assiniboine, or Kootenay National Park

## Trailhead

**Follow the Trans-Canada** Highway 8.3 km west from Banff to the Sunshine Interchange. Follow the Sunshine road 9 km to its end at the ski area parking lot. The trailhead kiosk is west of (behind) the gondola terminal, 200 m from the parking lot.

## Variations

- Day-hike Healy Pass, 18.8 km return
- Day-hike Simpson Pass, 15.2 km return
- Camp at Healy Creek CG and day-hike to the destinations
- An optional exit for backpackers from Healy Creek CG is to Simpson Pass, Wawa Ridge, and the Sunshine Road; 13.3 km

In the deep forest along Healy Creek and on the meadows above, you may find backcountry bliss. Keep this in mind as you assemble your pack in the busy parking lot. No other departure point in the Rockies so readily prompts me to put on my boots and my pack and to get away.

The trailhead kiosk is concealed behind the gondola terminal. On my last visit the only

*Healy Meadows features superb wildflower displays.*

instruction to hikers was a tiny backpacker sign on the north edge of the parking lot, bolted onto a stake and stuck into a garbage can filled with rocks. The sign pointed in the wrong direction.

**Trailhead to Simpson Pass Junction**

The road-width trail climbs gradually on the bank between Healy Creek and the Sunshine access road. At 0.9 km, the trail forks and narrows. Take the right-hand trail and begin a short descent to Sunshine Creek, which is eroded into Palliser Formation limestone. Karst fissures upstream capture much of the water, often leaving the lower reach of the stream dry.

Across Sunshine Creek, the climb resumes through a wonderful subalpine forest of Engelmann spruce, subalpine fir, and a few lodgepole pines. The delicate blooms of pink wintergreen and the tiny red fruits of grouseberry add colour to the forest floor. False azalea, with its pink, urn-shaped blooms, is common. Mountain arnica, showy fleabane, bracted lousewort, twinflower, yellow columbine, Sitka valerian, western meadowrue, northern black currant, Labrador tea, northern gentian, bracted honeysuckle, bronzebells, paintbrush, one-flowered wintergreen — the list of plants that typify the subalpine forest floor is nearly complete here. Listen for the songs of golden-crowned kinglets, winter wrens, black-capped chickadees, red-breasted nuthatches, pine siskins, Tennessee warblers, boreal chickadees, and varied thrushes; for the trilling of

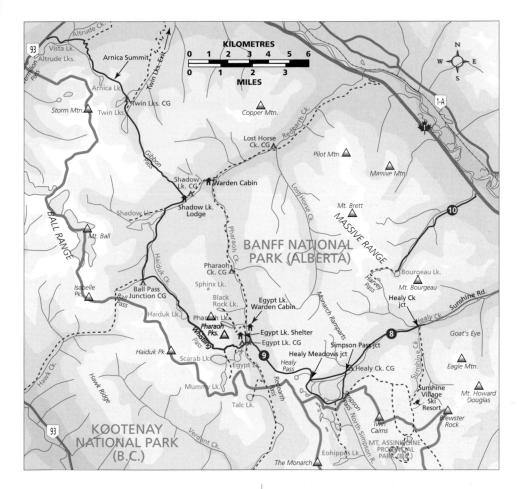

dark-eyed juncos; for the rasping calls of Clark's nutcrackers; and for the tapping of three-toed woodpeckers. The middens of red squirrels dot the forest floor, and their chattering greets you from the trees.

If you hit the trail late, the bridged creek crossing at km 3.3 makes a pleasant lunch stop. Here, Healy Creek has eroded a shallow canyon into the upturned edges of fossil-rich dolomite of the Cairn Formation.

For the next 2.4 km, the trail follows the north bank of Healy Creek, crossing three avalanche slopes before Healy Creek campground. Pressure-treated wood structures span sidestreams that are but trickles. They were constructed as part of a clean-up of the trail in the late 1980s. At that time, horse-use was banished, sections of trail were re-routed, and stone and gravel were incorporated into the tread in wet areas. In the upper valley, there are sections of inlaid natural stone that are

both attractive and highly effective. Look for low larkspur, white camas, and meadow buttercup in the avalanche clearings. The ruin of a cabin foundation lies about 30 m south of the trail, on the far side of the last avalanche slope. I've seen pine grosbeaks here.

You reach the campground — a fine destination for novice backpackers — 200 m beyond the third avalanche slope. Just past the campground, the presence of white mountain heather in the understory indicates the transition to the upper subalpine ecoregion. The Simpson Pass junction is 400 m beyond the campground. If you want to make a loop hike in the upper valley — including Simpson Pass, Healy Meadows, and Healy Pass — turn south (left) to cross the bridge over Healy Creek. If you want to hike directly to Healy Pass, head west (straight ahead), climbing 1.9 km to the Healy Meadows junction. Skip ahead in the text to that point.

## A Lunker of a Calling Card

George Simpson was Banff's first tourist. If he were alive today, he might be a CEO who played squash before jogging to the office, worked out at lunch, "downsized" half his staff in the afternoon, and fit in a 100 km bike ride before dinner. In the 1820s and 1830s he trooped relentlessly through Prince Rupert's Land and was said to have met every employee of the Hudson's Bay Company. He had the 19th century equivalent of his own corporate jet — an eight-seater express canoe. One seat was dedicated to a piper, who would herald his lordship's arrival at far-flung forts and trading posts. In 1841, freshly knighted for his services to the British Empire and to commerce in general, and then Governor of the Hudson's Bay Company, Simpson set out to make the first circuit of the globe by essentially a terrestrial route. He did it in less than two years, a feat achieved in no small part by the pace he kept across the Rockies — sometimes covering 80 km a day. His mean and uncompromising behaviour earned him the tag, The Little Emperor. He wrote: "It is strange that all my ailments vanish as soon as I seat myself in a canoe." Presumably, this was because someone else was paddling the breakneck pace. Dip, dip, and swing.

Simpson's party, led by the Cree guide Alexis Piché, crossed what is now known as Simpson Pass in 1858. (Simpson had called it Shuswap Pass.) Sir George left his calling card. In 1904, a party of Banffites camping on the pass found Simpson's initials and those of companion, John Rowland, and the date 1841 carved in a fallen tree. The relevant portion of the tree, now known as the Simpson Register, is housed at the Whyte Museum in Banff.

*Sir George Simpson*

## Simpson Pass Junction to Simpson Pass

The trail climbs away from Healy Creek as a narrow track. During wet weather, water often runs straight down the tread. Seeps abound near trailside. Judging from the tracks I've seen here, some of the seeps may be licks frequented by moose. Wildflowers decorate the trail edges. Halfway to the pass, the trail breaks in and out of glades that feature the first of the larches. After 1.4 km, the trail swings south to descend slightly over the last 200 m to Simpson Pass, with views ahead of The Monarch (2904 m).

Simpson Pass is a narrow breach in the forest, well below treeline — a frost meadow where cold air stunts the growth of trees. Larches dot the glade, along with wildflowers and the diggings of a colony of Columbian ground squirrels. The ancient stumps of axe-felled trees suggest the handiwork of a former occasional resident of the area — Bill Peyto — trail guide, park warden, prospector, and Banff legend.

If you are hiking the optional backpacking exit, head northeast (left) from the junction on

### Glacier Lily

*Glacier lilies*

Healy Pass and the surrounding meadows are renowned for their early summer displays of glacier lilies. The nodding, yellow flower is the first to appear in the upper subalpine ecoregion, growing through receding snowbanks. Its bloom is testimony to nature's remarkable means of ensuring that plants survive in harsh climates. Here, the growing season is less than two months, and the average annual temperature is -4°C. The glacier lily stores nutrients synthesized from last year's sunshine in its corm, releasing them in a burst in late spring, promoting rapid growth. Grizzly bears relish the protein-rich corm, and will excavate entire meadows in quest of this food.

Simpson Pass. The trail climbs into the forest and makes an undulating traverse beneath a limestone cliff for roughly 2 km, before trending southeast and climbing to the Monarch viewpoint on Wawa Ridge (2362 m) at km 3.3. Carry on east for 300 m to the Twin Cairns/Meadow Park junction. Continue straight ahead (east) to descend a ski run of the Sunshine Village ski area in 1.7 km. From the base of the ski run, make your way to the access road and turn north (left); it is 6.0 km of steady downhill to the parking lot.

## Simpson Pass to Healy Meadows Junction

To continue to Healy Meadows and Healy Pass, head west (right) from the junction in Simpson Pass. The trail angles north as it climbs steeply into the forest alongside a stream. The bedrock here is Cathedral Formation limestone, but the scrunching under your feet is quartz grit of the Miette and Gog formations, eroded from above and carried here in runoff. Early season hikers will be treated to astounding displays of glacier lilies from this point onward.

You reach the Eohippus Lake junction in 400 m. Continue straight ahead, where the trail soon levels and emerges from forest at the southern end of the Healy Meadows. These meadows loosely connect with those of Healy Pass, Lost Horse Creek, Harvey Pass, Citadel Pass, and Sunshine to form an extensive alpland — known as Sunshine Meadows — that covers approximately 40 km$^2$. Twenty-two rare plants have been recorded here, and cotton-grass graces the shores of the lakes. I've seen spotted sandpipers at the first lake. The meadows are bug heaven in July.

For the next 2 km, the sometimes spongy trail undulates north, winding through draws and cutting through stream courses, with the Monarch Ramparts off to the west. Vibrant pink and scarlet paintbrush highlight the wildflower displays. In the last basin before the Healy Meadows junction, an ocean of glacier lilies rings a wet meadow. Mountain marsh marigold, western anemone, red-stemmed saxifrage, mountain sorrel, and sticky false asphodel grow beside the inlet streams. The trailside boulders here are quartz-veined gritstone of the Miette Group of

## Bill's Place

*Bill's place in 1913...*                    *...and in 2002*

**The environs of Simpson Pass** were a favourite haunt of Bill Peyto (PEE-toe), who began his association with the Rockies in 1893 or 1894 as a trail guide working for Tom Wilson. Peyto set up his own company in 1901, when he achieved fame by guiding mountaineer James Outram to the base of Mt. Assiniboine on the occasion of its first ascent. After serving in the Boer War, Peyto became a Banff park warden in 1913. During his trail guiding years, Peyto trapped and prospected near Simpson Pass in the off-season. He built a cabin in the meadows — a palace by backcountry standards — which served as his base. The cabin still stands.

Peyto's best known prospecting claim — staked in 1917 — was at Talc Lake, a short distance away in what is now Kootenay National Park. The government of the day denied Peyto permission to develop the talc claim, citing that the would-be mine was located in a national park. The bureaucrats were a mineshaft shy on knowledge about the land in their care. The claim was outside of Banff, and Kootenay National Park was not established until 1920. By that time, Peyto had given up hassling with the feds. Ironically, the National Talc Company took over the claim and was granted permission to mine it.

Although it is popular to characterize Peyto as a wild man and a gruff recluse, archival photos show a gentler side — with wife and children in later years, near his Simpson Pass hideaway.

formations — the oldest rock exposed in this part of the Rockies. The view downvalley includes the distant Fairholme Range, and Mt. Bourgeau (2930 m). A short climb brings you to the Healy Meadows junction, with its quartzite "couch" nearby — a wonderful place to lounge on a pleasant day.

### Healy Meadows Junction to Healy Pass

You can exit from this junction by turning northeast (right) to descend 7.9 km to the parking lot. For Healy Pass, turn northwest (left). You soon leave the forest behind as you climb along the stream that drains the basin beneath the pass. The wildflower meadows here are on every experienced hiker's short-list of "best wildflower gardens in the Rockies." Look for the blooms of low larkspur and blue columbine. And look up every now and then. This is a great place for spotting raptors on the wing.

Healy Pass provides a wonderful prospect over the southern Rockies. The quartzite bluff of the Monarch Ramparts extends southeast from the pass, bordering Healy Meadows. Mt. Assiniboine (3618 m), highest in the southern Rockies, soars skyward 30 km to the south. From Mt. Assiniboine to Crowfoot Mountain in the north, the view encompasses a 110 km length of the Continental Divide.

To the west, the cluster of exquisite lakes in the vicinity of Egypt Lake will catch your eye. The arrangement of the three largest — Mummy, Scarab, and Egypt — is known as a cirque staircase. Glacial ice that flowed from the south created the three basins, each at a progressively lower elevation. Today, only a remnant glacier remains at the western end of Scarab Lake. To the southwest, you can see the cliffs of the unnamed peak above Talc Lake. They feature a fossil-rich outcrop of the Stephen Formation — popularly known as the Burgess Shale.

### Healy's Many Fortunes

**John Gerome Healy** was a classic character of the old west. He could list half a dozen professions and enterprises behind his name when he arrived in the Rockies in 1884. He prospected along Healy Creek and near Copper Mountain. Like most of his kind, Healy soon moved on. However, unlike many of his contemporaries, Healy's fortunes changed. He established a successful trading company in Dawson City, lived long and died a wealthy man.

### Return

The way home is a steady downhill trundle. Return to the Healy Meadows junction (1.5 km). Continue straight ahead and follow the trail, steeply at first, through ancient forest down the Healy Creek valley to the Simpson Pass junction, from where you hike familiar ground to the parking lot — total distance, 7.9 km.

# 9. Lakes and Larches

### Route

Overnight, 3–6 days

| Route | Elevation (m) | Distance (km) |
| --- | --- | --- |
| Parking lot | 1690 | 0 |
| Trailhead | 1692 | 0.2 |
| Healy Pass jct | 1706 | 0.9 |
| Healy Creek CG | 1973 | 5.7 |
| Simpson Pass jct | 1981 | 6.1 |
| Healy Meadows jct | 2095 | 7.9 |
| Healy Pass | 2330 | 9.4 |
| Pharaoh Creek jct | 1992 | 12.4 |
| Egypt Lake CG | 1997 | 12.6 |
| Whistling Pass | 2292 | 15.9 |
| Haiduk Lake | 2067 | 18.1 |
| Ball Pass jct and CG | 1921 | 21.4 |
| Shadow Lake | 1851 | 25.7 |
| Gibbon Pass jct | 1814 | 26.6 |
| Shadow Lake CG | 1814 | +0.1 |
| Gibbon Pass | 2300 | 29.7 |
| Lower Twin Lake | 2058 | 32.4 |
| Twin Lakes jct | 2058 | 32.6 |
| Upper Twin Lake and CG | 2088 | 33.4 |
| Arnica Summit | 2287 | 35.0 |
| Arnica Lake | 2149 | 35.8 |
| Vista Lake | 1570 | 39.4 |
| Kootenay Parkway | 1707 | 40.8 |

**Maps**
NTS: 82 O/4 and 82 N/1
Gem Trek: Banff and Mt. Assiniboine, or Kootenay National Park
**See map on p.49**

### Trailhead

**Follow the Trans-Canada** Highway 8.3 km west from Banff to the Sunshine Interchange. Follow the Sunshine road 9 km to its end at the ski area parking lot. The trailhead kiosk is west of (behind) the gondola terminal, 200 m from the parking lot.

*Egypt Lake*

Continental Divide. This is a spectacular terrain of cliff, meadow, glacier, and tarn — the hallmark scenery of the Canadian Rockies.

## Trailhead to Healy Pass

The road-width trail climbs gradually on the bank between Healy Creek and the Sunshine access road. At 0.9 km, the trail forks and narrows. Take the right-hand trail to continue west, where you begin a short descent to Sunshine Creek. The ensuing climb in the Healy Creek valley is through an ancient subalpine forest. You cross the creek at km 3.3, reach the campground at km 5.7, and the Healy Meadows junction at km 7.9. From this junction, near which you see your first larches of the hike, it is a steady climb through marvelous meadows to Healy Pass at km 9.4. For more detailed information on the Healy Creek valley, see Classic Hike #8.

## Healy Pass to Egypt Lake Campground

Healy Pass provides a wonderful prospect over the southern Rockies. The quartzite bluff of the Monarch Ramparts extends southeast from the pass, ringing the Healy Pass meadows. Mt. Assiniboine (3618 m), highest in the southern Rockies, soars skyward 30 km to the south. From Mt. Assiniboine to Crowfoot Mountain in the north, the view encompasses a 110 km length of the Continental Divide.

To the west, the cluster of exquisite lakes in the vicinity of Egypt Lake will catch your eye. The arrangement of the three largest — Mummy, Scarab, and Egypt — is known as a cirque staircase. Glacial ice that flowed from the south created the three basins, each at a progressively lower elevation. Today, only a remnant glacier remains at the western end of Scarab Lake.

Leaving Healy Pass, the trail descends rapidly through wet subalpine meadows and glades of larch forest to reach the Pharaoh Creek junction in 3 km, just south of the Egypt Lake warden cabin. Turn south (left) and you will cross a bridge over Pharaoh Creek in 150 m. The trail ascends the creekbank to the Egypt Lake campground and shelter. A reservation and permit are required for overnight use of the shelter. Given the area's popularity, this building is often overrun. Plan on spending a few days at Egypt Lake to enjoy the day-hiking options.

## Egypt Lake to Ball Pass Junction

From Egypt Lake campground, the Lakes and Larches trail tackles the headwall above Egypt

B ecause it is central to many short and wonderful day-hikes, Egypt Lake is the most popular backpacking destination in Banff National Park. The Lakes and Larches trail includes the Egypt Lake region, along with Healy Pass, and a series of passes on the eastern flank of the

## Variations

- Camp at Egypt Lake and return over Healy Pass, 25.2 km
- Exit from Egypt Lake along Pharaoh Creek to Redearth Creek, 31.9 km, 2–3 days
- Exit along Redearth Creek from Gibbon Pass junction, 40.0 km, 3–4 days
- Exit at Twin Lakes junction, 40.4 km, 3–4 days
- Hike the trail in reverse
- Hike from the northern trailhead to Twin Lake CG, 7.4 km; an excellent novice backpack
- By crossing Ball Pass and descending 9.7 km along Hawk Creek, you can link a portion of this outing with the Rockwall, making possible a trip of 88.8 km, 6–9 days
- Hike the trail in reverse and combine it with Mt. Assiniboine (Classic Hike #7) to create an outing of 98.9 km, 6-10 days

## Talc Lake (Natalko Lake), 4.2 km

From Egypt Lake campground, backtrack to the Pharaoh Creek bridge. Cross the bridge and turn south (right). Follow the east bank of Pharaoh Creek on a rough and often ill-defined trail, for 2.3 km to a junction. Turn west, cross the wet meadow, and pick up the trail that ascends the opposite bank. The trail between here and Talc Lake is an old cart track, constructed by the National Talc Company. Boulders cleared from the track are lined up along the trail edges. In this vicinity, the trail enters Kootenay National Park.

Talc Lake occupies an austere setting, walled by cliffs that feature the Cathedral -Stephen -Eldon sequence of sedimentary formations. The fossil-rich Stephen Formation is popularly known as the Burgess Shale. A 100 m high waterfall cascades to the west shore. The presence of a small drift glacier harks back to colder climes and the glacial origin of the cirque that contains the lake. You can see the portals of the talc mine in the cliffs to the south. You can inspect the old foundations and refuse from the mine by hopping the outlet of Talc Lake and walking south.

Those capable of routefinding and travel on difficult boulder slopes can head north from Talc Lake to cross a rocky saddle ("Natalko Pass," 2303 m) that grants access to the valley east of Mummy Lake. Distance for this loop hike is 9.5 km return from Egypt Lake campground. Otherwise, return the way you came.

## The National Talc Company

Talc is magnesium silicate, one of the softer minerals. It is used in talcum powder, explosives, and insulators. The Talc Lake claim was staked by outfitter and guide Bill Peyto in 1917. He was thwarted in his attempt to develop the claim by the government's erroneous contention that it lay within Banff National Park. (Kootenay National Park did not exist at that time.) The National Talc Company took over the claim, and mined talc during the 1920s. The claim then passed to Western Talc Holdings, and finally to Wartime Metals, which mined it in 1943. The talc was shipped by horse and cart to Massive, a railway siding in the Bow Valley. One marvels today at the energy of this enterprise, in what was then a remote corner of the Rockies.

## Pharaoh Lake/Black Rock Lake, 2.4 km

The mountain wall north of Egypt Lake is riddled with northeast facing cirques. Pharaoh Lake occupies the largest, and is backed by the quartzite cliffs of the Pharaoh Peaks. Walk north from the campground on the west side of Pharaoh Creek for 500 m to a junction. Turn west (left) and ascend a steep, rough trail for 800 m to the lakeshore. To continue to Black Rock Lake, rock-hop the outlet of Pharaoh Lake, and follow a track northwest for 1.1 km. The last 100 m is alongside a delightful stream. There is a massive rockslide at the west end of the lake. "Black Rock" describes the lichen-covered cliff to the south.

## Egypt Lake/Scarab Lake/Mummy Lake, 3.5 km

From the trail sign in front of the Egypt Lake shelter, head south through the campground on the Whistling Pass trail for 300 m to the Egypt Lake junction. Turn south (left) and follow a rough, undulating trail for 150 m to the north shore of Egypt Lake. The lake, which is 32 m deep and has an area of 16 ha, is home to cutthroat trout and eastern brook trout. A waterfall that drains Scarab Lake cascades over the colourful quartzite cliffs to the west.

The Egyptian theme for the names in this area originated with the Interprovincial Boundary Survey in 1922. It all started with a flight of fancy — a supposed resemblance (when viewed from above) of the outline of nearby Scarab Lake to that of a beetle. The scarab beetle was an Egyptian symbol of resurrection. With their minds in Egyptian mode, the surveyors dropped the names Egypt, Mummy,

and Pharaoh nearby.

Backtrack to the Whistling Pass trail. Turn west (left). The next 1.4 km of trail is poor and involves a steep ascent of the headwall above Egypt Lake. The trail descends slightly from the top of the headwall through a stand of larches to reach the Scarab Lake junction in 200 m. Turn south (left). Descend to the outlet of Scarab Lake in 600 m.

Rock-hop the outlet of Scarab Lake to continue south on a rough track. After an initial climb, the trail drops into a meadowed basin. Follow cairns through rockslide debris, angling upward toward a break in the cliff that grants access to rocky slopes above the east shore of Mummy Lake. This large lake occupies an extremely barren setting, beautiful in its simplicity. Travel is difficult along the boulderfields on the lakeshore.

*Whistling Pass was named for the whistling of the hoary marmots that live in the boulderfields nearby. They are still whistling.*

beaten into screes and boulderfields. If hiking in early summer, you will encounter snow on this north facing slope. Several easy rock-hops of the adjacent stream lead to a boggy area on the south shore of Haiduk Lake. Follow the east shore on a rough trail to another inlet at the north end. Spectacular views north to Mt. Ball and south to the waterfalls that drain the cirque below Haiduk Peak (2920 m), compete for your attention.

The trail parallels an extensive wet meadow for 300 m before crossing Haiduk Creek to its west bank on a log bridge. For the next 2 km, you descend gradually through subalpine forest before swinging west to plunge down forested moraines to the Ball Pass junction and campground.

## Ball Pass Junction to Gibbon Pass Junction

The first section of the trail to Shadow Lake features open views as it skirts wet meadows along the west fork of Haiduk Creek. Cross the principal meltwater stream from Ball Glacier on a bridge, slightly west of where the horse trail fords the stream. After you cross to the east bank of Haiduk Creek, the trail becomes wet, muddy, and rocky, slowing your pace. This trying section ends just before the outlet of Shadow Lake, where the trail has been gravelled.

The outlet of Shadow Lake is the setting for one of the more inspiring scenes in the Rockies — the awesome, glacier-draped, northeast face of Mt. Ball. The lake is 25 m deep, has an area of 57 ha, and is home to cutthroat trout and eastern brook trout. Haiduk Creek has created a sizeable alluvial fan at the inlet on the south shore, almost dividing the lake in two. As its name suggests, the lake spends the latter part of each day in the shadow of Mt. Ball. The best lighting is in early morning. If you will be camping at the nearby campground, return to the outlet for sunrise. East of the outlet, you have an unusual view of Pilot Mountain (2935 m), a well known landmark in the Bow Valley.

Lake. The 1.4 km climb is steep. The trail is covered in rubble, and water frequently runs down the tread. Persevere, for scenic rewards lie just ahead.

From the top of the headwall, the trail descends slightly to contour around a rockslide at the base of the southern Pharaoh Peak (2711 m). Continue straight ahead (west) at the Scarab Lake junction. The trail swings northwest and works its way through rock benches and sparse forest, climbing to the rocky saddle of Whistling Pass. The pass was named for the whistle of the hoary marmot. You may see these large rodents in the quartzite boulderfields nearby.

The views from Whistling Pass include glacier-capped Mt. Ball (3311 m) to the north, the highest mountain on the 80 km length of the Continental Divide between Mt. Assiniboine and Moraine Lake. Haiduk (HAY-duck) Lake lies on the floor of the U-shaped valley north of the pass. Although the lake was named by the Interprovincial Boundary Survey, its name is not Egyptian. Surveyor A.O. Wheeler named it with what he believed to be the Polish word for "lively" — in reference to the sun sparkling on its waves. The pass is a good place to see gray-crowned rosy finches. These alpine-dwelling birds are opportunistic feeders. They often congregate on snow patches to eat insects, snow worms, seeds, and spiders, which are easy to see on the white background.

The steep descent to Haiduk Lake is on a trail

The Shadow Lake campground is 1.2 km east of the lake, just east of Shadow Lake Lodge and the Gibbon Pass junction. If you want to exit the Lakes and Larches trail at this point, follow the Redearth Creek trail 13.4 km northeast to the Trans-Canada Highway. The Lost Horse Creek campground is at km 6.2.

## Ball Pass, 2.7 km

*Ball Pass*

 **This short sidetrip** takes you to the crest of the Continental Divide, offering detailed views of the south face of Mt. Ball, and a panorama over the valley of Redearth Creek. The first 1.5 km climbs gently to the upper reaches of the west fork of Haiduk Creek. Rock-hop the stream and commence the steep ascent. The route ahead looks unlikely, as the trail aims straight toward the boulderfield and cliff beneath the pass. However, a well-conceived series of switchbacks breaks through the headwall to deliver you easily to the craggy north entrance of the pass. The red, iron-rich soil underfoot is a possible origin of the local name, "Redearth."

Mt. Ball dominates the view. Its cascading glacier flies in the face of climate change, clinging magnificently to the south slopes of the mountain. James Hector brought the name "Ball" to the Rockies to commemorate John Ball, a British public servant who rallied government support for the Palliser Expedition. Ball later became an accomplished mountaineer, and first president of the Alpine Club of England. It is likely that Hector intended the name for the peak now known as Storm Mountain.

Walk 500 m south across the pass to obtain a view over the upper Hawk Creek valley in Kootenay National Park. The source of Hawk Creek is a stream that discharges from the ground, southwest of the pass.

The original Shadow Lake Rest House was built by the Canadian Pacific Railway in 1928, as part of a system of backcountry shelters for its clientele. Brewster Transport purchased the building in 1938 and sold it to Bud Brewster in 1950. In 1991, the lodge was redeveloped, with six new outlying cabins built. In 1993, additional development was proposed which saw an increase in capacity (including staff) to 40, making this one of the larger backcountry facilities in the Rockies.

## Gibbon Pass Junction to Arnica Lake

The steady climb to Gibbon Pass earns you the delights of another upper subalpine landscape. Numerous animal trails crisscross the expansive, larch-dotted alp of the pass. You may see mountain goats here. On the slope east of the pass, treeline is approximately 2400 m, well above the local norm of 2200 m. The slope is southwest facing and is in the lee of Storm Mountain. This may create an area with soils that are warmer and drier than normal. On the pass itself, young Lyall's larch trees are colonizing the tundra, transforming it to upper subalpine forest. Gibbon Pass was named in 1929 for John Gibbon, public relations manager with the CPR and founder of the Trail Riders of the Canadian Rockies.

From Gibbon Pass, the trail makes a gradual, sideslope descent north along the eastern side of the valley. After about 2.5 km, it switchbacks rapidly down to the outlet of lower Twin Lake. This is the first of another series of lakes that occupy northeast facing cirques — this time beneath Storm Mountain (3161 m). The cirques are separated by arêtes — narrow rock ridges that descend from the summit area. All of these arêtes, and many of the gullies between, have been climbed by mountaineers. The arête between the Twin Lakes is one of the premier alpine rock climbing routes in the Rockies.

The trail is boggy in the vicinity of Lower Twin Lake, where cotton-grass grows in abundance. Cross the outlet on a bridge to an important trail junction. Ahead, the "up and down" nature of this hike continues, with two stiff climbs and two descents in the remaining 8.2 km to the Kootenay Parkway. If you have had enough at this point, make a direct, downhill exit by following the trail northeast (right) from this junction, for 7.8 km to Castle Junction on the Trans-Canada Highway.

Upper Twin Lake and the Twin Lakes campground are 800 m north of the junction. The campground is a popular overnight destination for backpackers travelling south from the

*Shadow Lake at the foot of Mt. Ball*

*Upper Twin Lake and Storm Mountain*

Kootenay Parkway. Rock-hop the outlet and ascend steeply to Arnica Summit, a forested saddle on the northeast buttress of Storm Mountain. A steep descent brings you to Arnica Lake. *Arnica* is the genus name of common, subalpine wildflowers that feature opposite leaves, and showy, yellow blooms. There are fifteen species in the southern Rockies.

### Arnica Lake to the Kootenay Parkway

Leaving Arnica Lake, the trail descends onto the north flank of Storm Mountain. After passing the east shore of a rockslide depression lake, the trail

## Succession

The heat of the Vermilion Pass Burn cracked open the resin-sealed cones of lodgepole pines, resulting in a mass seeding and the subsequent growth of a dog-hair pine forest. Lodgepole pines are not shade tolerant. A dog-hair forest usually thins in 30 to 60 years, allowing for the transition to a forest dominated by Engelmann spruce and subalpine fir. This process of transformation is called succession, and is usually complete at this elevation within 130 years. However, the north-facing slope and the windiness of this location create harsh growing conditions. Thirty-five years after the burn, the average height of the young pines was just over 2 m.

emerges onto the southern edge of the Vermilion Pass Burn. This lightning-caused forest fire consumed 2630 hectares of subalpine forest in July 1968. The open area of the burn offers fine views east to Mt. Ishbel (2908 m), Castle Mountain (2850 m), and Protection Mountain.

You reach the lowest elevation on this hike just 1.4 km from trail's end, at Vista Lake. This deep valley is a curious landscape feature. It was not eroded over eons by the tiny creek we see today, but by a meltwater surge from a detached block of glacial ice at the end of the Wisconsin Glaciation. This meltwater also eroded the canyon west of the lake. Altrude Creek drains Vista Lake. It was named when a surveying crew combined the Latin words for "high" (*altus*), and "beautiful" (*pulchritude*).

From the outlet of Vista Lake, a well-graded trail climbs to the Kootenay Parkway, bisecting a hoodoo-like formation en route. The final Bow Valley advance of the Wisconsin Glaciation ended near here. Irregular mounds of moraine dot the forest. This hoodoo may have been eroded from such a moraine. It is the only formation of its kind visible in the area.

Trail's end is at the Vista Lake/Twin Lakes trailhead on the Kootenay Parkway, 39 km by road from the starting point. If you need to use a pay phone, hike 2 km east to Storm Mountain Lodge.

# 10. Bourgeau Lake

## Route

Day-hike

| Route | Elevation (m) | Distance (km) |
|---|---|---|
| Trailhead | 1410 | 0 |
| Wolverine Creek bridge | 1780 | 5.5 |
| Bourgeau Lake | 2175 | 7.4 |

Maps
NTS: 82 0/4
Gem Trek: Banff and Mt. Assiniboine
**See map on p.49**

## Trailhead

**West side of** the Trans-Canada Highway, 11.6 km west of the Mt. Norquay (Banff) interchange; 43.9 km east of Lake Louise. Westbound travellers must cross the two eastbound lanes of the divided highway. Use caution.

*Mt. Bourgeau and Bourgeau Lake as seen from the Harvey Pass trail*

Tucked away in a glacial cirque beneath Mt. Bourgeau (boor-ZJOWE), Bourgeau Lake is a gem of a destination. The elevation gain is considerable, but the well-graded trail makes for relatively easy access to the upper subalpine environs at the lake. Because it ascends a shaded valley, consider leaving this hike for mid-July or later, when the route will probably be clear of lingering snow. This is among the newer trails in Banff. It was cut in the late 1950s after the completion of the Trans-Canada Highway.

### Trailhead to Bourgeau Lake

For the first 2.5 km, the trail winds through forest on the slopes above Wolverine Creek. There are subtle changes in the vegetation at almost every turn. Most noticeable is the dog-hair forest of lodgepole pines and Douglas-firs, evidence of a 1904 forest fire. The trail passes between two stately Douglas-firs, one of which shows bark blackened by the fire. Beyond this point, Engelmann spruce is the most common tree. You may see spruce grouse here. About a kilometre from the trailhead, there is a wonderful squirrel midden. Although we tend to think of them as tree-dwelling creatures, red squirrels nest on the ground in these accumulations of seed shells shucked from spruce cones.

The first avalanche slope features fine views northeast to the Bow Valley and the Sawback Range, on whose slopes you can see charred forest that resulted from the 1998 Hillsdale fire, and from prescribed burns in 1991 and 1993. The meandering course of the Bow River reveals oxbow lakes, including Muleshoe Lake. Hole-in-the-Wall, a solution cave eroded by glacial meltwater, sits high and dry on the southwest face of Mt. Cory (2801 m).

The cliffs across Wolverine Creek dip northeastward toward the Bow Valley. Look for mountain goats on the terraces. The rock is limestone of the Livingstone Formation. The dip reveals the eastern arm of an anticline. The cliffs are an outlying ridge of Mt. Brett (2984 m). Dr. R.G. Brett was a businessman and politician, prominent in the affairs of Banff and the province of Alberta from 1886 to 1925.

Roughly a kilometre beyond the first avalanche slope, the trail crosses a tributary stream and curves gradually south. This stream, and the south fork of Wolverine Creek crossed at km 5.5, are often choked with trees avalanched from the surrounding mountainsides. The first creek is bridged. However, any bridge across the second creek would be destroyed by avalanches, so gabion (gah-bee-ON) bags have been installed as

## Variation

- You can extend this hike to Harvey Pass, 4.8 km return from Bourgeau Lake

stepping stones.

*Gabion* is French for "cage." Gabion bags are wire mesh baskets filled with rocks from the stream bed. By nature of their tremendous weight and low profile, gabions resist avalanching snow. They also dissipate the force of water by allowing most of the flow to pass between the rocks. Gabions are often successfully used for bridge footings and shoring in sites prone to erosion.

A waterfall tumbles from the hanging valley west of Wolverine Creek. After crossing the creek at km 5.5, you climb steadily on switchbacks to the subalpine wet meadow adjacent to Bourgeau Lake. The trail becomes muddy and indistinct. Do your best to keep to the beaten path. Cold air collects in the hollow of this meadow, where the damp soils are subject to frequent frosts. Trees cannot grow to any great height. However, on the slightly higher

*Eugene Bourgeau*

ground surrounding the meadow, a stunted forest of subalpine fir and a few Lyall's larches eke out a chilly existence in the shade of Mt. Bourgeau.

Bourgeau Lake is dammed by a rockslide. Its waters drain beneath the debris. The lake sits in a pocket of Banff Formation limestone. The massive cliffs that ring the lake are also limestone, but of the slightly younger, Livingstone Formation. This rock consists principally of the fossilized remains of crinoids — marine animals related to the starfish of today.

## A Modest Man, an Imposing Mountain

**James Hector** named Mount Bourgeau for Eugene Bourgeau, botanist with the Palliser Expedition of 1857–60. Bourgeau was a likable man and a first-rate botanist. He was only in the Rockies for one season, but he collected 460 species — including 50 varieties gathered above 2560 m. He carted 60,000 specimens back to Kew Gardens. The 2930 m mountain was first climbed in 1890 by surveyor J.J. McArthur and Tom Wilson. Although the mountain appears formidable, a "walk-up" route exists along the west slopes from Harvey Pass. The lake was named in 1912.

## Harvey Pass (2430 m), 2.4 km

**When the slopes** beyond Bourgeau Lake are free of snow, you can extend this outing by following any of several paths along the northwest shore to the west end of the lake. Look for low larkspur, a member of the buttercup family with mauve flowers. The leaves contain poisonous alkaloids. Ascend a rough track on the north side of the inlet stream, and follow cairns. A stiff climb brings you to a tarn set in a beautiful alpland. Continue straight ahead. Another, shorter climb leads to a large basin that features yet another tarn. You may be fortunate to see bighorn sheep here. A 1981 estimate gave a population of 120–130 sheep for the vicinity of Mt. Bourgeau. Sixty-five mountain goats were also reported to live in this area, but in recent years, the numbers of both species seem to have declined. The meadows and the slopes leading up to them are frequented by grizzly bears.

A faint track swings south and climbs a compacted scree slope to the climax of this exceptionally scenic hike — Harvey Lake, nestled in the hollow of Harvey Pass. The pass was named for Ralph Harvey, who accompanied Jim Brewster here in the 1920s. Mt. Assiniboine (3618 m) soars skyward in the view south. From the southern brink of the pass, enjoy the wonderful vista over the larch-filled forest of Healy Creek, Sunshine Meadows, and the lake-dotted terrain near Simpson Pass.

## Who Maintains the Trails?

Most hiking trails in the Rocky Mountain parks are maintained by trail crews employed by each park. The crews keep the trails clear of fallen trees, avalanche debris, and rocks; and ensure that tread surfaces remain well-drained. They also sometimes construct bridges, boardwalks, and campground facilities, and install and maintain signs. Most tools and materials are packed to the worksites each day. However, a helicopter is sometimes used to reach remote worksites, or for projects involving heavy materials. Rewarding physical work in spectacular mountain scenery creates great interest annually in the few available trail crew positions.

In US national parks, the Wilderness Act precludes the use of motorized equipment for backcountry maintenance, minimizing disturbances to wildlife and visitors. One benefit that might result from Parks Canada budget cuts is a revival of traditional, non-motorized trail maintenance techniques.

# 11. Johnston Canyon and the Ink Pots

## Route

Day-hike

| Route | Elevation (m) | Distance (km) |
|---|---|---|
| Trailhead | 1430 | 0 |
| Lower Falls | 1463 | 1.1 |
| Upper Falls | 1483 | 2.7 |
| Moose Meadows jct | 1524 | 3.2 |
| Trail summit | 1760 | 4.6 |
| Ink Pots | 1631 | 5.9 |

**Maps**
NTS: 82 0/4 and 82 0/5
Gem Trek: Banff and Mt. Assiniboine, or Kootenay National Park

**Best lighting:** late morning to mid-afternoon in Johnston Canyon; anytime at the Ink Pots

*An ingenious walkway allows you to walk within the cleft of Johnston Canyon.*

## Trailhead

**East side** of the Bow Valley Parkway (Highway 1A), 23.6 km east of Banff; 6.5 km east of Castle Junction. The trail departs the northeast corner of the parking lot.

People have been visiting Johnston Canyon since the prospector it was named for staked a claim here in the 1880s. Because the features of interest are next to the trail, this is an excellent outing for poor weather days. You may see mule deer, red squirrels, porcupines, gray jays, dippers, and common ravens. Johnston Canyon is one of three known Alberta nesting sites for black swifts. The Johnston Creek valley near the Ink Pots is frequented by coyotes, wolves, grizzly bears, and elk.

### Trailhead to Upper Falls

From the parking lot, cross Johnston Creek and turn north (right). The trailhead is at an elevation that is normally part of the montane ecoregion. However, canyons chill the air within, creating micro-environments more typical of higher elevations. The vegetation on shaded, north-facing slopes in lower Johnston Canyon is distinctly subalpine in character. On sun-exposed, south-facing slopes, lodgepole pines and a few Douglas-firs

prevail — indicator trees of the montane forest.

In Johnston Canyon, you walk through a sequence of sedimentary layers — rocks of the Rundle Group of formations — that were deposited 300 to 350 million years ago. The lower canyon is cut into limestone and dolomite of the Livingstone Formation. The vicinity of the Upper Falls is eroded into fossil-rich limestone of the Mt. Head Formation. The more sinuous, upper canyon is cut into shales and siltstones of the Etherington Formation. The Ink Pots lie within the siltstones, mudstones, and shales of the 208–245 million-year-old Sulphur Mountain Formation.

The trail in the lower canyon has been designed to accommodate the tremendous number of visitors. The most recent trail work was completed in 2003. In places, a concrete slab catwalk is suspended from the canyon wall on steel girders. Although it might seem intrusive, you gain an appreciation of the effects of flowing water that would not be possible from the canyon rim.

You reach the Lower Falls at km 1.1. On the opposite side of the creek you can walk through a natural tunnel to a balcony drenched by the spray of the falls. The shattered cliffs nearby have been coated with an artificial compound to prevent rockfall.

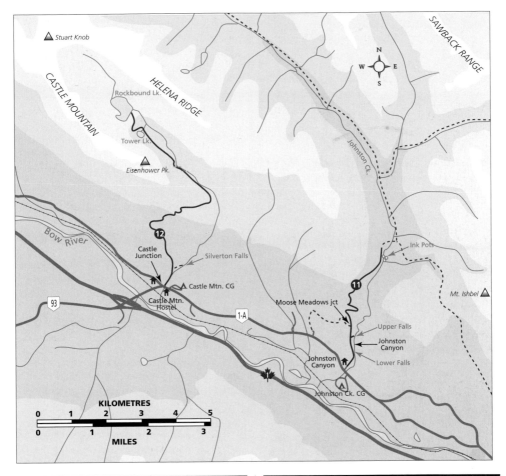

## The Hillsdale Slide

At the end of the Wisconsin Glaciation 12,000 years ago, Johnston Creek flowed east of here along the base of Mt. Ishbel. The mountain's slopes had been undercut during the glaciation. After the ice retreated, layers of the mountain broke free and slid to the valley floor in an event known as the Hillsdale Slide. This landslide blocked Johnston Creek, forcing it to seek another course to the Bow River. The creek was captured by a fault in the bedrock, visible from a high bank in the upper canyon.

So goes one theory. Another holds that Johnston Canyon may be the course of an ancient underground stream. The cavern was exposed to daylight by erosion during the Wisconsin Glaciation.

## Migrating Waterfalls

**Johnston Canyon** has a maximum depth of 30 m. It features seven waterfalls, each of which marks where a layer of dolomite bedrock has been uncovered by the flowing water. Dolomite is limestone that has been transformed. Water seeped into the limestone sediments before they lithified. Calcium in the limestone was replaced with magnesium. The magnesium-enriched rock — more properly described as a mineral — is harder than limestone. It naturally becomes the brink of the waterfalls in this canyon. At the base of each waterfall, the incessant pounding of the water has created a plunge pool. The plunge pool eventually undercuts the brink, causing it to collapse. In this way, the waterfall "migrates" slightly upstream, where the process is repeated.

## Lower Falls to Upper Falls

Many people turn back at the Lower Falls, so the trail beyond is less crowded. The character of the canyon also changes. It is often wider and V-shaped, in contrast to the narrow, deep slot of the lower canyon. At km 2.7, you can descend a catwalk to the base of the 30 m high Upper Falls. The canyon wall opposite features a travertine drape. Travertine is crumbly limestone, precipitated from lime-rich water. Algae remove carbon dioxide from the water during photosynthesis, depositing a film of calcium carbonate as a waste product. The calcium carbonate eventually builds up into banded limestone. This is the largest of the six travertine drapes in Johnston Canyon, and may be the largest in the Rockies. Twenty-five species of algae have been identified here.

## Upper Falls to the Ink Pots

Back on the main trail, you climb to the crest of the Upper Falls and a viewpoint at the canyon's edge. Please keep within the guardrails. Five people have died from falls into the canyon here. The

trail reverts to a natural surface just beyond. Twenty metres past the "end of interpretive trail" sign, a short spur trail leads west (left) to an abandoned canyon. Johnston Creek formerly flowed here as a waterfall. Downward erosion along the current stream course captured and redirected Johnston Creek, leaving this channel dry.

The trail angles away from the canyon, and the sound of rushing water soon fades. The forest becomes drier. At km 3.2, the trail joins the horse and skier route from Moose Meadows. Turn north (right ) for the Ink Pots. The trail climbs and becomes narrower before it descends to the willow plain on Johnston Creek at the Ink Pots. You see the high, shale banks of the upper canyon in places along the way. They are capped by a 20 m overburden of glacial till.

East of the Ink Pots, Mt. Ishbel (2908 m) is prominent. Its slabby layers and serrated ridges again feature limestones of the Rundle Group of sedimentary formations. Mt. Ishbel epitomizes the sawtooth mountain form. It's no wonder that James Hector coined the name "Sawback" for the surrounding mountains. You can see the hills and dales of the Hillsdale Slide to the south. To the north, grassy terraces on Castle Mountain provide excellent range for bighorn sheep and mountain goats.

### Inky Springs

*The Ink Pots*

**The Ink Pots** are the outlets of seven cold mineral springs. Fed by rainwater and snowmelt that has percolated into the surrounding bedrock, the spring water emerges at a constant temperature of 4.8°C. The combined volume of flow is 1800 litres per minute. The bases of the Ink Pots are covered in fine sediments with the consistency of quicksand. Two of the springs run murky due to sediments disturbed by the rising water — hence the name, The Ink Pots. The area around the Ink Pots was "hardened" in 1996. Please keep to the designated paths to avoid trampling vegetation.

### Swift and Secretive

**Of the eight species** of swallows and swifts in the Rockies, the black swift is the largest — about 20 cm from the beak to the tips of its deeply notched tail. It is also the least commonly observed. The feathers are black, with silvery-white highlights on the head. Forming life-long pair bonds, the look-alike males and females nest in moist canyons, behind waterfalls, or in hollow trees. Their young fledge in late summer. Swifts spend more of their time airborne than do swallows, collecting even nesting material and drinking water on the wing. They do not perch during their occasional rests, preferring to cling to vertical surfaces. Swifts feed principally on winged insects. Their foraging height is determined by the weather, for insects fly closer to ground during poor weather. During extended heavy rains, which prevent winged insects from flying, a black swift may fly hundreds of kilometres to find food, leaving its nestlings unattended. The young become torpid at such times, generally surviving until the local return of good weather summons Mom and Dad. Winter migration takes black swifts to Mexico and Costa Rica.

# 12. Rockbound Lake

## Route

Day-hike

| Route | Elevation (m) | Distance (km) |
|---|---|---|
| Trailhead | 1450 | 0 |
| Silverton Falls jct | 1450 | 0.3 |
| Silverton Falls | 1515 | +0.7 |
| Tower Lake | 2128 | 7.7 |
| Rockbound Lake | 2210 | 8.4 |

**Maps**
NTS: 82 0/5
Gem Trek: Banff and Mt. Assiniboine, or Kootenay National Park
**See map on p.61**

**Best lighting:** mid-morning to mid-afternoon

## Trailhead

**East side of** the Bow Valley Parkway (Highway 1A), 29.5 km west of Banff, 200 m east of Castle Junction.

Nestled beneath the colossal ramparts of Castle Mountain, Rockbound Lake is part of an elemental landscape of water, rock, and sky,

*Rockbound Lake is ringed on two sides by limestone cliffs.*

inspiring in its simplicity. Wildflower displays, larches, intriguing geology, and human history add interest to this outing.

### Trailhead to Tower Lake

The first 5 km of trail is fireroad width. You climb steadily through the lodgepole pine forest that cloaks the floor of the Bow Valley. This forest grew in the aftermath of an 1892 forest fire. At approximately km 2.4, the trail angles sharply east (right) at an unmarked junction. Straight ahead is an unmaintained path to the former site of the Castle Mountain fire lookout. Storm Mountain (3161 m) is prominent in the view west. The forested mounds on the floor of the Bow Valley are piles of moraine. These mark the ultimate halting place of

## Castle and Controversy

**Castle Mountain** is one of the better known and better named landmarks in the Rockies. James Hector first described it in 1858, and called it a textbook example of a "castellated mountain." The lower cliff is Cathedral Formation dolomite and limestone, the middle terrace is Stephen Formation shale, and the upper cliff is Eldon Formation limestone. This sequence, known as the "Middle Cambrian sandwich," creates the castellated appearance of many mountains in the eastern main ranges.

In 1946, politicians decided to rename Castle Mountain in honour of Dwight D. Eisenhower, WWII commander of Allied forces in Europe, and later US president. Canadians were generally unimpressed, but being polite folks, waited until a decade after

*Castle Mountain*

Eisenhower's death to do something about it. The name, Castle Mountain, was reinstated in 1979. As a compromise, the tower is now called Eisenhower Peak. It is not the highest point on Castle's 6.5 km long ridge, for the true summit (2804 m) is the one farthest north. You can't see it from this trail.

the Bow Valley glacier during the last advance of the Wisconsin Glaciation.

As the trail climbs over the treed ridge south of Castle Mountain, the forest becomes more subalpine in character. After it swings north behind the ridge, the trail narrows, the grade eases, and the tread surface becomes poor. If you are hiking early in the season, you will find it a challenge to stay on the trail. As a consolation to the mud underfoot, the moist glades at trailside feature stunning displays of white globeflowers.

The trail undulates over a series of forested recessional moraines, then becomes vague as it crosses a wet meadow just before Tower Lake. This shallow lake mirrors the southernmost summit of Castle Mountain (2752 m) — "the tower." This summit was first climbed in 1926. Rockslides near the lake are home to hoary marmots. The surrounding forest contains Lyall's larch. The needles of this deciduous conifer turn golden yellow in late summer.

### Tower Lake to Rockbound Lake

Rock-hop the outlet of Tower Lake. The trail switchbacks steeply up the limestone headwall to Rockbound Lake, passing through an ancient stand of Engelmann spruce trees. Drummond's anemone and alpine spring beauty are common wildflowers here. The trail braids and becomes indistinct as it approaches Rockbound Lake.

Rockbound Lake is a perfect glacial tarn. Cliffs of Eldon Formation limestone, up to 220 m high, provide a spectacular backdrop. Cutthroat trout, rainbow trout, and eastern brook trout in the lake attract osprey. You may see these raptors as they circle the lake before plunging to the water to catch fish. The osprey is specially adapted for this task, with an opposable outer talon that works much the same as a human thumb. It's no contest — one study found that osprey catch fish on 90 percent of their attempts.

Rockbound Lake marks the southernmost point of the Castle Mountain Syncline, a U-shaped fold in the bedrock that extends 260 km north to Mt. Kerkeslin in Jasper National Park. The Cathedral Formation limestone slab underlying the lake is tipped upward toward the south, damming the waters. You can walk east along this natural pavement to the high water outlet of the lake. Most of Rockbound Lake's outflow now drains underground through karst fissures eroded into the bedrock.

### Silverton Falls

Make the sidetrip to Silverton Falls on your

*Silverton Falls*

return, as the falls are shaded in the morning. Turn southeast (left) at the junction 300 m before you reach the trailhead. Follow the sidetrail to the bridge across Silverton Creek, but do not cross the creek. Face downstream at the bridge and take the unmarked trail that ascends the slope to the north (right). This leads to an unfenced viewpoint that overlooks the upper cataracts of the falls. Use caution.

"Silverton" refers to the railway and mining boom town of Silver City that flourished nearby from 1882–84. In its heyday, Silver City boasted a population of 2000 people, making it larger than Calgary. A round-trip visit to Silverton Falls adds 1.4 km to the Rockbound Lake outing.

## A Shattered Landscape

**Explorer A.P. Coleman,** a geology professor by vocation, called the valley above Rockbound Lake, "Horseshoe Valley." This valley is renowned for its "clint and grike," karst landscape — extensive limestone pavement that has been shattered by millennia of frost action. The "clints" are limestone blocks and the "grikes" are the fissures that separate them. The words come from the dialect of Yorkshire, England, where this type of landscape is common. Karst topography accounts for 12 percent of the world's landmass. The front ranges and main ranges of the Rockies, being predominantly limestone on the surface, contribute more than their share.

*The Boom Lake hike is an easy ramble through ancient forest to the shore of an impressive lake.*

# 13. Boom Lake

## Route

**Day-hike**

| Route | Elevation (m) | Distance (km) |
|---|---|---|
| Trailhead | 1723 | 0 |
| Taylor Lake jct | 1814 | 2.3 |
| Boom Lake | 1894 | 5.1 |

**Maps**
NTS: 82N/1 and 82 N/8
Gem Trek: Banff and Mt. Assiniboine, or Kootenay National Park

**Best lighting:** morning

## Trailhead

**Boom Creek** picnic area, north side of the Kootenay Parkway, 7.0 km west of Castle Junction, 97.7 km east of the junction with Highway 95.

The hike to Boom Lake is one of the easier Classic Hikes — an undemanding stroll through an ancient subalpine forest. The lake is the match of any in the Rockies. Its shores are a wonderful place to wile away the hours.

**Trailhead to Boom Lake**

After crossing Boom Creek on a bridge, the broad trail — formerly a tote road to a mine — begins its gradual climb. Continue straight ahead at the

Taylor Lake junction at km 2.3. The trail continues its rolling ascent for another 2 km before it descends gradually, becoming narrower, rocky, and rooted for the last 200 m. The trail emerges on the north shore of Boom Lake about 600 m west of the outlet. Rockslide debris makes travel difficult farther along the lakeshore.

## Bryophytes

**The damp forest** along the Boom Lake trail is ideal habitat for bryophytes — a group of essentially rootless, non-vascular plants with poorly developed plumbing. For this reason, they must grow in wet places and they do

*Feathermoss*

not grow very tall. Bryophytes — the name comes from the Greek words, *bryo*, which means "moss" and *phyton*, which means "plant" — grow from spores. They are among the overlooked miracles of the forest floor. Because you usually have to get nose-to-gametophyte with these plants in order to make acquaintance, most people pay them little heed. But bryophytes are worth getting to know — even superficially — if only for the roll call of names, some perfunctory, some unusual, some as beautiful as the plants they describe: alpine apple-moss, stairstep moss, alpine star-moss, rock star-moss, silver worms, fire moss, grooved gnome-cap moss, rolled-leaf pigtail moss, knight's plume, common dung-moss, and electrified cats-tail moss.

**65**

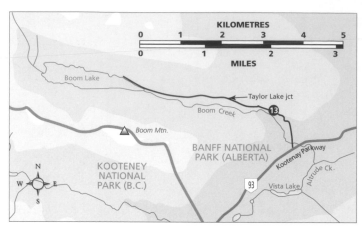

Boom Lake is 2.7 km long, 366 m wide, and 30 m deep. With an area of roughly 100 ha, it is the tenth largest lake in Banff National Park. Its waters are remarkably clear, given its proximity to glacial ice. Measurements have documented a reduction of silt in the water during the past century — an indication that the glaciers feeding the lake are dwindling.

The lake is home to cutthroat trout. The log booms are natural formations created from avalanched trees swept into the lake. The trees then drifted toward the outlet and became lodged, perhaps on submerged moraines. The first boom is several hundred metres east of where the trail reaches shoreline. The cold, damp, north-facing avalanche slopes on the south side of the lake support stands of Lyall's larch, a tree usually found 300 m higher.

The prominent ice-clad mountains northwest of the lake are Mt. Bident (3084 m) and Quadra Mountain (3173 m). People familiar with these mountains as viewed from the Moraine Lake Road or from Consolation Lakes may have difficulty recognizing them here. The upper ramparts of these mountains feature the "Middle Cambrian

## The Subalpine Forest

**The Boom Lake trail** is located a few kilometres east of the Continental Divide, in an area of high precipitation. Engelmann spruce and subalpine fir are the most common trees in this subalpine forest. The spire-like form of the subalpine fir, with its downsloping branches, helps shed the heavy snow load. Labrador tea, dwarf birch, feathermosses, clubmosses, and liverworts are prominent in the undergrowth.

This vegetation community is typical of the climax stage of a subalpine forest. It provides ideal habitat for mice and voles, which are standard fare for great horned owls, and for American martens — the most abundant carnivores in the Rockies. Moose use this forest for cover. You may see ruffed grouse, three-toed woodpeckers, and pileated woodpeckers. Varied thrush, hermit thrush, and golden-crowned kinglet are common songbirds. The bark of some Engelmann spruce trees is reddish-purple where the brown outer scales have been

*The subalpine forest*

removed by woodpeckers in quest of grubs and insects.

The damp and decay is in contrast to the lodgepole pine forest you saw at the trailhead. The smaller pines seeded after the 1968 Vermilion Pass Burn. Spruce and fir will probably replace the pines within 130 years. This process of transformation in the forest is called succession. Each forest type favours certain species of vegetation and wildlife. Nature uses fire to promote succession and revitalize stagnant forests. The mosaic of new and old, burned and unburned, creates the diversity of habitats required to maintain all species in the forest ecosystem.

The Boom Lake trail travels between the extremes of forest succession habitats in the Rockies. The forest at the trailhead is four decades old. Near Boom Lake you will see Engelmann spruce trees that measure a metre in diameter at the base and 40 m in height, indicating ages of 350–450 years.

sandwich" — cliffs of Cathedral Formation limestone, a terrace of Stephen Formation shale, capped by a final tier of Eldon Formation limestone. The basin beneath is heaped with moraines, indicating the extent of glacial ice less than two centuries ago.

The rockslide boulders and the dark cliffs that ring the lake are Gog Formation quartzite. This rock was created from quartz-rich sediments deposited in prehistoric seas during the Early Cambrian. Gog quartzite frequently contains iron. Many of the quartzite boulders at the water's edge are "rusted" brown with iron oxide. These rocks are home to colonies of pikas, tiny members of the rabbit family whose call is a shrill "Eeeeep!"

# 14. The Beehives and the Plain of the Six Glaciers

## Route

**Day-hike**

| Route | Elevation (m) | Distance (km) |
| --- | --- | --- |
| Parking lot | 1735 | 0 |
| Trailhead | 1732 | 0.6 |
| Mirror Lake | 2027 | 3.0 |
| Little Beehive jct | 2104 | 3.7 |
| Lake Agnes connector jct | 2170 | 4.2 |
| Little Beehive | 2253 | 4.8 |
| Lake Agnes | 2118 | 5.8 |
| Big Beehive jct | 2260 | 7.1 |
| Big Beehive | 2270 | 7.4 |
| Highline jct | 2010 | 8.9 |
| Plain of the Six Glaciers jct | 1950 | 10.7 |
| Plain of the Six Glaciers teahouse | 2135 | 12.1 |
| Victoria Glacier viewpoint | 2150 | 13.7 |
| Parking lot | 1735 | 21.2 |

**Maps**
NTS: 82 N/8
Gem Trek: Lake Louise and Yoho, or Guide to Lake Louise Day Hikes

**Best lighting:** most features are best lit in the morning

## Trailhead

**Consider using** public transportation — check at the park information centre. From Lake Louise Village, follow Lake Louise Drive 5.5 km to the parking lots at the lake. Paved walkways lead to the lakeshore. Walk along the lakeshore to the trail junction west of the Chateau. You want the Lake Agnes trail. It branches uphill to the north (right).

## Variations

- Exit from the Highline junction, 12.0 km total
- Exit from the Plain of the Six Glaciers junction, 15.0 km total

If you have time for only one hike near Lake Louise, this should be your choice. As you climb to the modest summits of Little Beehive and Big Beehive, you will see much of what is scenically special in the area, and you will be reminded frequently of its rich human history. However, this is not a hike for those seeking solitude. The outing incorporates two of the more popular trails in the Rockies — Lake Agnes and the Plain of the Six Glaciers. The trail on the north side of Big Beehive is often snowbound into July.

### Trailhead to Little Beehive

The broad Lake Agnes trail climbs steadily through subalpine forest for 1.6 km to a switchback that overlooks Lake Louise and the delta at its inlet. If the glacial melt season is on, you may see plumes of glacial sediment dispersing into the lake. The quartzite cliffs of Fairview Mountain (2744 m) rise across the lake. The trail narrows, turns sharply north and crosses a section of the wooden pipeline that once provided drinking water from Lake Agnes to the Chateau. At the horse-hiker barrier, turn west (left) to reach Mirror Lake. The quartzite buttress of Big Beehive forms the backdrop for this pond, which is impounded by moraine and has no visible surface outlet. Mirror Lake and nearby Lake Agnes were referred to by the Canadian Pacific Railway as "the lakes in the clouds" in promotional material in the late 1800s.

The trail continues north from Mirror Lake, switchbacking through larch trees on an avalanche slope on Mt. St. Piran. The mountain is named for the English parish that was the birthplace of Willoughby Astley, the first manager of Chalet Lake Louise. Astley supervised the cutting of many trails in the area, including this one.

*Cloud shadows dapple the surface of Lake Louise in this view from the Big Beehive.*

At the junction at km 3.1, turn sharply northeast (right) onto the Little Beehive trail. You ascend higher onto the avalanche slope, where western anemone, Sitka valerian, arnica, common fireweed, common yarrow, white rhododendron, fleabanes, dwarf dogwood, cinquefoil, and pink mountain heather grow. There are fine views southwest to Big Beehive, Fairview Mountain, Haddo Peak (3070 m) and glacier-clad Mt. Aberdeen (3151 m). The icy summit of Mt. Temple (3543 m) rises above them all.

After 500 m you reach another junction. Turn northeast (right), and follow the trail 700 m across an avalanche slope onto the larch-covered knoll of Little Beehive. You can see Lake Louise and the Chateau from the cliff edge at the far side of the avalanche slope. Partway across, you pass a large quartzite boulder that is surrounded by red-stemmed saxifrage.

Little Beehive commands a superlative view of the Bow Valley, from Hector Lake in the north to Pilot Mountain (2935 m) in the south. This site was an obvious choice for a fire lookout, which operated from 1942 until 1978. The lookout building was removed in 1985. Parks Canada has installed a display that describes the role of forest fires in this ecosystem. Unfortunately, Cyclone Mountain and Fossil Mountain are misplaced on the accompanying diorama.

## Little Beehive to Lake Agnes

On your descent from Little Beehive, continue straight ahead at the first junction. As you approach the Lake Agnes teahouse, the trail passes alongside a bluff of Gog Formation siltstone. As with most rocks in the area, the bluff dips to the southwest. Within this overall plane, some layers of sediments are at widely varying angles. This is called cross-bedding. These layers record the edges of shifting deltas when the sediments were deposited in the Early Cambrian, or where streams cut through sediments after they had been deposited. Beyond the bluff, the trail climbs a staircase to the teahouse on the shore of Lake Agnes.

## Lake Agnes

Walter Wilcox, an early visitor to Lake Agnes, called it "a wild tarn imprisoned by cheerless cliffs." True to Wilcox's description, the lake is a glacial tarn, occupying a hollow 20.5 m deep. The wilderness character of the lake is now lost to the throngs of visitors, but the scene is impressive nonetheless. From south to north, Big Beehive (2270 m), Devil's Thumb (2458 m), Mt. Whyte (2983 m), Mt. Niblock (2976 m), and Mt. St. Piran (2650 m) form a tight cirque around the lake. Sir William Whyte was second vice-president of the CPR, and John Niblock was a railway superintendent in the 1890s. The lake was their favourite fishing hole in the Rockies. Fishing is no longer allowed.

The Lake Agnes teahouse was one of a series constructed by the CPR to entice its hotel clients into the mountains. The first structure here was built in 1901. The present teahouse was privately reconstructed in 1981. It is open daily from mid-June to early October (check at the Lake Louise

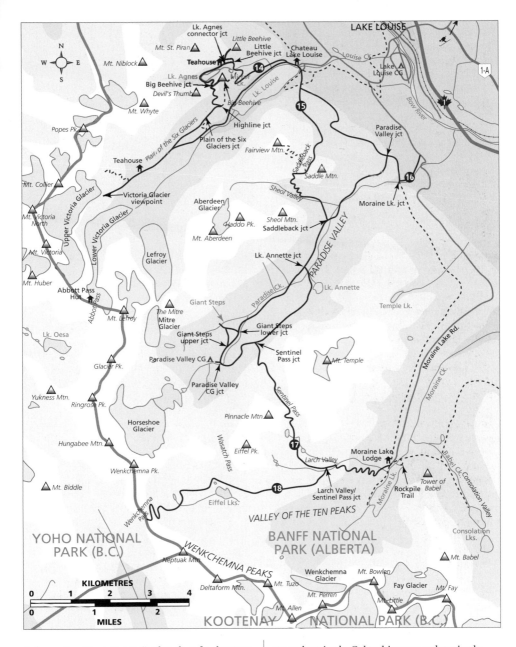

Information Centre), serving lunch, refreshments, and baked goods. You can learn more about the history of the teahouses at an interpretive display on the south side of the lake's outlet. Look for striations — grooves etched by glacial ice — in the quartzite bedrock nearby.

The upper subalpine forest at Lake Agnes provides the seeds, berries, fungi, and insects eaten by Clark's nutcrackers, gray jays, golden-mantled ground squirrels, Columbian ground squirrels, least chipmunks, and red squirrels. Please do not feed these birds and animals. Your "kindness" will ultimately kill them. Reliant on handouts, the non-hibernating species may not cache enough food to tide them through the winter. Those that do hibernate may go to sleep with bodies run-down by junk food diets, never to reawaken.

## Lake Agnes to Big Beehive

From the teahouse, head west through boulder-fields along the north shore of the lake. Hoary marmots and pikas are common here. Damp areas support dense growths of false hellebore and red-stemmed saxifrage. At the west end of the lake, the trail swings south beneath the shattered cliffs of the Devil's Thumb. Use caution if you must cross any lingering snow. The coarse sand eroded from the quartzite bedrock scrunches under your feet.

The trail switchbacks steeply up to the saddle between Big Beehive and Devil's Thumb. Take care not to dislodge rocks onto people below. Scan the cliffs of Mt. Niblock and Mt. St. Piran opposite, for mountain goats. From the crest of the climb, rough paths lead northeast (left) for 300 m to a shelter on the Big Beehive. Here, you obtain a stunning overview of Lake Louise, more than 500 m below. Lake Louise is 2 km long, has an area of 85 ha, and a maximum depth of 70 m. It is the 11th largest lake in Banff National Park. The lake occupies a hanging valley. It is dammed by a moraine that was pushed up alongside the Bow Valley Glacier during the Wisconsin Glaciation.

*Walter Wilcox, an early visitor to Lake Agnes, called it a "wild tarn imprisoned by cheerless cliffs."*

### Who Was Agnes?

*Lady Susan Agnes Macdonald*

**Lake Agnes** is named for Lady Susan Agnes Macdonald, wife of Prime Minister John A. Macdonald. Lady Agnes had been informed by the CPR that when she visited the lake in 1890, she would be the first woman to do so. Unfortunately, chalet manager Willoughby Astley, unaware of this arrangement, had guided another woman to the lake a few days earlier. By coincidence, the other woman's name was Agnes Knox. A member of the first lady's party defused the situation, pointing out that by giving the name "Agnes" to the lake, everyone would be happy.

### A Meat-Eating Vegan

*Common butterwort*

**Common butterwort** is a small, attractive plant with a tallish stem for its size. It sports a purple flower and a rosette of pale green, basal leaves. Nothing peculiar so far, but the common butterwort is a plant that could have come from a John Wyndham novel. Although it practices photosynthesis, it is one of seven insectivorous plants in the Rockies. Common butterwort grows on soils that are poor in nitrogen. It supplements its nitrogen supply through carnivory. Its leaves are coated in a sticky, acidic enzyme that traps and digests insects, turning them into bug slurpee. Yum. The exoskeletons cannot be digested, and so remain as black specks on the leaves. Although the butterwort's table of insect fare necessarily includes only small insects, occasional prey may have just finished pollinating the plant's flower. How's that for gratitude?

*The Plain of the Six Glaciers tea house*

hat. At the series of switch-backs just before the teahouse, look upslope for mountain goats. Common butterwort, one of seven species of carnivorous plants in the Rockies, grows in the seeps nearby. Golden eagles have nested near here in recent years. Look for them overhead.

The Plain of the Six Glaciers teahouse was constructed by Swiss Guides employed by the CPR in 1924. The building is just out of harm's way, beside a large avalanche path. Originally, the teahouse served as a staging area for mountaineers. Overnight accommodation is no longer offered. Lunch, refreshments, and baked goods can be purchased in season, which generally runs from mid-June to late September. Check at the Lake Louise Information Centre before your hike, to inquire whether the teahouse is open.

## Big Beehive to the Plain of the Six Glaciers

Return to where the main trail cuts across the Big Beehive and turn south (left). The trail switchbacks steadily down to join the highline route from Lake Agnes to the Plain of the Six Glaciers. Turn southwest (right), and follow this trail 1.8 km to the Plain of the Six Glaciers trail junction. Turn southwest (right).

The view to the south features The Mitre (2889 m), named for its resemblance to a bishop's

### Teahouse to Victoria Glacier Viewpoint

The teahouse is the ultimate destination for many hikers. But if you have the stamina, it is well worth extending this hike southwest for 1.6 km to the exposed crest of a lateral moraine that overlooks the Lower Victoria Glacier. Here, you are face to

## In Plain Sight of Ice

The Plain of the Six Glaciers is the forefield of Lower Victoria Glacier, from where six glaciers are visible: Lower Victoria, Upper Victoria, Lefroy, Upper Lefroy, Aberdeen, and Popes. (You can see a seventh glacier, which does not flow into this valley, on the north peak of Mt. Victoria.) The complex of moraines surrounding the plain records stages of glacial advance and retreat.

*Upper Victoria Glacier*

extent of the ice by the trim-line. All forest between the trimline and the present glacier position was destroyed during the Little Ice Age advance.

The surface of Lower Victoria Glacier is covered in moraine and rockfall debris. For many years, the glacier toe contained a large ice cave. Undermined by glacial retreat, this cave collapsed in 1992. In recent years the glacier has receded rapidly. Although the lengthwise retreat is notable, of more significance is the downwasting or loss of mass. If the trend continues, the terminus may become separated from the main mass of the glacier, creating a feature known as a dead-ice moraine.

The sharp-crested, lateral moraine that you hike along on the approach to the teahouse formed after 1909. Photographs show that the glacier covered this area in that year. Lower Victoria Glacier has receded 1.3 km since the maximum of the Little Ice Age in the early 1800s. You can gauge the former face with an ice age landscape. Massive limestone and quartzite cliffs glisten with glacial ice. Rockfalls and avalanches echo about. The moraine you stand on is ice-cored. Use caution.

In the view southwest, Abbot Pass (2925 m) separates Mt. Lefroy (3423 m) and Mt. Victoria (3464 m). Abbot Pass Hut sits atop the pass, built by Swiss Guides in 1921–22. Although most of this building is made from stone quarried on-site, more than two tonnes of supplies were packed by horse across the glacier, and then winched and carried by the guides to the pass. Named for Phillip Stanley Abbot, who died on Mt. Lefroy in 1896, the hut was the highest inhabitable building in Canada until the Neil Colgan Hut was constructed above Moraine Lake in 1982. Travel beyond the viewpoint is for experienced and properly equipped mountaineers only.

It is 7.5 km from this viewpoint to the parking lot via the Plain of the Six Glaciers trail. Continue straight ahead at all trail junctions. If the short section of trail along the edge of a bluff is not to your liking, you can bypass it on moraines to the south. If you reach the lake in early evening, you may witness the comings and goings of beavers. They often venture onto the trail to nibble the shoreline willows, oblivious to human traffic.

### Glacier Types

**Glacial ice forms** in areas where more snow accumulates in winter than melts in summer. The shape of a glacier depends on its location and on features of the surrounding landscape. *Icefields* form on flat areas at high elevation. *Outlet valley glaciers* flow from icefields into valleys below. *Alpine valley glaciers* occupy high mountain valleys and are not fed by icefields. *Cirque glaciers* occupy and erode bowl-shaped depressions in mountainsides. A small cirque glacier is called a *pocket glacier*. *Catchment glaciers* form at high elevations where indentations in a mountainside trap windblown snow. If the indentation is deep, the glacier may be called a *niche glacier*. Where ice avalanches from a cliff and coalesces on the valley floor, the resulting body of ice is called a *regenerated glacier*.

Any of these glacier types can also be called a *hanging glacier* if the ice terminates on a cliff. A *rock glacier* is a lobe-shaped accumulation of rock that insulates permanent ice within. Except for icefields and outlet valley glaciers, you can see all these glacier types from the Plain of the Six Glaciers trail.

# 15. Saddleback Pass

### Route

Day-hike

| Route | Elevation (m) | Distance (km) |
|---|---|---|
| Parking lot | 1735 | 0 |
| Trailhead | 1738 | 0.1 |
| Saddleback Pass | 2330 | 3.8 |
| Saddleback jct, Paradise Valley | 1845 | 7.6 |
| Paradise Valley jct | 1814 | 10.4 |
| Parking lot | 1735 | 14.9 |

**Maps**
NTS: 82 N/8
Gem Trek: Lake Louise and Yoho, or Guide to Lake Louise Day Hikes
**See map on p.69**

### Trailhead

**Consider using** public transportation. Inquire at the Lake Louise Information Centre about any restrictions on this trail. From Lake Louise Village, follow Lake Louise Drive 5.5 km to the parking lots at the lake. Paved walkways lead to the lakeshore. The Saddleback Pass trailhead is southeast of the World Heritage Site monument.

### Variations

- Hike to the pass and back, 7.6 km return
- Cross the pass to make a loop through lower Paradise Valley, 14.9 km
- Competent hikers can add an ascent of Fairview Mountain, 3.0 km return from the pass

Cleared in 1893, the trail to Saddleback Pass was among the earlier recreational hiking trails in the Rockies. For more than a century, its ascent has served many as an introduction to the alpine wonders of the Lake Louise area, and as a test of fitness. Few trails are so intent of purpose. With an average grade of 16 percent, this trail makes a beeline for the "saddle" connecting Fairview Mountain and Saddle Mountain, leaving many hikers breathless along the way.

Saddleback Pass is set among pleasant glades in a treeline larch forest. For the adventurous, a beaten path leads to the summit of Fairview

*The ice-capped summit of Mt. Temple looms over boulderfields and larch forest on Saddleback Pass.*

## EEEEP!

*Pika*

**Eeeep! So goes the call** of the pika (PEE-kah or PIE-kah), one of two members of the rabbit family in the Rockies. (The other is the snowshoe hare.) The quartzite boulderfields below Saddleback Pass are perfect terrain for this tiny mammal. Less than 20 cm long, the pika has a gray coat and a minuscule tail. It has been affectionately described as "a tennis ball with ears." Pikas live in colonies. You will probably hear a pika long before you see it. The shrill call warns its fellows of your presence.

Pikas eat grasses, lichens, leaves, and wildflowers. As the animal does not hibernate, it must stash food to tide it through the winter. It spends the summer gathering vegetation and drying it on flat rocks, before hiding the hay in its bouldery home. People who study such things say that a pika can pack away 35 kg of hay — more than 150 times its body weight. But the fare gets boring, so the pika augments its winter diet with partially digested pellets of its own dung. Hmmm... pass the ketchup, please. Eagles, hawks, owls, and members of the weasel family are the pika's principal predators.

Mountain. By continuing over Saddleback Pass, you can extend this hike into a loop outing through Sheol and Paradise valleys.

## Lake Louise to Saddleback Pass

The first hundred metres set the tone for this outing, as you toil upward across the shaded northeast slope of Fairview Mountain. More than 4 m of snow falls here annually. The damp, climax subalpine forest of Engelmann spruce and subalpine fir has not burned since 1630. Feathermosses are prominent in the undergrowth.

Continue straight ahead at the Fairview Lookout and Moraine Lake trail junctions. The trail crosses a broad swath in the forest, created by avalanches from the quartzite cliffs of Fairview Mountain. From the switchback at the south edge of this avalanche path, look back for the view of the Chateau Lake Louise and distant Mt. Hector (3394 m), rising above the expansive, glacially carved trough of the Bow Valley.

At about km 2, the trail forks. Both trails lead to Saddleback Pass, converging again in 400 m. The left-hand trail is less steep and offers views across the Bow Valley to the Slate Range. You can see the slopes of Whitehorn Mountain (2669 m), crisscrossed by the ski runs of the Lake Louise ski area. After it swings south to approach the pass, the trail crosses more avalanche terrain and switchbacks through the first stands of Lyall's larch. The winding route into the pass circumvents snow patches that linger in early summer. Please do not shortcut the switchbacks.

The icy crest of Mt. Temple (3543 m) looms majestically over a foreground of larch trees on Saddleback Pass. The dark, rocky peak to the west of the pass is Sheol Mountain (2779 m). *Sheol* is the Hebrew abode of the dead. The mountain was named because of its gloomy appearance from the valley at its base.

The CPR built a teahouse on Saddleback Pass in 1922. It had an unreliable water supply and operated for only one summer. You may find weathered boards in various locations on the pass — the remains of the building's siding. Sections of the water line from Sheol Valley still run across the flanks of Fairview Mountain.

### Fairview Mountain (2744 m) Option

From the cairn on the pass, a steep track leads 1.5 km northwest onto the slopes of Fairview Mountain. First climbed by surveyor J.J. McArthur in 1887, Fairview is today the most frequently ascended mountain in the Rockies. During good weather, when the slopes are free of snow, virtually any reasonably fit and well-prepared hiker can make the ascent. As the mountain's name implies, the summit panorama is among the finer near Lake Louise. Be sure to descend from Fairview by retracing your route of ascent. Accidents, sometimes fatal, are common on this "easy" mountain when hikers attempt to "take a shortcut" down the northeast face to Lake Louise. Hardly a summer goes by without a search and rescue call-out. Lightning killed an experienced hiker on Fairview's summit in 2002.

## Loop Hike Option

To extend this outing into a loop hike, continue southwest over Saddleback Pass to descend the switchbacks into Sheol Valley. As you lose elevation, the relatively minor summit of Sheol Mountain gains in stature, gloomily blocking the afternoon sun. The trail crosses the creek that drains Sheol Valley. The descent continues to the Saddleback trail junction, 3.8 km from the pass. Turn northeast (left) and follow this pleasant trail 3.1 km to the Paradise Valley trail junction, making two crossings of Paradise Creek. Turn northwest (left) at the junction, from where it is 4.4 km through subalpine forest to the parking lot near the trailhead.

# 16. Paradise Valley

## Route

Day-hike or overnight

| Route | Elevation (m) | Distance (km) |
|---|---|---|
| Trailhead | 1729 | 0 |
| Moraine Lake trail jct | 1799 | 1.1 |
| Paradise Valley jct | 1825 | 1.3 |
| Saddleback Pass jct | 1845 | 4.2 |
| Lake Annette jct | 1910 | 5.7 |
| Lake Annette | 1980 | 6.3 |
| Sentinel Pass jct | 2119 | 8.8 |
| Paradise Valley CG jct | 2012 | 9.4 |
| Paradise Valley CG | 2020 | +0.3 |
| Giant Steps upper jct | 2015 | 9.6 |
| Giant Steps | 2012 | 10.3 |
| Giant Steps lower jct | 1985 | 11.1 |
| Trailhead | 1729 | 19.3 |

**Maps**
NTS: 82 N/8
Gem Trek: Lake Louise and Yoho
**See map on p.69**

**Best lighting:** morning

## From Yale to Paradise

**Sheol, Fairview, Saddle, Paradise** and many other names in the Lake Louise area were given by members of the Yale Lake Louise Club. These five schoolmates spent a blissful and somewhat perilous summer on the heights around Lake Louise in 1894. Although most of them lacked significant mountaineering experience, their adventures included the first ascents of Mt. Temple and Mt. Aberdeen, the discoveries of Paradise Valley and Moraine Lake, and the first crossings of Sentinel, Wastach, Wenkchemna, and Mitre passes. Two members, Walter Wilcox and Samuel Allen (who had visited the Rockies together in 1893), each published maps of the area. Many of the names Allen applied were of Native origin. Wilcox (seated on the right in the photo) also authored *Camping in the Rockies* — later called *The Rockies of Canada* — a best selling book that went through numerous printings and editions, establishing him as the authority of the day on the Canadian Rockies.

*The Yale Lake Louise Club*

## Trailhead

**Consider using** public transportation. Parks Canada may close the Paradise Valley campground. Inquire at the Lake Louise Information Centre. From Lake Louise Village, follow Lake Louise Drive 3 km to the Moraine Lake Road. Turn south (left). Follow this road 2.3 km to the Paradise Creek trailhead.

## Variations

- Hike to Lake Annette, 12.6 km return
- Hike to the Giant Steps, 18.0 km return
- Hike the loop in reverse
- Use the campground as a base to explore the upper valley
- Add a visit to Sentinel Pass. See Classic Hike #17.

*Mt. Temple towers over Paradise Valley.*

With its alluring combination of forest, lakes, glaciers, meadows, waterfalls, and imposing mountains, Paradise Valley provides one of the more complete hiking experiences in the Canadian Rockies. From the backcountry campground at the head of the valley, you can leisurely explore the Giant Steps, Sentinel Pass, Wastach Pass, and Horseshoe Glacier. This outing is an excellent choice for novice backpackers, and is best between mid-July and mid-September.

### Trailhead to Lake Annette

The trail begins with an ascent over forested moraines, pushed up where the ancestral Paradise Valley and Bow Valley glaciers merged

## Mt. Temple — A Mountain Crucible

**The north face** of Mt. Temple (3543 m) dominates the view from the first bridge over Paradise Creek. Mt. Temple is the highest peak in the Lake Louise area, third highest in Banff National Park, and eleventh highest in the Rockies. The summit is more than 1700 vertical m above the valley floor. Mt. Temple is also one of the bulkier mountains in the range, occupying 15 square kilometres.

Mt. Temple has long been a testing place for mountaineers. It was first climbed in 1894 by members of the Yale Lake Louise Club, led by schoolmates Walter Wilcox and Samuel Allen. They followed a route from Sentinel Pass on the opposite side of the mountain. The imposing north flank was first climbed in 1966, and now features many challenging mountaineering routes. The mountain was named for Sir Richard Temple, patron of a British scientific expedition to the Rockies in 1884.

during the Wisconsin Glaciation. The open subalpine forest features yellow columbine, false hellebore, fleabane, arnica, and dwarf dogwood. The undergrowth is dominated by clubmosses, spike mosses, feathermosses, grouseberry, and false azalea.

Continue straight ahead at the bike-ski trail junction. The trail follows the crest of an ancient creek bank through a dog-hair pine forest to the Moraine Lake trail. Turn north (right). Follow this trail 300 m to the Paradise Valley junction, ascending a rolling sequence of ancient creek terraces. Turn west (left) at the junction. The Paradise Valley trail climbs a short distance over more moraines, and then begins a gradual descent to the first crossing of Paradise Creek.

Boggy areas along the south bank of Paradise Creek feature elephant head, cotton-grass, fleabane, cinquefoil, and yellow paintbrush. The trail recrosses the creek to reach the Saddleback Pass junction. Continue straight ahead for 1.5 km to the Lake Annette junction. Turn south (left), and again cross Paradise Creek. Just past the bridge you may see ancient tree stumps — too many to have been used for building bridges. The stumps suggest that there may have been a cabin nearby in the early 1900s.

The trail climbs moderately to the outlet of Lake Annette. The slope west of the trail is covered in white mountain heather, and white globeflowers grow along the outlet stream. Look for dippers here.

Bordered by boulderfields, moraine, and larch forest, Lake Annette sits at the base of Mt. Temple's stupendous north face. A kruppelholz forest of subalpine fir rings the north shore of the lake. The upper part of each tree is a lifeless spike, killed by the chilling blast of avalanches from Mt. Temple. The gnarled mat of the

*Lake Annette occupies a shallow depression at the base of Mt. Temple.*

lower trees has survived, insulated within the snowpack. Lake Annette was named by Walter Wilcox for a woman he presumed was the wife of Willoughby Astley, the first manager of the Chalet Lake Louise. Annette was Astley's mother.

## Lake Annette to Upper Paradise Valley

From Lake Annette, the trail climbs steeply southwest onto a bench covered in rockslide debris. This is a good place to see pikas and perhaps a wolverine. This section of trail is usually snowbound and muddy until mid-July. The apex of the trail features a grand prospect ahead to the tremendous cirque of Horseshoe Glacier and the

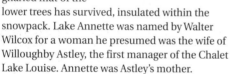

## Porcupine

**The porcupine,** a.k.a. "prickle pig," is a common resident of upper subalpine forests. With its coat of some 30,000 barbed quills, a porky is so well protected, it doesn't have to worry about moving quickly out of harm's way. You will often encounter these rodents as they slowly flee, quills fluffed, reluctant to leave the trail. The porcupine's principal natural food is the sugary cambium layer beneath the bark of coniferous trees — particularly subalpine fir. But porcupines have a remarkable taste for junk food: plywood, antifreeze, brake fluid, salty boots, and backpacks. Your other common experience of porcupines is likely to be at night, when they might serenade you with their surprising vocabulary of whimpers and cries. If not singing, they may keep you awake by chewing on the outhouse door.

peaks that surround the head of Paradise Valley. Highest is Hungabee Mountain (hun-GAH-bee) (3493 m). This Native name was bestowed by explorer Samuel Allen in 1894. Appropriately, it means "chieftain." You can see the Slate Range to the northeast and the glacier serac wall on the north face of Mt. Temple to the southeast.

Near the end of the 3 km traverse beneath Mt. Temple, the quartzite towers that flank Pinnacle Mountain (3067 m) come into view. Highest of the pinnacles is the Grand Sentinel. At the base of Mt. Lefroy across Paradise Valley, "Mitre Glacier" terminates in a classic moraine-dammed lake. The cliffs of Mt. Ringrose (3281 m), Glacier Peak (3283 m) and Mt. Lefroy (3423 m) are alive with snow avalanches on warm afternoons. At the Sentinel Pass junction, turn northwest (right), and descend over a rock glacier to Paradise Creek. En route, Neptuak Mountain (3237 m) is framed through Wastach Pass to the southwest. A wooden sign points toward the pass, however there is no maintained trail in that direction.

After you cross the bridge over Paradise Creek, the trail forks. The left-hand fork leads to the campground in 300 m. Almost everyone who has camped here has a good porcupine story. Keep your boots inside your tent and don't go barefoot.

From the campground, a maze of paths leads northeast, merging into a single trail to the Giant Steps, a kilometre distant. Those not camping should take the right-hand fork at the campground junction. This provides a more direct approach to the Giant Steps, which you reach by turning north (left) in 200 m at the subsequent junction.

**Exit**

To complete this loop hike, keep left at junctions on your return from the Giant Steps to reach the Paradise Valley trail in 800 m. Turn northeast (left). Descend the valley to the Lake Annette junction, crossing Paradise Creek twice on bridges. From the Lake Annette junction, retrace the first 5.1 km to the trailhead.

## The Giant Steps

*The Giant Steps*

**The Giant Steps** are a series of gently dipping, quartzite slabs in the north fork of Paradise Creek. Scratches on the slabs are striations caused by rocks embedded in the underside of Horseshoe Glacier when it most recently advanced across this area. By looking at the striations, you can see the glacier's direction of flow. Some of the quartzite blocks in and alongside the stream were broken off by the glacier. Depressions in the slabs have filled with thin soils that support miniature gardens of lichens, mosses, and wildflowers. Please avoid stepping on them.

The trail emerges at the uppermost cascades. To reach the lower falls, backtrack to the approach trail and follow faint paths downstream. Use caution on the slippery rock, and be on the lookout for ice on cold days.

# 17. Sentinel Pass

## Route

Day-hike or overnight

| Route | Elevation (m) | Distance (km) |
|---|---|---|
| Trailhead | 1888 | 0 |
| Larch Valley/Sentinel Pass jct | 2241 | 2.4 |
| Sentinel Pass | 2611 | 5.8 |
| Sentinel Pass jct (Paradise Valley) | 2119 | 8.1 |
| Lake Annette | 1966 | 11.2 |
| Paradise Creek trailhead | 1729 | 16.9 |

**Maps**
NTS: 82 N/8
Gem Trek: Lake Louise and Yoho
**See map on p.69**

## Trailhead

**Consider using** public transportation. Parks Canada may close the Paradise Valley campground. Check at the Lake Louise Information Centre for any restrictions on this trail. From Lake Louise Village, follow Lake Louise Drive 3 km to Moraine Lake Road. Turn south (left). Follow this road 12 km to its end at Moraine Lake. The trailhead is on the lakeshore, south of the lodge.

Few destinations better exemplify the primal nature of the Rockies than the barren cleft of Sentinel Pass. Sandwiched between the shattered ramparts of Pinnacle Mountain and Mt. Temple, the pass is the highest point reached by maintained trail in the Rockies. It offers you a toehold normally in the domain of mountaineers. The steep slopes on either side of the pass can be treacherous when snow covered. Most years, if you hike this trail before mid-July, you should carry an ice axe and be proficient in its use.

**Trailhead to Sentinel Pass**

From the trailhead kiosk in front of the lodge, follow the trail southwest for 35 m to a junction. The Sentinel Pass/Wenkchemna Pass trail branches north (right), and immediately begins its steep climb. In the next 2.5 km, the trail gains 352 m to the entrance to Larch Valley. Moraine Lake is visible through the trees. The climb, which takes you to the crest of an ancient lateral moraine of the

Wenkchemna Glacier, concludes with a series of ten switchbacks that lead to a trail junction and a well-placed bench. The trail to Larch Valley and Sentinel Pass branches north (right).

Larch Valley occupies a broad glacial cirque that is centred on a bedrock fault south of Sentinel Pass. The trail winds its way into the lower valley and crosses a footbridge to a meadow. As early morning visitors will discover, the meadow is a frost hollow where cold air collects. Trees along the northern edge of the

*Mt. Fay, as seen from Sentinel Pass, the highest point in the Rockies reached by maintained trail.*

meadow display branches stunted by the cold. The meadow contains earth hummocks, formations caused by a churning action during repeated freezing and thawing of the soil when it was underlaid by permafrost. Directly southwest is Deltaform Mountain (3424 m), highest of the Wenkchemna Peaks. American explorer Walter Wilcox named the mountain for its resemblance to delta (Δ), the fourth letter of the Greek alphabet.

The trail swings north and climbs to treeline, passing some ancient larches and glades filled with western anemone. The three lakes in the tundra below Sentinel Pass were called Minnestimma Lakes by Samuel Allen, a companion of Walter Wilcox. *Minnestimma* means "sleeping waters." From the outlet of the middle lake, the trail heads east and begins the stiff climb along the lower flank of Mt. Temple to the switchbacks

## Variations

- Hike to the pass and return the same way, 11.6 km
- Cross Sentinel Pass to Paradise Valley. Exit from Paradise Valley via Lake Annette to the Moraine Lake Road, 16.9 km. See Classic Hike #16.
- Cross Sentinel Pass to Paradise Valley. Visit the Giant Steps and exit along the valley bottom trail to the Moraine Lake Road, 19.4 km. See Classic Hike #16.
- Same as previous, but camp at the Paradise Valley campground, 20.0 km. See Classic Hike #16.
- You can begin this outing with a short sidetrip (500 m return) along the interpretive trail to the top of the Moraine Lake Rockpile. See Classic Hike #18.

that lead into Sentinel Pass.

## Sentinel Pass

Sentinel Pass was first reached in 1894 by Samuel Allen, who ascended from a camp in Paradise

## Mr. Fay's Mountain

**By most accounts,** Professor Charles Fay of Tufts University was a gentleman and an accomplished mountaineer. Founder of the Appalachian Mountain Club and the American Alpine Club, Fay made 25 visits to the Rockies between 1894 and 1930, the year of his death. However, there is one story that portrays Fay out of character. To honour Fay's contribution to the exploration of the Rockies, the Geographic Board permitted him to choose a mountain to name for himself. Fellow mountaineer C.S. Thompson suggested the peak above Moraine Lake that Samuel Allen had first called Heejee ("Peak One.") Fay concurred, thus supplanting Allen's name, the first of seven times that this would happen in Valley of the Ten Peaks.

On his visit in 1904, Fay intended to make the first ascent of "his mountain." Two guides, the Kaufmann brothers based at Chalet Lake Louise, apparently conspired to rob him of this prize. While one of the guides led Fay on a poor route destined for certain failure, another led British mountaineer Gertrude Benham to success by a different route. Although there is no official record of what transpired, it is thought that Fay was so incensed that he promptly had the Kaufmanns fired by their employer, the Canadian Pacific Railway. Fay considered applying to have his name bestowed upon another peak so that he might attempt its first ascent. This he did not do, settling instead for a consolation prize — the second ascent of Mt. Fay, two weeks after Benham's.

*The Grand Sentinel*

## Lyall's Larch — Gold in the Hills

**Larch Valley** is named for the tree, Lyall's (LIE-alls) larch — also called subalpine larch and alpine larch. (This last name is an oxymoron, as the alpine ecoregion is defined, in part, by the absence of trees.) Of the three larch species in Canada, the Lyall's is the least extensive in range. In the Rockies, you won't find it north of Clearwater Pass, 28 km north of Lake Louise. It grows only in the upper subalpine forest, frequently forming pure stands at treeline. The mature tree is 5–10 m tall, has a ragged top, and brown bark with reddish-purple tones. Bright green needles grow from black, knobby twigs that are covered in dark woolly down. The wood burns easily, but because the tree usually grows in rocky terrain, larch forests are seldom consumed by forest fires. Some trees in Larch Valley may be more than 400 years old.

Lyall's larch is a deciduous conifer — it sheds its needles in late summer. Then the tree goes dormant with the buds for next year's growth already formed. Before shedding, larch needles turn golden yellow, transforming the treeline forests of the southern Rockies into a wonderful sight. Up to 500 visitors a day flock to Larch Valley at this time. Steer clear, for there are better places to see larches. The tree was catalogued by Eugene Bourgeau. Its taxonomic name, *Larix lyalli*, commemorates David Lyall, a Scottish surgeon and naturalist who accompanied the Franklin Expedition.

Valley. A few days later, Allen, Wilcox, and L.F. Frissell returned to the pass and climbed Mt. Temple, the first time a mountain exceeding 3353 m (11,000 ft) had been climbed in Canada. Theirs has become "regular route" on the mountain. On a fair summer day, as many as a hundred mountaineers may make the trip to Mt. Temple's summit by this route.

Wilcox described the pass as a vast ruin of nature. The chief agent of erosion at work here is mechanical weathering. Water expands nine percent when frozen, so the repeated freezing and thawing of water in cracks forces the fissures open. Eventually, boulders, cliffs, and mountainsides succumb to this incessant process.

The view south from the pass features the Wenkchemna Peaks, from Mt. Fay (3234 m) in the east, to Deltaform Mountain in the west. The large (120 m high) pinnacle to the north of the pass is the Grand Sentinel, a favourite objective of rock climbers.

### Sentinel Pass to Paradise Valley

North from the pass, the trail is poorly defined as it switchbacks steeply down through scree and boulders on the west side of the valley. Take care not to dislodge rocks onto people below. After the initial descent, the trail angles across the valley floor (follow cairns) to the east side. The grade lessens and the way becomes obvious. The pinnacles on the north slope of Pinnacle Mountain may be silhouetted against the sky or looming from the mist, offering intriguing possibilities to photographers.

## Paradise Valley Options

**At the trail junction** 2.3 km north of Sentinel Pass, you have two options for concluding this hike. If you would like to visit the Giant Steps or camp in the backcountry campground in Paradise Valley, continue straight ahead at this junction. The trail descends across a rock glacier to Paradise Creek, where a sidetrail leads to the Giant Steps. It is 10.9 km to the Moraine Lake Road via the Giant Steps.

For a shorter exit, turn northeast (right) at this junction and follow the highline route beneath the north face of Mt. Temple to Lake Annette, and then to the Moraine Lake Road. Distance for this option is 8.8 km. Either way, you should have transportation prearranged. The Paradise Creek parking lot is 9.7 km by road from Moraine Lake, and 5.3 km from Lake Louise Village. See Classic Hike #16.

# 18. Wenkchemna Pass

See map on p.69

## Route

Day-hike

| Route | Elevation (m) | Distance (km) |
|---|---|---|
| Trailhead | 1888 | 0 |
| Larch Valley/Sentinel Pass jct | 2241 | 2.7 |
| Eiffel Lakes | 2287 | 6.0 |
| Wenkchemna Pass | 2600 | 9.7 |

**Maps**

NTS: 82 N/8

Gem Trek: Lake Louise and Yoho

**See map on p.69**

## Trailhead

**Consider using** public transportation. Check at the Lake Louise Information Centre for any restrictions on this trail. From Lake Louise Village, follow Lake Louise Drive 3 km to Moraine Lake Road. Turn south (left). Follow this road 12 km to its end at Moraine Lake. The trailhead is on the lakeshore, south of the lodge.

The Wenkchemna Pass trail travels the length of the Valley of the Ten Peaks to a barren, rocky saddle on the crest of the Continental Divide. The hike is dominated by the imposing northern aspect of the Wenkchemna Peaks. Forests of Lyall's larch, intriguing geology, and human history add to the appeal of this outing. Wenkchemna Pass is the second highest point reached by maintained trail in the Rockies. In most years it is snowbound until early July.

### Trailhead to the Eiffel Lakes

From the trailhead kiosk in front of the lodge, follow the trail southwest for 35 m to a junction. The Sentinel Pass/Wenkchemna Pass trail branches north (right), and immediately begins its steep climb. In the next 2.5 km, the trail gains 352 m to the entrance to Larch Valley. Moraine Lake is visible through the trees. The climb, which takes you to the crest of an ancient lateral moraine of the Wenkchemna Glacier, concludes with a series of ten switchbacks that lead to a trail junction and a well-placed bench. The trail to Larch Valley and Sentinel Pass branches north (right). Continue straight ahead (west) for Wenkchemna Pass.

For the next 2 km, the trail travels at treeline across the southern flank of Eiffel Peak (3084 m), offering views ahead to Wenkchemna Pass and back to the western end of Moraine Lake. In 1893, Walter Wilcox and colleague Samuel Allen were the first to see the upper part of this valley. Wilcox was so taken aback by the austere appearance of the Wenkchemna Peaks and the chaos of rubble at their bases, that he coined the name Desolation Valley.

Samuel Allen named ten of the mountains in

## When Is a Moraine Not a Moraine?

**You can begin** this hike with a short sidetrip (500 m return) to the top of the Moraine Lake rockpile. Samuel Allen called the lake, Heejee Lake, in 1893. Walter Wilcox paid the first visit to its shores in 1899. He called it Moraine Lake, because he thought that it was dammed by a glacial moraine.

*Moraine Lake and the Wenkchemna Peaks from the Rockpile*

debris that was transported on the surface of a glacier. This would make it a rockslide, a moraine, and a pile of erratics.

Most of the boulders in the rockpile are Gog Formation quartzite and siltstone. You can see fossilized worm burrowings and an example of ripple rock. This rock records the action of wavelets on a prehistoric shoreline, 560 million years ago.

The rockpile is now thought to be rockslide debris, although some geologists think it may be rockslide

*The Wenkchemna Pass trail traverses the length of the Valley of the Ten Peaks to the lofty pass on the Continental Divide.*

(3237 m), on the southeast.

After you cross an avalanche slope, the Eiffel Lakes come into view. These lakes, fringed with larch trees, occupy depressions in rock-slide debris. They were a favourite destination of Wilcox, who would pack his 11x14 plate camera here late in the summer, when he thought the scenery was at its best. Wilcox called them the "Wenkchemna Lakes." The name "Eiffel" refers to a tower of rock on the north side of Eiffel Peak. This tower supposedly resembles the well-known structure in Paris. The lakes do not support fish.

The debris that harbors the Eiffel Lakes originated in two rockslides, one from the north face of Neptuak Mountain, another from near Wenkchemna Pass. One of the boulders has an estimated weight of more than 1000 tonnes. The total volume of the rockslides is more than 10 million cubic metres. The prominent peak to the northwest is Hungabee Mountain (3493 m), which is the second highest in the area after Mt. Temple, and commands the head of nearby Paradise Valley.

### Eiffel Lakes to Wenkchemna Pass

West of the Eiffel Lakes, the trail is rough as it crosses boulderfields. The going becomes easier as the trail winds through an upper subalpine meadow bisected by several streams — the last water sources before the pass. From the meadows, the trail angles southwest and then switchbacks upward through more boulderfields. The quartzite boulders underfoot rest on the surface of a rock glacier — an accumulation of ice that allows the entire mass to creep slowly downhill.

this valley with the Stoney words for the numbers 1 through 10. *Wenkchemna* means "ten." Allen's application of nomenclature was arbitrary, as eighteen mountains flank the valley. Only three of the Wenkchemna Peaks still bear Allen's names. Tonsa or "Peak 4" (3054 m) is directly south across the valley from Eiffel Peak. Wenkchemna Pass is bordered by Wenkchemna Peak (3173 m) on the north, and by Neptuak Mountain, "Peak 9"

## A Valley of Rock and Ice

**Most of the rubble** on the floor of the Valley of the Ten Peaks is surface moraine that covers the 4 km² of Wenkchemna Glacier. This peculiar body of ice is sustained primarily by snow and ice avalanches from couloirs on the north faces of the Wenkchemna Peaks. The more easterly part of the glacier is now stagnant and detached from the active glacial ice. Insulated by the moraine on its surface, this huge mass of ice will slowly melt if the glacier does not advance again and reincorporate it.

The rubble-covered glacier features conical talus (TAY-luss) piles, mounds of rock created by avalanches. These piles have been carried from the base of the cliffs by the moving ice. The glacier's surface is dotted with kettle ponds, formed by slumping and melting of ice-cored moraines. A sinuous terminal moraine winds along the glacier's northern margin. Walter Wilcox was right — it is a scene of desolation, but not without beauty.

## Variation

- Strong hikers can add a visit to Sentinel Pass, 26.2 km total. See Classic Hike #17.

There are several small kettle lakes northwest of the trail. You may see white-tailed ptarmigan as you approach Wenkchemna Pass. These ground-dwelling grouse-like birds feature plumage that changes colour from white in winter, to a mottled brown, gray, and black in summer. The tail is always white. On the final section of trail you toil across a scree slope before descending slightly onto Wenkchemna Pass.

The trackless west slope of the pass plunges to the upper reaches of Tokumm Creek in Yoho National Park. The rock formation in the meadows there is called Eagle Eyrie. Golden eagles do frequent this area, and when seen from ground level, the rock formation resembles a bird of prey. The summit of Neptuak Mountain, southeast of the pass, is the only point in Canada where the boundaries of three national parks meet — Yoho, Banff, and Kootenay. Looking northeast, the massive bulk of Mt. Temple (3543 m) dominates all other mountains in the area.

## Meadow Chalice

*Western anemone*

**The meadows** on this hike are flush with western anemone. You will have to arrive early in the hiking season to see the showy, creamy-white blooms — sometimes tinged with blue — that poke through the edges of receding snowbanks. Most hikers only see the seedheads, which endure the remainder of the season. When covered with dew or backlit by the sun, these shaggy tops are a favourite with wildflower photographers. Anemone is derived from the Greek, *anemos*, which means "wind." "Chalice flower" is one of the folk names for this plant — a reference to the deep, cup-shaped bloom. The confines at the centre of the flower trap solar heat, evidently making the location more attractive to pollinating insects and helping to ensure propagation.

# 19. Skoki

## Route

**Overnight, 3–5 days**

| Route | Elevation (m) | Distance (km) |
|---|---|---|
| Trailhead | 1698 | 0 |
| Temple Research Station | 1990 | 3.7 |
| End of gravel road | 1995 | 3.9 |
| Halfway Hut | 2195 | 7.1 |
| Hidden Lake CG jct | 2195 | 7.2 |
| Hidden Lake CG | 2198 | +0.1 |
| Boulder Pass | 2345 | 8.7 |
| Deception Pass jct | 2348 | 10.5 |
| Baker Lake CG | 2210 | 13.2 |
| Baker Creek jct | 1955 | 13.9 |
| Baker/Red Deer Divide | 2180 | 15.0 |
| "Jones' Pass" jct | 2160 | 16.7 |
| Red Deer Lakes CG | 2088 | +2.3 |
| "Jones' Pass" | 2210 | 19.0 |
| Skoki Valley jct | 2195 | 19.6 |
| Skoki Lodge | 2164 | 20.0 |
| Merlin Meadows CG | 2119 | 21.2 |
| Skoki Valley jct | 2195 | 22.8 |
| Deception Pass | 2485 | 25.8 |
| Boulder Pass | 2345 | 28.2 |
| Trailhead | 1698 | 36.9 |

**Maps**
NTS: 82 N/8, and 82 N/9, and 82 O/5, and 82 O/12
Gem Trek: Lake Louise and Yoho, or Banff and Mt. Assiniboine

## Trailhead

**Parks Canada** is considering restricting access in the Skoki area. Check at the Lake Louise Information Centre. From the Lake Louise interchange on the Trans-Canada Highway, turn east onto Whitehorn Drive and follow signs for the Lake Louise ski area. Turn south (right) after 2 km onto the Fish Creek Road. Follow this gravel road 1 km until it becomes restricted access. Park in the parking lot on the south (right).

The area known as Skoki (SKOWE-key) encompasses a series of compact, lake-dotted valleys — Ptarmigan, Baker, Skoki, and upper Red Deer — in the Slate Range northeast of Lake Louise. Much of the hiking terrain is at or above treeline. Grizzly bears, wolves, moose, wolverines, mule deer, elk, coyote, bighorn sheep, and mountain

*The Skoki trail winds through this rockslide as you climb to Boulder Pass. Mt. Temple is in the distance.*

## Trailhead to Boulder Pass

The Skoki trail commences with a stiff climb along the Temple access road. Don't let the road and its occasional traffic fool you; this area is frequented by grizzly bears. Travel accordingly. Views are limited, except from the top of "Ford Hill," where Mt. Victoria (3464 m) and other summits near Lake Louise are visible to the west. Continue straight ahead at junctions until the road ends 200 m beyond the Temple Research Station at the Lake Louise ski area. Angle steeply uphill across the ski run to where the trail proper begins.

The trail follows Corral Creek through upper subalpine forest. You may see red squirrels, porcupines, gray jays, Clark's nutcrackers, American martens, and mule deer. Some work on the Skoki trail was done by Ukranian prisoners during WWI. At km 6.8, the forest thins. Cross Corral Creek to its west bank. Use caution if the bridge is frosty. Directly ahead are the three highest summits of the Slate Range, from west to east — Mt. Richardson (3086 m), Pika Peak (3052 m), and Ptarmigan Peak (3059 m). Mt. Richardson was named by James Hector for John Richardson, surgeon and naturalist with the Franklin Arctic expeditions of 1819 and 1825. The Slate Range is home to approximately 40 mountain goats.

Halfway Hut (also called Ptarmigan Hut) is the next waypoint on the trail. The cabin was constructed in 1931 as a stopover for ski guests of Skoki Lodge, and for guides and packers making supply trips. The building is halfway between the Lake Louise railway station and Skoki Lodge. Many sober and reputable travellers have reported unusual sights and sounds near Halfway Hut. The ghosts of four skiers killed in avalanches are said to haunt the building. They schuss down from Ptarmigan Peak to convene a nightly poker game in winter. Today, the hut is a day-use shelter

goats frequent these valleys.

This outing describes a counterclockwise loop hike. You can add day-hikes from the campgrounds. Mountaineers can make straightforward ascents of more than a dozen nearby summits. Completing the charm of the Skoki area is its vibrant human history. You share the entire loop with horses.

## Hidden Lake, 1.3 km

**I recommend** the sidetrip to Hidden Lake if you are staying at the nearby campground, or day-hiking from the trailhead to Boulder Pass. The trail departs from the campground and follows the north fork of Corral Creek. Wildflowers fill the glades in the treeline larch forest. Rock-hop the stream just below the lake's outlet, and follow the wet track to the lakeshore.

Hidden Lake is a typical glacial tarn, 32.3 m deep. Cutthroat trout inhabit the waters. Mountain goats and bighorn sheep ramble along the cliffs north of the lake. Redoubt Mountain (2902 m) looms across the valley to the southeast.

## Variations

- Day-hike to Hidden Lake and Boulder Pass, 12.8 km return
- Day-hike to Boulder Pass and Deception Pass, 22.0 km return
- Hike the loop in reverse
- Base yourself at one of the four campgrounds and visit other destinations on day-hikes

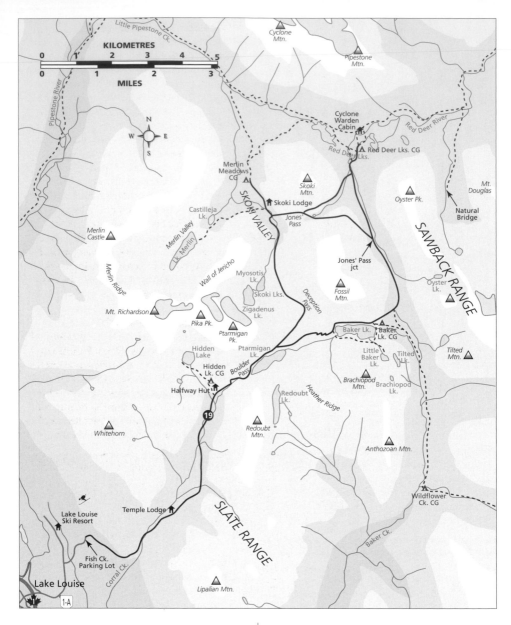

only. It is located on the site of a prehistoric Native encampment. There are fine views of Mt. Temple (3543 m) and some of the Wenkchemna Peaks. Porcupines and Columbian ground squirrels frequent the surrounding meadows. I once saw a female wolverine with three cubs here.

The Hidden Lake junction is 100 m north of Halfway Hut. For most hikers, the adjacent backcountry campground is less than four hours' travel from the trailhead, making it possible to

start this hike in the afternoon in early summer, with the assurance of reaching a campground before dark.

The initial 500 m of trail between Halfway Hut and Boulder Pass can be very muddy. The final kilometre winds through massive quartzite boulders of rockslide debris from Redoubt Mountain (2902 m). The mountain was named because of its "redoubtable," fortress-like appearance. If you look back during the climb, you may see the large boulder that perfectly mimics the shape of distant Mt. Temple.

Boulder Pass is the gateway to the spectacular upper subalpine environment of Skoki. The centrepiece in the view is Ptarmigan Lake, which laps against the eastern side of the pass. On rare calm days, the lake mirrors Fossil Mountain (2946 m) and the distant summits of Mt. Douglas (3235 m) and Mt. St. Bride (3312 m), the two highest mountains in the Sawback Range. True to the name of the lake and nearby peak, you may see white-tailed ptarmigan — a ground-dwelling, alpine grouse — on the pass.

## Little Baker Lake, 1.2 km

**Little Baker Lake** is one of three lakes tucked under the east flank of Brachiopod Mountain. Rock-hop the outlet of Baker Lake and follow beaten paths through larch forest to the southeast. Look back at Fossil Mountain to see the incredible Z-shaped, overturned fold in the upper part of the south face.

The maze of paths here defies sensible description. Pass a small unnamed pond (not shown on the topographic map) along its east shore, and continue to Little Baker Lake. You have views to Tilted Lake en route. Brachiopod Lake is farther south. This seasonal pond usually dries up by late summer.

### Boulder Pass to Baker Lake

The Skoki trail is rocky and wet in places as it contours along the north shore of Ptarmigan Lake. Kruppelholz tree islands of spruce and fir dot the tundra. Cotton-grass grows along the lakeshore. You should be prepared for poor weather in this vicinity. When the clouds are down on the hills, Ptarmigan Lake can be one of the bleaker places in the Rockies. Summer snowfalls are common and winds are often strong and bitterly cold. The Deception Pass junction is 1.9 km from Boulder Pass. Continue straight ahead for Baker Lake.

The trail contours through several shale gullies southwest of Fossil Mountain, before descending through stunted subalpine forest to Baker Lake. Follow the north shore of the lake through willows to the Baker Lake campground near the outlet. The lake is popular with backcountry anglers and bugs. Porcupines and snowshoe hares frequent the tenting area. Look for dippers in the outlet stream.

### Baker Lake to Red Deer Lakes

At the junction 50 m east of Baker Lake campground, keep northeast (left). From the junction, the trail contours through open subalpine forest dotted with larches, and then descends to the treeless tundra of the valley floor and another junction. Turn north (left). The wildflowers here are exceptional, and include elephant head and dense clumps of vibrantly coloured paintbrush.

## A Textbook Landscape

**The vicinity** of Ptarmigan Lake marks the transition from the eastern main ranges to the front ranges. The eastern main ranges were created 120 million years ago. The mountains contain resistant limestone, dolomite, and quartzite cliffs alternating with layers of recessive shale. The strata are horizontal or dip slightly to the southwest.

If you look at Ptarmigan Peak, you can see that it rests on a massive sandwich of alternating resistant and recessive sedimentary layers. This rock sandwich is the Pipestone Pass Thrust Sheet, an assemblage of rocks that slid 60 km upward and over younger rocks during mountain building. The steep drop between Ptarmigan Lake

*Ptarmigan Lake*

and Baker Lake marks the leading edge of this thrust sheet.

In contrast, the younger rocks of mountains farther east were thrust skyward 85 million years ago when the front ranges were created. The sedimentary formations of front range mountains, such as Fossil Mountain, dip steeply to the southwest, creating sawtooth and overthrust mountains.

By looking at the profile of Ptarmigan Peak from the shore of Ptarmigan Lake and comparing it with mountains to the east, it is easy to grasp the complex concept of thrust sheets, and the differences between the eastern main ranges and front ranges.

Cyclone Mountain (3041 m) and its eastern outlier, Pipestone Mountain (2970 m), are prominent directly north. Cyclone was named in 1910 by a mountaineering party who studied routes on the mountain while a thunderstorm gathered over its summit. The sedimentary formations of Pipestone Mountain feature an anticline.

About 2 km from the campground, you cross the unremarkable height of land that separates Baker Creek from the Red Deer River. Perhaps because it is almost unrecognizable as a mountain pass, this well-travelled feature is yet to be officially named — the name "Cotton-grass Pass" has been suggested. Broad mountain passes are frequently boggy like this one. Without a steep gradient to direct the flow of streams and springs, water collects into pools and marshes. The sedges and willows that grow in these areas make them excellent habitat for moose.

At the trail junction 3.5 km from Baker Lake campground, turn west (left) if you do not want to include the Red Deer Lakes in this outing. The trail climbs over the shoulder of Fossil Mountain into "Jones' Pass."

To continue to Red Deer Lakes, continue straight ahead at this junction and the one

## Ken Jones — The Mountain Life

*Ken Jones*

**The unofficial name** for the pass between Skoki and Fossil mountains was suggested by the late Jon Whyte. In 1936, Skoki Lodge was enlarged and a new ridgepole was sought for the roof. Outfitter and woodsman Ken Jones scoured the Skoki area for a tree of suitable length, finding one at Douglas Lake, more than 13 km to the east. Using a horse team, it took Jones a week to skid the tree to Skoki Lodge via "Jones' Pass." Ken Jones is testimony to the youth-giving properties of a mountain life. He made a visit to the lodge in the spring of 2003, at age 90.

## Natural Bridge, 6.1 km

*Natural Bridge*

**Despite their crumbly** and heavily eroded nature, the Canadian Rockies offer few examples of natural windows, bridges, and arches. Perhaps the best known are Goat's Eye above Healy Creek, and Yoho's Natural Bridge on the Kicking Horse River. If you've come this far, you might want to make the day-trip to Banff's Natural Bridge, just off the Red Deer Valley. The outing involves two fords, the first one moderately difficult.

From Red Deer Lakes campground, head north for 500 m to the junction with the Red Deer trail. Turn east (right). Negotiate the horse fence and carry on past the Cyclone warden cabin. Climb into the woods beyond the cabin, and hike through ancient forest to the marked junction, 2.5 km beyond. Turn south (right) to enter the valley between Oyster Peak and Mt. Douglas. Ford the Red Deer River. Just 400 m south, you must ford (easy) the outlet stream of the side valley. The trail climbs moderately beyond this ford for 2.5 km to the Natural Bridge, where an unnamed creek has undercut a lip of resistant Palliser Formation limestone.

## Lake Merlin, 2.9 km

*As with many lakes set in limestone bedrock, Lake Merlin drains underground.*

paintbrush.

The trail draws alongside the south shore of Castilleja Lake before commencing an excruciatingly steep climb south on scree slopes. At the top of this climb, follow cairns west to the Lake Merlin headwall. Ascend a scree gully through the headwall and then descend west over limestone pavement to the lakeshore. Take care not to knock rocks onto your companions while you are in the gully. With your boots, you've just traced a dominant theme of eastern main range mountains: the alternation of resistant and recessive formations of rock. Castilleja Lake is set in blocky quartzite. The gully is crumbly shale of the Mt. Whyte Formation. The solid pavement above is Cathedral Formation limestone.

The glaciated north face of Mt. Richardson creates an exceptional backdrop for Lake Merlin. The lake takes its name from nearby Merlin Castle, an assembly of quartzite pinnacles that mountaineer J.F. Porter likened to an Arthurian castle. Merlin was a prophet and magician of Arthurian legend. Porter may have had another intention in mind when he gave the name, for Lake Merlin demonstrates some of nature's magic. If you walk along the lake's northeast shore, you may be puzzled at the absence of an outlet stream. But you probably noticed that Castilleja Lake received an inlet stream from above. As with many lakes set in limestone in the Rockies, Lake Merlin is a karst feature. It drains underground through the underlying Cathedral Formation.

When Porter's party visited the lake, they noticed evidence of an abandoned surface outlet, along with driftwood that marked an ancient high water level. This indicates that Lake Merlin's subterranean outlet is, in geological terms, of recent origin. The driftwood has not yet completely decomposed, so the change to underground drainage probably occurred within the last 200 years. With care, you can search the upper headwall northeast of the lake for a natural "window" that allows a glimpse within the bedrock to the underground stream. It's a remarkable sight, for the stream is an underground waterfall. Merlin indeed!

**In a landscape** overflowing with lakes, Lake Merlin is without question Skoki's most scenic. However, the trail to the lake will not be to everyone's liking. It's an up-and-down affair, routed across boulderfields and up a steep limestone headwall. The destination more than compensates for the demands of the approach. Lawrence Grassi, renowned for his trail construction in the Lake O'Hara area in Yoho, worked on part of this trail.

The trailhead is at creekside, directly opposite the front door of Skoki Lodge. The purplish rock in the creek bed is ancient Miette Formation shale. The trail winds through pleasant upper subalpine forest for 300 m to a junction. Turn west (right). You then climb onto a sideslope of quartzite boulders that have appropriately tumbled from the Wall of Jericho. The blooms of red-stemmed saxifrage, mountain sorrel, yellow columbine, and arnica brighten the rocky slopes. Views north include Mt. Willingdon (3373 m), Cataract Peak (3333 m), Cyclone Mountain, and unnamed summits on the west side of the Drummond Icefield.

The trail crosses a low ridge west of the boulderfield. I once encountered a wolverine here. It fled off-trail into a dead end and turned to face me, snarling. I timidly backed away to let the animal pick its route. It was gone in a flash. Descend from the ridge on a rocky trail, following cairns where necessary. Unfortunately, a number of paths have been marked, only serving to confuse the route. During the descent, your eyes will probably be fixed on remarkably coloured Castilleja (cass-TIH-lee-ah) Lake. *Castilleja* is the genus name of the wildflower, following. The trail enters a 250-year-old spruce-fir forest where the tread soon deteriorates into horse-churned muck. You must make several awkward stream hops during the next 700 m, after which the sidetrail to Red Deer Lakes campground branches east (right).

The nearby Red Deer Lakes are popular fishing holes, and were formerly stocked to promote angling. Research has indicated that the rainbow trout, eastern brook trout, and cutthroat trout present are no longer reproducing. Continued fishing will ultimately deplete the lakes. There is a maze of muddy trails on the surrounding willow plain. Mt. Hector (3394 m), the highest peak in this part of Banff National Park, dominates the view west. The middle Red Deer Lake was called Hatchet Lake by participants of the 1915 Alpine Club of Canada camp, because of the shape of its shoreline. The Red Deer River was known to the Cree as "Elk River," because of the numerous elk (wapiti) in the upper reaches of the watershed. Europeans know the elk as "red deer." The first explorers applied this name to the river and lakes.

## Red Deer Lakes to Merlin Meadows Campground

From Red Deer Lakes campground, backtrack south 700 m to a junction. Turn west (right), hop the creek, and follow the trail heading west into "Jones' Pass." The trail from the Baker/Red Deer Divide merges with this trail at an avalanche slope just before the crest of the pass. This area is often fragrant with the resin of trees downed in avalanches during the previous spring. Straight ahead (southwest) is the Wall of Jericho (2910 m), and Ptarmigan Peak. West from the pass, sections of trail have been gravel-capped. The trail swings northwest and descends to the Skoki Valley junction. Turn north (right). You reach Skoki Lodge in 400 m. Merlin Meadows campground is 1.2 km farther north.

## Return

The homeward trail departs south from Merlin Meadows campground. Continue straight ahead at the junction 400 m south of Skoki Lodge. The trail climbs 300 m in the next 3 km, to Deception Pass. The pass was named by skier Cyril Paris for a reason that will soon be obvious: it's farther to the crest than it looks.

Deception Pass provides a tremendous panorama of the Slate Range, Ptarmigan Lake, the Bow Range near Lake Louise, and more distant points north and south. White-tailed ptarmigan are common here. Skiers in winter find ascent

and descent of this pass either a peril or a pleasure, depending on their fondness for terminal velocity.

Descend south on slopes of compacted shale to the Boulder Pass trail. Turn west (right). The remainder of the trail is on familiar ground, retracing the first 10.5 km of this outing along the shore of Ptarmigan Lake and over Boulder Pass, to the Fish Creek parking lot.

## Skoki Lodge

*Skoki Lodge*

**The first detailed** exploration of the Skoki area was made by the J.F. Porter mountaineering party in 1911. Porter bestowed many names still in use today. *Skokie* is a Native word that Porter brought from his Illinois home. It means "marsh." He gave it to the west meadow near today's Merlin Meadows campground.

In 1930, ski enthusiasts Cliff White and Cyril Paris of Banff sought a place to build the first ski lodge in the Rockies. With its abundant snowfall and variety of skiing slopes, they chose the Skoki Valley. Originally intended to be a ski club cabin only, the lodge opened in the winter of 1931 and soon became a commercial enterprise. It now operates seasonally in summer and winter. Tea, coffee, soup, and baked goods may be available to hikers for a fee during posted hours — usually late morning to late afternoon — just the thing to cheer up a rainy day.

# 20. Mosquito Creek

## Route

**Day-hike or overnight**

| Route | Elevation (m) | Distance (km) |
|---|---|---|
| Trailhead | 1828 | 0 |
| Mosquito Creek CG | 1990 | 5.4 |
| Molar Pass jct | 2195 | 6.9 |
| Molar Pass | 2365 | +3.4 |
| "Mosquito Lake" | 2302 | 8.8 |
| Molar Meadows | 2310 | 9.0 |
| North Molar Pass | 2593 | 11.5 |
| Upper Fish Lake CG | 2210 | 14.8 |

**Maps**
NTS: 82 N/9
Gem Trek: Bow Lake and Saskatchewan Crossing

*Molar Pass*

## Trailhead

**Mosquito Creek** on the Icefields Parkway, 23.6 km north of the Trans-Canada Highway. The parking lot is on the west side of the Parkway, south of the bridge. The trailhead is on the east side of the Parkway, north of the bridge. Use caution crossing the road.

With its high starting elevation, the Mosquito Creek trail grants quick access to a lofty and sublime alpine environment with many pockets to explore. I have stomped and skied along this trail perhaps twenty times and have never tired of its destinations. You share all routes with commercial horse parties, so avoid this trail during wet weather, when muck and mire prevail. The valley, meadows, and passes are frequented by grizzly bears. Travel accordingly.

### Trailhead to Molar Pass Junction
The trail climbs steeply up the bank of Mosquito Creek — the steepest grade in the first 7 km — and then angles across the right of way cleared in

## Variations

- Day-hike to Molar Meadows, 18.0 km return
- Day-hike to Molar Pass, 20.6 km return
- Day-hike to North Molar Pass, 23.0 km return
- Camp at Mosquito Creek campground and explore both passes
- Backpack to Fish Lakes campground, 14.8 km

the 1930s for the "Wonder Road," precursor of the Icefields Parkway. The next 1.9 km is through open coniferous forest with a variety of subalpine wildflowers in the undergrowth. The forest in this valley last burned in 1830, in a large fire that also consumed much of the upper Bow Valley. The rooted and rocky trail drops to creekside and then travels across willow plain. Rock-hop as required.

The trail crosses the north fork of Mosquito Creek on a two-log bridge, and continues through forest to the Mosquito Creek campground at km 5.4. The campground is set among Eldon Formation boulders that tumbled here in a rockslide. Given the horse traffic in this area, you should treat all drinking water.

The trail beyond the campground is notorious for its muck holes and braiding, especially during early summer and after rains. The trail crosses the creek on a bridge and follows the bank for roughly a kilometre. It then recrosses the creek, reaching the Molar Pass junction 500 m farther.

### Molar Pass Junction to Molar Pass
For 1.5 km beyond the junction, you hike on a wet and sometimes sketchy trail through glades of open upper subalpine forest. The exceptional wildflower displays here more than compensate for the poor trail. The cliffs to the west are part of the group of summits at the head of Noseeum Creek. The northeast cliffs of the highest peak, "Noseeum Peak" (2988 m), feature a niche glacier. The craggy entrance to Molar Pass looms ahead, perhaps prompting you to question just how you are going to get up that cliff.

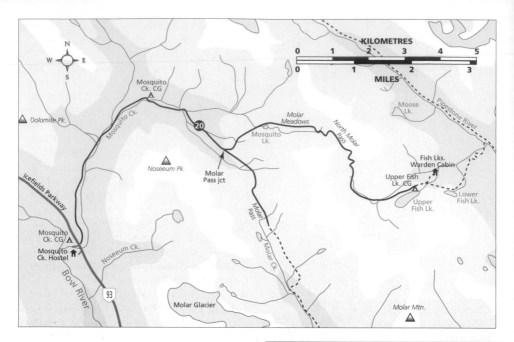

## Aquatic Gardens

*Mountain marsh marigold*

The grade steepens as the trail climbs onto drier ground above the creek. Rock-hop a stream that cascades down titled slabs of quartzite bedrock. Mountain sorrel, leather-leaved saxifrage, alpine forget-me-not, and dense blooms of yellow columbine grow here. The trail switchbacks cleverly through the cliff at the northern entrance to Molar Pass. From the top of this climb you have an exceptional view north over upper Mosquito Creek, and onto the extensive, rolling alpland of Molar Meadows to the northeast.

Molar Pass is a heath and avens tundra — 2 km long —that separates the headwaters of Mosquito Creek and Molar Creek. The view south improves as you traverse the hillside on the east side of the pass. We once watched a grizzly bear here from a kilometre away. Eventually, you can see the summit of Mt. Hector (3394 m), the peaks of the Slate Range, Molar Mountain (3022 m) and its outlying tower (2901 m). James Hector named Molar Mountain in 1858. When viewed from near Lake Louise, the mountain and its tower resemble pointed teeth.

Most of the bedrock in Molar Pass is Cathedral Formation limestone. The axis of the pass lies along a bedrock fault. To the west, above the pass, a ledge of Stephen Formation shale is topped by massive cliffs of Eldon Formation limestone. This sequence — Cathedral-Stephen-Eldon — is the "Middle Cambrian sandwich" of sedimentary

**Upper subalpine areas** with limestone bedrock often contain seeps — outlets for rainwater and snowmelt that have drained underground. As it percolates downwards, the water is intercepted by resistant rock layers. These channel the water laterally to the surface. The bedrock on the way to Molar Pass is Gog Formation quartzite, but the culprit limestone is just uphill to the east. When this trail has been churned into quagmire by horses, no amount of drainage control and no heat spell will keep the incessant trickle of water off the tread. One of the joys of these failures of trail design is the tiny gardens of moisture-loving plants that thrive in and around the slop. Look for elephant head, white globeflower, yellow paintbrush, dwarf false asphodel, red-stemmed saxifrage, yellow saxifrage, cotton grass, fringed grass-of-Parnassus, and mountain marsh marigold. Step gently.

*Molar Meadows*

## A Cold and Rocky Home

*Yellow mountain saxifrage*

**At approximately km 3,** the Mosquito Creek trail crosses an alluvial fan that marks the entrance of a tributary stream from the north. Vegetation on this fan is scant. Not only does the rocky soil make tree growth difficult here, but the tributary stream and Mosquito Creek channel cold air into the valley bottom, shortening the growing season.

Mountain fireweed (riverbeauty), yellow mountain saxifrage, red-stemmed saxifrage, yellow paintbrush, elephant head, and common butterwort are wildflowers that thrive in this cold, damp environment. Common butterwort is one of seven insectivorous plant species in the Rockies. The pale green leaves at the base of the plant trap and digest insects.

This habitat is also good for sedges. Sedges resemble grasses, but have triangular, solid stems. One of the more common sedges in the Rockies is cotton-grass. Its brilliant white tufts contain minuscule flowers. The tufts grace the banks of subalpine streams and marshes in late July and August.

formations that builds many imposing mountain walls in the central Rockies. The fissured limestone pavement of the pass is known as a "clint and grike" landscape, with underground drainage called karst. The "clints" are limestone blocks and the "grikes" are the fissures that separate them. The words come from the dialect of Yorkshire, England, where this kind of landscape is common. True to fashion, the four lakelets on the benches west of the pass drain underground.

When you start to descend into the upper reaches of Molar Creek, it's time to turn around. Your ramblings in Molar Pass will add a few kilometres to the length of this hike.

### Molar Pass Junction to North Molar Pass

Continue straight ahead at the junction and begin a steep climb through treeline. Above is the alpine tundra of Molar Meadows, an exquisite backcountry landscape. The flower-filled meadows are a favourite haunt of grizzly bears. An unnamed quartzite spire rises above the southern edge of the meadows. The castellated towers of Dolomite Peak (2782 m) are prominent in the view west. "Mosquito Lake" (unnamed on the topographic map), its shores fringed with cotton-grass, completes this idyllic scene. The lake is an ideal place to rest before the hard work ahead — the climb to North Molar Pass — 280 m of elevation gain in the next 2.7 km. Of course, you could simply park it here in wildflower heaven.

Rock-hop the lake's outlet and climb away from the north shore. The trail crosses a beautiful alpland, the match of any in the Rockies. On the final approach to North Molar Pass, you may be intrigued by the two rock types visible. Weathered and lichen-covered blocks of Gog Formation quartzite are south of the trail. Pink and buff coloured fragments of Cathedral Formation limestone are to the north. You follow the seam between these two formations directly to the pass.

The ascent culminates in a steep track, scraped out of the rubble. The narrow, barren crest of North Molar Pass (2593 m) is the third highest point reached by maintained trail in the Rockies. The pass is named for its proximity to Molar Mountain (3022 m), the summit of which is framed perfectly in the view southeast, just before you cross the pass. After taking in the view, those day-hiking from the Icefields Parkway should turn back at this point. If you are day-hiking from the Mosquito Creek campground, assess your stamina for the 373 m descent to Upper Fish Lake, which you will have to climb on your return.

## North Molar Pass to Upper Fish Lake

A perennial snow and ice patch clings to the southeast side of North Molar Pass. Give this treacherous feature a wide berth by crossing high on the slope to the north, then descending steeply to pick up the trail. After an initially abrupt drop, you cross the stream that

*Upper Fish Lake*

drains the pass. The trail then begins a rambling, braided descent through sedge and heath meadows toward Upper Fish Lake. Where the trail again angles to the edge of the stream, rock-hop to the east side. The location of this crossing is sometimes marked by a cairn. It is otherwise easy to miss. Cross the stream again in 1 km on a log bridge upstream from a small canyon cut into Cathedral Formation limestone.

From the rise just beyond this crossing, you get your first full view of Upper Fish Lake, 100 m below. Cataract Peak (3333 m) rises beyond the lake on the east side of the Pipestone Valley. Cataract is among the higher mountains in the front ranges. It is surprising that this fine peak was not climbed until 1930.

## Skunked at Fish Lakes

**When the Fish Lakes** were stocked with cutthroat trout, they offered good prospects to anglers. Stocking of lakes in Banff to support angling was discontinued in 1988. Angler success soon decreased rapidly. The Fish Lakes and two other unnamed lakes nearby were closed to angling in 1992 to allow fish stocks to recover through natural regeneration. In these cold, unproductive waters, recovery may take decades. If the Fish Lakes are reopened to angling, it may be as a "catch and release" fishery only. Stocking of fish in national parks is now restricted to native species, and only to assist in recovery or re-establishment of native populations, not to support angling.

## The Ghost Deer

**The Clearwater-Siffleur** caribou herd is the most southerly in the Rockies. When the first edition of *Classic Hikes* went to press in 1994, the herd was thought to contain about two dozen animals. It seemed to be expanding its range. In 1990, I saw caribou tracks in the upper valley of Mosquito Creek. Reports of sightings came from near Lake Louise and in the Skoki area. At the time, there was a legendary member of the herd — a white bull that I had seen in 1990 and in 1992. The ghostly appearance of that bull may have been an omen, for by early 2002 wildlife biologists had all but given up on the herd, considering it extirpated. There had been no sightings for almost two years. The resurgence of wolves,

and climate warming are two of the theories put forward for the rapid decline. This is not the first time the herd is known to have crashed. Guide and outfitter Jimmy Simpson reported caribou tracks in the Siffleur Valley in 1902, and that Stoney hunters had killed all but two of the herd two years earlier. After that, caribou seem to have disappeared from local record until the 1970s. As for the current fate of the herd, in August 2002, a park warden sighted a caribou cow and calf in a remote valley not far from here. Where there is a female with young, there must necessarily be a male, so tenuous hope for the Clearwater-Siffleur caribou herd continues.

The Upper Fish Lake campground is set in a grove of spruce, fir, and larch, 100 m north of the upper lake. The larch trees here are near the northern limit for the species. With fishing no longer allowed at the Fish Lakes, this heavily used campground may see less traffic, and the surrounding vegetation may recover from the abuses of undisciplined firewood gathering. The district warden cabin is 200 m north of the lake.

If you would like to add more distance to your outing, rock-hop the outlet of Upper Fish Lake and continue to tiny, Lower Fish Lake in 1 km. The trail beyond — among the muddier in the Rockies — descends steeply to the Pipestone Valley, a haven for wolves, grizzly bears, and caribou.

# 21. Dolomite Pass

## Route

Day-hike or overnight

| Route | Elevation (m) | Distance (km) |
|---|---|---|
| Trailhead | 1944 | 0 |
| Lake Helen | 2363 | 6.0 |
| Trail summit | 2500 | 6.9 |
| Lake Katherine | 2370 | 8.1 |
| Dolomite Pass | 2393 | 8.9 |

**Maps**
NTS: 82 N/9
Gem Trek: Bow Lake and Saskatchewan Crossing

## Trailhead

**East side of** the Icefields Parkway, 32.5 km north of the Trans-Canada Highway; opposite the Crowfoot Glacier viewpoint.

For more than 5 km, the Dolomite (DOE-loh-mite) Pass trail traverses an exceptional alpine environment. The wildflower displays in the meadows before Lake Helen are superb. Dolomite Pass and the valleys it connects are travel routes and prime summer habitat for grizzly bears. Fortunate hikers may also see wolves and mountain caribou. The trail is used by commercial horse parties.

Most locals, and those who make the trail signs, refer to Lake Helen as "Helen Lake." In the case of geographical features (other than rivers

*Wildflower meadows above Helen Creek*

and passes) that were named in English for people, the generic part of the name is supposed to come first, followed by the specific: Lake Louise, Mt. Victoria, Glacier des Poilus. When the feature is not named for a person, the arrangement is supposed to be the other way around: Glacier Lake, Castle Mountain, Saskatchewan Glacier. Scan your maps and you'll find many exceptions to the rule, but Lake Helen follows it.

**Trailhead to Lake Helen**
The first 3 km of trail ascends steadily as it contours around the south end of the outlying ridge of Cirque Peak. From treeline you have expansive views into the Bow Valley. Mt. Hector (3394 m) is the prominent glacier-clad peak, 14 km south. Crowfoot Glacier is directly west, above the outlet of Bow Lake. Early travellers in the Bow Valley called it "Trident Glacier," because its terminus featured three separate lobes of ice, two of which draped the headwall toward Bow Lake. The present name likens the glacier's form to the foot of

## Variations

- Hike to Lake Helen, 12.0 km return
- Experienced backpackers familiar with bear safety may random camp in the valley of Dolomite Creek, north of the pass.

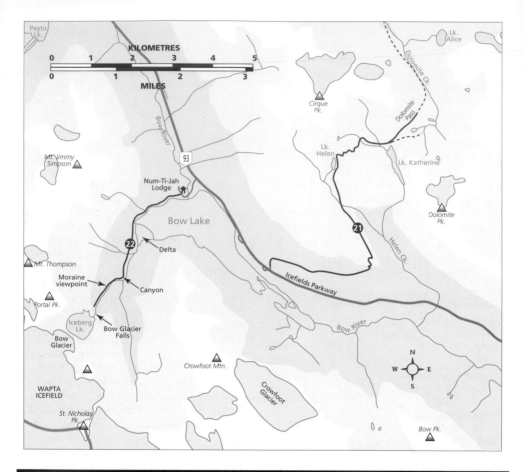

## Crowfoot Glacier

*Almost everywhere you look in the Rockies, glaciers are disappearing.*
*Crowfoot Glacier ca. 1912-15 (left), and in 1995 (right)*

the American crow, which has three splayed toes. The extent of glacial recession makes the origin of the name less obvious today, as two of the "toes" have virtually disappeared. One of them fell off in the 1920s, in an avalanche reportedly (but not likely) heard as far away as Lake Louise.

After a series of switchbacks, you make a hairpin turn north into the valley of Helen Creek. Cirque Peak (2993 m) is straight ahead, and the castellated summits of Dolomite Peak (2782 m) tower over Helen Creek to the east. The true summit of Dolomite Peak is the fourth tower from north. It was first climbed in 1930. Some of the other towers were first ascended on days-off by workers employed in the construction of the original Icefields Parkway, between 1931 and 1939.

The meadows nearby are a sea of colour in

## Dolomite Peak

*Dolomite Peak*

**Dolomite rock formed** when water seeped into limestone sediments before they lithified. Calcium in the limestone was replaced with magnesium. The magnesium-enriched rock — more properly described as a mineral — is usually tougher than the original limestone and more colourful too. Unlike The Dolomites of the Italian Alps, Dolomite Peak does not contain massive dolomite cliffs. However, it does display an interesting sequence of sedimentary formations. From the shore of Lake Katherine to the summit of the peak, the formations are Pika Formation limestone, Arctomys Formation shale, Waterfowl Formation limestone, Sullivan Formation shale, and finally, cliffs of Lyell (lie-ELL) Formation limestone. These formations are Middle Cambrian to Late Cambrian in age. The recessive shales have been eroded into ledges; the more resistant limestones have endured as cliffs. Their alternation creates the "layer cake" or castellated form of Dolomite Peak.

mid- to late-July, bedecked with an array of upper subalpine wildflowers: western anemone, bracted lousewort, paintbrush, fleabane, glacier lily, Sitka valerian, mountain heather, yellow columbine, and arnica. After the first frosts of August, the pungent stench of valerian fills the air — one of the harbingers of autumn in the Rockies.

The trail crosses the base of a quartzite rockslide — a good place to look for hoary marmots — and then descends into a ravine. Rock-hop the stream and continue north on a braided trail across the alpine tundra toward Lake Helen. Braids develop when hikers and horses avoid muddy sections of trail. As few as 20 pairs of feet travelling across untracked tundra may create a permanent trail. Despite trail restoration efforts, thoughtless hikers and riders continue to beat new braids into the soil. Please — get your boots wet and muddy — keep to the most beaten path, thereby preventing the development of additional braids, and allowing the marginal braids to recover.

For many, Lake Helen is the ultimate destination on this hike. The knoll just south of the lake provides pleasing views south to the Bow Valley. The lake-dotted alpland in the foreground is reminiscent of highland Britain. Indeed, one member of the first party to cross Dolomite Pass suggested the name "Doone" for features in this area. *Doone* is Gaelic for "down." Confusingly, "The Downs" are limestone uplands of central Britain. In the view north, the quartzite cliffs at the head of the valley are nesting grounds for golden eagles.

### Lake Helen to Dolomite Pass

The trail to Dolomite Pass continues north from Lake Helen to the base of Cirque Peak. The switchbacking climb over the mountain's south ridge is the high point on this hike. The rock underfoot is brownish limestone of the Pika

## The Crowfoot Dyke

**The Crowfoot Dyke** is the most accessible exposure of igneous rock in the central Rockies. You can see it on the Icefields Parkway — a dull, green outcrop of diabase — 1.1 km south of the trailhead. A dyke is an intrusion of molten rock that flowed underground along cracks in existing sedimentary rock, and then consolidated. The Crowfoot Dyke was created between 570 and 730 million years ago. It extends 2.8 km east from the outlet of Bow Lake to the banks of Helen Creek, passing beneath the trail.

Formation. Views of Dolomite Peak and the environs of Dolomite Pass are superb. On clear days, you can see Mt. Assiniboine (3618 m), 110 km to the south. I have seen caribou tracks in the screes. Many hikers are confused as to why they must now *descend* to approach Dolomite Pass. The explanation is simple. Unlike most trails that follow streams directly to their sources on mountain passes, this trail traverses into Dolomite Pass from another drainage, crossing this high ridge on the way.

The steep descent east from the ridge crosses an outcrop of purple Arctomys (ARK-toe-miss) shale. In the southeast face of Cirque Peak you can see a prominent anticline, an arch-shaped fold in a layer of this formation. From the meadows at the north end of Lake Katherine, Mt. Temple (3543 m) is visible to the south, as is the glaciated horn of Mt. Daly (3152 m). You may be surprised to see hoary marmots in these open meadows, away from their customary sanctuary of boulderfields. It seems that these particular animals are content to burrow deeply into the meadows, rather than using boulders for partial cover.

Rock-hop the lake's inlet and climb the hillside to the east into Dolomite Pass. The trail becomes vague. The travelled route is on the rise north of the small lake that drains east into Dolomite Creek. Random camping is allowed east and north from this point but is not recommended. There are no trees in which to cache your food. The only reasonable option for food storage is atop the large boulders nearby.

Dolomite Pass was first crossed in 1898 by a party from Boston's Appalachian Mountain Club. The mountaineers named a number of nearby features for family members. Alice was the wife of party leader, Reverend H.P. Nicholls. Helen and Katherine were two of his daughters. Other names were given for descriptive reasons: Observation Peak (3174 m) for the view from its summit; Cirque Peak for the cirque glacier on its north flank; and Dolomite Peak for its resemblance to The Dolomites, a group of mountains in The Alps, renowned for their sheer north facing cliffs. If you continue a kilometre northeast from Dolomite Pass, you will be rewarded with views to the south of another lake and the glacier on the northeast side of Dolomite Peak.

*Bow Glacier Falls thunders down the headwall beneath Bow Glacier.*

# 22. Bow Glacier Falls

## Route

**Day-hike**

| Route | Elevation (m) | Distance (km) |
|---|---|---|
| Parking lot | 1940 | 0 |
| Trailhead | 1938 | 0.4 |
| Bow Lake delta | 1938 | 2.4 |
| Mouth of Bow Canyon | 1966 | 3.6 |
| Moraine viewpoint | 1996 | 4.0 |
| Base of Bow Glacier Falls | 2103 | 5.0 |

**Maps**
NTS: 82 N/9 and 82 N/10
Gem Trek: Bow Lake and Saskatchewan Crossing
**See map p.94**

**Best lighting:** before early afternoon

## Trailhead

**The west side of** the Icefields Parkway, 35.1 km north of the Trans-Canada Highway. Follow the Num-ti-Jah Lodge access road west for 400 m to the public parking lot. Walk the gravel road west toward the lake, curving northwest (right) in front of the lodge to the trailhead on the lakeshore.

For more than a century, the shores of Bow Lake have been a favourite of outdoors-minded visitors. No wonder. This relatively short hike is a marvel for its variety — it offers a lakeshore stroll with fine views, an ascent alongside a canyon, a rough track across a moraine field, and a spray-filled vista of a thundering waterfall. Despite the attractions, on a fair morning with the lake calm, you'll be tempted to plunk down at your first view of the lakeshore and go no farther. The landscape is much less claustrophobic than at Lake Louise and Moraine Lake, with the scenery on par. But the environs of Num-ti-Jah Lodge are teeming, and you will soon want to move on to escape the throngs just discharged from their buses. Don't worry; most of them are heading to the restroom and won't be joining you.

## Trailhead to Moraine Viewpoint

As you walk past the lodge, you may see barn swallows overhead; they nest in the various buildings. The rocky and rooted trail follows the north shore of Bow Lake at the base of Mt. Jimmy Simpson (2970 m), crossing the runouts of avalanche slopes and rockslides. Most of the rocks are quartzite of the Gog Group of formations. Look and listen for pikas. Flag trees dot the lakeshore. Bearing branches only on their leeward sides, they "flag" the prevailing wind from the Wapta Icefield. This wind whips whitecaps on the lake in summer, and shapes frozen waves of snow, called sastrugi, in winter. Bow Lake is frozen, on average, from the first week of November until the second week of June. The trail margins are coloured by an array of subalpine wildflowers. Look for the intricate blooms of shooting stars. When the lake level is high, a few short sections of trail may be under water.

The striking pyramidical form of St. Nicholas Peak (2970 m), is prominent in the view southwest across the lake. St. Nicholas was the Swiss birthplace of Peter Sarbach, the guide who led the first mountaineers onto the Wapta Icefield, in 1897. *Wapta* is a Stoney word for "river." Jean Habel, a German mountaineer, named the feature in 1897, but his reason for applying the generic name "river" to an icefield is not clear — unless he meant, "river of ice." To the southeast, glacier-clad Mt. Hector (3394 m) dominates the upper Bow Valley. J.N. Collie named this fine peak for James Hector, naturalist, geologist, and doctor of the Palliser Expedition.

You reach the delta on the west shore of the lake at km 2.4. A short section of trail here may be flooded, especially in late afternoon on a hot day. Skirt the wet area by keeping right, against the base of the cliffs. Elephant's head grows in the glacial silt at the water's edge. The trail carries on along the inlet stream. I have seen dippers and a spotted sandpiper here.

You climb over the first of three forested moraines and drop back to the floodplain. Cross a small tributary stream on a log bridge. The trail

## Deltas

*The delta on northwest shore of Bow Lake*

Many streams and rivers in the Rockies are glacially fed. Where the angle of a stream bed is relatively steep, cobbles and gravels are transported. But where the angle lessens, larger particles drop out of the flow, creating a rocky, fan-shaped landform. If this landform occurs on the side of a valley, it is called an alluvial fan. If it occurs on the shore of a lake, it is known as a delta. The name comes from the resemblance of the landform to delta (Δ) the fourth letter of the Greek alphabet.

Bow Lake features two deltas. The most obvious is on the northwest shore, where meltwater from Bow Glacier enters the lake. The growth of vegetation is hindered by the constant deposition of silt and gravel, by the shifting of the meltwater streams, and by the cold air channelled along the water.

Less obvious is the delta where the lodge sits. The stream that created this delta is now but a trickle. It no longer transports glacial sediments. Vegetation has stabilized the underlying gravels. This delta was probably created thousands of years ago by a meltwater surge from a glacier near Bow Pass. This glacier has since disappeared.

skirts the end of a second forested moraine 400 m later, by hugging the bank of the stream. If the water level is high, an alternate trail climbs over and descends the moraine. Keep to creekside for 200 m to where the trail reaches the third forested moraine. Skirt this along the creek or climb over it. Another 400 m stretch of floodplain, carpeted with mountain avens, intervenes before the trail delivers you to the mouth of Bow Canyon.

The climb alongside the canyon is withering but short. Use care if the trail is wet or snowy — especially on the way down. The canyon is about 20 m deep, and is carved into Eldon Formation limestone. Its central portion features a chockstone that spans the chasm. The trail levels near the upper end of the canyon, with a pleasing view ahead — past an ancient whitebark pine — to Bow Glacier Falls. Carry on for 50 m to the viewpoint on the crest of the Little Ice Age moraine of Bow Glacier.

## Viewpoint to Bow Glacier Falls

The viewpoint marks the halting place of Bow Glacier in about 1850 — the end of the Little Ice Age. The terminal moraine of that advance is smeared against the knoll under your feet. Just over a kilometre away, Bow Glacier Falls thunders down a cliff of Pika Formation limestone. If you study the cliffs alongside the upper cataract of the falls, you will see why the water flows where it does. Trace one of the layers in the cliff, from south to north (left to right). You will see that the layers are offset at the waterfall, indicating that the stream course has been captured by a fault in the rock. Mt. Thompson (3065 m) and its outlier, Portal Peak (2790 m), flank the falls to the north. The peak to the south of the glacier is officially unnamed. Locals know it variously as "Polaris," "The Hamburger," and "The Onion." Yellow columbine, pink wintergreen, white camas, daisy fleabane, and arrow-leaved groundsel grow at the viewpoint. Be careful not to trample them.

The viewpoint provides the postcard shot of the falls, but for the full sensory experience, pick your way across the forefield and immerse yourself in the spray. Head north (right) from the viewpoint a short distance, then descend sharply west (left) from the moraine crest to the forefield. A promising track begins in the direction of the

## Vanishing Act

*Bow Glacier in 1898...*

*...and in 2002*

**The first mountaineers** to travel the Wapta Icefield did so by ascending Bow Glacier in 1897. When I first learned of their route, I thought it preposterous, plagued with cliffs, steep moraines, and even steeper ice. But I wasn't thinking Little Ice Age. Those mountaineers ascended Bow Glacier just after that mini-ice age loosened its grip and the glacier began to recede from the vicinity of today's viewpoint. They did have to deal with steep ice on the headwalls, but getting that far was relatively easy.

As the accompanying photographs show, the change in the landscape in just over a century is astounding.

Photographs taken about 1930 show that the toe of the glacier had receded partway up the lower headwall, where the falls are today. Today, the glacier has almost receded to the top of the second headwall, and its terminus is thinning rapidly. The basin between the two headwalls contains a tarn known to locals as "Iceberg Lake."

## Jimmy Simpson

**Trail guide** and outfitter Jimmy Simpson spent the winters of the early 1900s hunting and trapping in the remote country north of Bow Lake, and came to know the area better than anyone. His adventures are legendary. Simpson poached what was then a world record bighorn ram and claimed he heard an orchestra in the sky one winter night. Simpson said that he regularly dreamed of the locations of sheep and goats. Next day he would lead his clients there for a successful hunt. (This area was not part of Banff National Park at the time.) In 1920, he began construction of a simple log cabin on the lakeshore. The rustic abode became popular with mountaineers. With construction of the Icefields Parkway in the 1930s, Simpson built the forerunner of today's Num-ti-Jah (numm-TAH-zjaah) Lodge. The lodge's name is a Stoney expression for the American marten, a member of the weasel family common in subalpine forest. The original octagonal cabin, known as "The Ram Pasture" in deference to Jimmy's personality and his prowess as a hunter, still stands.

## Ill Winds

**Atmospheric contaminants** — including DDT, toxaphene, and PCBs — are present at low concentrations in the snow and ice of Bow Glacier. These pollutants are carried from as far away as Eurasia before condensing on the icefields of the Rockies. Deep layers of the icefields were contaminated more heavily in the mid-20th century, when these chemicals were also widely used in North America. With climate warming, some of the contaminated deeper layers are beginning to melt, releasing the pollutants into headwater streams. These streams also carry radioactive fallout from the atmospheric nuclear bomb tests of the 1950s and 1960s.

The pollutants are currently present at concentrations measured in parts per trillion — not high enough to render the water unfit to drink. But this might change as climate warming accelerates the melting of glaciers. Because of their tendency to accumulate in the fatty tissues of cold water organisms and to be biomagnified in food chains, toxaphene and other chemicals can reach fairly high concentrations in the lake trout of Bow Lake — 10–20 times higher than in nearby lakes that don't receive glacial meltwater. A similar process of atmospheric pollution and biomagnification is taking place in the Arctic, where concentrations of pollutants have reached values high enough to harm those who eat fish and marine mammals.

falls, but where a tributary stream comes down from Mt. Thompson, piling an alluvial fan into the valley, the route becomes vague. Rock-hop and boulder-hop as required. You may get your feet wet, but the direction to your destination is obvious. Keep to the most beaten path. Pick your way carefully to avoid trampling the moisture-loving plants that grow here — particularly yellow mountain saxifrage.

Any of the thousands of boulders at the base of the falls can serve as your ultimate stopping place. The closer you get to the stream, the wetter you will likely be, as spray from the falls coats the area — not such a bad thing on a hot day. But if it's cold, watch for ice on the rocks. Keep off snow patches. Lesser waterfalls cascade over the colourful, banded cliffs to the north. This amphitheatre was one of the honing grounds for waterfall ice climbers during the development of that pursuit in the late 1970s. The forefield is underlaid by rock of the Eldon Formation, but being a place where the glacier has dumped rocks brought from elsewhere, it is a sedimentary melting pot. Look for, but please don't collect, "zebra rock" (the alternately banded gray limestone and white dolomite of the Lyell Formation) and "tiger rock" (black limestone striped with apricot dolomite of the Cathedral Formation).

# 23. Chephren Lake/ Cirque Lake

### Route

**Day-hike**

| Route | Elevation (m) | Distance (km) |
|---|---|---|
| Trailhead | 1684 | 0 |
| Mistaya River bridge | 1661 | 0.4 |
| Chephren/Cirque jct | 1737 | 1.7 |
| Chephren Lake | 1720 | 3.9 |
| Chephren/Cirque jct | 1737 | 6.1 |
| Cirque Lake | 1791 | 9.0 |
| Chephren/Cirque jct | 1737 | 11.9 |
| Mistaya River bridge | 1661 | 13.2 |
| Trailhead | 1684 | 13.4 |

**Maps**
NTS: 82 N/15
Gem Trek: Bow Lake and Saskatchewan Crossing

At **Waterfowl Lake** campground, on the west side of the Icefields Parkway, 56.4 km north of the Trans-Canada Highway. Don't go into the campground, but continue south (straight ahead) on the access road for 400 m. The trailhead is at the southwest corner of the parking area.

*Cirque Lake*

What makes a hike "classic?" Is it the trail itself — its location and route, or its history? Or is it the scenery, the vegetation? Is it sharing the experience with a companion, or is it a welcome period of solitude accompanied by exertion? It can be any or all of these things, and it can be different from day to day on the same trail. What is a certainty about this excursion is that it is not the trail itself that makes this hike a classic. I won't belabour descriptions of the muck and mire that await. At best, you will have damp feet by day's end; after a rain, you will likely be soaked — as I once was — from the elbows down. But the twin destinations — two gems tucked away in their glacial pockets — are classic in every regard, and the austere mountain walls echo with the history of early pack trips along Bear Creek.

### Trailhead to Chephren/Cirque Junction

The trail begins as a gravel path that skirts the south edge of the campground. As with most campgrounds on the Icefields Parkway, this one occupies an alluvial fan — in this case the fan created by Noyes Creek. The bulk of this landform was deposited by a surge in glacial melt at the end of the Crowfoot Advance, 6000–7000 years ago. The fan spans most of the floor of the Mistaya (miss-TAY-yah) Valley, impounding the waters of Upper Waterfowl Lake.

In 400 m you reach the bridges that cross the narrows between the Waterfowl lakes. Those staying in the campground can begin the hike here. The campground and surrounding area are a customary hangout for bears. Travel accordingly.

The trail climbs south from the bridges, initially through open spruce-fir forest, with buffaloberry, dwarf dogwood, feathermosses, and clubmosses in the understory. The forest here last burned in 1858. Listen for varied thrushes and

- Hike to Chephren Lake, 7.8 km return
- Hike to Cirque Lake, 9.2 km return
- Visit both lakes, 13.4 km return

robins. On my last visit, I heard a loon calling from Upper Waterfowl Lake. A section of pine forest follows, the understory bedecked with prolific blooms of Labrador tea. The trail angles southwest and begins to climb and descend a series of terraces — probably the courses of ancient creeks that once drained the glaciers west of here. Fringed grass-of-Parnassus, elephant head, rein orchids, and hooded ladies'-tresses grow in the intervening pockets of wet meadow. Finally out of earshot of the Icefields Parkway, you cross three of these meadows before reaching the junction at km 1.7.

### Junction to Chephren Lake

Turn northwest (right) for Chephren Lake. Patches of ground lichens of the *Cladonia* genus cover the forest floor, along with clubmosses. Such ground cover is atypical for this low an elevation at this latitude, and can be attributed to the glacial chill and high amount of precipitation here. Much of the trail is routed alongside wet meadows. The saturated soil, the tree roots, and the lack of significant grade on the tread hinder drainage. Things soon go from wet to wetter. Persevere; it's worth it. Views of Howse Peak (3290 m) with its niche glaciers, and Mt. Chephren (3266 m), along with displays of orchids, provide distraction. You might hear rockfalls from the flanks of the mountains. Watch your step to avoid squashing the orchids. Look for the tracks of deer and moose in the mud. There's lots of it to inspect.

About 2 km from the junction, the trail turns

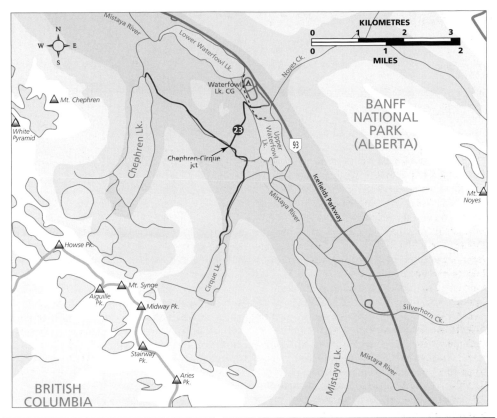

## The Trail North

**The first packtrains** to travel north in the Mistaya Valley did so on a difficult trail along the east side of the river. The trip from Lake Louise to Saskatchewan River Crossing required five to seven days. When the packtrains reached the North Saskatchewan River, they were obliged to make three hazardous fords — Mistaya River, Howse River, and North Saskatchewan River — in order to continue north. In 1923, Jimmy Simpson cut a trail along the west bank of the Mistaya River in the lower part of the valley. Packtrains could then ford the river easily between the Waterfowl lakes, eliminating one of the trio of crossings downvalley. The first party to use the new route was that of mountaineer James Monroe Thorington, guided by Simpson, while on their way to the first ascents of Mt. Saskatchewan and North Twin, and ascents of Mt. Athabasca and Mt. Columbia. The Chephren Lake trail follows the 1923 route as far as the sharp turn just before the lake.

## Swamp Critters

**What better place,** than in the shadow of majestic glacier-clad mountains, to talk about herptiles, the universally overlooked creatures of the slime? Herptiles include two classes of species, both cold-blooded: amphibians — which have smooth skin, soft eggs, a larval stage, and an adult stage; and reptiles — which have scaly skin, hard-shelled eggs, and only one life stage. There are four amphibian species in this part of the Rockies. You are most likely to see the boreal toad. You'll find it near water in mid-to-late spring, when it mates. Later in the summer, you might find toads well away from water. The Columbia spotted frog is the larger of the two frog species in this part of the Rockies. It is greenish-brown with dark spots. The wood frog is the other hopping amphibian. The long-toed salamander is a carnivorous, lizard-like creature about 10 cm long, with glossy dark skin, and a yellowish-green stripe down the back. It is most often found in low elevation valleys. Of reptiles there is but one — the wandering garter snake.

Herptiles are barometer species. Some populations have disappeared. Climate change and environmental stresses have been key. All of the Rockies' herptiles are pushing the elevational limits for their species, making them particularly vulnerable.

sharply southwest (left), and descends steeply to the logjam at the outlet of Chephren Lake. In terms of straight-line distance, you aren't far from the highway and a goodly number of people, but in just over an hour, the trail has transported you to a very lonely piece of the Mistaya Valley.

Chephren Lake is 2.6 km long and 750 m wide. Fed principally by meltwater from two glaciers nestled under Howse Peak, the lake sports the blue-green hue typical of glacial lakes. Two meltwater streams drain the glacier south of the lake, bisecting a red quartzite cliff. A prominent lateral moraine flanks the east side of the glacier. Above, Aiguille (eh-GEEL) Peak (2999 m) — *aiguille* is French for "needle"— looms over the southeast ridge of Howse Peak. Joseph Howse was a trader for the Hudson's Bay Company. He crossed Howse Pass — at the western base of the peak — in 1810. If it has snowed recently, you may be treated to avalanches from Howse Peak's northeast face. Looking west, you can see a small cirque glacier beneath Mt. Chephren, along with the horseshoe moraine it has pushed up. The view north down the outlet stream includes Mt. Murchison (3333 m) and its many outliers. To the northwest, you can see the summit of Epaulette Mountain (3095 m), named for the glacial crest on its "shoulder." Kingfishers, sandpipers, and violet-green swallows frequent the lake. Mountaineers and anglers have beaten paths along both shores, but if you

*Chephren/Cirque junction*

found the travel exasperating this far, don't consider exploring them.

After you've had your fill of mountain-watching and lake-watching, return to the Chephren/Cirque junction. You'll be pleasantly surprised at the subtle, downhill grade. Turn northeast (left) if you've had enough; head southeast (straight ahead) to carry on to Cirque Lake.

## Junction to Cirque Lake

The Cirque Lake trail, initially much drier than the route to Chephren Lake, descends through open forest with dwarf dogwood, wild strawberry, feathermosses, and clubmosses in the understory. Early season hikers will be treated to the blooms of calypso orchids. Red squirrels are numerous. At

## An Array of Lakes

The west side of the Mistaya Valley contains a series of large lakes, unmatched in the Rockies — Peyto, Mistaya, Cirque, Chephren, Upper Waterfowl, and Lower Waterfowl. Only from the bridge between the Waterfowl lakes can you see more than one of these bodies of water from a single valley-bottom viewpoint. But as the photograph taken on the summit of Mt. Weed shows, mountaineers obtain wonderful vistas of the lakes. All of them feature deltas at their inlets. The delta of Upper Waterfowl Lake has filled almost half of the lake's original area.

*A mountaineer's view of the Mistaya Valley*

*Chephren Lake*

the base of many conifers, you will see piles of scales shucked from cones by the squirrels as they harvest the seeds. Rock-hop the outlet of the wet meadow that extends toward Chephren Lake. A little farther on you walk on a creekbank between two streams. Rock-hop the second stream and continue southeast a short distance to where the

## The Matterhorn of the Mistaya

*Mt. Chephren*

**Mt. Chephren** (KEFF-ren) is a prominent landmark in the Mistaya Valley and the upper North Saskatchewan Valley, visible from Bow Pass to Parker Ridge. It is a classic horn mountain, its crest whittled from horizontal layers of limestone and quartzite by the action of glaciers on two of its three flanks. J.N. Collie named it Black Pyramid in 1898, to contrast it with glacier-capped White Pyramid (3275 m) to the southwest. The name was changed in 1918, to prevent confusion with its neighbour and with Pyramid Mountain in Jasper. Chephren was the son of Cheops, builder of the Great Pyramid. He reigned in the 26th century BC, and was apparently immortalized in the face of the Sphinx. The mountain was first climbed in 1913.

trail swings southwest (right), about 1.1 km from the junction. Wild rose and pink wintergreen grow nearby.

The climb begins and soon delivers you to a small pond, impounded by grasses and sedges. Moose frequent this area. Views northwest include White Pyramid (3275 m). Just beyond, the trail cuts through an ancient stand of Engelmann spruce, with arnica and horsetails beneath. You climb steeply up a forested moraine along the outlet stream from Cirque Lake. The cool of the creekbank is wonderful on a hot day. The trail makes a short switchback away from the creek. At the top, continue straight ahead to sidehill just above the water. I have seen spruce grouse here.

This is a trail where the view of your final destination is delivered in increments. At first you see the headwall at the southeast end of Cirque Lake, but it takes some time to reach the lakeshore. Look back for views of Mt. Noyes (3084 m) and the unnamed towers above Noyes Creek. There are pleasing trailside groupings of yellow columbine and hybrid yellow-western columbine, along with twinflower, false hellebore, and orchids. Near the outlet of the lake, you cross the base of an avalanche slope. Beside the trail, the water flows through an extensive meadow of sedges before the creek proper begins. Trail's end is a quartzite boulderfield on the northwest shore of the lake. The avalanche slopes above are excellent bear habitat.

Cirque Lake is scarcely a third the size of its northern neighbour but shares a similar setting. Your eye will be drawn to the hanging niche glacier between Aries Peak (2996 m) and Stairway Peak (3000 m), and to the valley glacier at the far end of the lake. *Aries* is Latin for "ram," in this case referring to bighorn sheep. The name was given to balance features to the south named *Capricorn*, Latin for "goat." Midway Peak (2917 m) is so named because it lies about halfway between Stairway Peak and Mt. Synge (2972 m). This latter mountain commemorates an Irish engineer who, in 1852, drew a map showing a railway route across Canada. He was ridiculed at the time, but only 30 years later, after the expenditure of millions of dollars surveying and the loss of at least 38 surveyors, the route was essentially adopted, with no credit to Synge.

Take care on the steep sections during your return, as they can be slick when wet.

# 24. Sarbach Lookout

## Route

Day-hike

| Route | Elevation (m) | Distance (km) |
|---|---|---|
| Trailhead | 1520 | 0 |
| Mistaya Canyon | 1479 | 0.5 |
| Sarbach Lookout jct | 1493 | 0.7 |
| Mistaya River overlook | 1517 | 1.7 |
| Sarbach Lookout site | 2043 | 5.3 |

**Maps**
NTS: 82 N/15
Gem Trek: Bow Lake and Saskatchewan Crossing

## Trailhead

**West side** of the Icefields Parkway, 70.1 km north of the Trans-Canada Highway, 5.1 km south of the junction with Highway 11.

Banff's fire lookout system, completed between 1941 and 1950, contained seven lookouts. Connected by telephone to warden stations in the valleys below, the keepers who staffed the lookouts were often able to provide early warning of forest fires. Aerial smoke patrols during times of high fire hazard rendered the lookouts obsolete in the 1970s. Although the lookout towers in Banff were all abandoned by 1978 and removed by 1985, the trails to most lookout sites are still maintained. They provide easy access to lofty viewpoints. The Sarbach (SAR-back) Lookout site is unique in that it grants an overview of three of Banff's larger valleys.

### Trailhead to Mistaya River
The initial 450 m of trail is road width as it descends to Mistaya Canyon. After you have gawked at the spectacular canyon, cross the bridge. Turn north (right) in 15 m. The trail ascends a bank of glacial till. Till overlies the bedrock here to a depth of more than 30 m. Because most till in the Rockies came from limestone bedrock, it contains a high percentage of calcium carbonate (lime). Water percolating through the till creates a natural cement that binds the rock particles together. These gravel banks are deceptively tough. In places, rainwater and snowmelt are eroding hoodoos into them.

*Mt. Murchison from Sarbach Lookout*

At the junction in 200 m, turn southwest (left) onto the Sarbach Lookout trail. The forest on this river terrace is an ancient one of Engelmann spruce and lodgepole pine that last burned in 1640. The lodgepole pines here are as old and as tall as you will see anywhere in the Rockies. One spruce at trailside shows charred heartwood exposed by a lightning strike. At first glance, the tree appears dead. However, a few upper branches are still growing. In the absence of recent fire, new habitat in this forest is created by blowdowns that remove weakened trees. The downed trees are piled like jackstraws. They provide abundant fuel for the inevitable day when the forest will burn.

At km 1.7, the trail regains the bank of the Mistaya River, from where you have a fine view south to the tremendous mountain wall along the western slope of the Mistaya Valley. The glacier-draped cliffs of The White Pyramid (3275 m), Epaulette

## Mistaya Canyon

**Mistaya Canyon** is cut into Cambrian-aged Eldon Formation limestone. It features a natural arch and potholes eroded by rocks trapped in depressions. The river has exploited a joint set — an arrangement of parallel cracks in the bedrock. This creates the dogleg course of the canyon, visible north of the bridge. In places, the canyon is scarcely 2 m wide. Rather than attempting to cross the Mistaya River in places where it was wider, Stoneys would cross here on felled trees during their hunting trips into the mountains. *Mistaya*, a Stoney word for "grizzly bear," supplanted the original name of the same meaning, *Ojinjah Wapta*.

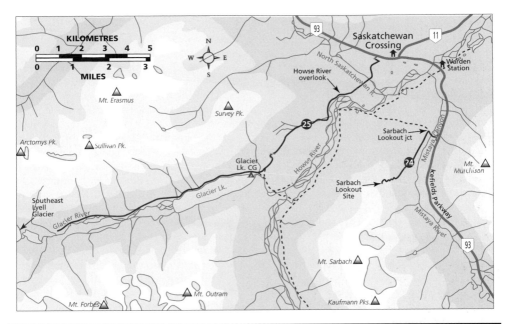

## Whitebark Pine

Whitebark pine is an indicator tree of the upper subalpine ecoregion. The tree bark is silver and smooth on young trees, gray and scaly on older trees. Needles are in bunches of five. The tree is extremely slow growing and may not produce cones until it is 80 years old. This is a tree that prefers the icy blast of cliff edges. It helps to stabilize steep slopes, moderates the rate of snow melt, and provides food, cover, and shelter for many species of wildlife. Botanists call it a keystone species, vital to the ecosystem. Found throughout mountainous western North America, whitebark pine is declining over much of its range. Its survival is threatened by the combined effects of blister rust, fire suppression, and pine beetle epidemics.

*Whitebark pine*

The cones of the whitebark pine do not open on their own to disperse seeds. Enter the Clark's nutcracker. The bird relies on the tree to provide its food — pine nuts — and the tree relies on the pointy-beaked bird to crack the seeds from their casings and disperse them. A Clark's nutcracker can hold up to 100 seeds in a pouch under its tongue. It caches the seeds — 22,000 to 33,000 per summer

(yes, someone has counted them) — in various places to tide it through the winter. Usually, the bird chooses sun-exposed sites that are likely to be snow-free. These are just the kinds of sites that the tree prefers, so when the nutcracker forgets to come back to a particular site, some of the seeds — which it has buried at the perfect depth for germination — begin to grow into trees. Ronald M. Lanner wrote a book about this close-knit relationship, entitled *Made for Each Other: A Symbiosis of Birds and Pines.* The seed caches are raided by grizzly bears, who also relish the protein-rich pine nuts.

The stand of whitebark pine on Mt. Sarbach exhibits the diverse forms possible for this species. The tree is a gnarled and twisted kruppelholz where fully exposed to the elements. Where protected in the forest it has a robust form, attaining heights of 10–12 m. "Spike tops" indicate where the crowns of trees have suffered die-off from the chill of winter winds. The whitebark pine is one of the longer-lived tree species in the Rockies. Ages in excess of 1000 years have been recorded.

Mountain (3095 m), the Kaufmann Peaks (3110 m and 3095 m), and Mt. Sarbach (3155 m) create an archetypal Rockies image. If you were to keep going straight ahead here, you wouldn't get far — trust me — but you would be following the original trail cut in 1923 on this side of the valley. It hasn't been cleared since the 1940s.

## Mistaya River to Sarbach Lookout

The trail veers southwest (right) from the river. For the next kilometre you cross boggy terrain toward the north ridge of Mt. Sarbach. You may see moose here. The "snow course markers" on trees indicate locations where snow core samples were taken by the Water Survey of Canada. By melting the snow, its water equivalent was determined. Data obtained from snow at these sites was combined with other data from the Rockies, allowing a prediction of the annual run-off to be calculated. The project was abandoned in the early 1980s — a bad move, in hindsight, what with climate change and perpetual drought on the prairies.

To this point, the trail from the Mistaya River has climbed gradually. Now the hard work begins — 370 m of gain over 2.5 km. There are limited views before the lookout site. However, the blooms of arnica, few-flowered anemone, and calypso orchids brighten trailside. You will know that the relentless climb is nearing its end when the trail swings onto the north end of the ridge and whitebark pine becomes the most common tree in the surrounding forest.

The last 200 m of trail is bordered with rocks — the handiwork of a tower keeper. Snow patches linger until early July. Remarkably, there is a record of mountain caribou tracks here. A Sacramento rain gauge, tree stumps, and the cabin foundation are now all that remains of the fire lookout, which was built in 1943 and used until 1971. Even without the advantage of a tower, the site commands a grand perspective of the three valleys that merge below — the Mistaya to the south, the Howse to the west, and the North Saskatchewan to the north and east.

The mountains of the Amery Group are immediately north. Mt. Wilson (3260 m) looms to the

## A Geo-Political Rift

James Hector named Mount Murchison for Roderick Murchison, President of the Royal Geographical Society in 1856, and the man who recommended Hector to the Palliser Expedition. Murchison was no piker when it came to geology, having authored and co-authored the original geological theories of, respectively, the Devonian and the Silurian periods. Hector was a keen observer of geology and landforms — he later went on to head the Geological Survey of New Zealand. Palliser described him as "the most accurate mapper of the original country I have ever seen." Everywhere in his travels in the Rockies, Hector made journal entries that describe the landscape. Many of these observations described the effects of glaciation, against which Hector bumped his moccasins day after day. Of glacial markers in the landscape near the Waterfowl Lakes, he wrote: "... all point to a time when the glaciers which now only occupy the higher valleys were more extended." This makes the naming of Mt. Murchison all the more ironic, because back across the pond, Murchison was staunchly resisting the theories of Swiss-born naturalist, Louis Agassiz (ah-GASS-ee), who in 1837 had proposed that much of the landscape of Europe looked the way it did because of ice-age glaciations. Agassiz, like Hector, had evidence: striations — grooves in bedrock, scratched by rocks embedded in moving ice, far distant from any then-current gla-

*Mt. Murchison*

ciers; glacial erratics — oddball rocks dropped far from their places of origin; and moraines that were far removed from any then-contemporary glaciers. Of course, it all seems so obvious today. But Murchison's intolerance caused heated disputes among European geologists and contributed to a scientific rift on the Continent that has yet to heal.

Murchison never saw "his" mountain. If he had, he might have hopped off his high horse in a moment, for Mt. Murchison is as ice-embattled, cirque-pocked, and crest-whittled a mountain as any — a billboard for ice-age glaciations.

northeast, above the right-angle bend in the North Saskatchewan River. The mountain was named for Tom Wilson — trail guide, outfitter, and the first white visitor to the shores of Lake Louise. Wilson's heyday was the late 1800s. In the early 1900s, he became a fixture at the Banff Springs Hotel and at Chateau Lake Louise, regaling guests with stories of the trail, mostly tall but some true.

## Mt. Murchison

The stupendous form of Mt. Murchison (3333 m) blocks everything else from view across the Mistaya Valley. Mt. Murchison is a massif, a miniature mountain range that contains ten summits. James Hector reported that Natives considered Mt. Murchison to be the highest mountain in the Rockies. The impression is understandable, although far from true — Mt. Murchison does not even rank among the 50 highest summits. The northerly summit towers 1920 m above the North Saskatchewan River. Although the first ascent of Mt. Murchison was claimed in 1902, the highest summit (second from the north) was evidently not reached until 1985.

Mt. Murchison is a wonderful example of a castellated mountain. Resistant limestone and dolomite cliffs alternate with recessive ledges of shale. If you trace the sedimentary formations on the lowest tier of cliffs, you will see where they become fractured vertically and offset in a normal fault. The formations on one side of the fault have moved downward relative to the other.

Glaciers have eroded cirque basins into Mt. Murchison's flanks. Waterfalls cascade from them. The largest is "Murchison Falls" — a winter playground for ice climbers. The mountain's many summits are glacially sculpted horns. Farther south in the Mistaya Valley, Mt. Chephren (3266 m) and the White Pyramid also exhibit horn mountain shapes.

The summit of Mt. Sarbach is hidden from view, 5 km south of the lookout site. The mountain was first climbed in 1897 by J.N. Collie, G.P. Baker, and Peter Sarbach. Sarbach, the first Swiss Guide to work in Canada, spent only one summer in the Rockies. He led a number of other important first ascents, including Mt. Lefroy and Mt. Victoria at Lake Louise, and Mt. Gordon on the Wapta Icefield. You may see mountain goats on the slopes above the lookout site. Once, as I gazed across the valley at Mt. Murchison, my eye caught movement downslope, where a massive grizzly bear was feeding on buffaloberries.

# 25. Glacier Lake

| Route | | |
|---|---|---|
| Day-hike or overnight | | |
| Route | Elevation (m) | Distance (km) |
| Trailhead | 1443 | 0 |
| North Saskatchewan River bridge | 1418 | 1.1 |
| Howse River overlook | 1433 | 2.3 |
| Glacier Lake CG | 1457 | 9.1 |
| Head of Glacier River valley | 1493 | 18.6 |

**Maps**
NTS: 82N/15 and 82 N/14
Gem Trek: Bow Lake and Saskatchewan Crossing
**See map on p.105**

**Best lighting:** morning at Glacier Lake

| Trailhead |
|---|
| **West side** of the Icefields Parkway, 1.2 km north of the junction with Highway 11, 76.4 km north of the Trans-Canada Highway, 148.8 km south of Highway 16. |

When fur trader and map maker David Thompson visited Glacier Lake in 1807, he wrote: "All the Mountains in sight from the end of the Lake are seemingly of Ice." Thompson saw the Little Ice Age maximum of the glaciers, but even after two centuries of glacial recession, the colossal icefall of the Southeast Lyell Glacier, which tumbles from Division Mountain west of the lake, is still an impressive sight.

The Glacier Lake trail is often snow-free early in the hiking season. Although the trailhead and destination are at nearly equal elevations, there is enough up and down to make the outing an ideal early season "shake down" trip. You may random camp in the valley west of the lake. The area is frequented by bears.

## Trailhead to Glacier Lake

The trailhead is in a dense lodgepole pine forest, the product of a July 1940 forest fire — the Survey Peak Burn. It consumed 40 km² and forced closure of the just opened Icefields Parkway. Buffaloberry and bearberry, whose fruits are favourite foods of bears, are common in the undergrowth near the trailhead. I have often seen ruffed grouse along the first kilometre of trail.

The trail descends a series of ancient river terraces to an I-beam bridge over the North Saskatchewan River at km 1.1. Here, the river's course has been captured by a bedrock fault, creating a small canyon. The North Saskatchewan River is 1216 km long. More than 80 percent of the water it carries to Hudson's Bay (via Lake Winnipeg and the Nelson River) originates in glaciers. The 49 km section within Banff National Park was proclaimed a Canadian Heritage River in 1989. Canadian Heritage Rivers are those that have played an important role in the human and natural history of Canada. The trail climbs away from the river and continues through burned forest to the edge of a terrace above the Howse River at km 2.3.

This terrace "feels" different than most at similar locations in the Rockies. Usually what's immediately underfoot on the bank of a glacial river is the rubble of moraine. Not here. This riverbank and those across the valley are silty. The silt is called loess (LURSS), scoured over millennia from the valley floor by the prevailing southwest wind and piled here into dune-like mounds where the river turns east. These loess deposits are the most extensive in Banff. The lower Howse Valley is also noted for its kettle lakes. Seven appear on the topographic map.

Mt. Outram (OOT-rum) (3240 m) is southwest in the view from the overlook. It was named for reverend and mountaineer James Outram, who made first ascents of many high peaks in the Rockies in 1901 and 1902. Tucked in behind Mt. Outram is Mt. Forbes (3612 m), seventh highest mountain in the Rockies, and the highest mountain entirely within Banff National Park. James

## Glaciers: The Beginning and End of Lakes

If you look at the topographic map, you will see that Glacier Lake occupies the eastern end of a 13 km long plain. At the conclusion of the Wisconsin Glaciation, the lake may have filled the entire valley. Over time, rubble and sediment carried by the Glacier River have filled much of the lake. As with most glacially formed and fed lakes in the Rockies, if glacial recession continues, the day will come when either the filling will be complete or the glaciers will vanish. Either way, Glacier Lake will cease to exist.

Outram teamed up with the party of Scottish mountaineer J.N. Collie to make the first ascent of Mt. Forbes in 1902. James Hector of the Palliser Expedition named the mountain, not for the eminent geologist of his day, but for Edward Forbes, his professor of natural history at the University of Edinburgh.

The trail swings west from the viewpoint and

## The Howse Valley: A Once and Future Highway?

*The Howse Valley*

**As its heavily braided** appearance suggests, most of the flow of the Howse River is glacial in origin. It consists of meltwaters from numerous glaciers and from three icefields that cover more than 100 km² — Freshfield, Mons, and Lyell. Howse Pass, 16 km south, was part of the first fur trade route across the Rockies. It saw use between 1800 and 1810, when it was closed by hostile Pikanii. The Howse Valley is a haven for many large mammals: elk, mule deer, moose, black bears, grizzly bears, wolves, mountain goats, and coyotes. Joseph Howse was a fur trader who crossed the pass in 1810.

Although the Banff National Park Management Plan precludes the construction of new roads, two communities east of the Rockies — Red Deer and Rocky Mountain House — have for years advocated extending Highway 11 across Howse Pass. Such a highway would decrease transportation times and costs between some places in Alberta and BC, but would destroy one of the last wilderness enclaves in the Rockies while diverting only 8 percent of the traffic from the Trans-Canada Highway. An economic analysis of the proposed highway's effects has also shown a net economic loss for communities in central Alberta, because the road would divert traffic from the Highway 2 corridor. The idea of constructing a road over Howse Pass has very little support in BC.

*Glacier Lake at dawn*

descends to riverside. Look back for the view southeast, where the many-summitted massif of Mt. Murchison (3333 m) towers above the mouth of the Mistaya Valley. The trail veers away from the river. You spend the next 5 km climbing and descending a forested spur of Survey Peak to reach the shore of Glacier Lake and the campground near its outlet.

Glacier Lake is 3.75 km long, 750 m wide, and with an area of 263 ha, is the fourth largest lake in Banff National Park. Its waters are dammed by a moraine created where the ancestral Southeast Lyell and Freshfield glaciers merged. Glacier Lake was named in 1859 by James Hector. He also named a mountain north of the lake for John Sullivan, mathematician and secretary to the Palliser Expedition. Hector and a companion climbed the peak, wearing only moccasins on their feet, so it is not likely that the challenging mountain that we call Sullivan Peak (3022 m) today was their objective. You may see osprey circling over the lake, in quest of lake trout, rocky mountain whitefish, and bull trout.

## The Glacier River Valley

The rough trail along the north shore of Glacier Lake originated earlier this century as a mountaineering approach to Mt. Forbes and the Lyell Icefield. Although the trail is infrequently cleared and is sketchy in places, the route to the head of the valley is obvious. Beyond the inlet, the trail works its way across alluvial flats, following the north bank of the Glacier River and passing the site of the 1940 Alpine Club of Canada Camp. About 9.5 km from the campground, look for a faint track that climbs steeply northwest (right) onto a series of knife-edged, lateral moraines. From this hard-won vantage you have astounding views of the icefall of the Southeast Lyell Glacier and its marginal lake, along with the tremendous glaciated fang of Mt. Forbes.

## The Southeast Lyell Icefall: A Cascading River of Ice

*The Southeast Lyell Icefall*

Just over a century ago, the head of the Glacier River Valley was buried in glacial ice. Mountaineers J.N. Collie and Hugh Stutfield described the icefall in 1902: "Incomparably the finest we have seen in the Rockies, it is a larger scale than anything of the kind in Switzerland. It is of immense width, with a band of cliffs, surmounted at their northern end by blue ice-pinnacles, dividing the upper from the lower glacier for the greater part of the distance. The meltings of the higher snows fall over these cliffs in a series of waterfalls, and the roar of the ice avalanches was constant and deafening."

**109**

# 26. Sunset Pass/ Sunset Lookout

## Route

Day-hike or overnight

| Routes | Elevation (m) | Distance (km) |
|---|---|---|
| Sunset Lookout Trailhead | 1438 | 0 |
| Sunset Lookout jct | 1860 | 2.9 |
| Sunset Lookout site | 2043 | +1.6 |
| Norman Lake CG | 1973 | 3.6 |
| Sunset Pass | 2165 | 7.6 |
| Pinto Lake viewpoint | 2134 | 8.2 |

**Maps**
NTS: 83 C/2
Gem Trek: Bow Lake and Saskatchewan Crossing

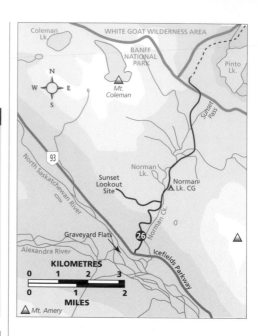

## Trailhead

**East side** of the Icefields Parkway, 91.6 km north of the Trans-Canada Highway, 16.4 km north of the junction with Highway 11, 32.9 km south of the Icefield Centre, 133.6 km south of Highway 16.

The Sunset Pass trail is a backcountry artery into the remote northeast corner of Banff National Park, used principally by backpackers and horse parties bound for Pinto Lake in the adjacent White Goat Wilderness Area. But the two destinations within Banff make fine outings. The sidetrail to Sunset Lookout offers a breathtaking prospect over the North Saskatchewan Valley. The willow meadows of Sunset Pass typify the upper sub-alpine ecoregion. Strong hikers can visit both destinations in a long day.

### Trailhead to Sunset Lookout Junction

With no preamble, the trail climbs steeply away from the parking lot. The climb abates where the trail cuts through an old stream course, but then resumes with purpose. The surrounding forest is an open one, dominated by lodgepole pines. Buffaloberry, dwarf dogwood, wild strawberry, and birch-leaved spirea are common in the undergrowth. The glossy leaves of buffaloberry are pale and fuzzy on the underside, with rust-coloured spots. By late July, the yellow flowers yield red and amber berries — a staple food of bears. If the berry crop is on, you should make lots of noise

and look for recent bear sign. When I surprised a grizzly bear here, the bear made a no-contact charge, passing within two metres. There are many rub-trees and scratch-trees alongside the trail. Some clearly show the claw marks of bears.

As you ascend this slope, you'll notice that the trail crosses ridges of limestone bedrock, that dip to the northeast. This is not common in the main ranges, where the strata usually lie in horizontal layers or dip slightly to the southwest. These rocks are in the western arm of the Castle Mountain Syncline, a U-shaped fold whose axis runs through the meadows just this side of Sunset Pass. When you reach the meadows near Norman Lake, you'll be able to see the syncline in the slopes of Mt. Coleman, to the north.

The steep slope you are travelling is a product of glacial overdeepening of the North Saskatchewan Valley. Tributary valleys, such as Norman Creek, were not as deeply eroded by glacial ice during the Wisconsin Glaciation and were left hanging above the main valley floor. With the energy created by its steep gradient, Norman Creek has carved an impressive canyon, with a

## Variations

- Hike to the lookout site, 9.0 km return
- Hike to the pass, 16.4 km return
- Visit both destinations, 19.6 km return
- Camp at Norman Lake and explore

*The upper North Saskatchewan Valley from Sunset Lookout*

series of waterfalls. Just after km 1.0, three side-trails lead south from the corners of switchbacks to the edge of the canyon. The second sidetrail has the best view. Use caution; the area is unfenced. The creek may have been named for John Norman Collie, one of the leading alpinists of his day. Collie climbed extensively in the European Alps and on Nanga Parbat in the Himalaya, and made six mountaineering trips to the Rockies between 1897 and 1910.

From the canyon, the trail works its way north before switchbacking intensely upward to the Sunset Lookout junction. A few stately Douglas-fir trees grow among the pines on this slope. This may be the northern limit for the Douglas-fir in Banff National Park. Wildflowers here include fine displays of arnica and glacier lilies. The forest becomes more enclosed and the grade moderates just before the Sunset Lookout junction. Turn north (left) for the lookout.

## Sunset Lookout

The sidetrail to Sunset Lookout makes a rambling ascent through old subalpine forest. Squirrel middens, valerian, fleabanes, arnica, bracted lousewort, grouse-berry, and patches of glacier lilies dot the forest floor. I've heard blackpoll warblers here. You'll know that you are just about at the lookout site when you see stumps at trailside. The trail angles west to the cliff edge and descends steeply for 60 m to the look-out site, with its staggering view of the North Saskatchewan Valley, more than 500 m below. This is no place for acrophobics; it is more suited to mountain goats, which are often seen nearby. The foundations and lightning conductor cables of the lookout pose a genuine tripping hazard. Be careful.

On my last visit, I spooked a golden eagle during my descent to the lookout site. The raptor took off, banking away to the south. As I marvelled at its flight, it was joined by a lesser shape — a rough-legged hawk. For the next five minutes, I was witness to their territorial duel as they scrapped — talon, beak, and feather — over the void.

Sunset Lookout was built in 1943. It operated until 1978, when smoke patrols by helicopter rendered it and the other towers in the fire lookout system obsolete. The site was well chosen. Mt. Saskatchewan (3342 m), guardian of the southeastern edge of Columbia Icefield, dominates the view west, where the upper reaches of the Alexandra River are visible. The valleys of the North Saskatchewan, Mistaya, and Bow align to the south, allowing an unrestricted view to Bow Peak,

## The Graveyard

**From Sunset Lookout** you can compare the North Saskatchewan River and the Alexandra River, which merge below on the Graveyard Flats. The North Saskatchewan is a glacially charged stream, with multiple braids and extensive gravel flats. Although it too has glacial origins, the Alexandra River shows a more meandering course, with abandoned channels, sloughs, and ox-bow lakes. Pick a channel on the Alexandra and follow it. See if it rejoins the main river or dead-ends in a pocket of moose habitat.

*Graveyard Flats*

The gravels of the Graveyard Flats offered the best camping place in the upper North Saskatchewan valley. Natives dressed the kills of their hunts there. Explorer Mary Schäffer named the flats after she found animal skeletons in 1907. *Saskatchewan* is Cree for "swift current." The North Saskatchewan River is 1216 km long. The portion within Banff National Park was designated a Canadian Heritage River in 1989. Princess Alexandra was the wife of King Edward VII.

60 km distant. Some glaciologists speculate that before mountain building, the North Saskatchewan River flowed south along this alignment, rather than beginning its exit from the mountains at Saskatchewan River Crossing. The northern vista includes Hilda Peak, Nigel Pass, and the environs of Columbia Icefield. Few other viewpoints in the Rockies reveal the trough-like, glacially-scoured form of the major valleys so clearly.

The limestone of the lookout site is a miniature rock garden. Look for these wildflowers: stonecrop, harebell, yarrow, paintbrush, dwarf raspberry, yellow-flowered false dandelion, Mackenzie's hedysarum, four-parted gentian, wild strawberry, bearberry, daisy fleabane, red-stemmed saxifrage, cinquefoil, and woolly pussy-toes. The orange lichen, *Xanthoria elegans,* grows on the rock. On the trail nearby, you'll brush your pack against whitebark pines. Note the needles in bunches of five. Clark's nutcrackers frequent the area, gleaning the seeds from the cones of these trees.

### Sunset Lookout Junction to Sunset Pass

Continue straight ahead at the lookout junction. (If you are returning from the lookout, turn northeast, or left.) The trail undulates through flower-filled glades to the edge of a large subalpine willow meadow, and an unsigned junction. Keep right and descend to a bridge over Norman Creek. The campground is in the stand of trees just beyond.

Mt. Coleman (3135 m) dominates the north side of the valley. A.P. Coleman was a geology professor from the University of Toronto. He made seven journeys into the hinterland of the Rockies between 1884 and 1908, naming many features and contributing greatly to the growing knowledge of the landscape. His book of 1911, *The Canadian Rockies, New and Old Trails,* is a landmark of Rockies' history. The north side of the mountain features a spectacular glacier and two large lakes that drain underground.

The trail to Sunset Pass follows the southeast side of wet meadows and willow plain for several kilometres, before angling northeast into forest. You might get your feet wet here and there, as you hop channels in the wet meadows. The trail reaches the height of land and the national park boundary to the north of Sunset Pass proper. It then descends slightly onto a limestone bench above the headwaters of the Cline River. Michael Cline was a fur trader in the Rockies in the early

*Pinto Lake*

1800s, when he made annual trading trips through the front ranges from Jasper House to the Kootenay Plains.

### Pinto Lake Viewpoint

After you travel 600 m along the bench northeast of Sunset Pass, walk east from the trail to the edge of the cliff. This provides a wonderful prospect over Pinto Lake and the Cline River valley. The lake was named for one of A.P. Coleman's most troublesome packhorses on his 1893 expedition. Pinto went missing on the journey home. No one was sad to see him go. Still, to quote Coleman: "… we immortalized him by giving his name to an exquisite lake near the head of Cataract River." If you are day-hiking, do not descend to Pinto Lake. It's much farther than it looks (5 km), and — if you have also been to the lookout site — will result in a 34 km outing by the time you return to the Icefields Parkway, possibly today, probably tomorrow.

### Mr. Amery's Mountain

**The prominent mountain** to the southwest of Sunset Lookout — its flanks riddled with glacial cirques — is Mt. Amery (AY-muh-ree) (3329 m). The mountain was named in 1927 for L.S. Amery, a British statesman, publisher, and mountaineer. Two years later, Amery came to Canada with the express purpose of making the first ascent of "his" mountain. In wretched weather, guide Ernest Feuz (FOITS) Jr. led Amery and a partner by a difficult route to the summit — or so they thought. A 1985 ascent found no evidence of the cairn they claimed to have built, and no suitable rocks with which to build one. In the poor visibility of his ascent, it is possible that Mr. Amery did not quite reach the true summit.

# 27. Saskatchewan Glacier

## Route

**Day-hike**

| Route | Elevation (m) | Distance (km) |
|---|---|---|
| Trailhead | 1599 | 0 |
| Crest of knoll | 1765 | 1.9 |
| Valley floor | 1737 | 2.5 |
| End of defined trail | 1768 | 5.6 |

**Maps:**
NTS: 83 C/3
Gem Trek: Columbia Icefield
Inland Waters Directorate: Columbia Icefield

**Best lighting:** morning and early afternoon

## Trailhead

**You have two** parking choices on the Icefields Parkway. Add either of these distances to the length of the hike. Use great care when walking along the roadside.
**1.** In the Cirrus Mountain viewpoint 600 m east of the trailhead; 107.6 km north of the Trans-Canada Highway, 16.9 km south of the Icefield Centre, 117.6 km south of Highway 16.
**2.** At the "Big Bend" parking area, 750 m west of the trailhead; 108.9 km north of the Trans-Canada Highway, 15.6 km south of the Icefield Centre, 116.2 km south of Highway 16.

From either parking area, walk on the gravel highway shoulder, facing traffic, to the sideroad that descends south to an old bridge. Use caution when crossing the highway. Do not attempt to park at the bridge. There is insufficient room for vehicles, the grade is steep, and access to and from the modern road is hazardous.

Few people travelling the Icefields Parkway at "The Big Bend" realize that they are within 7 km of Saskatchewan Glacier, one of the larger glaciers in the Rockies. This trail grants access to the forefield of the glacier, where you can explore the rough terrain of a recently glaciated

## Variation

• Explore the forefield beyond the end of defined trail

*Saskatchewan Glacier*

landscape. This is the only unmaintained outing described in *Classic Hikes*. Bulldozed as a jeep road in 1941, the North Saskatchewan River and the surrounding forest are reclaiming the tread. Although most of the route is easy to follow, there are specific hazards on this hike, beginning with the walk along the Icefields Parkway. When you are on the route, you have to deal with an un-fenced canyon, unsigned junctions, an overgrown section, an avalanche slope, high water levels, and washouts. For these reasons, this is recommended to experienced hikers only.

### Trailhead to Saskatchewan Glacier Forefield

Cross the old bridge over the North Saskatchewan River. The bridge was completed in 1938 during construction of the "Wonder Road," the precursor to the Icefields Parkway. Fifteen metres south of the bridge, look for a faint trail that climbs the slope and then angles upstream above the west bank of the river. Don't use the lower trails, as they take you perilously close to the brink of the canyon, and farther on they may be flooded by the river. The silver spar trees of the surrounding forest resulted from a 1905 forest fire. The understory features bearberry, the leaves of which turn bright red in late summer.

After 400 m, keep right where the jeep track comes in from the south. Follow the riverbank, and descend northwest (right) onto the river flats 300 m later. Follow cairns across the flats for 400 m to the edge of the forest. If you look back to

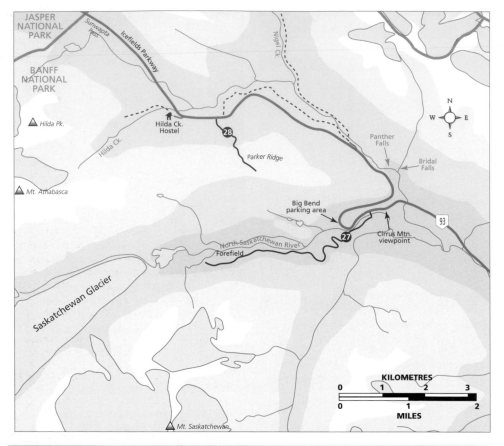

## North Saskatchewan River Canyon

**The canyon** at the trailhead is a masterpiece of natural sculpture, eroded into fossil-rich dolomite of the Flume Formation. In depth and beauty, it is as impressive as many of the better known chasms in the Rockies. At its narrowest, the canyon is less than half a metre wide. The silt-laden waters of the North Saskatchewan River have eroded many potholes and fanciful shapes into the resistant rock. If the day is typical, glacier-driven, catabatic winds will fling the spray skyward, creating rainbows that dance in the air. Please use caution here — the canyon is unfenced.

*North Saskatchewan River Canyon*

## Witness

*Saskatchewan Glacier as seen from Parker Ridge in 1924...*          *...and in 2002*

**Geologically speaking,** 18 years of acquaintance with a glacier is not much of an interval on which to base a description of significant change. My first visit to this valley was in May 1984, during a ski mountaineering trip to Castleguard Mountain. I hiked to the toe of the glacier, put on my skis, and ascended the ice without difficulty. On repeat visits, including two more ski mountaineering trips in successive years, I noted degrees of glacial recession, and how access to the ice was becoming more difficult. Nothing prepared me for the jolt when I visited this valley in July 2002, after an absence of nine years. The toe of the glacier, which in 1984 was in contact with the marginal lake, had receded fully 1 km. Mountaineering access to the ice now appears impossible on the south, and extremely hazardous — being threatened by unstable moraines — on the north. The lake is much smaller. The river, on a hot day at the end of a month-long heat wave, was much lower than I expected. At a braided section in the forefield, I was able to ford it at two in the afternoon — something that should be unthinkable. I wish that this was merely a point of interest only to mountaineers, glaciologists, and curious guidebook authors, but in less than one-third of my lifetime, I have witnessed monumental effects of climate change. The core glacier system of the Canadian Rockies, the source of three of the continent's great rivers, is rapidly dwindling.

## A Mighty River of Ice

**Saskatchewan Glacier** is one of eight outlet valley glaciers of the Columbia Icefield. The glacier extends almost 9 km from the icefield rim, making it the longest glacier in the Rockies. Its meltwaters create the first reach of the North Saskatchewan River.

The most recent significant advance of glaciers in the Rockies was during the Little Ice Age, which began between AD 1200 and 1400, and ended in the mid-1800s. Most glaciers reached their maximum size of that advance in the early 1700s, receded slightly, readvanced to near maximum in the mid-1800s, and have since retreated dramatically. Saskatchewan Glacier reached its maximum later than most other glaciers. In 1854, the toe extended to where the track descends from the knoll to the forefield.

A glaciated valley often preserves evidence of the former size of a glacier. A terminal moraine marks the greatest lengthwise extent of the glacier, and recessional moraines mark positions of halt during its retreat. The maximum thickness of the ice is revealed by a feature called trimline. The obvious trimline on the north side of this valley is more than 100 m above the valley floor, giving an approximate indication of the thickness of Saskatchewan Glacier in the mid-1800s. Forest within the trimline was obliterated by the moving ice. In this peri-glacial climate and on poor soils, the forest has not had time to become re-established. The sparse forest outside the trimline survived the most recent advance.

Today, in the lower reaches of the valley, the Saskatchewan Glacier forefield lacks prominent terminal and lateral moraines, such as those that flank Athabasca Glacier. Lateral moraines are created when the ice fills a valley from side to side. Here, the lateral moraines were undercut when the ice retreated. They collapsed onto the glacier's surface and became part of the ground moraine — the chaos of rubble on the valley floor. Closer to the glacier you can see the lateral moraine on the north side of the valley. If you detect a glistening in its slope, you're right. It is an ice-cored moraine. You can see where parts of it have collapsed.

your left, you can see "Sideways Falls" at the lip of the valley north of Mt. Saskatchewan. The track makes a sharp turn southeast (left) into the forest and begins its winding ascent over the knoll that conceals Saskatchewan Glacier. Before you duck into the trees, look back for a fine view of the twin summits of Cirrus Mountain (3270 m), with the Castle Mountain Syncline evident in its slopes.

After a climb of about a kilometre, the trail descends the west side of the knoll onto an ava-

*Drumlins dot the forefield. In the background, you can see the Little Ice Age trimline.*

lanche slope that may be covered with snow or debris. There are fine views ahead to a cascading glacier on the southeast slopes of Mt. Andromeda (3450 m). Look and listen for the Clark's nutcrackers that frequent the whitebark pines nearby. This place, with its double-whammy of avalanches and catabatic winds, is a tough place to be a tree. One massive whitebark pine survives miraculously in the middle of the avalanche path.

The descent concludes at the former site of the Saskatchewan Glacier Hut. You can make a detour north on a beaten path for 150 m to river's edge for a fine view upvalley. Back on the main trail you head west, but the promise of easy travel is short-lived. The track is washed away 300 m beyond. There is a maze of trails here, covering about 600 m through the shintangle of willows and pines on the riverbank. The best way to negotiate the first part of this mess is to skirt it by heading south for 30 m to the edge of a rockslide. Head west along the rockslide until it ends, and then make your way back toward the riverbank. Eventually, the willows thin and you walk through open pine and spruce forest. About 1.5 km from the hut site, a prominent cairn marks the descent from the riverbank to the forefield. Here, unless the ice recedes another 500 m before this book goes to print, you obtain your first view of Saskatchewan Glacier.

## Saskatchewan Glacier Forefield

The track across the forefield is defined by low mounds of rubble pushed up alongside the bulldozer blade, and by the odd cairn. After about a kilometre of bouldery travel, the track passes through an area of recessional moraines that date to the 1920s. I have seen a mountain goat here on the valley floor. There are several drumlins to the north — piles of teardrop-shaped glacial debris. The blunt end of each drumlin faced into the flow

## The Saskatchewan Glacier Hut

**In 1942 the US Army** constructed buildings near Saskatchewan Glacier to serve as a base for testing oversnow vehicles called "Weasels." The base was flattened by snow the following winter. The remains were salvaged by the Canadian Army, which built a hut for mountain warfare training in 1943. This building was leased by the Alpine Club of Canada the following year, and became known as the Saskatchewan Glacier Hut. By the 1960s, the building was in disrepair, and the river began to undermine its foundation. Noting that the "matter of alpine huts and wilderness shelters is becoming very controversial," Parks Canada did not renew the lease in 1972. The hut was demolished and the access road was closed to vehicles. A clean-up in 1994 removed almost all traces of the habitation. The small log frame structure that remains predates the hut. Analysis of the logs in this building (see the "Tree-time-knowledge" sidebar) indicates that it was probably built in 1926. It may have housed camping supplies for outfitters. If you poke around, you might find other relics, including the leaf springs of a truck.

of ice; the tapered end faced away. The method by which drumlins form is not agreed upon by glaciologists, but they may result from deposits made by subglacial streams.

The point where the bulldozer track reverts to a footpath marks the location of the glacier terminus in the early 1940s. Follow cairns west from here, keeping to the south edge of the forefield. Snowmelt from the cirques above streaks the dark cliffs with waterfalls. Rock-hop the tributary streams as required. Many of the larger boulders in the forefield show striations — scratches and grooves caused by rocks embedded in the underside of the moving ice. Mountain fireweed and yellow mountain saxifrage decorate the gravels. On my last visit, I watched an American pipit here, hanging like a kite on the glacial wind. This is also good habitat for horned larks.

The more you walk toward the glacier, the farther away it seems to get. Blame it on glacial recession. Some hikers are content not to travel all the way to the marginal lake near the glacier toe. About 5.4 km from the trailhead, a faint path veers north, descending at first, and then climbing onto a knoll of debris near the centre of the valley. The cairn here offers a fine viewpoint. The strip of lengthwise rubble visible on the northern edge of Saskatchewan Glacier is a medial moraine, created where two tributary glaciers merge. If you look back at Parker Ridge on the north side of the valley, you can count six sedimentary formations from valley bottom to ridgecrest — most dating to the Late Devonian.

It is 1.7 km from the knoll to the shore of the marginal lake. If you choose to carry on and are confronted with a river crossing, don't force the issue. Glacial rivers are difficult and dangerous to ford. The lake fills a depression in the bedrock. Marginal lakes are common in the Rockies — Athabasca, Bow, Robson, and Cavell glaciers also feature them. Since the bed of this lake was uncovered in the 1960s, the glacier has receded more than 2 km. Islands in the lake are the crests of submerged recessional moraines. On my most recent visit to the lake, I marvelled at the presence of a nesting pair of spotted sandpipers. Hummocks and hollows near the lake are miniature kames (conical shapes of moraine) and kettles (depressions where detached ice blocks melted during glacial retreat).

If you are thinking about a glacial stroll, don't; access to the glacier has become difficult and dangerous in recent years, and is not possible from the south side of the river. To complete your appreciation of Saskatchewan Glacier, I recommend Parker Ridge, Classic Hike #28.

## Tree-time-knowledge

Most coniferous trees in the Rockies are long-lived. Those that grow near glaciers help to reveal much about the climate and glacial events of the recent past. Glaciologists look for ice-contact trees — those killed or scarred by ice during glacial advances. By coring the trees and counting the tree rings, and by comparing the findings to master keys derived from other sites in the Rockies,

*Driftwood on the shore of the marginal lake*

Upvalley, there is no forest, so trees could not have been avalanched into the lake. How did the wood get here? This is glacier-released wood, freed from Saskatchewan Glacier as the ice receded. Glaciologists have studied this wood, dating the oldest fragment to 3180 years ago — indicating that the trees, from forests that once grew upvalley, were overrun during what is known as the

they can assign probable dates to former positions of the ice. The process is called dendrochronology, a name derived from three Greek words — *dendros* for "tree," *chronos* for "time," and *logos* for "knowledge" — tree-time-knowledge.

The current spate of glacial retreat in the Rockies offers glaciologists an exceptional window into the past. If you hike to the marginal lake you may see driftwood piled into the bays along its eastern edge.

"Peyto Advance." In 1999, a meltwater shaft in the terminus of the glacier revealed the stumps of a forest shorn by the ice. Subalpine fir was the dominant species. Downvalley, ice-contact trees on the glacier's lateral moraine indicate three glacial advances during the Little Ice Age. Saskatchewan Glacier reached its maximum size roughly a century later than the other major outlet valley glaciers of Columbia Icefield.

# 28. Parker Ridge

## Route

Day-hike

| Route | Elevation (m) | Distance (km) |
|---|---|---|
| Trailhead | 1997 | 0 |
| Ridgecrest | 2285 | 1.9 |
| Saskatchewan Glacier viewpoint | 2270 | 2.4 |

**Maps**
NTS: 82 C/3
Gem Trek: Columbia Icefield
Inland Waters Directorate: Columbia Icefield
**See map on p.114**

**Best lighting:** morning

## Trailhead

**South side** of the Icefields Parkway, 115.5 km north of the Trans-Canada Highway; 9 km south of the Icefield Centre, 109.6 km south of Highway 16.

My visit to Parker Ridge during fieldwork for this edition was an afterthought. I had been to the ridgecrest perhaps a dozen times before; why go again? But as I drove by on a fair day, I couldn't resist. I thought that I would nip up and down in an hour and a half. I spent four. The day was jewel-bright, cut from perfection. The meld of mountain, meadow, and ice in view was quintessential Rockies. And miracle of all, there was no wind.

### Trailhead to the Ridgecrest

The trailhead is located in a treeline forest where vegetation growth is hindered by high elevation, cold glacial air, near constant winds, poor soils, avalanches, and a northeast aspect. From the parking lot, the trail crosses a subalpine meadow — a frost hollow, typical of areas adjacent to glaciers. Cold air from Hilda Glacier collects here, creating a local growing season so short that mature trees cannot develop.

The horn mountain shapes of Mt. Athabasca (3491 m) and its outlier, Hilda Peak (3060 m), are prominent to the west. The summits of these mountains protruded above the kilometre-thick ice sheets of the Great Glaciation. Since the retreat of the ice sheets, alpine glaciation has continued to whittle away at the upper mountainsides, creating the horns.

The climb begins across the meadow. The trail enters ancient forest. At one point you squeeze between two massive Engelmann spruce trees that are likely at least 400 years old. However, most of the vegetation here is in stunted, kruppelholz form. (*Kruppelholz* is a German term that means "crippled wood.") The gnarled, dense, evergreen mats with silvery bark are subalpine fir trees. Taller, Engelmann spruce grow from within the mats. Although they appear to be shrubs, these are mature trees, possibly hundreds of years old.

The treeless areas on the northeast slope of Parker Ridge are either avalanche swept rock, or tundra comprised of sedges, white mountain avens, mountain heather, snow willow, arctic willow, moss campion, woolly everlasting, and purple saxifrage. Vegetation here is low in stature to reduce wind exposure and to enable the plants to absorb heat from the dark soils. Thick, waxy leaves help retain moisture. Fuzzy stems are natural insulation.

More than 6 m of snow falls annually at Parker Ridge. Because of the shaded, northeast aspect and cold temperatures resulting from the

## Keeping on Track

The Parker Ridge trail was built in the 1960s with ease of access in mind. Gentle switchbacks carved the slope. Unfortunately, those impatient with the trail have shortcut the switchbacks, cre-

*Watch for these signs.*

ating trenches that channel runoff. On your way to the ridgetop you will see dozens of signs that block the shortcut trails, encouraging you to keep on track. The signs were installed when the trail was rehabilitated in a costly project. Seeds from plants on Parker Ridge were grown in greenhouses, and the resulting seedlings were transplanted back to the ridge to revegetate redundant trails. Please help to protect this fragile landscape, and the considerable investment, by keeping to the gravelled path.

*Saskatchewan Glacier is the centrepiece in the view from Parker Ridge. The short hike to the ridgecrest is one of the more rewarding outings in the Rockies.*

terminate in a marginal lake, the principal headwaters of the North Saskatchewan River. The braided river courses through the rubble of the valley below, an area occupied by the glacier less than a century ago.

Compared to Athabasca Glacier, the surface of Saskatchewan Glacier is relatively unspectacular. It has no icefalls and few large crevasses. Of interest is a medial moraine, a strip of lengthwise rubble on the glacier's surface. This type of moraine forms where two tributary glaciers merge. Mt. Saskatchewan (3342 m) is the high peak protruding above rounded summits, 8 km south of Parker Ridge.

Immediately south (left) of the head of the Saskatchewan Glacier is Castleguard Mountain (3070 m). South of this mountain is the entrance to Castleguard Cave, one of the larger cave systems in Canada. More than 18 km of passages have been explored. Some of these follow ancient drainages beneath Columbia Icefield to terminate in dead-ends that are choked with glacial ice. If the day is clear, the view beyond Castleguard Mountain will include the lofty summit of Mt. Bryce (3487 m), 19 km distant.

If you look uphill (west) along the crest of Parker Ridge, you will notice how the outlying ridge is rounded in appearance, becoming much more rugged toward Mt. Athabasca. The rounded parts of the ridge were completely covered by moving ice during the Great Glaciation, while the jagged areas were probably not. If you choose to explore along the ridge to the cairn at the high point (2350 m), please stay on the beaten path. The ridgecrest features kruppelholz forms of whitebark pine, a common tree in windy locations. The limestone bedrock of the Southesk

elevation and the proximity to Columbia Icefield, this snow takes a long time to melt. A few of the drifts along trailside are perennial features. Needless to say, the slopes of Parker Ridge are popular with skiers in winter and spring. If you look north you may be able to pick out the summit of Mt. Alberta (3619 m), fifth highest peak in the Rockies.

**The Ridgecrest**

A blast of icy wind may greet you where the trail gains the open ridgecrest. Follow the beaten path southeast (left) for 500 m for a full view of Saskatchewan Glacier. With a length of 9 km, this outlet valley glacier of the 325 km² Columbia Icefield is the longest in the Rockies. It descends 750 m in elevation from the icefield rim to

Syringopora *fossils spotted with* Xanthoria elegans *lichen*

Formation contains coral-like fossils called *Syringopora*. Please do not remove the fossils.

Mountain goats, white-tailed ptarmigan, gray jays, Clark's nutcrackers, pikas, and ravens are among the frequently observed wildlife on Parker Ridge. If you are fortunate, a grizzly bear or wolverine may lumber over the crest, or a golden eagle may wheel overhead. I saw a harrier skim by on my last visit. The ridge was probably named for Herschel Parker, an American mountaineer who made several first ascents of mountains near Lake Louise at the turn of the century.

## The Glacier Trail

*"First Passage;" packtrain on Saskatchewan Glacier, 1923*

In the early 1900s, mountaineering parties intent on ascending peaks at the southern edge of Columbia Icefield followed the Alexandra River southwest to a base camp in Castleguard Meadows. If they wanted to continue farther north, they were obliged to return along the Alexandra River to the North Saskatchewan River, before crossing Sunwapta Pass — a journey of approximately three days. This backtracking frustrated outfitter Jimmy Simpson and his clients. The supplies used descending the Alexandra could be better used exploring new ground. On the 1923 expedition of mountaineer James Monroe Thorington, Simpson took a one-day shortcut from Castleguard Meadows to Sunwapta Pass; he led the packtrain down the Saskatchewan Glacier and over Parker Ridge.

It was a day-long effort. The horses fussed, but less than expected. The ploy was repeated on the Smithsonian Institution, Columbia Icefield expedition of 1924. For two decades thereafter, the crossing of Saskatchewan Glacier with horses became standard fare. In the late 1920s, outfitter Jack Brewster incorporated a visit to Castleguard Meadows via Saskatchewan Glacier into his pack trips from Jasper to Lake Louise — an outing known appropriately as "The Glacier Trail."

## Rock Lichens: Old Timers

**In some areas,** the thin soils of Parker Ridge support only rock lichen colonies. Rock lichens are hardy organisms — an example of a symbiotic relationship — that contain fungi and algae. The fungi house the algae, and the algae produces food for both. One byproduct of this relationship is humic acid, which accelerates the chemical breakdown of rock and the creation of soil. Rock lichens grow outward at an incredibly slow, consistent rate, so the diameter of a lichen patch can be used to estimate its age and the

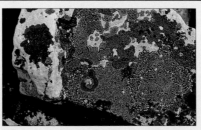

*Rock lichen*

dates of recent glacial retreats. It is thought some rock lichen colonies in the Rockies may have begun life at the end of the Wisconsin Glaciation, 11,000 years ago. Two of the more common rock lichens are the brilliant orange *Xanthoria elegans*, found on a variety of rock types; and the green and black map lichen (*Rhizocarpon geographicum*), found principally on quartzite boulders. Rock lichens are eaten by caribou, bighorn sheep, and mountain goats.

# Jasper National Park

*Jonas Pass as seen from the climb to Jonas Shoulder on the Brazeau loop*

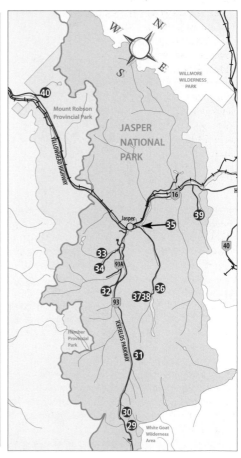

Established in 1907 as Canada's sixth national park, Jasper is the largest of the Rocky Mountain parks. It includes 10,878 km² of the front ranges and eastern main ranges and has almost 1000 km of maintained trails. The Classic Hikes in Jasper feature long backcountry outings as well as day-hikes to spectacular alpine landscapes.

Jasper townsite provides a full range of supplies, accommodation, and services. The townsite is 362 km west of Edmonton on Highway 16; 237 km north of Lake Louise via the Icefields Parkway. Access is by car, passenger bus, or train. Columbia Icefield is 102 km south of Jasper; 126.5 km north of Lake Louise. The park has 10 frontcountry campgrounds with 1758 campsites. There are five hostels. Park information centres are in Jasper townsite and at Columbia Icefield. The warden office is in the industrial compound. Emergency assistance may be available at the Icefield Centre, at warden stations at Poboktan Creek on the Icefields Parkway, at Maligne Lake, and at Pocahontas.

**121**

# 29. Brazeau

## Route

Overnight, 5–7 days

| Route | Elevation (m) | Distance (km) |
|---|---|---|
| Trailhead | 1864 | 0 |
| "Camp Parker" | 1910 | 2.1 |
| Nigel Pass | 2225 | 7.2 |
| Boulder Creek CG | 2030 | 10.7 |
| Four Point CG | 1910 | 13.9 |
| Jonas Pass jct | 1910 | 14.0 |
| Jonas Pass | 2320 | 23.8 |
| Jonas Shoulder | 2490 | 29.6 |
| Jonas Cutoff CG | 2140 | 32.8 |
| Poboktan Creek jct | 2115 | 33.0 |
| Poboktan Pass | 2304 | 36.0 |
| John John CG | 2020 | 40.3 |
| John John Creek bridge | 1830 | 44.5 |
| Brazeau Lake outlet bridge | 1805 | 48.3 |
| Brazeau Lake CG | 1805 | +0.4 |
| Brazeau Valley jct and bridge | 1720 | 51.2 |
| Brazeau River CG | 1720 | 51.3 |
| Brazeau River east bank | 1790 | 54.5 |
| Wolverine South CG | 1860 | 59.8 |
| Brazeau River west bank | 1875 | 62.1 |
| Four Point CG | 1910 | 66.2 |
| Boulder Creek CG | 2030 | 69.3 |
| Nigel Pass | 2225 | 72.8 |
| Trailhead | 1864 | 80.0 |

**Maps**
NTS: 83 C/3, and 83 C/6, and 83 C/7

## Trailhead

**East side of** the Icefields Parkway at Nigel Creek; 111.8 km north of the Trans-Canada Highway, 113.4 km south of Highway 16, 12.7 km south of the Icefield Centre. Southbound travellers should use caution making the awkward turn into the trailhead parking area. Walk north from the parking area on the old road. The trail veers east (right) to cross Nigel Creek on a bridge, 50 m north of the gate.

The Brazeau (brah-ZOE) Loop traverses three upper subalpine passes, the shattered crest of a mountain ridge, and the delightful, broad Brazeau Valley — with a stop at one of the larger backcountry lakes in the Rockies. The area is

*The Brazeau loop traverses three alpine passes. This is the upper Brazeau Valley from Nigel Pass.*

home to grizzly bears, elk, moose, wolves, coyotes, wolverines, cougars, deer, and mountain caribou. This is a great hike for birding. Take your time and enjoy this exquisite landscape. Backpacking in the Rockies does not get any better.

### Trailhead to Nigel Pass
Fifty metres north of the parking lot, the trail crosses to the east bank of Nigel Creek. For the next 7.1 km it follows the creek to its sources in the extreme northeastern corner of Banff National Park. In the early going, the trail alternates between ancient upper subalpine forest and avalanche slopes, which support exceptional wildflower displays. At km 2.1 the trail climbs onto the

## Variations

- Locals are split on which direction to hike this loop. If the forecast is for a few days of fair weather, hike it in the direction described so you have good weather (albeit heavier packs) on the passes. If the forecast is not so favourable, hike it in the opposite direction and hope for improvement.
- Day-hike to Nigel Pass, 14.4 km return
- For a fine three-day trip, camp at Boulder Creek (10.7 km) and spend a day exploring near Nigel Pass
- For a superb three-day trip — perhaps the best in the Rockies — camp at Four Point (13.9 km) and day-hike to Jonas Pass (9.9 km) and Jonas Shoulder (15.6 km)
- Exit along Poboktan Creek from Jonas Cutoff CG; 54.2 km, 4 days

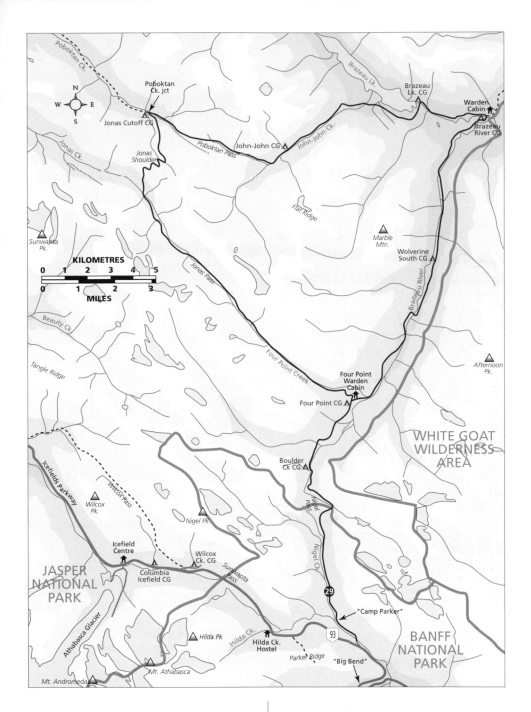

bank above the confluence of Hilda Creek and Nigel Creek. This is "Camp Parker." Many trees nearby feature carvings — the handiwork of travellers along the Icefields Parkway in the 1940s, when it was called the "Wonder Road." The

237 km journey from Lake Louise to Jasper was at least a two-day adventure in those days. This grove of trees was near the halfway point, and was a popular resting and camping place. Please don't add graffiti — much of the older "artwork" has

*A tree carving at Camp Parker*

*The limestone barrens of Nigel Pass, with Nigel Peak beyond*

been disfigured in recent years.

The horn shapes of Mt. Athabasca (3491 m) and its outlier, Hilda Peak (3060 m), form the backdrop to the west. To the northwest is the southern summit of Nigel Peak. It displays the U-shaped fold of the Castle Mountain Syncline, a bedrock feature that extends 260 km through Banff and Jasper.

The trail swings north into the upper valley of Nigel Creek. Although close to the Icefields Parkway, this area is frequented by grizzly bears. Make lots of noise while you cross the avalanche slopes. The last kilometre of the climb is on a steep, eroded trail that leads to a craggy limestone bluff that overlooks the Brazeau River. This point is a kilometre to the east of, and slightly higher than Nigel Pass. Here, you are astride the boundary between Banff and Jasper, and between two geological provinces of the Rockies — the eastern main ranges to the west, and the front ranges to the east.

Parker Ridge, Mt. Saskatchewan (3342 m), and the rounded peaks adjacent to Saskatchewan Glacier are prominent in the view south from Nigel Pass. To the southeast, you can see Cataract Pass and the source of the Brazeau River. The glaciated summit of Nigel Peak (3211 m) rises above massive limestone cliffs to dominate the view west.

## Nigel Pass to Four Point Campground

Leaving Nigel Pass, make a straightforward ford of the Brazeau River. We were once entertained here as a ptarmigan hen, fleeing our presence, coerced

## Backcountry Construction, *Au Naturel*

*A typical backcountry bridge in Jasper, built from trees felled nearby*

**The use of** natural materials for bridges prevails in Jasper's backcountry. In other parks, pressure-treated wood structures have been the norm for many years. By the time pressure-treated wood is purchased and flown to the work site (along with the trail crew), these structures involve a tremendous expense. Although supposedly "maintenance free" for 30–50 years, pressure-treated wood structures succumb to the vagaries of heavy snow loads, flash-floods, and undercut stream banks just as readily as bridges built from materials found on-site. The chemical compound typically used in the wood — copper-chromate-arsenic — is lethally poisonous. The manufactured look of pressure-treated timbers is often an eyesore in remote settings. It would be nice to see a revival of the philosophy and woodworking skills associated with using natural and "found" materials for trail structures in the backcountry.

*Jonas Pass epitomizes the alpine high country of Jasper's front ranges.*

showy white tufts of cotton-grass in late summer.

Follow the meandering course of the Brazeau River to a small canyon, where you cross the river to Boulder Creek campground. Beyond the campground, the trail undulates in forest alongside the canyon. There are many rocks and roots underfoot. Buffaloberry bushes line the trail. You cross Boulder Creek in 600 m, on an artfully constructed log bridge.

Most hikers travel as far as Four Point campground on the first day. Although in a pleasant setting, the campground shows the wear and tear of heavy use. Please do your part to minimize impacts at the campgrounds on this loop.

## Four Point Campground to Jonas Cutoff Campground

As camping is not allowed in Jonas Pass, you must complete the entire distance to Jonas Cutoff campground — 18.9 km — on the second day. All but the concluding 3.2 km are uphill. Start early to allow plenty of time to enjoy the alpine glory of Jonas Pass.

The Jonas Pass junction is 100 m northeast of Four Point campground. Turn northwest (left). The trail climbs into the hanging valley of Four Point Creek over a series of recessional moraines. Each moraine marks a position of temporary halt during the northward retreat of the glacier that once filled the valley. In the forest and on the river flats nearby, there are several drumlins — teardrop shaped mounds of glacial debris.

After a steady climb of 4 km, the trail levels in open forest. The valley bottom is a frost hollow, devoid of trees but bedecked with wildflowers. The shrub thickets and tundra here are important habitats for mountain caribou. On our first visit to Jonas Pass, we watched in amazement as a lone caribou descended the slopes east of the pass. We hid behind a boulder. From this rocky blind we observed the animal at close range for fifteen minutes.

As it approaches Jonas Pass, the trail is routed between Four Point Creek and a rocky bench to the west. The cliffs on the west side of the valley are riddled with glacial cirques. Meltwater from these glaciers is the source of the five silty, tributary streams that you must rock-hop. The third

her chicks into crossing the river. Although ptarmigan are ground-dwelling birds, as this hen and her brood demonstrated to us, they are capable of short bursts of flight when they feel threatened.

The trail climbs away from the river and for the next kilometre winds through rockslide debris dotted with hardy alpine flowers — moss campion, sawwort, cinquefoil, white mountain avens, and yellow hedysarum. Just before it commences a steep descent, the trail crests a small bluff that offers a panorama of the upper Brazeau Valley. This is a graphic overthrust landscape — the steeply tilted southwest-facing slopes of the front range peaks terminate above northeast-facing cliffs. The peaks are separated by parallel valleys, creating a symmetry that has led more than one visitor to comment, "All the mountains look the same." The colourful quartzite ridge to the north divides the drainages of Boulder Creek and Four Point Creek. Particularly pleasing are the meanders, verdant wet meadows, and waterfalls along the Brazeau River. The meadows are lush with the

## Beauty, Eh?

The pinkish-purple bloom of mountain fireweed is often the only splash of colour on the gravels of glacial streams. About one-tenth as tall as common fireweed, the long-lasting blooms persevere throughout the summer. This plant has other common names — alpine fireweed, broad-leaved willowherb, and the one that best describes it — riverbeauty. Whether you view dense blooms covering river gravels or the flowers of an individual plant, you'll agree.

stream is among my favourites in the Rockies. It cascades over the quartzite bedrock, its banks coloured by dense blooms of mountain fireweed, paintbrush, and groundsel. Look for the mauve bloom of the alpine harebell on drier slopes.

The crest of Jonas Pass is typical of upper sub-alpine passes in the Rockies. Four lakelets and numerous seasonal ponds mark the imprecise height of land. Trees cannot grow in the pass itself, because it is a frost hollow. The soil is frozen for much of the year, preventing the supply of water required for tree growth. However, just upslope on either side of the pass, a few islands of kruppelholz mark the uppermost limit of the forest. Alpine gentians grow in profusion among the boulders in the pass. I have seen horned larks and a pair of green-winged teals. In 1992, a group of hikers watched spellbound as a cougar stalked a caribou herd nearby.

From Jonas Pass, the trail angles away from the upper reaches of Jonas Creek toward Jonas Shoulder. Several small tributary streams filter from the base of rockslides and cross the trail.

These are the last water sources for 5 km.

The initial climb toward Jonas Shoulder is very steep. However, the grade moderates as the trail contours north. You can see three rock glaciers across the valley. They extend from the base of the cliffs onto the meadows near Jonas Creek. A rock glacier is an assemblage of rockslide debris that contains just enough ice to allow the entire mass to creep downhill. One study found 119 rock glaciers in Jasper National Park, but there are probably more than that. Many are stagnant or in decline, but these rock glaciers may be advancing.

During this climb, you enjoy a wonderful prospect south to Jonas Pass. The ridge east of the pass culminates nearby in a quartzite tower. Sunwapta Peak (3315 m), its north face cloaked in glacial ice, looms to the west. The mountain was first climbed in 1906 by guide and outfitter Jimmy Simpson. An unwilling mountaineer but a legendary hunter, Simpson was probably lured summitward while in pursuit of mountain goats or bighorn sheep. Use binoculars to look for caribou in the upper reaches of Jonas Creek.

## Mountain Caribou

The caribou has a brown coat with lighter patches on the neck, rump, belly, and lower legs. The neck is fringed on its underside. Males and females both sport antlers. Those of the male feature a forward-reaching "shovel." When they run, caribou carry their heads high and tilted back, and lift their legs in a distinctive prance. If you are close enough, you will hear the clacking made by tendons in the animal's legs. The caribou's large hooves help support it in

*Mountain caribou*

deep snow. They leave a track that is more rounded than that of other deer family members — like two half moons. The caribou's staple foods are ground lichens and rock lichens in summer, and tree lichens in winter. The caribou that frequent the Brazeau and Maligne areas of Jasper stay within the park all year, making them, at least on paper, the only truly protected caribou in southern Canada.

The population of mountain caribou in Alberta

crashed from an estimate of 9000 animals in 1960, to less than 7000 today — perhaps to as few as 3600. The southernmost herd — the Clearwater-Siffleur herd — is not expected to survive. In 2000, the Committee on the Status of Endangered Wildlife in Canada upgraded the status of Canada's southern mountain caribou to "threatened" — a species that is likely to face extirpation if limiting factors are not reversed. Many of the 19 herds are small, isolated, and pressured by recreational development, by logging, and by petroleum exploration — three key ingredients in the extirpation recipe.

Seasonal or permanent closures of some areas are clearly required to help protect the species. Please abide by any new regulations. Only a concerted effort by Parks Canada, governments, industry, hunters, and recreationalists will ensure the local survival of caribou.

The climb ends even more steeply than it began, on the crest of Jonas Shoulder — the ridge that separates the Jonas and Poboktan (poh-BOCK-tan) valleys. This is the 10th highest point reached by maintained trail in the Rockies. *Poboktan* is Stoney for "owl." A.P. Coleman gave the name in 1892, when his party saw owls in the valley below.

The trail on the Poboktan side of Jonas Shoulder is snow-covered in early summer. Descend with care. The trail angles sharply south (right), then switchbacks steeply down on scree. After crossing an intervening ridge, the trail rambles over boggy meadowland, paralleling the stream and descending rapidly north toward Poboktan Creek. Please keep to the beaten path to avoid creating braids in the trail. You will get your boots wet here. Shortly after you enter forest, look for a signed trail that branches west (left) to Jonas Cutoff campground. The campground is 200 m before the Poboktan Creek bridge and trail junction.

## A.P. Coleman — A Professor of Mountaineering

*A. P. Coleman*

**The first non-Native** party to cross Jonas Pass was led by A.P. Coleman in 1893. Coleman was a geology professor at the University of Toronto. He made seven trips into the uncharted wilds of the Rockies between 1884 and 1907. Initially, his quest was to find Mt. Hooker and Mt. Brown, fabled guardians of Athabasca Pass, and reputed to be the highest mountains in the Rockies. In his last expedition, he made an attempt on Mt. Robson.

During his journey of 1893, Coleman received advice on the route from a Stoney elder, Chief Jonas. Coleman named many other features using Stoney, Cree, and Iroquois words. Coleman's considerable exploits and detailed observations were recorded in *The Canadian Rockies, New and Old Trails*, published in 1911.

Campfires are no longer allowed. You can exit here, along Poboktan Creek; 21.4 km to the Icefields Parkway, with two campgrounds enroute.

## Jonas Cutoff Campground to Brazeau Lake

The splendours of this loop hike continue into the third day. At the Poboktan Creek junction, turn southeast (right), to commence the climb to Poboktan Pass. The trail crosses and recrosses the creek on bridges, and then angles steeply away from the east bank to climb through treeline. Last time we hiked here, we had a head-on encounter with a grizzly bear. During the ascent you will see weathered posts, 5 m long, lying near the trail. These were formerly part of a backcountry telephone system, erected by park wardens in the 1920s. The advent of portable radios rendered the system obsolete, and the wires were removed. Backcountry wardens now pack satellite phones.

Poboktan Pass is the third upper subalpine setting visited on this hike — a heath and avens tundra, dotted with kruppelholz, carpeted with wildflowers and frequented by caribou and grizzly bears. The pass divides waters that flow north to the Arctic Ocean via the Athabasca, Slave, and Mackenzie rivers, from waters that flow east to Hudson's Bay via the Brazeau, Saskatchewan, and Nelson rivers. Duncan McGillivray, a fur trader with the North West Company in 1800, was the first non-Native to cross Poboktan Pass. Directly southeast of the pass, Flat Ridge (2820 m) features several rock glaciers on its north slopes.

The trail from Poboktan Pass descends at first gradually, then abruptly into the forest along John-John Creek. John-John Harrington was father of Mona Matheson, Jasper's first female trail guide. She married Charlie Matheson, a park warden who was stationed in the Brazeau District during the 1930s. For those who have wiled away the hours on Poboktan Pass, or who would otherwise like a short day on the trail, John-John campground makes a pleasant, creek-side stopping place.

From the campground, the trail follows the north bank of John-John Creek toward Brazeau Lake, then descends steeply through a forest of spruce and lodgepole pine to cross John-John Creek. Across the bridge, the trail enters the debris of the Brazeau Lake Slide.

The trail continues southeast beyond the slide, climbing into lodgepole pine forest that offers only partial views of nearby Brazeau Lake. A steep descent east through spruce-fir forest leads to a bridge southeast of the lake's outlet. Be thankful for this bridge. The raging river would otherwise not be negotiable, except perhaps to daring souls on horseback. Look for harlequin ducks in the fast-flowing water and bald eagles in the nearby trees. Across the river, turn northwest (left) to reach Brazeau Lake campground and the trail to the lakeshore. Turn southeast (right) to continue the loop.

From the campground, a rough track leads along the northeast shore of Brazeau Lake. With a length of 5 km, a maximum width of 900 m, and an

*The alpine meadows of Pobokton Pass are frequented by caribou, bighorn sheep, and grizzly bears.*

area of 360 ha, the lake is among the larger bodies of water in the backcountry of the Rockies. It is fed by meltwater from the 25 km2 Brazeau Icefield to the north. In that direction you can see Mt. Henry McLeod (3315 m) — named for a railway surveyor who was the first non-Native known to see Maligne Lake — a feat he accomplished, remarkably, in 1875. Look for moose in the bay across the lake from the campground.

## Brazeau Lake to Four Point Campground

From the outlet of Brazeau Lake, follow the northwest fork of the Brazeau River southeast for 2.9 km to a junction. Turn south (right), and cross the river on a high bridge to the Brazeau River campground. The following 3.2 km of trail undulates over ancient rockslides forested with

lodgepole pines, and makes for tedious travel.

After traversing high above the cleft of a canyon, the trail descends to the main branch of the Brazeau River and crosses to its east bank. The hiking immediately improves, with expansive vistas of the broad Brazeau Valley and surrounding peaks. Marble Mountain (2960 m) is to the north. By technical definition, "marble" is limestone or dolomite that has been recrystalized through heat or pressure. True marble is rare in the Rockies. In common usage however, marble refers to any carbonate sedimentary rock that can be polished. The effects of erosion by glacial ice and flowing water have created an abundance of this kind of "marble" in the Rockies.

The Brazeau River cuts across the northwest-

## The Brazeau Lake Slide: The Walls Came Tumbling Down

When park warden Charlie Matheson rode down John-John Creek on a routine patrol in July 1933, he was the first person to see the aftermath of the tremendous Brazeau Lake Slide. He found the trail obliterated by a morass of mud and rocks. The debris was "still quivering." Needless to say, the backcountry telephone line was destroyed. Matheson reported that the water of Brazeau Lake had an odd taste for about a month, probably due to sediments from the slide.

The Brazeau Lake Slide is the largest landslide in the Rockies that is known to have occurred in the 20th century. The slide was caused by separation of one or more of the underlying rock layers on the slope above. A build-up of pressure caused by water or ice within crack systems may have forced the lay-

ers apart. The rock that failed is Cambrian-aged, Pika Formation limestone and dolomite. The bedding plane of the slide slope dips at 27 degrees to the northeast — the direction of the lake. This steepness is typical of slopes that produce this kind of landslide.

Because the dead trees in the slide debris lie parallel to the direction of flow, the slide was probably not an instantaneous catastrophe, such as the famous Frank Slide. (The wind blast from an instantaneous slide flattens trees at right angles to the flow.) The conical mounds in the runout of the slide are called *mollards*. Vibration of the ground during the slide caused sifting and sorting of rock and sediments, building the mollards. As unlikely as it seems, the effect has been duplicated in laboratory experiments.

*Brazeau Lake is one of the larger backcountry lakes in the Rockies.*

# 30. Wilcox Pass

## Route

**Day-hike**

| Route | Elevation (m) | Distance (km) |
|---|---|---|
| Trailhead | 2040 | 0 |
| Wilcox Pass | 2355 | 4.5 |
| North end of pass | 2320 | 7.4 |
| Tangle Falls | 1830 | 12.0 |

**Maps**
NTS: 83 C/3 and 83 C/6
Gem Trek: Columbia Icefield
Inland Waters Directorate: Columbia Icefield
(partial coverage)

## Trailhead

**Wilcox Creek** campground, on the east side of the Icefields Parkway, 121.5 km north of the Trans-Canada Highway; 103.7 km south of Highway 16; 3.0 km south of the Icefield Centre. The trailhead is on the left, just off the highway.

southeast grain or strike of the Rockies, as do the Bow, Athabasca, North Saskatchewan, Red Deer, and Clearwater rivers. These rivers are antecedent streams, older than the mountains. Their downward erosion kept pace with uplift during mountain building, so the rivers maintained their unlikely courses.

Wolverine South campground is a wonderful stopping place for those who would like to extend their time in the Brazeau Valley. Views to the southwest include Mt. Athabasca (3491 m) on the fringe of Columbia Icefield, 20 km distant. We saw a golden eagle and a Swainson's hawk here. Wolf tracks decorated the mud. The trail recrosses the Brazeau River on a bridge, and alternating between shrub meadows and pine forest, completes the loop back to Four Point campground. From here, it's a day's hike over familiar ground to the Icefields Parkway via Nigel Pass.

## Joseph Brazeau

**The features bearing** the name "Brazeau" commemorate Joseph Brazeau, a trader, clerk, and postmaster with the Hudson's Bay Company. Brazeau worked at fur trade outposts along the eastern edge of the Rockies from 1852 to 1864. With his knowledge of Native languages, Brazeau was of great assistance to the Palliser Expedition. James Hector named the river for him in 1860. The lake and mountain were named by A.P. Coleman in 1892 and 1902, respectively. The mountain had appeared on earlier maps as "Mt. McGillivray," commemorating fur trader, Duncan McGillivray.

When Walter Wilcox travelled north from Lake Louise in 1896, his party hit a roadblock in the upper Sunwapta Valley. The terrific, rocky jumble of the Mt. Kitchener Slide and the resulting gorge on the Sunwapta River made travel north from Sunwapta Pass into the Sunwapta Valley impossible for horses. Wilcox's guide, Fred Stephens, detoured by climbing over a pass to the northeast to regain the Sunwapta Valley farther north. The Wilcox Pass/Tangle Creek trail retraces this historic route, offering panoramic views of the peaks and glaciers near Columbia Icefield. If you plan to descend into Tangle Creek, pre-arrange transportation for the end of the hike. Those who don't mind a stiff hill climb after a good hike might consider stashing a bike.

### Trailhead to Wilcox Pass

From the trailhead at the entrance to Wilcox Creek campground, the trail climbs steeply into an ancient forest of Engelmann spruce. They aren't giants, but many of these trees — stunted by the glacial chill — are 300 to 350 years old. The oldest known Engelmann spruce in Jasper National Park — approximately 700 years — grows 3 km west of here. The high stumps you see are from trees cut for bridge timbers during

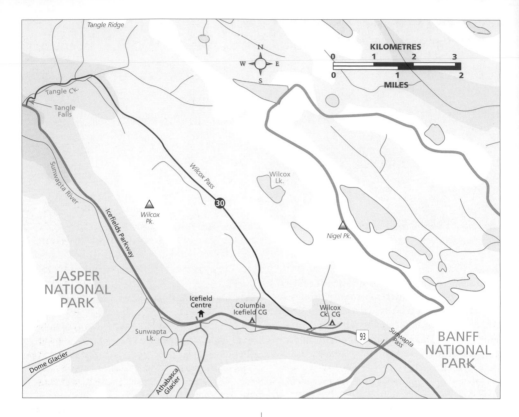

construction of the original Icefields Parkway in the late 1930s.

You reach treeline in just a kilometre, at the edge of a cliff that overlooks the Icefields Parkway. In the view south, from left to right, the features are Mt. Athabasca (3491 m), Mt. Andromeda (3450 m), Athabasca Glacier, Snow Dome (3451 m), Dome Glacier, and Mt. Kitchener (3480 m). Mt. Athabasca was first climbed in 1898 by J.N. Collie and Hermann Woolley. From its summit, they claimed the "discovery" of Columbia Icefield. Today, Mt. Athabasca is probably the most frequently ascended alpine peak in the Rockies. Look for climbers on the icy faces of this mountain and on Mt. Andromeda.

The trail veers north from the edge of the cliff and begins a rambling ascent along the principal stream that drains the pass, through stands of

## Variations

- Hike to the pass, 9.0 km return
- Hike to the north end of the pass, 14.8 km return
- Traverse the pass to Tangle Falls, 12.0 km

ragged kruppelholz. Nigel Peak (3211 m) rises to the east.

Wilcox Pass is alpine tundra at its best — a broad, U-shaped valley, 3 km long. The large cairn that marks the height of land is the ultimate destination for most hikers, but the slopes either side of the pass beckon. You might consider following a faint trail that curves around the end of the northwest ridge of Nigel Peak to Wilcox Lake. Wildflowers and wildlife abound. Flocks of bighorn sheep — often exclusively composed of rams — congregate on lingering snow patches, seeking escape from heat and bugs. I have only taken the safety off a bear spray twice in the backcountry. Once was here, when a bighorn ram approached head down, with menace in his eye. I finally scared him off by calling him things that I won't recount. Other wildlife species that frequent the pass include mountain goat, grizzly bear, moose, wolverine, and golden eagle. In early August, many of the ponds in the height of the pass are decorated with the showy, white tufts of the sedge, cotton-grass. If you do not wish to carry on to Tangle Creek, retrace your route to the trailhead.

*Wilcox Pass*

*Bighorn sheep frequent Wilcox Pass.*

## Wilcox Pass to Tangle Falls

The trail becomes indistinct as you head northwest across the pass. Work your way upslope toward Mount Wilcox — following occasional cairns — to gain the rocky bench about 20 m above the level of the pass. Please walk side by side and spread out to avoid repetitive trampling of vegetation. Continue north on this bench, usually without benefit of defined trail. The thistle-like, purple blooms of sawwort, and tiny, yellow, alpine hawksbeard colour the screes.

At the north end of the bench, look for a faint track that descends northeast to upper Tangle Creek. This track soon becomes a well-beaten trail. The glaciated summits of Mt. Woolley (3405 m), Diadem Peak (3371 m), and Mushroom Peak (3210 m) are grouped together in the northwest. *Diadem* is Latin for "crown," and refers to the snowy crest of the mountain. Mushroom Peak was also named for a snow feature — a cornice noticed on the summit by N.E. Odell, who made the first ascent, solo, in 1947.

The domed summit of Tangle Ridge (3000 m) is due north. Later in the descent, you obtain a view of Mt. Alberta (3619 m), tucked in behind Mt. Woolley. Mt. Alberta is the fifth highest mountain in the Canadian Rockies and one of the more

## Disappearing Ice and Disappearing Water

**You can see** eight glaciers in the view south from the approach to Wilcox Pass: Boundary and "Little A" on Mt. Athabasca; "A-A" between Mt. Athabasca and Mt. Andromeda; two unnamed cascading glaciers on Mt. Andromeda; Athabasca; "Little Dome," and Dome. Athabasca Glacier receded 1.6 km, and decreased 57 percent in area, and 32 percent in volume between 1870 and 1971. Glaciologists estimate that in 1998 the glacier lost 5 percent of its mass in one scorching summer.

The glacially streamlined form of Mount Wilcox (2884 m) borders the west side of Wilcox Pass. Wilcox and his companion, R.L. Barrett, made the first ascent in 1896. Wilcox Lake is concealed from view on the east side of the pass, at the foot of Nigel Peak. The lake has no surface outlet, indicating underground drainage in the limestone bedrock. A large spring along Nigel Creek, 5 km south, is thought to be the emergence of the underground stream.

## Good Stew, Nigel!

**Nigel Vavasour** was cook on the 1898 expedition that made the first ascent of Mt. Athabasca and claimed "discovery" of Columbia Icefield. The expedition included mountaineers John Norman Collie, Herman Woolley, and Hugh Stutfield, and was guided by Bill Peyto. On the way north from Lake Louise, the party lost many supplies when testy packhorses plunged into the North Saskatchewan River. The larder was almost empty before serious climbing could begin. While Collie and Woolley claimed glory on the heights of Mt. Athabasca, Stutfield and Peyto undertook a more mundane pursuit. They hunted bighorn sheep near Nigel Pass in an area that they called the "Wild Sheep Hills." The hunt was successful, and the sheep stew that became the party's staple for the next two weeks must have been a success too, for Collie applied the cook's name to a number of features in the area.

*Tangle Falls*

# 31. Maligne Pass

## Route

Day-hike or overnight

| Route | Elevation (m) | Distance (km) |
|---|---|---|
| Trailhead | 1540 | 0 |
| Maligne Pass jct | 1710 | 6.1 |
| Avalanche CG | 2040 | 11.2 |
| Maligne Pass | 2260 | 15.2 |

Maps
NTS: 83 C/6, and 83 C/11, and 83 C/12

## Trailhead

**At Poboktan Creek** on the east side of the Icefields Parkway, 69.9 km south of Highway 16, 30.8 km north of the Icefield Centre, 155.3 km north of the Trans-Canada Highway.

difficult to climb. This is one of two maintained hiking trails from which it is visible.

You reach the sources of Tangle Creek in a large willow meadow. After entering the forest and crossing the creek to its south bank, the trail comes to an opening on a rise. In the view west beyond the icebound summits of Stutfield Peak (3450 m), you might pick out the shoulder of North Twin (3684 m), third highest mountain in the Rockies. There is an old campsite in the clearing below this rise, with teepee poles still stacked against the trees. The following clearing contains the ruins of a cabin. The building may have been built by Jimmy Simpson or Bill Peyto in the early 1900s, to serve them on their winter trap lines.

The trail soon emerges from forest atop a grassy slope, 120 m above the Icefields Parkway. Bighorn sheep frequent this area. Descend south to the grade of the "Wonder Road," forerunner of the Icefields Parkway. Follow this track north to Tangle Falls and trail's end. The bedrock of the falls is Cambrian-aged Mistaya Formation limestone. Untracked bush is known to outfitters as "shin tangle." Tangle Creek and falls were named in 1907 by explorer Mary Schäffer, after a trying descent from Wilcox Pass. From Tangle Falls it is 9.8 km south along the Icefields Parkway to the original trailhead.

On a fair day, Maligne Pass is a glory — the match of any alpine environment in the Rockies. Although only a single ridge separates you from the Icefields Parkway, the pass is a remote place, the wilderness haunt of grizzly bears and caribou. You share the trail with horses.

**Trailhead to Maligne Pass Junction**
The trail begins behind the kiosk on the north edge of the parking lot. Descend to Poboktan Creek, which you cross on an I-beam bridge in 100 m. Turn east (right) at the junction across the creek. For decades, the Poboktan Creek trail has been an artery into the Brazeau backcountry. In places, the wide trail isn't pretty — it's chewed by horse traffic — but the vegetation at trailside provides distraction. You begin in a forest dominated by Engelmann spruce. Twinflower, northern gentian, dwarf dogwood, yellow columbine, and fireweed grow in the understory. After about 700 m, the trail draws alongside the rambunctious creek. If the water is up, you may hear boulders rolling down the creekbed. And no, for once, the Native name of this creek does not mean "turbulent water." *Poboktan* is a Stoney word for "owl." Mountaineer A.P. Coleman gave the name to the creek and to the pass at its head, in 1892.

The first 2 km of trail reveals a subtle aspect of the geological blueprint of the Rockies. As you hike beside Poboktan Creek, you might expect that you are ascending the Poboktan Valley. But

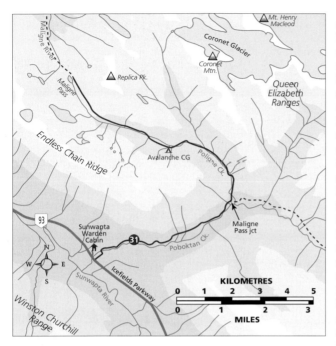

around the edge of a quartzite boulderslide on the southeast end of Endless Chain Ridge and enters an open forest of mature lodgepole pines. You will see small pines growing in the understory. When a forest survives long enough for trees of the same species to propagate, it is said to be a climax forest. The lodgepole pine is a fire-dependent tree and is relatively short-lived (75–200 years) in the Rockies. It is not often that lodgepoles become a climax forest species. However, they have an affinity for quartzite bedrock, so this type of forest is common in the front ranges of Jasper. Bracted lousewort, Labrador tea, fleabanes, white camas, paintbrush, dwarf blueberry, wild strawberry, and crowberry grow beneath the trees. I saw a pair of ravens here, gleaning tiny, red grouseberries from trailside.

About 5 km from the trailhead, you have views southeast through the trees to Poboktan Mountain (3323 m), the highest peak in the valley. The trail draws alongside the creek again at a small beach — a pleasant place to take a break. Looking down the creek you can see the northerly peaks of the Winston Churchill Range on the west side of the Sunwapta Valley. The British statesman did not climb in those mountains, but he did climb the Matterhorn when a young lad. In a wet spot just beyond the beach, I saw the tracks and leavings of a large wolf and a smaller one, and a moose. You climb away from the creek again — travelling a section of trail that has been ditched and mounded to improve drainage — to where Poligne Creek comes rushing down from the north. Turn north (left) at the junction just before the creek.

## Maligne Pass Junction to Maligne Pass

Poligne (derived from POboktan and MaLIGNE) is a better handle than "Maboktan" would have been, but it seems a shame that the creek that drains the southern aspect of Maligne Pass has such a perfunctory name. By the time you reach the pass, you will be well acquainted with this watercourse — having crossed it and its tributary eight times on bridges. The first of these is just 200 m north of the junction, where the creek

take a look at the topographic map. You are still in the Sunwapta Valley; the true mouth of the Poboktan Valley is about 2 km from the trailhead, where Endless Chain Ridge and the Waterfall Peaks align. The explanation is simple. The ice-age glacier that most recently carved the Sunwapta Valley was much larger than the one that carved the Poboktan Valley. At the end of the Wisconsin Glaciation, Poboktan Creek probably emptied from its valley in a waterfall. Subsequent downward erosion of the creek has blurred that abrupt transition, enabling the tributary to run across the floor of the main valley. Between the trailhead and the mouth of the Poboktan Valley, you climb over a series of low rises. These landforms might be ancient recessional moraines of the glacier that once occupied the Poboktan Valley, or they could be more recent features — old river terraces of the Sunwapta River. (Yes, *Sunwapta* is Stoney for "turbulent water.")

If you look south through the trees, you may catch glimpses of the rim of Columbia Icefield on Mount Kitchener (3480 m). The trail contours

## Variations

- Day-hike the pass, 30.4 km return
- Camp at Avalanche CG and explore the pass over the next day or two

emerges from a slabby canyon. Grind away up the east bank on the steepest grade of the hike.

At the top of this climb, the trail swings north and descends slightly. In the forest, note the transition from lower subalpine to upper subalpine that took place on the climb. You soon cross to the west side of the creek to bypass a section where avalanche slopes run right to the valley floor. The trail is rough and wet here. Judging from the tracks I saw, the area is frequented by caribou. Perhaps they enjoy munching on the sedges. The third crossing of Poligne Creek delivers you onto the shingle flat of a tributary that emerges from a rock glacier. There are fine boulders of Gog conglomerate here — 600-million-year-old concrete made from pebbles cemented together with quartz. The fourth creek crossing spans the mouth of the north fork of Poligne Creek, a tributary that has a reputation as a bridge basher. When I hiked it, the trail had been re-routed

north to bypass a spot where the old bridge was washed out and partially buried. Note how most backcountry bridges in Jasper are built from trees felled on-site. The location of usable trees often dictates the placement of the resulting bridge.

You now have creeks on either side of you for a short distance as the trail swings northwest. Cross Poligne Creek again to its west bank. The forest thins dramatically as you traverse a sideslope, with the boulder gardens and the cascades of the creek below. The bedrock here is Gog Formation siltstone and conglomerate. Look and listen for dippers. Coronet Mountain (3152 m) is to the east. It was named by American alpinist Howard Palmer for the shape of a snow formation high on the peak. Another footbridge takes you over to the east bank, with a view upvalley and across valley to the "back side" of Endless Chain Ridge. But what will likely catch your eye is underfoot — a bank of rusty, quartzite sand, eroded from the

## Straight Up and Narrow

Lodgepole pine forests cloak the major valley bottoms of the montane ecoregion in the Rockies — Bow, Athabasca, Kicking Horse, Kootenay, Kananasksis, and Waterton. Lodgepole forests often indicate where large forest fires occurred in the recent past. The cones require temperatures above 45°C to open and to release their

*A stand of lodgepole pine*

seeds; hence the tree's reliance on forest fires for propagation. The resulting dog-hair forests of tightly-spaced saplings crowd out other tree species. The long needles of the lodgepole pine are in pairs. In late June, lodgepoles release their pollen in thick clouds. That's the yellow scum you see on lakes and puddles. This tree is not the same as jack pine, which grows east of the Rockies.

Lodgepoles are susceptible to infestation by mountain pine beetles, which have affected more than half of this species in some valleys. The beetles engrave tunnels in the cambium layer of the tree, where the sapwood that sustains new growth is located. The tunnels cut off the sap flow, killing the tree. Parasitic, pine dwarf mistletoe also afflicts lodgepole pines, sometimes causing a tree's branches to grow in dense clumps called brooms.

If the needles of a lodgepole are reddish-brown, the tree may have been afflicted by red-belt. Warm chinook winds parch the needles in winter when the sap is frozen. The tree is unable to replenish the needles, so they die and fall off.

For Natives who travelled in the mountains, the lodgepole pine was an obvious choice for making travois and teepee poles. A mature tree, unless it is slow-growing, is free of branches on the lower two-thirds of its trunk. European explorers copied the practice of tent-making with this tree. I have seen stacks of ancient poles in many places along trails in the Rockies. You may be puzzled by the contradiction inherent in the typically arrow-straight trunks of this tree species, and its Latin species name, *contorta*. The tree was first catalogued in coastal California, where it is typically twisted in form. The coastal variety is now known as shore pine.

The age record — from a tree in Yoho's McArthur Creek valley — is 454 years. The tallest lodgepole known is 46.34 m, in BC's Manning Provincial Park. The lodgepole pine is the provincial tree of Alberta.

*The alpine glory of Maligne Pass*

Sketchy, vague, spongy, mucky — it's all these things. But where there's this much moisture in the subalpine ecoregion, there is usually a great display of wildflowers, and in this regard you won't be disappointed. Frosted paintbrush, valerian, elephant head, arnica, fleabane, blue-bottle gentian, groundsel, alpine speedwell, and bracted lousewort cover the tread. Watch where you step.

Gog bedrock. I saw stonecrop growing here, its yellow bloom flaming against the reddish-brown sand. The trail becomes something akin to muskeg just before it crosses Poligne Creek above a small canyon. Avalanche Campground is 40 m downstream on the west bank, set in a small clearing.

The trail beyond the campground is an immediate disappointment and may try your patience.

## Alpine Speedwell

*Alpine speedwell*

**Many flowering plants** of the alpine region have blue or purple flowers, which helps them withstand intense solar radiation. You'll have to take off your sunglasses to spot the tiny blooms of alpine speedwell (*veronica wormskjoldii*). As with many plants, the common name of this one recalls its use as a folk medecine cure. It was prescribed for everything from blood disorders to kidney stones.

If you have hiked Jonas Pass from south to north, you may get a sense of the familiar as you approach Maligne Pass. The aspect is similar, as is the elevation, and the fact that both passes are sandwiched between quartzite mountains. As well, both passes are frequented by caribou and grizzly bears. Keep alert.

About a kilometre beyond the campground, you make the last bridged creek crossing of the ascent. The trail is very poor just beyond but then improves as it climbs away from the valley bottom — something it probably should have done a kilometre back. Lakes on the west side of the valley drain into Poligne Creek in a series of waterfalls. Pause during the climb to look downvalley for the great view toward Poboktan Pass. At the conclusion of the climb, you leave the last of the trees behind and begin a sidehill traverse into the pass. On my second visit to the pass, I got hung up in traffic here. A large porcupine, fleeing my presence, set off — as porcupines often do when seeking to escape — directly along the trail. I was finally obliged to say, "Excuse me," as I stepped around it in order to carry on.

## Maligne Pass

Like a blue gem dropped into a setting of green, an unnamed lake about 350 m long and ringed by rock on two shores, nestles in Maligne Pass. When you first see the lake, you also get your first view north to the glaciated summit of Mt. Unwin (3268 m). Sid Unwin was guide to the party of Mary Schäffer in 1908, in their quest for Maligne Lake. After weeks on the trail with no sight of the fabled lake, Unwin set off alone one afternoon to ascend the eastern side of the upper Maligne

**135**

River valley, hoping for an instructive view. In this aim he was successful. Schäffer named the peak for him, and Unwin has been credited with the first ascent, although it is more likely that he reached the lesser, subsidiary summit to the west. As was the case with so many of his contemporaries, Unwin was soon dead; he fell in combat in WWI.

The trail skirts above the lake's east shore to the crest of the pass, which is marked with an artful cairn. Views ahead now include the series of peaks that flank the east side of the upper Maligne River. Closest is the massive humpback form of Mt. Mary Vaux (3201 m), named by Schäffer for her companion on the expeditions of 1907 and 1908. A member of a Philadelphia family famous for its late 19th century scientific interest in the Rockies and Selkirks, Mary Vaux had a particular interest in botany. She was the first woman to climb a mountain (Mt. Stephen) over 10,000 feet in Canada. She later married Charles Walcott, director of the Smithsonian Institution. Vaux named Llysyfran Peak (3141 m), also in view, for a Welsh relative. Mt. Charlton (3217 m) is partially visible, to the east of Mt. Unwin. Henry Charlton was the advertising agent for the Grant Trunk Pacific Railway (GTPR). Mary Schäffer named the peak for him in 1911, when the GTPR subsidized her second trip to Maligne Lake. On the west side of the pass, the Endless Chain Ridge carries on with no end in sight. Schäffer named the ridge in 1907. She watched it parade by for the better part of a week as she rode the trail in the Sunwapta Valley.

The lake on the pass drains south into Poligne Creek. The tiny creek that crosses the trail just north of the cairn, drains north — the first gatherings of the Maligne River. *Maligne* is one of the older placenames in the Rockies. It's French for "wicked." The river was named by Father Jean de Smet in 1846. Wicked is hardly a sentiment to be applied to the environs of the pass, but de Smet had trouble crossing the river's mouth at its confluence with the Athabasca River.

I saw horned larks and American pipits in the meadows near the lake, and a mother blue-winged teal with a brood of six ducklings on the water. Other birds I heard near the pass were white-crowned sparrows, boreal chickadees, and mountain chickadees. Judging from my informal census, the benches west of the pass may be the hoary marmot capital of the Rockies. Scan the wet meadows north of the pass carefully — this is great habitat for caribou.

The steep screes of Replica Peak (2794 m) rise from the east side of Maligne Pass. Howard Palmer named the peak in 1923, but he intended the name for a presently unnamed mountain to the northeast, which he thought similar in profile to Coronet Mountain. As is so often the case, a cartographer put the name in the wrong place and there it stuck. A trek to the summit of Replica Peak — best accomplished from a departure point slightly downvalley to the south — will probably be on the minds of mountaineers. For those more content to ramble the meadowlands and benches, I'll let Maligne Pass divulge its many secret places to you.

## Carts before Horses

*The bridge at the outlet of Maligne Lake*

**If you have been** to Maligne Lake, you may have wondered at the skookum bridge over its outlet. It looks out of place. It is. In 1971, Parks Canada unveiled its Provisional Master Plans for the four mountain parks. Conceived by bureaucrats, without any involvement of the public, the plans called for the upgrading of existing fireroads and the construction of many new roads: Howse Pass, Cascade Valley, Red Deer/Pipestone, Fortress Lake, Redearth Creek, Wapta Falls, Ottertail, Amiskwi, Otterhead, Kicking Horse, Beaverfoot, Yoho Valley, and Maligne Pass/Poboktan Creek. Some of the road alignments were partially cut — the first kilometre of the Wapta Falls trail in Yoho is an example. The public was outraged and the plans were dropped. Those who love wild places owe a great deal to the fledgling environmentalists who spoke out against those proposals more than three decades ago. The public consultation process we have today is a legacy of the debacle of 1971, along with a bridge built for a road that — thanks to new legislation — should never again be entertained.

# 32. Fryatt Valley

## Route

**Overnight, 3–4 days**

| Route | Elevation (m) | Distance (km) |
|---|---|---|
| Trailhead | 1215 | 0 |
| Athabasca River | 1210 | 7.2 |
| Athabasca Valley vpt. | 1240 | 8.6 |
| Lower Fryatt CG | 1280 | 11.6 |
| Fryatt Creek bridge | 1605 | 15.9 |
| Brussels CG | 1660 | 17.2 |
| Fryatt Lake | 1715 | 18.7 |
| Headwall CG | 1780 | 21.1 |
| Sydney Vallance Hut | 2000 | 22.0 |
| Upper Fryatt Valley | 2035 | 23.2 |

**Maps**
NTS: 83 C/12 and 83 C/5

*Fryatt Creek collects in this pool, known as "The Roman Bath," at the mouth of the upper Fyatt Valley.*

## Trailhead

**Follow the Icefields Parkway** to the junction with Highway 93A at Athabasca Falls, 29.8 km south of Highway 16, 70.9 km north of the Icefield Centre. Turn west and follow Highway 93A, 1.1 km to the Fryatt Valley/Geraldine Lakes road. This gravel road may be gated, however the gate should not be locked unless the area is closed. Follow this road 2.1 km south to the signed trailhead for Fryatt Valley.

After a long approach during which the scenic interest builds gradually, the Fryatt Valley hike culminates in a wonderland of lakelets, pools, meadows, glaciers, disappearing rivers, and savage peaks — all that is classic about the Canadian Rockies. Black bears and grizzly bears frequent the approach trail. On our first venture to the Fryatt trailhead we saw an enormous grizzly just 40 m from the parking area... "let's go somewhere else today." You share the trail with mountain bikers as far as the first campground.

## Bear Alley

**Buffaloberry is a** common shrub in the pine forests that cloak the Athabasca Valley, and a principal reason why bears frequent the Fryatt Valley trail. The shrub's glossy, dark green leaves are pale and fuzzy underneath, with rust-coloured dots. The red and amber berries, which ripen in late July and early August, are a summer staple of bears. At that time, they may comprise up to 95 percent of a black bear's diet. An adult grizzly bear may eat 200,000 of these berries a day — a fact that will leave you asking two questions. How does a bear eat something as small as a buffaloberry? Not one at a time. It threshes the branches of the shrub through its jaws, getting a

*Buffaloberry*

mouth full of berries and leaves. How do we know that a bear eats that many berries? Some dedicated researcher followed one around, picked through its scats, and, using some unknown formula, rendered the estimate. To us, the buffaloberry is sweet, but has a repulsive aftertaste.

If the berry crop is on, you should make lots of noise while hiking this trail. Bears will often be preoccupied with feeding, and may not hear you approach. If a bear perceives you as a threat to its food source, it might become aggressive. Scats containing red berries, tracks in muddy areas, and damage to the shrubs will warn you that a bear is about.

## Trailhead to Lower Fryatt Campground

The hike begins with an easy fireroad walk along the west bank of the Athabasca River, through a fire succession forest of lodgepole pine. The resin-sealed cones of the lodgepole generally require the heat of a forest fire to open. Thus, a mass seeding of lodgepole pines takes place after a fire, producing even-aged stands of trees. The fire that helped create most of these trees took place in 1889, when much of the Athabasca Valley in what is now Jasper National Park burned.

Wetlands surround the trail. These sloughs were formerly kettle lakes, created by melting blocks of ice at the end of the Wisconsin Glaciation. The lakes have filled with sediments that now support aquatic vegetation — making good habitat for moose. At km 2.0 the trail crosses the braided outlet stream from the Geraldine Lakes. This stream is prone to flash-flooding. Over millennia, the stream has built a large alluvial fan from the shales it has carried down the mountainside. Trail crews have difficulty maintaining the bridges. The adjacent trail often becomes a watercourse. You may have to rock-hop the stream and pick your way for a short distance. Trembling aspen and cottonwood poplar trees grow here.

The pleasant stroll through the forest continues. At km 7.2, the trail draws alongside the Athabasca River, with the Icefields Parkway just 150 m away on the opposite bank. The sediment-choked waters are a formidable barrier to travel. In the 1800s, the voyageurs of the fur trade called their route across Athabasca Pass, *la grande traverse* — "the great crossing" — in reference to the difficult ford of this river. From the riverbank, you can well imagine the harrowing prospect of having to cross this torrent on foot or in a makeshift raft.

At km 8.0 the trail veers away from the river and climbs over a knoll covered in a dog-hair forest of lodgepole pine. The trail emerges from the forest above the confluence of Lick Creek and the Athabasca River, atop a bank of glacial till. Till is a thick blanket of sediment and rubble left behind by glaciers. Till banks in this part of the Athabasca

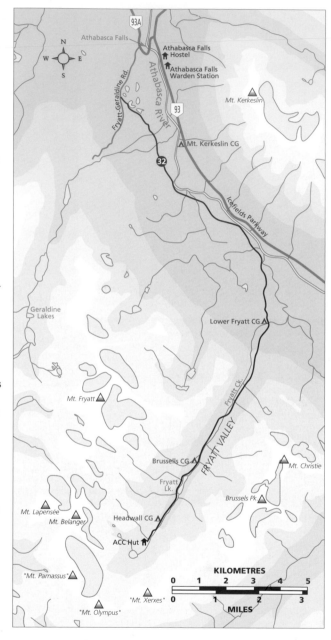

Valley are rich in sulphur-bearing minerals. Deer, elk, and mountain goats congregate here to lick at the sediments, thereby obtaining a natural dietary supplement. The minerals are especially important to mountain goats during late spring, when they shed their winter coats. You may see goat wool clinging to shrubs and tree bark, and tracks and pellet-like droppings on the trail nearby.

The tremendous breadth of the Athabasca Valley fills the view south. It is hard to imagine that this valley was filled with glacial ice a kilometre thick during the Great Glaciation. Although the eastern slope of the valley is now home to the Icefields Parkway, the western slope — travelled by this trail — is still unspoiled. We watched a pair of golden eagles wheel overhead — their graceful flights a perfect symbol of the wilderness nature of this valley.

Lower Fryatt campground is at km 11.6. This stopping place is on an alluvial fan beside the considerable torrent of Fryatt Creek. It is likely to be chilly here at night, as cold air will drain along Fryatt Creek from the valley above. This is the end of the mountain bike trail.

## Lower Fryatt Campground to Upper Fryatt Valley

Cross the creek on a good bridge, and prepare for the climb ahead. The forest becomes more subalpine in character as you ascend the shaded slope toward the mouth of the Fryatt Valley. The entrance to the valley is guarded by a quartzite spire to the north. The layers of rock on this outlying peak of Mt. Fryatt dip steeply to the southwest, indicating that they are part of the western arm of an anticline. The Athabasca Valley has been eroded downward through this massive, arch-shaped fold. There are many streams to hop at the valley mouth. Two of these are silty. They

### From Icefield to Ocean

*Athabasca River*

**From its sources** on the northern edge of Columbia Icefield, the Athabasca River flows 1230 km to Lake Athabasca in northeastern Alberta. Its waters eventually reach the Arctic Ocean via the Mackenzie river system. *Athabasca* is Cree for "place where there are reeds," referring to the delta at the river's mouth. The name was one of the earlier to be used by Europeans in the Rockies, possibly in 1790. The 168 km section of the Athabasca River within Jasper National Park was designated a Canadian Heritage River in 1989.

### Left Hanging

*The west flank of the Athabasca River is rent by a series of hanging valleys. Brussells Peak rises above Fryatt Valley in this view from the Icefields Parkway.*

**Fryatt Valley** is a textbook example of a hanging valley. During the Wisconsin Glaciation, glaciers in tributary valleys did not erode as deeply as the ancestral Athabasca Glacier eroded the Athabasca Valley. As a result, when the glacial ice receded, the tributary valleys were left hanging above the floor of the Athabasca Valley. If you look at the topographic map, you will see this graphically depicted. The contours on the southwestern slope of the Athabasca Valley — either side of Fryatt Creek — describe a uniform cliff, more than 15 km in length. Through this cliff, Fryatt Creek and the streams that drain other valleys to the north and south, plunge toward the Athabasca Valley.

drain a glacially fed lake on the north slope of Mt. Christie.

The grade eases, and the trail soon crosses to the northwest bank of Fryatt Creek on an imaginatively installed log bridge. From here you obtain your first, tantalizing views of the upper Fryatt Valley. Although the surrounding mountainsides rise steeply, the valley floor here feels open after travel through the confined forest below. The trail is rocky and vague in places. Rock-hop and follow cairns.

I recommend Brussels campground if you want to day-hike to the upper Fryatt Valley. Although Headwall campground is closer to the main attractions on this hike, it is a poor camping place and best avoided.

The alluvial fan beyond Brussels campground is a product of debris flows and meltwater surges from the tributary valley to the north. The fan almost completely fills the valley floor, forcing Fryatt Creek to the south. The constriction creates a natural dam that impounds the waters of Fryatt Lake. You obtain your first view of this charming body of water as the trail climbs over the fan. The waterfall that drains the upper valley graces the headwall beyond. The glaciated summits are the "Three Blind Mice" (2720 m) to the south (left), and "Mt. Xerxes" (ZURK-seas) (2970 m). Brussels Peak appears formidable viewed from here. At the base of its southwest ridge you can see a series of pinnacles that resembles a miniature Stonehenge.

Rock-hop streams on the alluvial fan, and descend to Fryatt Lake. Follow a rough track along the northwest shore to Headwall campground. Headwall is a graphic example of where *not* to place a campground in the Rockies. It is among cow parsnip at the base of a large avalanche slope, a possible haven for grizzly bears. Tent sites are close to the trail. The campground is shaded in the evening and early morning. Brrrr!

Beyond the campground, you climb steeply to the base of the 200 m high headwall that separates the upper and lower valleys. This headwall is one of the more unpleasant sections of "trail" in the Rockies. Outrageously steep and poorly defined in places, the trail is more a scramble than a hike. But the grunt is over in less than a kilometre. From the top of the climb, your are rewarded with magnificent views northeast over Fryatt Valley. But you will soon want to turn your back on them. The views are even better to the southwest.

## Upper Fryatt Valley

From the top of the headwall, the raw beauty of

*Now you see it, now you don't.*
*Fryatt Creek plunges underground in the upper valley.*

the Rockies is revealed with splendour and grace in the upper Fryatt Valley. Fryatt Creek collects in a delightful pool — known as "The Roman Bath" — above the headwall. Fringed with meadow and subalpine forest, this pool creates an idyllic foreground for the exquisite arrangement of glaciated mountains beyond. Switching themes from Roman to Persian to Greek to voyageur, the mountains are, from south to north: "Mt. Xerxes" (2970 m), named for the ruthless Persian king of

## Boats, Bolts, and Pitons

**The names of the** mountains that flank the Fryatt Valley have interesting histories. Mt. Christie (3103 m) was named in 1859 by James Hector of the Palliser Expedition, for William Christie, who was then in charge of Fort Edmonton. Christie assisted Hector during the winter of 1858–59, when, unbelievably, Hector set out for Athabasca Pass. Mt. Fryatt (3361 m) was named by the Interprovincial Boundary Commission in 1920 for Charles Fryatt, captain of *The Brussels*, a Belgian merchant vessel that ran interference in the English Channel during WWI. Fryatt was captured by the Germans and executed. The striking, turreted form of Brussels Peak (3161 m) honours Fryatt's ship. This summit is one of the more challenging climbs in the Rockies, and was among the last major peaks close to a highway to fall to climbers. The controversial first ascent took place in 1948, aided by the placing of pitons and bolts. Many mountaineers of the day considered such tactics to be "cheating." Three decades later, the use of such climbing aids was commonplace. Today, the climbing elite again frowns on using bolts and pitons for the route up, but they are approved when used for anchoring rappels on the way down.

*The Ramparts rise in a fortress-like wall in this view from the outlet of Amethyst Lakes.*

486–465 BC; "Mt. Olympus" (2940 m), named for the mythical dwelling place of the Greek gods; "Mt. Parnassus" (2840 m), named for a Greek mountain of the same name; and Mt. Belanger (bell-ON-zjay) (3120 m), named for André Belanger, a fur trader who crossed Athabasca Pass in 1814, and who subsequently drowned in the Athabasca River just east of the Rockies.

The Alpine Club of Canada's Sydney Vallance Hut, built in 1970, is located nearby. Follow the trail southwest from the hut to the first tributary stream. Keep straight ahead, hop the stream and cross a wet meadow to cliffs where cairns define the route.

The limestone bedrock of the upper valley exhibits remarkable karst features. The first example was the pool above the headwall. It drains underground into the waterfall. Now you will see where Fryatt Creek disappears into, and emerges from, various underground channels. The final act in the scenic drama of the Fryatt Valley is revealed when the trail winds through a boulder garden and descends to the shore of an unnamed lake at the foot of extensive moraines below "Mt. Olympus." This is the epitome of cliff, tarn, meadow, and glacier that, for so many hikers, characterizes the Canadian Rockies.

The upper Fryatt Valley offers tremendous opportunities for wandering and exploration. If you choose to travel off-trail, please spread out to avoid repetitive trampling of the fragile upper subalpine vegetation. Do not venture onto glacial ice unless you are experienced and properly equipped for glacier travel.

# 33. Tonquin Valley

| Route | | |
|---|---|---|
| **Overnight, 3–5 days** | | |
| **Route** | **Elevation (m)** | **Distance (km)** |
| Astoria trailhead | 1738 | 0 |
| Astoria CG | 1692 | 6.8 |
| Chrome Lake jct | 1695 | 8.2 |
| Switchback CG jct | 2100 | 13.8 |
| Switchback CG | 2100 | +0.2 |
| Surprise Point jct | 1979 | 16.8 |
| Clitheroe CG | 1980 | +0.1 |
| Surprise Point CG | 1900 | +2.2 |
| Amethyst Lakes CG | 1982 | 20.2 |
| Moat Lake jct | 1985 | 22.7 |
| Maccarib CG | 1997 | 23.6 |
| Maccarib Pass | 2210 | 31.1 |
| Portal Creek CG | 1980 | 33.5 |
| Portal trailhead | 1480 | 43.7 |

**Maps**
NTS: 83 D/9 and 83 D/16
Gem Trek: Jasper and Maligne Lake

The prize vista of the Tonquin Valley is the lofty, unbroken precipice of The Ramparts that towers above the Amethyst Lakes. It's a postcard view, known around the world. Despite the scenic attraction, some will find the Tonquin overrun with hikers, horses, and mosquitoes. There is no question that solitude is hard to find. The

## Trailhead

**Follow the** Icefields Parkway 6.7 km south from Jasper to Highway 93A. Turn right and follow Highway 93A south for 5.2 km. Turn right onto the Mt. Edith Cavell Road, and follow this 12 km to the Tonquin Valley trailhead parking lot, opposite the youth hostel. Large recreational vehicles and trailers are not allowed on the Mt. Edith Cavell Road. Use the trailer drop-off. A shuttle service is available from Jasper (fee charged).

backpacking quota is often filled, and two horse outfitters' lodges bring two dozen more people into the area daily, along with horse flies. Day-rides take place near the Amethyst Lakes, where you may encounter strings of 15 to 20 horses and riders.

The Tonquin Valley receives twice as much precipitation as Jasper townsite. The wet meadows near the lakes breed mosquito swarms as thick as anywhere in the Rockies. Although Parks Canada has spent a great deal of money rebuilding portions of trail to sustain the impacts of horse use, there remain sections that make for poor hiking during spring runoff and summer rains. Yes, the Tonquin Valley is a beautiful place. But if you want your experience to be blissful rather than baneful, avoid this outing during early season and during spells of poor weather. Keep

## Chrome Lake Approach

**Unless you plan** to go no farther than Surprise Point campground, continue straight ahead at the Chrome Lake junction. The approach to Chrome Lake from this junction is on a poor trail, but it will save you 2.1 km and some climbing if you continue beyond the lake to reach Surprise Point campground. Chrome Lake is 6.5 km along the trail. The Eremite Valley junction is 300 m farther. Turn north (right) to climb to Surprise Point campground in 1.9 km. If you use this option and continue with the remainder of the Tonquin loop, you increase the total distance to 46.0 km.

## Variations

- Hike the route in reverse
- Camp at Clitheroe (16.9 km) or Surprise Point (19.0 km), and explore
- Day-hike from Portal trailhead to Maccarib Pass, 25.2 km return

alert for the duration of this hike. Bear warnings are often posted for the Astoria, Portal, and Eremite valleys. Jasper has two known instances of human deaths caused by grizzly bears; both took place on these trails.

### Trailhead to Surprise Point Junction

The road-width trail descends to the outlet of Cavell Lake. From the bridge, you have an inspiring view south to Mt. Edith Cavell (3363 m), the highest mountain in this area. The mountain was named by surveyor A.O. Wheeler to commemorate an English nurse, Edith Cavell. Remaining in Brussels after it fell to the Germans in WWI, she was executed in 1915 for allegedly assisting the escape of prisoners of war.

Keep right at the junction across the bridge. The next 4.7 km are a novelty for the beginning of a hike. The trail descends gradually over this distance, crossing Verdant Creek on the way. The mature forest at trailside consists of Engelmann spruce and whitebark pine, with an understory dominated by buffaloberry. This shrub's red and amber berries are a favourite food of black bears and grizzly bears. You may see bear scats and tracks along the trail. Throne Mountain (3120 m) is the prominent peak to the west. A deep glacial cirque has been eroded between the two northeast-trending ridges, creating the mountain's "arm rests."

Cross the Astoria River on a bridge and follow the north bank 1.8 km to Astoria campground. The fruits of crowberry, grouseberry, bearberry, and bunchberry (dwarf dogwood) colour the undergrowth nearby in late summer. Because horses frequent the Tonquin loop, you should treat water from all sources before consumption. Be sure to take your water upstream from the trail at this campground, to minimize the chance of contamination by horse dung and urine.

## A Mountain Fortress

**The Ramparts** are a precipice of Gog Formation quartzite — 900 m high in places — that extends in an arc for 14 km along the Continental Divide. Seven of The Ramparts' named summits exceed 3050 m. The surveyors of the Interprovincial Boundary Survey were inspired by the fortress-like appearance of the mountain wall, and so coined the names: Parapet, Dungeon, Redoubt, Drawbridge, Bastion, Turret, and Barbican. Moat Lake, at the foot of the northern Ramparts, completes the motif.

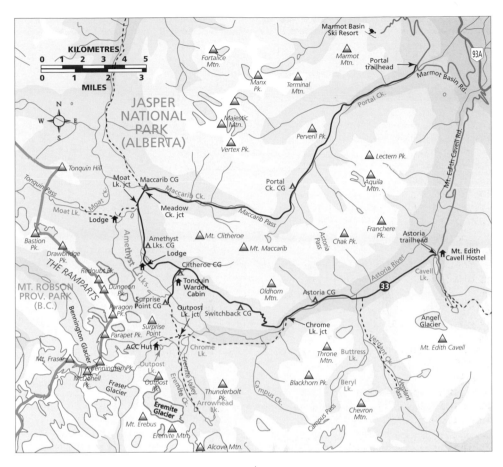

Beyond the Chrome Lake junction the trail is poor and wet beneath the quartzite rockslide on Oldhorn Mountain (2988 m). On the west side of this slide, the trail switchbacks upward to gain entry to the Tonquin Valley. By the early 1980s, the trail here was so ravaged by horse use that extensive rehabilitation was necessary. Heavy machinery was flown in, and sections of trail were crowned and ditched to improve drainage. Soil blanket was installed beneath the tread to prevent deep mud holes from re-developing. Much of the tread surface is gravel, transported here by helicopter. Although the expensive finished product looks out of place in the subalpine meadows, it has — although it's hard to believe on some days — significantly reduced the muck and mire underfoot.

The trail levels near the Switchback campground junction, from where you obtain your first, tantalizing view of The Ramparts and Amethyst Lakes. Continuing northwest, the trail makes a treeline traverse through delightful meadowland on the slopes beneath Oldhorn Mountain. The views continue to improve, and now include Chrome Lake to the south, and Moat Lake to the northwest. After a short descent, the trail reaches the Surprise Point junction. You have three options for camping nearby. The Amethyst Lake campground is 3.3 km north (right); Surprise Point campground is 2.2 km southwest (left); and Clitheroe campground is 100 m west (left).

*Clitheroe* is an Old English name, with Germanic origins and various translations — "hill by the water," "song thrush hill," and "hill of loose stones." Any of them fits.

## Surprise Point Junction to Surprise Point

The trail to Surprise Point campground passes through Clitheroe campground and soon deteriorates into a horse-churned quagmire. The character of the trail improves as it angles south into a large meadow that contains the Tonquin warden cabin. In front of the cabin, turn west (right) into

## Chrome Lake/Outpost Lake/Eremite Valley, 20.8 km return from Surprise Point CG

If you don't mind rough trails, you can combine these three destinations into an energetic and rewarding day-hike from either Surprise Point or Clitheroe campgrounds.

### Chrome Lake

Head south on a rooted, rocky and muddy trail, that descends 2.1 km to a junction northwest of Chrome Lake. A 200 m sidetrip to the east (left) takes you to the swampy shore of the lake. Look for bog orchids and spotted frogs. The upper Eremite Valley, your ultimate destination on this day-hike, is to the south. Backtrack to the junction, and head west on the Outpost Lake trail for 400 m to another junction. Straight ahead (south) is the Eremite Valley.

*The rough track to the Eremite Valley ends at a series of Little Ice Age moraines, with stunning views of rugged, glaciated peaks.*

### Outpost Lake

Turn west (right) if you would like to make the 2.4 km return sidetrip to secluded Outpost Lake. The trail crosses Penstock Creek and climbs steeply onto a knoll of rockslide debris and the forested lakeshore. The Alpine Club of Canada's Wates-Gibson hut is nearby. The building is named for Cyril Wates and Rex Gibson, two mountaineers who were active in this area from the 1920s to the 1940s. The present hut is the third structure in this vicinity; it dates to 1967. You'll find the foundation and chimney of its predecessor, constructed in 1947, along the east shore of the lake.

Outpost Lake contains the only non-silty drinking water on this hike. There are many mountaineer's paths in this area. One leads to a sedge meadow south of Surprise Peak. The meadow is frequented by northern bog lemmings, one of the more uncommon mammals in Jasper National Park. This rodent prefers damp habitats in the upper subalpine ecoregion. Backtrack to the Outpost Lake junction.

### Eremite Valley

From the junction at Chrome Lake, the Eremite Valley trail follows Penstock Creek south. Mt. Bennington (3265 m) is the prominent peak to the west, named for Bennington, Vermont, the birthplace of fur trader and explorer, Simon Fraser. Meltwater from glaciers on the north side of the peak is a principal source of the 1280 km Fraser River.

The origin of Penstock Creek's unusual name is soon revealed. Just north of its junction with Eremite Creek, Penstock Creek flows underground through a cave — a natural penstock. Cross the creek easily on the natural bridge that results. In 2002, there was a bridge over Eremite Creek, just beyond. After this crossing, do not follow the well-beaten trail toward Chrome Lake. Pick up a faint trail heading south. It is on the west side of the bedrock ridge that separates Eremite Creek from Chrome Lake.

After a kilometre of hiking through willows, the trail ascends slightly into a flower-filled glade, before descending again to the creek. This area has been the site of five Alpine Club of Canada mountaineering camps since 1941. Camping and fires are no longer allowed here, nor anywhere else in the Eremite Valley. Beyond, the trail climbs steeply into upper subalpine forest. Eremite Glacier occupies a deep cirque to the west. Fine waterfalls cascade over the ice-worn cliffs beneath it. Where the trail drops into a small draw, take the east (left) branch, and resume the climb over rockslide debris and through a shintangle of kruppelholz fir.

### Upper Eremite Valley

The upper valley is packed with spectacular scenery. A chaos of moraines marks the maximum extent of various glaciers during the Little Ice Age. Arrowhead Lake is dammed by the curving east lateral moraine of Eremite Glacier. The lake is not a typical glacial tarn, but a murky, shallow flat where sediment-choked meltwater collects.

About 4.5 km south of the Outpost Lake junction, the Eremite trail disappears in a meadow bisected by meltwater streams. Boulder-hop the streams, and scramble onto the moraines to the south for a marvelous view of the peaks, glaciers, and tarns at the head of the valley. An *eremite* is a religious recluse, or hermit. The name was applied to the 2910 m mountain west of the valley in 1916, by surveyor M.P. Bridgland. He considered the mountain to be "a solitary peak."

*Sunset from Surprise Point Campground*

bugs. The only appealing water source is Lower Amethyst Lake, more than 200 m distant. (Bring a water billy.) Surprise Point (2378 m), southwest of the campground, was named because a party from the Interprovincial Boundary Survey was surprised at how long it took them to reach its lowly summit.

The sedges in the wet meadows bordering the Amethyst Lakes are important summer food for mountain caribou. Caribou are cold-adapted animals. During the summer, they escape the heat by congregating on perennial snow patches in nearby side valleys.

forest, and follow signs for Surprise Point.

The trail emerges from the forest into an extensive wet meadow on the east shore of Lower Amethyst Lake. Look for fish and waterfowl in the larger stream channels. Follow metal markers across a cotton-grass bog to the bridged outlet of the lower lake. This vantage offers one of the finer prospects of The Ramparts. Surprise Point campground is 400 m beyond, set on a rocky knoll surrounded by wetland.

The campground provides a panoramic view of the Tonquin Valley and the upper Astoria Valley. From here, Mt. Edith Cavell is almost unrecognizable — a rocky chisel scraping the sky. Unfortunately, the campground is often teeming with

## Surprise Point Junction to Maccarib Creek Campground

The Tonquin loop continues north from the Surprise Point junction on a rocky trail that descends toward the peninsula that separates the two Amethyst Lakes. The buildings in view are part of a horse outfitter's lodge. After it gains the east shore of Upper Amethyst Lake, the trail swings north alongside a marsh to the Amethyst Lake campground. Across the lake, you can see six glaciers on The Ramparts. Four of these glaciers created horseshoe-shaped terminal moraines when they advanced during the Little Ice Age.

If you choose to camp here, be aware that outfitters graze their horses nightly along the east and north shores of Upper Amethyst Lake. This puts the horses in competition with the caribou.

A braided trail leads north from the campground. This area is underlaid by bouldery glacial till, which makes for rough walking. The view of the northwestern arc of The Ramparts from this area was featured in A.Y. Jackson's 1924 painting,

---

### The Tonquin — A Blast from the Past

**Fort Astoria** was an outpost established in 1811 near the mouth of the Columbia River, by fur trade magnate, John Jacob Astor. *The Tonquin* was one of his ocean-going fur trade vessels. How did these names navigate upstream to the Rockies? The connection is tenuous. The Athabasca Pass fur trade route crossed the Rockies 30 km south of the Tonquin Valley. Some of Astor's employees followed the route in 1813. What is more curious about these names here is that Tonquin Creek does not flow in the Tonquin Valley, nor into any Alberta river. The creek is across the Continental Divide, in BC.

Astor sold *The Tonquin* to the Hudson's Bay Company. While the vessel was anchored in Clayoquot (KLAH-kwit) Sound off the west coast of Vancouver Island, Natives boarded and killed most of the crew. Some of the survivors blew-up the ship, killing all who remained on board.

---

### Moat Lake, 3.5 km

**The Moat Lake** junction is 2.5 km north of Amethyst Lake campground. Although the sidetrip to the lake is scenic, the developed trail has been severely damaged by horse traffic. The final 1.5 km involves a poorly defined track across a boulder meadow covered in willows. However, the rewards are a close-up view of the northern Ramparts, and a pleasing prospect of Mt. Clitheroe and Majestic Hill if you return in the light of late afternoon.

*The Rampart*s. Jackson was a member of The Group of Seven — artists who specialized in Canadian landscapes. The highest peak of The Ramparts, Mt. Geikie (GEEK-ee) (3270 m), is entirely in BC. It was named for Scottish geologist, Sir Archibald Geikie.

You'd never guess it, but on this section of trail, you cross a watershed divide. The Amethyst Lakes drain southwest into the Astoria River. To the north of here, waters flow north into Meadow Creek. That's right; the Amethyst Lakes occupy a mountain pass.

The Tonquin loop climbs away from the northeast shore of Upper Amethyst Lake through open spruce forest, and then descends to Maccarib (mah-KAH-rib) Creek. Cross the bridge and turn east (right) at the Meadow Creek junction. The sidetrail to Maccarib Creek campground is 50 m farther.

Maccarib campground is shared by hikers and non-commercial horse parties. Situated on a bench above the north bank of Maccarib Creek, it offers exceptional views west to The Ramparts, and east to Maccarib Pass. *Maccarib* is Quinnipiac for "caribou." Caribou frequent the area between the campground and Maccarib Pass.

## Maccarib Campground to Portal Trailhead

The trail to Maccarib Pass ascends gradually through upper subalpine wet meadows, crossing bridges over Maccarib Creek and its tributaries numerous times. Most of the trail has been

*Maccarib Pass is a good place to see caribou.*

rehabilitated. Gravel cap has been laid over soil blanket, and the edges have been reinforced with timber, creating a finished product called "turnpiking." Mt. Clitheroe (2747 m) forms the southern slope of the valley. It features a sizable rock glacier, comprised of quartzite boulders.

Groundsel and fireweed grow at trailside on the final climb to Maccarib Pass. The tundra of the pass stretches almost 2 km over the divide between Maccarib Creek and Portal Creek. Low-lying areas feature earth hummocks. These earth mounds were created by repeated freezing and thawing of the soil, when permafrost underlaid the area. The hummocks are vegetated with western anemone, woolly everlasting, and mountain heather. Snow willow, arctic willow, white mountain avens, and moss campion grow in the

## Goodair's Final Resting Place

**The grave of** park warden, Percy Goodair, is just north of Maccarib campground. Goodair was district warden in the Tonquin Valley in the 1920s, and worked from a cabin located here. On September 12, 1929, he met his end outside the cabin door. When his body was recovered, it was evident that it had been mauled and scavenged by a grizzly bear.

Mountaineer James Monroe Thorington characterized Goodair in 1925. "A quiet, pleasant man, he had had the usual interesting career of those whom one runs across in the far places. Studying medicine

*Goodair's grave*

in London, he enlisted and went to Africa during the Boer War, remaining afterward in the South African diamond fields, wandering as a prospector to strange corners of the earth, and at last finding a life in the Canadian wilderness that pleased and held him. We could quite understand it, and not without a touch of envy."

A mountain west of The Ramparts commemorates Goodair. Another mountain northeast of Lake Louise was named for him in 1986, when six national park wardens who had died in the line of duty were commemorated in the Warden Range.

hollows between them. White-tailed ptarmigan and Columbian ground squirrels are two of the creatures you may see on the pass. And keep a sharp lookout for grizzly bears. You can see Mt. Edith Cavell again to the southwest over Astoria Pass.

From Maccarib Pass, the trail switchbacks down to Portal Creek through rolling subalpine meadows. You reach the Portal Creek campground in 2.4 km. The mountains surrounding the valley are composed mostly of reddish, Gog Formation quartzite. In 1916, surveyor M.P. Bridgland named two mountains along the creek for golden eagles he saw in the vicinity — Chak Peak (2798 m) and Aquila Mountain (2880 m). *Chak* is Stoney for eagle, and *Aquila* is Latin. The slopes of Chak Peak contain a large rock glacier. Farther down the valley you might pick out Lectern Peak (2774 m), named for the rostrum of rock at its summit. On the horizon, far to the northeast, you can see the gray limestone peaks of the Colin Range, beyond Jasper.

Just over halfway down the valley, the trail ascends onto a rocky sideslope and contours across the flank of Peveril Peak, before descending steeply through lodgepole pine forest to cross the westerly tributary of Portal Creek. The remaining 3.7 km continues the steady descent, passing beside two outcrops of glacial till. Numerous animal trails and tracks indicate that these outcrops are used by goats and deer as mineral licks. From the second outcrop, you have a fine view west along Portal Creek to Peveril Peak (2686 m). This mountain's unusual name was in the title of a novel written by Sir Walter Scott. The last interesting feature on the Tonquin loop is a mass of downed trees to the south of the trail. The weathered trees appear to be ancient avalanche debris from the opposite side of the valley. This slope has since revegetated with mature forest, indicating that the avalanche probably took place at least 200 years ago.

Cross the bridge to the south bank of Portal Creek. The Tonquin loop ends a few hundred metres later at a parking lot on the Marmot Basin Road. Turn east (right) to descend this road, 6.5 km to its junction with Highway 93A. At this junction, turn north (left) for Jasper, or south (right) for the Mt. Edith Cavell Road junction. You should prearrange transportation for the conclusion of this hike. Otherwise, avoid arriving at the Marmot Basin road late in the day, unless you enjoy a heel-burning walk on the road.

# 34. Cavell Meadows

## Route

**Day-hike**

| Route | Elevation (m) | Distance (km) |
|---|---|---|
| Trailhead | 1753 | 0 |
| Cavell Meadows jct | 1790 | 0.6 |
| Cavell Meadows summit | 2160 | 3.8 |
| Cavell Meadows jct | 1790 | 7.0 |
| Trailhead | 1753 | 8.0 |

**Maps**
NTS: 83 D/9
Gem Trek: Jasper and Maligne Lake

**Best lighting:** morning

## Trailhead

**Check at the** park information centre regarding trail closures. Follow the Icefields Parkway, 6.7 km south from Jasper to Highway 93A. Turn right and follow Highway 93A south for 5.2 km. Turn right onto the Mt. Edith Cavell Road, and follow this 14 km to the Mt. Edith Cavell parking lot. The Path of the Glacier-Cavell Meadows trailhead is at the southeast corner of the parking lot. Large recreational vehicles and trailers are not allowed on the Mt. Edith Cavell Road. Use the trailer drop-off opposite the beginning of the road. A shuttle service is available from Jasper (fee charged). Avoid this hike during mid-day.

On the rolling alpland of Cavell Meadows, Angel Glacier and the precipitous north face of Mt. Edith Cavell (3363 m) provide the backdrop for a stunning mid-summer display of wildflowers. This outing describes a loop hike beginning on the Cavell Meadows trail and returning via the Path of the Glacier, an interpretive trail that explores the forefield of Cavell Glacier and Angel Glacier. The forefield was covered by glacial ice as recently as 1920. The Cavell Meadows is so popular and hiked so often when snow still lingers, that trail braiding has reached a level that can only be called environmental destruction. Voluntary closures are posted during the snowmelt season. Please abide by any new regulations. At press time, there were plans to rehabilitate the trail. You are exposed to the threat of ice avalanche on the

Path of the Glacier trail. Don't walk around the west shore of Cavell Pond or ascend the moraines beneath Angel Glacier.

## Trailhead to Cavell Meadows

From the parking lot, the trail climbs over a terminal moraine and works its way south through the quartzite rubble of the glacier forefield. This area was covered by ice less than 50 years ago. Life is taking hold. A cottonwood poplar grows from the rocks, right on the trail. At the junction in 600 m, turn east (left). The Cavell Meadows trail climbs steeply over a lateral moraine. This landform, and the terminal moraine you crossed earlier, were created by Cavell Glacier during the Little Ice Age. The coarse, quartz sand underfoot has been eroded from the quartzite boulders. Least chipmunks, golden mantled ground squirrels, and pikas live in the nooks and crannies of this moraine.

At the top of the moraine, there is an abrupt transition to subalpine forest. This is the trimline of Cavell Glacier. A century and a half ago, the ice of the glacier was thick enough to reach this far up the side of the valley, obliterating mature forest. Some trees near trimline show evidence of roots and trunks damaged by the moving glacial ice. You can see where two, lesser moraines nest within the outer moraine. Together, they record three glacial advances of nearly equal magnitude. There should have been two terminal moraines for you to climb over at the trailhead, nested one inside the other, but the older, outer moraine — which dated to 1705 — was destroyed when the parking lot was built in the 1970s.

You hike beside the moraine for 600 m. Dwarf false asphodel, cotton-grass, and red-stemmed saxifrage grow in wet areas. Enjoy the tremendous views of Angel Glacier and Cavell Pond from the nearby crest of the lateral moraine. The ice cliffs are 40 m thick. Angel Glacier formerly merged with Cavell Glacier, however, glacial recession caused it to break contact in the 1940s. After a few decades when it maintained a state of equilibrium, the ice is once again flying up the cliff. Soon, it will be an angel no more. You can see the lichen trimline of Angel Glacier clearly to the north of the hanging body of ice. The lighter-coloured rock was scoured of lichens during the Cavell Advance.

After paralleling the moraine crest for a few hundred metres, the trail heads into forest and resumes its climb. The forest here is an ancient one, dominated by Engelmann spruce and subalpine

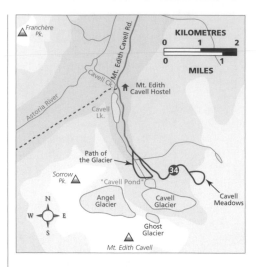

fir. One fir is half a metre thick at the base. In the winter of 1990–91, a snow avalanche from the north face of Mt. Edith Cavell created a wind blast strong enough to topple some of these trees. One tree cut from the debris by chainsaw showed 232 concentric rings, each recording a year's growth. Arnica and valerian comprise most of the ground cover. Red-breasted nuthatches and Clark's

## The Angel of Mercy

*Angel Glacier*

**Today, "Angel"** seems a most appropriate name for the wing-shaped glacier. However, the name was not prompted by the glacier's appearance. Mt. Edith Cavell was named for an English nurse who worked behind the lines with the Belgian Red Cross in WWI. She tended to the injured of both sides, but was executed for allegedly assisting the escape of captive troops. It was popular to refer to nurse Edith Cavell as "the angel of mercy," and this is how the name first became associated with the glacier.

*The Cavell Meadows trail climbs from glacial moraine to rolling alpine meadows, with fine views of Angel Glacier.*

many junctions, this instruction no longer works. Please keep to the most beaten of the many paths. Mountain heather, fleabane, paintbrush, Sitka valerian, western anemone, arnica, alpine veronica, bracted lousewort, groundsel, everlasting and white mountain avens are just a few of the many wildflowers that grow here. Amateur botanists are particularly fond of these meadows for their displays of mountain heather — pink, yellow, and white.

The upper meadows are part of the alpine ecoregion, and are occasionally visited by mountain caribou and grizzly bear. Some hollows here may hold snow until mid-August. The trickle of snowmelt on warm days provides a water source for moisture-loving plants such as leather-leaved saxifrage, white globeflower, and red-stemmed saxifrage. The reddish tinge in snowbanks is watermelon snow, caused by algae with a red pigment. Some of the steep slopes above the meadows contain rock glaciers — accumulations of rock that contain just enough ice to allow the whole mass to creep downhill.

## Cavell Meadows to the Path of the Glacier

From the high point, the trail loops back through the upper meadows to rejoin the approach trail at treeline. Please keep to the beaten path. At the Path of the Glacier junction, turn south (left). The

nutcrackers are common, along with red squirrels.

Two and half kilometres from the trailhead, the forest becomes a patchwork of tree islands, separated by glades of subalpine meadow. Although the elevation here (2060 m) is low for treeline, the chilling effects of glacial ice, the north-facing slope, and the winter-long shade of Mt. Edith Cavell, combine to inhibit the growth of forest. Soon the trail emerges from the trees. When I wrote the description for the first edition, I instructed hikers to keep right at junctions to follow the trail through a carpet of wildflowers to a cairned knoll. Unfortunately, there are now so

## The Little Ice Age — Cool Detective Work

**The most recent advance** of Cavell Glacier took place during the Little Ice Age, which here lasted from AD 1050 to the mid 1840s. Glaciologists have gained much of their understanding of recent glaciation in the Rockies from studies carried out here, and often refer to the Little Ice Age as the "Cavell Advance."

Glaciologists use vegetation near glaciers to help them assign dates to glacial events. They take core samples from mature trees near trimline. By counting the tree rings in the core, and cross-referencing to a master key for the area, they can determine the approximate age of the tree. If the tree is 300 years old, glacial ice has not covered its location for at least 300 years. If a number of trees close to a glacier are sampled, the date and extent of the most recent maximum advance of the ice can be plotted. Trees that grow on moraines formed during the Cavell

Advance, or those known to have been damaged by glacial ice, are particularly useful in this process, which is called dendrochronology.

Rock lichens also provide means for dating glacial events. Map lichen (*Rhizocarpon geographicum*), grows at a rate of 42 mm per century in its first 110 years, and 11.4 mm per century for the subsequent 140 years. These lichens have been growing on boulders in the forefield since the ice withdrew. By measuring the diameter of the lichens, glaciologists can determine how long it has been since the area was covered by ice.

What have glaciologists learned about Cavell Glacier? Between 1888 and 1975, the glacier receded 988 m. The maximum of the Cavell Advance here took place in 1705. This was the greatest advance of Cavell Glacier during the previous 2600 years.

trail descends to Cavell Pond in the cirque at the base of Mt. Edith Cavell. The hollow containing this lake was uncovered by the retreating ice in 1963. Icebergs or "growlers" calve from the glacier toe and are often afloat in the water. The surface of the glacier contains several talus (TAY-luss) cones, piles of rocky avalanche debris, transported from the base of Mt. Edith Cavell's north face by the moving ice.

The trail returns to the parking lot along the principal meltwater stream from the glacier. The rocky soils and cold environment make it difficult for vegetation to become established here. Willows, sedges, mountain fireweed, and a few stunted spruce trees are all that have taken hold. The contrast between the barren forefield and the lush, adjacent forest is striking. Barring another glacial advance, it will be centuries before the forefield supports mature subalpine forest again.

# 35. Maligne Canyon

*The Maligne River flows through the best known limestone canyon in the Rockies.*

## Route

**Day-hike**

| Route | Elevation (m) | Distance (km) |
|---|---|---|
| Sixth Bridge trailhead | 1015 | 0 |
| Fifth Bridge | 1030 | 1.6 |
| Fourth Bridge | 1055 | 2.9 |
| First Bridge | 1140 | 3.5 |
| Upper trailhead | 1145 | 3.7 |

**Maps**
NTS: 83 D/9 and 83 C/13
Gem Trek: Best of Jasper

**Best lighting:** The canyon is best on days with subdued lighting.

## Trailhead

**Follow Highway 16,** 3.7 km east of Jasper to the Maligne Lake Road. Turn east, cross the Athabasca River, and follow the road 2.3 km to the turnoff for Sixth Bridge. Follow this sideroad 1.2 km to the Sixth Bridge picnic area.

Maligne Canyon is one of Jasper's "must see" places. Tour buses discharge hordes of people; they move elbow to elbow in the upper canyon. How, you ask, can this be a "classic" hike?

The canyon's popularity is justly deserved. If you hike the full length, it rates as a stellar natural history walk. When you are storm-bound in Jasper, this is a great outing to make while waiting for the weather to clear in the high country. You share the first 1.3 km with bikes and the first 1.6 km with horses. If you take young children on this hike, hold their hands. Although the trail is fenced in many places, the route is often alongside the swift-flowing river or along the maw of the canyon — places not without hazard.

**Trailhead to Fourth Bridge**
From the parking area, cross the bridge to the northeast bank of the Maligne River. Turn southeast (right). The first 800 m along the riverbank is on a wide, flat, trail through a montane forest of white spruce, lodgepole pine, trembling aspen, and a few Douglas-firs. The fire-scarred trunks of the Douglas-firs testify to their ability to withstand moderate ground fires. Prickly juniper, buffaloberry, wild onion, bearberry, and very tall Scouler's willow make up most of the sparse ground cover. Red squirrels chatter from the trees. Short spur trails lead to pleasing views of the river.

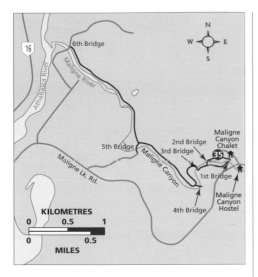

Look for dippers and the old warden office, which is on the opposite bank of the river.

The pleasant preamble done with, you reach the mouth of the canyon. Note the change in the character of the forest. Dampness and chill

## The Invisible River

*An emergence*

**Two rivers flow** through Maligne Canyon. If you were to compare the volume of flow at Sixth Bridge with the volume at First Bridge in mid-summer, you would see that the lower canyon contains eight times as much water as the upper canyon. The emergences of the Maligne karst system pump 24,000 litres per second into the canyon. This underground river may be the largest in the world. The entrances to the karst system — called sinks — are upvalley on the floor of Medicine Lake. It takes 70 hours for the water to travel from there to Maligne Canyon. Other emergences of the underground river feed some of the lakes near Jasper.

prevail; Engelmann spruce, subalpine fir, and lodgepole pine dominate. The trail climbs over a jumble of limestone boulders, from which issues a bit of the mystery and magic of the Maligne Valley. Yes, it's a spring, but it is also an outlet for the underground drainage of Medicine Lake, 17 km southeast. This outlet, called an emergence, is one of more than 20 between here and Fourth Bridge. The emergences gush when Medicine Lake is full; they trickle as the lake level drops.

Horsetails — a favourite springtime food of bears — grow alongside the first emergence. I have seen bear scats and tracks in the sand nearby. White birch also grows here. Please don't peel the bark. At km 1.3 the bike trail veers left. Continue straight ahead. At km 1.6, the trail from Fifth Bridge comes in from the west (right). Angle left, upstream, and turn right at the horse-hiker separation in 50 m.

The trail traverses an exposed till bank that is being colonized by trembling aspen, juniper, and wild rose. Across the river, you can see the sedimentary layers of the bedrock. They dip slightly to the north, but what is more important to the creation of the canyon is that the bedrock on the west side of the river is about 3 m higher than on the east side. This offset is a normal fault — a fracture in the bedrock that occurred after mountain building. The rocks east of the fault dropped down relative to those on the west. A lateral moraine deposited by the ancestral Maligne Glacier diverted the Maligne River onto the fault, where the flowing water readily exploited the weakness. In no time, geologically speaking — less than 10,000 years — Maligne Canyon came into being.

That's one canyon-creation theory. Another proposes that Maligne Canyon is itself the course of an ancient underground stream, exposed to daylight by glacial erosion during the Wisconsin Glaciation.

The trail drops into the damp forest at riverside. This is my favourite part of the canyon. Two of the larger emergences from the Maligne karst system enter beneath an overhang on the opposite bank. Beaten paths lead to the riverbank in places, but the wet, silt-covered rock is certain death if you misplace a step. The canyon winds; the trail makes brief climbs and descents, passing from open slope to confined chasm — a patchwork of micro-habitats. On the opposite bank, a waterfall cascades from the ancestral lateral moraine on the canyon rim, scouring away the soils to reveal a complete exposure of the bedrock. Fourth Bridge takes you across the canyon, but the trail does not continue on that bank.

### Fourth Bridge to Trail's End

The bedrock geology changes above the Fourth Bridge, and the canyon narrows dramatically as a result. Downstream, the canyon is wider, where it is being eroded into relatively weak shales of the Banff Formation. Upstream, the river has a tougher time eroding the more resistant limestone of the Palliser Formation. This limestone is fossil-rich, containing snail-like gastropods, clam-like brachiopods, squid-like cephalopods, crinoids (related to sea-stars), and corals.

*Potholes dot the riverbed above First Bridge. Boulders trapped in swirling eddies drilled these circular depressions into the limestone.*

The Maligne River takes a mighty drop beneath Third Bridge, where the canyon's depth is 10 m and you cross to the opposite bank. Here, the air also changes dramatically. Below the bridge, it's cool and damp where you've been hiking within the canyon. From here on, you climb along the canyon rim, where the air is noticeably warmer. If you've had any solitude on the trail to this point, you probably won't now, as many people hike here from the upper parking lot. Note how the bedrock has been polished smooth in places by the shuffling of millions of feet, some, amazingly, clad in high heels. The large boulders at trailside are glacial erratics, dropped here when the Maligne Valley glacier last receded 12,000 years ago.

### Canyon-Making 101

**So, glacial stream,** you'd like to cut a canyon for yourself. You come charging down the mountainside at a clip, pushing everything out of your way. You are one-quarter of the way there. What's that? Through no fault of your own, you've exposed a crack in the rock. Try flowing there for a while. We'll check on you in a few thousand years.... Look, you're making quite an impression, but don't take all the credit. The bedrock is limestone, and your water is naturally slightly acidic. Acid is the nemesis of limestone, which is rich in calcium. That acid, coupled with your abrasive load of glacial silt, has really put you in the groove. But don't be too smug, your glacier upstream is dwindling. Eight thousand years ago, you were chewing away at this limestone at the clip of 10 cm each year, but I bet you haven't even knocked off a single centimetre in the last decade.

Nooks and crannies on the opposite wall of the canyon are used as nesting places by ravens. Maligne Canyon is also one of three known nesting places in Alberta for black swifts. Look for them on the wing in the evening. These "cigars with wings" are easy to recognize in flight. The canyon is deepest — 55 m — at Second Bridge. It's so deep, it's hard to grasp the scale. Locals know the pocket of ice on the wall below as "The Icebox." Don't cross at Second Bridge, but take time to contrast the forests on either side of the river. A damp, canyon forest of spruce and fir grows on the shaded, south side of the river, whereas a drier forest of lodgepole pine and Douglas-fir grows on the sunny, north side of the river.

Carry on to First Bridge, where the canyon is 38 m deep and the entire river is forced through a 1 m slot. A chockstone spans the canyon just downstream; you get to cross on a bridge. The canyon is shallow from here on, but of interest for its many potholes — circular depressions drilled into the limestone by boulders caught in eddies — a process that required thousands of years. Some of the potholes now lie in abandoned channels. The depressions are gradually filling with soils to become miniature gardens. Alas, the upper canyon is showing the abuses of heavy visitation. Graffiti has appeared on rocks in the river bed, and a fenced area that displays fossils has been walked on so much, the outlines of the fossils have been obliterated.

### Return

I recommend that you walk back down the canyon, as you are certain to see things that you missed on the way up. If nothing else, you get to spend more time in the company of the lower Maligne River, a ribbon of blue-green beauty.

# 36. Opal Hills

## Route

**Day-hike**

| Route | Elevation (m) | Distance (km) |
|---|---|---|
| Trailhead | 1700 | 0 |
| Schäffer Viewpoint jct | 1695 | 0.2 |
| Loop trail jct | 1900 | 1.6 |
| Maligne Lake viewpoint | 2150 | 2.6 |
| Summit of meadows | 2160 | 3.2 |
| Loop trail jct | 1900 | 6.6 |
| Trailhead | 1700 | 8.2 |

**Maps**
NTS: 83 C/112 and 83 C/13
Gem Trek: Jasper and Maligne Lake

## Trailhead

**Follow Highway 16,** 3.7 km east from Jasper to the Maligne Lake Road. Turn east (right). Follow the Maligne Lake Road 44 km to parking lots on the east side of the lake. The trailhead is at the northeast corner of the uppermost parking lot.

The Opal Hills are a delightful island of green set amidst the gray limestone mountains that flank the east side of the Maligne Valley. This steep loop hike features interesting geology and, with a little effort, an exceptional view of Maligne Lake.

*Opal Peak from Opal Hills*

### Trailhead to Opal Meadows

From the trailhead, descend through lodgepole pine forest into a clearing known as the "hummock and hollow meadow." Keep left at the junction 200 m from the parking lot. You can see the Opal Hills through the treetops, but you'll soon have your head down as you begin a steep climb on a poorly conceived and heavily eroded trail. Persevere; the views ahead are worth the effort.

The loop junction is at km 1.6. The route described here takes the right-hand branch. The remainder of the climb is at times withering —

## Hummocks, Hollows, Rockslides and Moose

*Moose*

**In the Rockies,** "hummock and hollow" landscapes — such as the meadow near the trailhead — usually resulted from the melting of detached blocks of rubble-covered glacial ice at the end of the Wisconsin Glaciation. However, the mounds in this meadow are the remains of frost-shattered boulders of rockslide debris. The hollows are now thought to be bedrock karst features. The Maligne Valley is home to the second largest measured rockslide in the Rockies. Depressions in the debris have filled with water, creating many of the lakes and ponds in the area. The wet shrub thickets that develop nearby are excellent moose habitat. The Maligne Valley supports one of the few remaining concentrations of moose in the Rockies. Elsewhere, habitat loss caused forest fire suppression, and collisions with vehicles have led to a region-wide decline in moose.

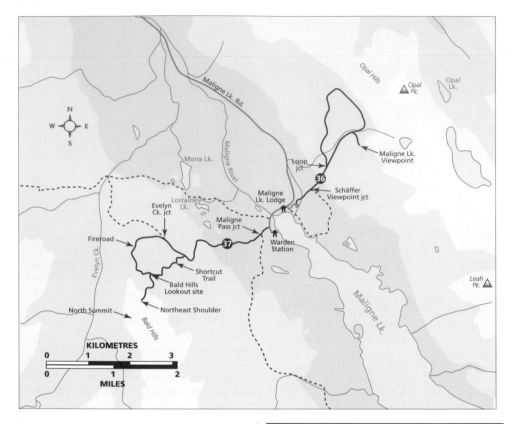

a 25° grade in places — but you hike downhill later on a trail less steep, which is consequently safer and easier on your knees.

Beyond the junction, the lodgepole pines give way to a mature forest of Engelmann spruce and subalpine fir. The trail parallels a shale ravine during the final climb to the meadows that

## Alpine Lousewort

**The Opal Hills** feature an inordinate number of blooms of alpine lousewort. You have to get nose to meadow to appreciate these tiny (5–15 cm tall), pinkish-purple beauties. The leaves are fern-like and, together with the stem, are covered in tiny filaments that help insulate the plant from the wind. There are nine lousewort species in the Canadian Rockies, including two that are more familiar — bracted lousewort and elephant's head. The name, "lousewort," comes from the myth that domestic animals that ate the plants of this genus would become infested with lice. Not so, but anything that eats large quantities of these plants is likely to become very sick, as they are poisonous.

## A Made-over Mountain

**Where are those** drab gray limestones, so typical of the Queen Elizabeth Ranges on the east side of the Maligne Valley? Has Opal Peak had a facelift? No, it was more like a face-drop. The Palliser and Rundle formation limestones, along with the Gog Formation quartzite that was beneath them, now rest on the floor of the Maligne Valley. All that rock went there in one or more colossal landslides, sometime after the Wisconsin Glaciation, following the retreat of the ancestral Maligne Valley glacier, some 10,000 years ago. The volume of the landslides is estimated at 498 million cubic metres, making it the second largest landslide complex yet identified in the Rockies. Although it isn't a gardener's first choice, the Sulphur Mountain Formation siltstone exposed by the landslide offers — after the weathering of millennia — much better soil than the limestones. Thus, green meadows contrast beautifully with the reddish-brown siltstone. Add the white snowbanks in the gullies, and you can see why Mary Schäffer coined the name, Opal Hills.

*Maligne Lake from Opal Hills viewpoint*

track climbs south onto a knoll. By contouring farther south, you are rewarded with a panoramic view of Maligne Lake, more than 400 m below. Maligne Lake is by far the largest of Jasper's 778 mapped lakes and ponds, and is the largest natural lake in the Rockies — 22 km long and 96 m deep, with an area of 2066 ha. It is fed by meltwaters from the 25 km² Brazeau Icefield, and by many other glaciers.

The loop trail keeps left at the viewpoint junction, crosses the shale ravine, and soon branches north into the meadows. With its abundance of upper subalpine

surround the Opal Hills. Looking west from the meadows, you have a fine view of the Maligne Valley. The Opal Hills are hummocks of landslide material from Opal Peak (2789 m). You won't find opals. Mary Schäffer named the hills for their colours — reddish rock and green tundra, striped with snow. But you will find gems of a different sort in the meadows — exquisite wildflower displays.

From the first junction in the meadows, a faint

and alpine wildflowers, and kruppelholz tree islands, the shallow, meadowed vale between the Opal Hills and Opal Peak is a delight. Bears like it, too, so keep alert.

## Return

At the north end of the meadow, the trail curves west and then south, re-entering the forest to commence the sideslope descent to the loop junction. Use caution on the steep grade to the parking lot, especially if the trail is wet.

## Mountain Woman

**Mary Schäffer** was a Quaker from Philadelphia who made her first visit to the Rockies in 1889. After a few summers of adjustment, she took to the backwoods life with passion and ease, and endeared herself to Stoney Natives, who called her *Yahe-Weha* —"mountain woman."

Following her husband's death in 1903, Schäffer made annual pilgrimages to the Rockies. Her initial focus was to collect botanical samples for a wildflower guide, which

*Mary Schäffer*

she was to illustrate. With the necessary collecting completed in 1905, adventure became the motivation. She journeyed to Wilcox Pass in 1906, and in 1907 made the first attempt to find a large lake

known to the Stoneys as *Chaba Imne*, which means "Beaver Lake." Using a crude map drawn by Stoney chieftain Sampson Beaver, Schäffer reached the lake from the south on her second attempt, in 1908. Her party built a raft, *The Chaba*, and spent three days mapping and exploring the lake, and naming many features. She returned in 1911, this time approaching from the recently constructed Grand Trunk Pacific Railway at Jasper. The accounts of her journeys, published in magazines and journals, made her a celebrity. Her book of 1911, *Old Indian Trails of the Canadian Rockies*, has been republished as *A Hunter of Peace*, and still makes for enchanting reading.

# 37. Bald Hills

## Route

Day-hike

| Route | Elevation (m) | Distance (km) |
|---|---|---|
| Trailhead | 1697 | 0 |
| Maligne Pass jct | 1710 | 0.3 |
| Shortcut trail jct | 1940 | 2.5 |
| Evelyn Creek jct | 1960 | 3.2 |
| Lookout site | 2170 | 5.2 |
| End of fireroad | 2180 | 5.7 |
| Northeast shoulder | 2280 | 6.2 |
| North summit | 2320 | 7.1 |

**Maps**
NTS: 83 C/12
Gem Trek: Jasper and Maligne Lake
**See map on p.154**

*Meadows in the Bald Hills feature astounding displays of white mountain heather.*

## Trailhead

**Follow Highway 16**, 3.7 km east from Jasper to the Maligne Lake Road. Turn east (right). Follow the Maligne Lake Road 44 km to the bridge over the lake's outlet. Cross the bridge and follow the road 250 m to the parking lot on the west shore of the lake. There are two trailheads west of the parking lot. The one for Bald Hills is to the south (left).

Few viewpoints in the Rockies offer as encompassing a panorama as do the Bald Hills. Adding to the attractions are interesting geology and tremendous wildflower displays. On a fair day, it would be difficult to pick a finer destination. You share the fireroad with horses. Bring all your drinking water; horse pastures border the only creek near the beginning of the fireroad.

### Trailhead to Lookout Site
Although all are unanimous in extolling the destination, I have heard some describe the hike to the Bald Hills as a boring fireroad plod. The tread is hard underfoot and you may have to dodge commercial horse parties, but there is much of interest in the surroundings during the ascent.

The forest is dominated by lodgepole pine. Near-homogenous stands of pine like this indicate a large forest fire in the not-too-distant past. You can see charred logs and stumps. Golden-crowned kinglets and black-capped chickadees buzz through the trees. Two plants prevalent in

pine forests are everywhere in the understory — twinflower and Labrador tea. Arnica, fleabane, buffaloberry, dwarf dogwood, northern sweet-vetch, and various willows are also common, along with invasive plants borne in the feed and dung of horses — dandelion, buttercup, and clover. Ruffed grouse and spruce grouse make occasional trailside appearances. Fritillary butterflies — smallish, with orange wings dotted with black — seem partial to this fireroad, perhaps attracted by various goodies in the horse dung.

You reach the Maligne Pass junction in 300 m. Continue straight ahead. A series of outbuildings — a horse staging area, a helipad, and a pumphouse — borders the right-hand side of the fireroad over the next 400 m. Ahead, you have a glimpse of the ultimate destination. Looking back, you can see the mountain known as "Sinking Ship," on the east side of Maligne Lake.

The fireroad veers north and winds through an area of rocky hummocks. These hummocks are landslide debris known as mollards. The debris came from the vicinity of the Opal Hills on the east side of the valley, in a series of monumental

## Variations

- You can make a loop to and from the lookout site by ascending the fireroad and descending the shortcut trail, or vice versa. The loop will be 1.3 km shorter than out and back via the fireroad. If you use the shortcut trail up and down, your outing will be 2.6 km shorter.
- Ascend the north summit, 1.8 km return from the lookout site

*When the visibility is good, competent hikers can carry on from the northeast shoulder to the north summit.*

rockslides that followed the retreat of the main valley glacier after the Wisconsin Glaciation. Some of the debris dams the outlet of Maligne Lake.

The fireroad levels just before the shortcut trail junction at km 2.5. The shortcut trail is steeper than the fireroad, and is rockier and rooted. It is a toe-jammer and knee-cruncher on the way down, but it shortens the climb to the lookout site from 2.7 km to 1.4 km.

Beyond the shortcut junction, the fireroad undulates for 700 m to the Evelyn Creek junction.

## Caribou Crunch

**The Bald Hills** are frequented by the only herd of caribou in Canada that spends all of its time within a national park. In years past, sightings were common but have become less so. The factors responsible include the resurgence of wolves in the Rockies, climate change, and human activity. For more than a decade, environmentalists had been advocating winter closure of the Maligne Lake area to reduce the human-caused stresses that are affecting the caribou — in particular, to eliminate the use of snowmobiles to trackset ski trails. In 2002–03, Parks Canada instituted the first of two planned winter-long closures of the Maligne Lake Road, during which time caribou and wolves were to be studied. Most of the 19 herds of southern mountain caribou face imminent extirpation, if pressures are not reversed. Based on sound ecological data, summer and winter management of caribou range near Maligne Lake is urgently required if the local herd of caribou is to survive.

Keep left for the Bald Hills. I saw the tracks of moose and deer here. The steepest section of fireroad follows, yielding a fine view back to the Opal Hills. Note the transition in the understory; pink mountain heather and yellow mountain heather are now common, marking entry to the lower subalpine ecoregion. Views to the north begin to open, with the Queen Elizabeth Range visible across the Maligne Valley, and Little Shovel Pass in the Maligne Range visible to the north. This snippet of view encapsulates the two great themes of the local geology — younger, gray, front range limestone to the east; older, colourful, main range quartzite underfoot. Mona Lake, named for Mona Harrigan, Jasper's first female trail guide, is revealed as a blue gem in the green mantle of the valley floor.

The grade moderates as the fireroad curves southwest to enter treeline glades. You pass a small pond. White mountain avens and white mountain heather are common. In this transitional forest, I heard a surprising chorus of birdlife: juncos trilling; hermit thrushes, a golden-crowned sparrow, and ruby-crowned kinglets singing; and a Cooper's hawk calling.

A hitching rail marks the former fire lookout site. To the southeast, you see the full length of Maligne Lake. From north to south, the peaks in view on the east side of the lake are: Opal Hills, "Sinking Ship," Leah Peak (2801 m), Samson Peak (3801 m), Maligne Mountain (with glacier), Mt. Paul (2805 m), Monkhead (3211 m), and Mt. Warren (3300 m). Mt. Charlton (3217 m) and Mt. Unwin (3268 m), on the near shore, complete the visible lakeside peaks.

### Lookout Site to North Summit

To carry on, take the left-hand of the two tracks that branch from the hitching rail. This track is the proper continuation of the fireroad. It initially heads south, passing the junction with the shortcut trail in 75 m (marked only by a cairn), before looping west to end at the base of the north summit. (If you come up the shortcut trail, turn south onto the fireroad if you want to go to the summit; otherwise turn north to descend the fireroad.) The meadows here are flush with the best displays of white mountain heather and blue-bottle gentian that I have seen in the Rockies.

If you are hiking early in the season, the slopes above may be entirely snow-covered. Otherwise, a beaten track ascends steeply south on the screes, turning west at its steepest point to gain the shoulder of this modest summit. From there, the grade relents as you walk onto the domed high point, with its panoramic views.

The rounded shapes of the Bald Hills indicate that they were completely covered by glacial ice during the Great Glaciation 75,000 years ago. With their harsh edges removed, the connecting ridges to the middle and south summits beckon to competent ramblers. To reach the middle summit, make a slight descent west to gain the well-beaten path on its north ridge. Views southwest from the middle summit include the head of Evelyn Creek, with a prominent rock glacier above its southerly fork. To the south, the keen eye will discern Mt. Columbia (3747 m), North Twin (3730 m), and Mt. Alberta (3619 m), respectively, second-, third-, and fifth-highest peaks in the Rockies.

# 38. Skyline

*Little Shovel Pass*

## Route

Overnight, 2–4 days

| Route | Elevation (m) | Distance (km) |
| --- | --- | --- |
| Maligne Lake trailhead | 1690 | 0 |
| Lorraine Lake jct | 1755 | 2.2 |
| Mona Lake jct | 1755 | 2.4 |
| Evelyn Creek CG | 1810 | 4.8 |
| Little Shovel CG | 2155 | 8.3 |
| Little Shovel Pass | 2240 | 10.3 |
| Snowbowl CG | 2080 | 12.2 |
| Big Shovel Pass | 2325 | 17.5 |
| Watchtower jct | 2300 | 17.9 |
| Wabasso jct | 2240 | 19.5 |
| Curator CG | 2120 | +0.8 |
| The Notch | 2510 | 22.1 |
| Trail summit | 2530 | 24.2 |
| Tekarra CG | 2060 | 30.9 |
| Signal CG jct | 2020 | 35.7 |
| Signal CG | 2015 | +0.1 |
| Signal Mountain trailhead | 1160 | 44.1 |

Maps
NTS: 83 C/12, and 83 C/13, and 83 D/16
Gem trek: Jasper and Maligne Lake

## Trailhead

**To take advantage** of the higher starting elevation, most parties hike the Skyline from south to north. Follow Highway 16, 3.7 km east from Jasper to the Maligne Lake Road. Turn east (right). Follow the Maligne Lake Road 45 km to the parking lot on the west side of the lake. The Skyline trailhead is the most northerly of the two on the west side of the parking lot. A shuttle service is available from Jasper (fee charged).

For almost two-thirds of its length, the Skyline travels at or above treeline. Rambling through expansive meadows, crossing high passes, and traversing ridgecrests of the Maligne Range, it provides panoramic views of the Athabasca and Maligne valleys, and the surrounding mountain ranges. It's no wonder that the Skyline is the most heavily used backcountry trail in Jasper.

Given its high elevation, in most years you should not hike the Skyline until after mid-July, when most of the snow will have melted. Avoid this outing during poor weather, for if it's stormy in Jasper, it will be miserable on the exposed ridges of the Maligne Range. Although you can complete the trail in two days, I recommend spending more time. The summits of the Maligne Range offer many possibilities for ridge walking and straightforward mountaineering.

### Trailhead to Little Shovel Pass
From the trailhead, a broad path climbs through an open coniferous forest dominated by lodgepole pine. The undergrowth features buffaloberry, feathermosses, twinflower, common fireweed,

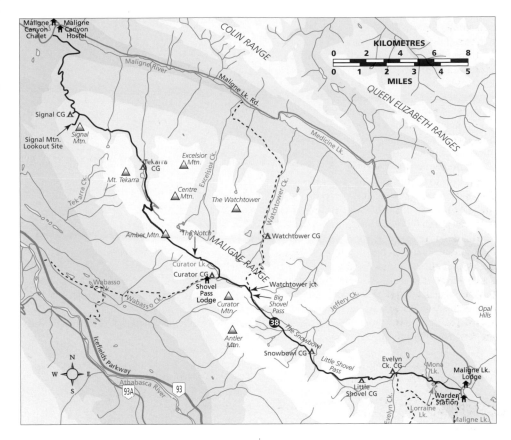

rocky mountain goldenrod, and grouseberry. The sweet, red fruit of this heath family member is favoured by ruffed grouse. You may see these birds here.

The trail winds through hummocky terrain, debris from the Maligne Lake rockslide. At km 2.2 and km 2.4, short sidetrails branch respectively southwest (left) to Lorraine Lake, and north (right) to Mona Lake. These lakes occupy hollows in the debris of the rockslide. Mona Harrigin Matheson was Jasper's first licensed female trail guide. Lorraine Magstad's parents worked at the Maligne Lake chalet in the late 1920s.

At km 4.8 the trail crosses Evelyn Creek to the

first campground. "Evelyn" refers to either the wife of the first resident Superintendent of Jasper National Park in 1913, or the Dutchess of Devonshire, who visited Jasper in 1920.

The trail climbs steeply away from the campground. Although the elevation here is subalpine, lodgepole pine is still the dominant tree. Engelmann spruce and subalpine fir are typically more common in the subalpine, however the

## Variations

- Hike the trail in reverse
- Day-hike to Little Shovel Pass, 20.6 km return
- Camp at Snowbowl campground (12.2 km) and explore
- Hike in from the north, camp at Tekarra campground (14.2 km) and explore

## The Making of the Skyline

The section of the Skyline south of Big Shovel Pass was first travelled by Mary Schäffer's expedition to Maligne Lake in 1911. The northern part of the trail was developed in 1937, when outfitter Fred Brewster sought to make a loop outing for his guided trips to Maligne Lake. Patrons journeyed by road from Jasper to Medicine Lake. From there, they were ferried across the lake. They then boarded horse-drawn carts to lodging at Maligne Lake. Return was on horseback along the Skyline to Jasper.

combination of quartizitic soils and southerly exposure here creates the perfect niche for lodgepole pines. Many of the pines are twisted and stunted, products of the colder climate at this higher elevation. Two more members of the heath family are now common in the undergrowth — crowberry and blueberry.

Beyond Little Shovel campground, the trail swings north onto the alpine tundra that leads to Little Shovel Pass. The blooms of ragwort, yellow paintbrush, and mountain fireweed colour the banks of the stream that drains the pass.

*Hikers cross Amber Mountain at the apex of the Skyline.*

Looking southeast from the crest of Little Shovel Pass, the ragged limestone summits of the Queen Elizabeth Range rise above Maligne Lake. Most prominent is Mt. Brazeau (3470 m), highest mountain in the front ranges. The pass is home to a colony of hoary marmots. Marmots usually prefer the protection of boulderfields. Here, in the absence of protective rocks, they excavate deep burrows on the open tundra. They must burrow to remain out of the grasp of grizzly bears, their principal predator.

## Little Shovel Pass to Curator Campground

The steady descent north from Little Shovel Pass leads into an extensive upper subalpine basin known as The Snowbowl. Sedges and willows here are important summer foods for mountain caribou. This uncommon member of the deer family has a dark brown coat with light patches on the neck, belly, rump, and legs. Mountain caribou are officially listed as a species at risk in Canada. Future protection of Jasper's caribou herds may include seasonal closures of hiking trails in calving areas to reduce stress on the animals

Snowbowl campground is a good base for day-hiking toward Antler Mountain (2557 m) at the head of the valley. Beyond the grove of trees that harbors the campground, the trail descends north into meadows and begins its rambling and often muddy ascent toward Big Shovel Pass. Moisture-loving wildflowers and sedges thrive here — fleabane, Sitka valerian, western anemone, ragwort, shooting star, white globeflower, mountain marsh marigold, cotton-grass, and elephant head. The pink petals of elephant head have three lobes,

which create the ears, trunk, and mouth of the "elephant." Several dozen miniature "elephant heads" are arranged atop the spike of this showy wildflower. The Latin species name, *groenlandica*, means "Greenland." That's where the species was first catalogued.

Curator Mountain (2624 m) is west of Big Shovel Pass, named for its position as custodian of the pass. An ice apron clings to its eastern slope; its cornice bears the unmistakable brilliant blue of perennial snow.

On the north side of Big Shovel Pass, the trail is a faint path beaten into the screes —easily lost when snow-covered. When the trail forks, keep right. Although the rocky slopes appear barren,

## Venerable Mountains

**The Maligne Range** is part of the eastern main ranges. Elsewhere in the Rockies, these ranges are usually among the highest and most rugged. The modest elevations and rounded summits of mountains along the Skyline indicate that they were completely covered by glacial ice during the Great Glaciation, when valley glaciers were a kilometre thick.

The Maligne Range is comprised almost entirely of early-Cambrian, Gog Formation quartzite. Map lichen grows profusely on this rock, making it appear dark from a distance. However, quartzite can be colourful when viewed close-up — buff, pink, purple, and white. Fresh exposures often feature reddish-orange stains caused by iron oxide. The Maligne Range mountains are in marked contrast to the higher, sawtooth and overthrust mountains of the front ranges to the east, which are composed principally of drab, gray limestones.

*The Skyline traverses the crest of the Maligne Range from Maligne Lake to Maligne Canyon. This view of Mt. Tekarra is near the north end of the trail.*

## Maligne Lake, the Hard Way

*The namesake shovels*

In 1908, outfitter Billy Warren led a party organized by Mary Schäffer to Maligne Lake. They reached the lake from the south, constructed a raft, explored the waters and named many surrounding features. Schäffer's account of the journey was widely circulated and well received, and brought celebrity status.

In 1911, the Grand Trunk Pacific Railway was completed as far as Jasper. With the advent of the railway, the Canadian government sought to publicize the newly created Jasper Forest Park in order to capitalize on tourism. Mary Schäffer was invited to return to the lake, to make an accurate map of it. Schäffer, who lamented the coming of the railway and the changes it would bring to the mountains she dearly loved, reluctantly agreed.

Instead of building another raft on the shores of the lake, it was decided that materials for a boat would be packed on horseback from Jasper. Rather than tackle the trackless wilds of the Maligne Valley with such a load, outfitter Jack Otto chose to cross the crest of the Maligne Range. After ascending Wabasso Creek, Otto led the party along the southern part of today's Skyline to the north shore of Maligne Lake.

This unlikely journey was undertaken at an even more unlikely time of year, mid-June, when snows were still deep in the high country. Otto sent an advance party to pack a trail over the high passes. Finding the snow more than they could handle, his men fashioned two impromptu shovels from spruce trees, and used them to scoop out a trail across the passes. The shovels, which Schäffer at first mistook for distant sheep, were left on the high point to greet the following party, and so the passes were named.

Surveyor A.O. Wheeler subsequently proposed the name "Bighorn Pass" for Big Shovel Pass, because sheep abound in the area. However, Schäffer's placename has endured. The original shovels are now in the collection of the Jasper-Yellowhead Historical Society.

**161**

closer inspection will reveal the blooms of moss campion, alpine harebell, Lyall's goldenweed, golden fleabane, and alpine hawksbeard, scattered across the screes.

About 500 m north of Big Shovel Pass, the trail from the Watchtower Basin descends the ridge from the east. Scamper up to the ridgecrest for the view over the hanging valley of Watchtower Creek. The striking summit of The Watchtower (2791 m) was first climbed in 1951. Watchtower Basin offers an escape route from the Skyline. It might get you out of the weather quickly, but the route, at least in the early going, is not easy. The initial descent is north. Then the trail switchbacks tightly to the south and contours around the swampy basin at the head of the valley. It is 13.2 km to Maligne Lake Road.

The Skyline descends to the Wabasso junction, 1.6 km north of Big Shovel Pass. Turn south (left) to camp at Curator campground. This badly eroded sidetrail loses 120 m of elevation in just 800 m. The pleasant campground is set in a grove of trees beneath a waterfall. Shovel Pass Lodge is in the meadow below the campground. The creek is frequented by horses from the lodge. Unless you want to go thirsty, you'll be obliged to sample the cocktail. Boil it first. This is the headwaters of Wabasso Creek, which Mary Schäffer followed to the Skyline in 1911. *Wabasso* is Cree for "rabbit." The Wabasso trail offers a 13.8 km exit from the Skyline to the Icefields Parkway.

## Curator Campground to Tekarra Campground

From the Curator campground junction, the Skyline winds north through boulderfields beside Curator Lake, and then climbs steadily to The Notch (2510 m). The Notch is the sixth highest point reached by maintained trail in the Rockies,

and was certainly an ambitious place to bring ponies. The Notch often sports a cornice of snow on its east side. Give it a wide berth.

The scree summits that flank this lofty pass are walk-ups that offer superb views of the Athabasca Valley. Mt. Edith Cavell (3363 m) is the prominent peak to the southwest. The Ramparts of the Tonquin Valley are beyond. Views south include Mt. Christie (3103 m) and Mt. Fryatt (3361 m), Brussels Peak (3161 m), and the northern fringe of Columbia Icefield. Directly below, Curator Lake sparkles like a blue gem in a setting of barren stone. On clear days, Mt. Robson (3954 m) towers above the horizon, about 90 km to the northwest.

The next 5 km are the apex of the Skyline, as it follows the backbone of the Maligne Range across the summit ridge of Amber Mountain at 2530 m. Do not attempt this section of trail during electrical storms. Even non-mountaineers will be tempted to walk off trail the few hundred metres to Amber Mountain's highest, most northerly point (2544 m). To the east, four parallel ranges of sawtooth mountains are stacked like rocky waves

Part Rock, Part Ice

*Rock glacier on Centre Mountain*

**The valleys east** of Amber Mountain contain a number of tarns whose blue-green waters indicate glacial sources. However, you won't see any glacial ice. The meltwater comes from rock glaciers, piles of rockslide debris that insulate ice within. There are 119 catalogued rock glaciers in Jasper National Park.

Signal Mountain Lookout, 0.9 km

**If you want** to top off the Skyline with one last great view, turn southwest (left) at the junction with the Signal Mountain fireroad. Follow the culmination of the fireroad as it climbs the last 100 m to the lookout site, with its grand prospect of the Athabasca and Miette valleys. Built in 1941, Signal Mountain Lookout was the first operational lookout in the national parks. This sidetrip is a particularly good option if you camp at Signal campground, where you could nip up to the lookout site for sunset or sunrise, or both.

*Curator Lake*

against the skyline. You can see Jasper townsite to the north. Amber Mountain was named because of the colour of its weathered screes. If you study these screes carefully you will see a geologic feature called patterned ground. The soil here is permafrost, although the surface thaws for part of the summer. These freeze and thaw cycles churn the screes, separating larger particles from smaller ones. On flat terrain this creates shapes called polygons; on slopes it creates stone stripes.

From the ridge north of Amber Mountain, the trail leaves the "skyline" and switchbacks down toward Centre Lake. You can see the rock glacier that feeds this lake, on the west slope of Centre Mountain (2700 m). Bighorn sheep, mountain caribou, white-tailed ptarmigan, and hoary marmots frequent this area. Mount Tekarra (teh-CAR-rah) (2694 m), with its massive east-facing cliffs of Gog Formation quartzite, dominates the view north. *Tekarra* was James Hector's Iroquois guide when the Palliser Expedition travelled to Athabasca Pass in 1859. During your descent to Centre Lake, you pass a gigantic limestone boulder — a glacial erratic. It's a good place to find shade on a hot day, or shelter on a windy day.

The remaining 2 km to Tekarra campground involve delightful upper subalpine hiking. Mountain fireweed and cotton-grass bloom in the adjacent stream course. The campground is located at the creek crossing, 500 m below the outlet of Tekarra Lake. From this convenient base, mountaineers may make ascents of Mount Tekarra, Centre Mountain, and Excelsior Mountain.

## Tekarra Campground to Signal Mountain Trailhead

From Tekarra campground, the trail ascends to treeline and contours around the north flank of Mount Tekarra. The sawtooth limestone slabs of the Colin Range are prominent across Maligne Valley. Between 1835 and 1849, Colin Fraser was in charge of Jasper House, a Hudson's Bay Company outpost in the Athabasca Valley. James Hector named a mountain for him in 1859.

Signal Mountain is the northern outlier of Mt. Tekarra. Its slopes command remarkable views north along a 30 km length of the Athabasca Valley, and west beyond Jasper into the Miette Valley. The mountains northwest of Jasper are the Victoria Cross Range. Five summits in this range were named for Canadian soldiers who were WWI recipients of the Victoria Cross, Britain's highest award for military valour. Signal Mountain was formerly the site of a fire lookout.

Turn north (right) where the trail joins the Signal Mountain fireroad. The Signal campground junction is in 50 m. The Skyline concludes with an 8.4 km fireroad walk, a real heel burner that descends steadily to Maligne Lake Road. On the way, you have views of Roche Bonhomme (ROSH-bun-OMM) in the Colin Range. The mountain's French name means "good fellow rock," and was probably given by the voyageurs of the fur trade in the early 1800s. The strata near the summit bear a striking resemblance to the face of a man looking skyward. The patch of dead trees below the summit is the remains of a 1985 forest fire.

**163**

# 39. Sulphur Skyline

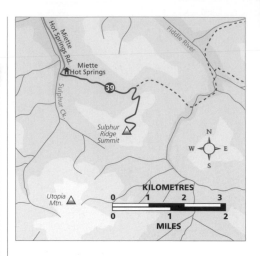

## Route

Day-hike

| Route | Elevation (m) | Distance (km) |
|---|---|---|
| Trailhead | 1372 | 0 |
| Sulphur Skyline jct | 1508 | 2.6 |
| Sulphur Ridge summit | 2060 | 4.6 |

**Maps**
NTS: 83 F/4
Gem Trek: Jasper and Maligne Lake

**Best lighting:** afternoon

## Trailhead

**Follow Highway 16** east from Jasper, 42.9 km to the Miette Hot Springs Road. Turn south (right) and follow this road 19 km to its end at the Miette Hot Springs parking lot. Two trails depart. You want the trailhead that is south (right) of the hot springs pool entrance. Some of the park trail signs refer to this outing as "Sulphur Ridge."

A handful of trails in the front ranges of Jasper and Banff climb from valley bottoms in the montane ecoregion to alpine ridges or summits. None does so in as short a distance as does the Sulphur Skyline trail. The stiff climb rewards you with a panoramic view of the wildly contorted peaks in northeastern Jasper. The ridgecrest is usually windy. Carry warm clothing and all your drinking water.

### Trailhead to Sulphur Skyline

Make an end-run around the sheep in the parking area to reach the trailhead. The trail begins as a broad, paved lane, leading southeast from the hot pool building. The mixed forest contains tree species of the montane and lower subalpine ecoregions — Douglas-fir, cottonwood poplar, trembling aspen, lodgepole pine, and white spruce. Scouler's willow — a tall shrub — is abundant, as is common juniper. Wildflowers include northern bedstraw, camas, arnica, yarrow, and harebells. Keep straight ahead where the paved surface ends at the water supply for the hot springs. The trail narrows and becomes rough. Keep left at the subsequent, unsigned junction. From open slopes you can look south to a shallow

cirque. The dome to the east (left) of the cirque is your destination.

The trail contours into the pass that separates Sulphur Ridge from the unnamed peak to the north. At the fork junction in the pass, keep south (right) and commence a steep climb. If you have your head down on this section you will miss the rapid transition from lower subalpine to upper subalpine forest. Kruppelholz spruce and fir trees testify to the windiness of this location. A band of bighorn sheep frequents these slopes. This trail was rebuilt in the 1990s. Log benches block the old switchbacks. White rhododendron grows here, along with a rarity on the Classic Hikes — the nodding, purple bloom of mountain monkshood.

The trail curves south as it gains treeline on the east shoulder of Sulphur Ridge, revealing a spectacular view southeast over the Fiddle River valley and the Nikanassin Range. The Nikanassin and the adjoining Miette Range to the north are oriented along the strike of the Rockies,

## First Range and First Fiddle

*Nikanassin* **is Cree** for "first range." It is the first row of the Rockies in this area when approached from the east. Pierre-Jean de Smet, a Jesuit missionary, called the Fiddle River, *La Rivière au Violon* (Violin River), in 1846. Various origins of the river's name are given. The most far-fetched claims that the wind makes the sound of a violin when it strikes the ridge of the nearby Fiddle Range. It is more likely that de Smet — who travelled with a fur trade brigade — was entertained at camp by a fiddle-playing voyageur. In typical western fashion, de Smet's "violin" was soon corrupted to "fiddle."

*The view from Sulphur Skyline reveals the rugged geology of Jasper's front ranges. Ashlar Ridge dominates the view north.*

River. The Athabasca is an antecedent stream — it cut through the strike alignment as the mountains were being created, making two sidevalleys out of what would have been one valley, and bisecting the parallel ranges of mountains in a similar fashion.

The trail levels briefly at treeline. There is a white quartzite boulder at trailside and quartzite rubble underfoot. If you think that the boulder looks out of place among the surrounding siltstone, you're right. The boulder is a glacial erratic, transported by glacial ice some 30 km from the main ranges to the west and deposited here when the ice receded. Erratics provide glaciologists with clues as to the ice age origins of glaciers. On my last visit, a mule deer was hanging around here, obviously accustomed to hand-outs.

The trail leaves the windblasted kruppelholz to traverse west beneath the summit dome of Sulphur Ridge, which sits atop the crest of an anticline. It then switchbacks tightly upslope to the summit — a withering climb on a rocky track. To the east, foothills and prairie stretch to the horizon. A sea of rugged front range limestone peaks floods the view in all other directions. Ashlar Ridge (1700 m) will catch your eye to the north. "Ashlar" is a form of masonry — thin dressed stones used to cover brick or rubble. The remarkable 300 m high upper cliff of the mountain is resistant Palliser Formation limestone. Utopia Mountain (2560 m) is 3 km southwest of Sulphur Ridge. The mountain was named because its summit provided a survey crew with refuge from the flies in the valley bottom.

Sulphur Ridge is an unofficial name for this minor summit, given in recognition of the pungent smell of nearby Miette Hot Springs. The springs are the hottest (53.9°C) and most aromatic in the Rockies. You won't catch a whiff of sulphur on the summit. However, on your return to the parking lot, you can follow the boardwalk south past the old hot springs building. Here, at the spring outlets, the sulphur aroma is prominent, as is the yellow colour of elemental sulphur, produced as the hydrogen sulphide reacts with oxygen in the atmosphere.

northwest-southeast. The mountains consist of resistant rocks in the upturned edge of a thrust sheet. The valleys on either side have been eroded into the weak shales along the thrust faults, and are known as strike valleys. Looking north, you can see how Fiddle River valley aligns with the Moosehorn valley, northwest of the Athabasca

## The Miette Reef — Legacy of Ancient Ocean

**The mountains** near Miette Hot Springs contain a remarkable formation called the Miette Reef. This reef was built by encrusting colonies of sponges — called stromatoporoids (strome-at-oh-PORE-oids) — that lived in warm, shallow seas during the Late Devonian. The Miette Reef amassed to a thickness of 200 m before being entombed in sediments that killed the stromatoporoids and the other reef-building lifeforms. The reef was once again brought to the surface during mountain building; this time, high and dry. The principal rocks are the gray and black dolomite of the Cairn Formation and the pale limestone and dolomite of the overlying Southesk Formation. The Miette is but one reef in a larger system called the Fairholme Reef Complex, into which most of southern Alberta's oil and gas wells have been drilled. Less than 10 km east of Sulphur Ridge — outside Jasper National Park — drilling crews are active, tapping petroleum resources in the foothills. You can see the seismic lines — narrow strips in the forest cut during petroleum exploration. You can't drill for oil or gas in the park, but if you tried, you'd go bust. The oil has long since drained from the Miette Reef.

# 40. Berg Lake

## Route

**Overnight, 2–6 days**

| Route | Elevation (m) | Distance (km) |
|---|---|---|
| Trailhead | 862 | 0 |
| Kinney Lake | 985 | 4.2 |
| Kinney Lake viewpoint | 1006 | 5.2 |
| Kinney Lake CG | 985 | 6.8 |
| Whitehorn CG | 1128 | 10.9 |
| Emperor Falls viewpoint | 1493 | 14.7 |
| Emperor Falls CG | 1631 | 15.4 |
| Marmot CG | 1646 | 18.1 |
| Hargreaves Glacier jct | 1650 | 18.5 |
| Berg Lake CG | 1646 | 20.2 |
| Toboggan Creek jct | 1645 | 20.3 |
| Rearguard CG | 1646 | 21.3 |
| Snowbird Pass jct | 1650 | 21.7 |
| Robson Pass CG jct | 1650 | 22.2 |
| Robson Pass CG | 1650 | +0.1 |
| Robson Pass | 1652 | 22.6 |

## Maps

NTS: 83 E/3
BC Ministry of Environment, Lands and Parks:
Mount Robson Park, 1:125,000

*Mt. Robson, the "Monarch of the Rockies," reflected in a pool on the Toboggan Creek fan, near Berg Lake.*

## Trailhead

**Follow Highway 16,** 84 km west from Jasper; 18 km east from Tete Jaune Cache, BC; to the visitor centre at Robson Junction. Obtain your permit here. Turn north and follow the paved sideroad 2 km to its end at the Berg Lake trailhead parking lot.

The Berg Lake trail is in Mt. Robson Provincial Park. Mt. Robson was established in 1913 as the second provincial park in BC. Basic supplies are available at Robson Junction. The park has five frontcountry campgrounds, three of which — Robson Meadows, Robson River, and Emperor Ridge — are near the trailhead. Mt. Robson is in the Pacific time zone, one hour behind Jasper and Banff.

Towering majestically above Berg Lake, the two-kilometre-high north flank of Mt. Robson epitomizes the Canadian Rockies. Clad with a magnificent array of glaciers, this monolith of rock, snow, and ice is without equal in a range of mountains celebrated for its scenery.

The Berg Lake trail, which brings you to the foot of Mt. Robson's awesome northern rampart, is by far the most heavily travelled backpacking route in the Canadian Rockies. Around 4000 people register each summer for overnight trips, staying an average of 2.7 days each. Another 50,000 make day-hikes. Strong backpackers can reach Berg Lake in a day. But seven well-spaced campgrounds allow you to break the approach conveniently into two days.

All campers should obtain a permit and pay a fee at the visitor centre on Highway 16. There are 98 tent sites on the trail, 18 of which can be reserved in advance for any given day. Phone 800-689-9025. The trail is open to mountain bikes as far as Kinney Lake campground. Horse packers occasionally use the trail. Helicopters land at Robson Pass two days a week. Flightseeing traffic is common overhead.

## Variation

- Camp at Kinney Lake, an excellent novice backpack, 6.8 km

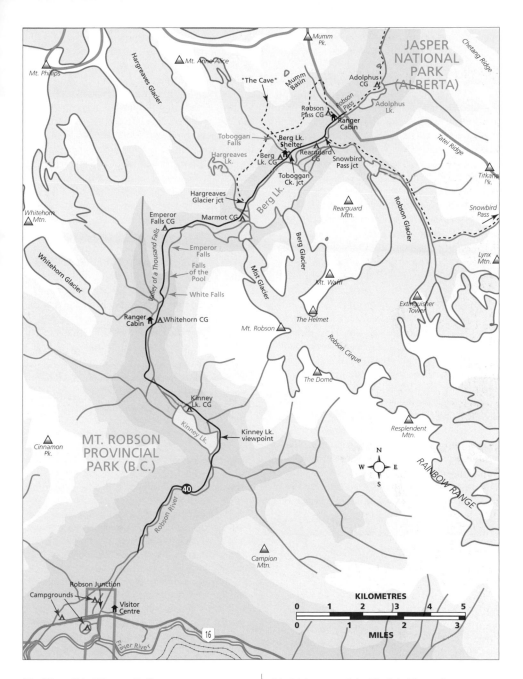

## Trailhead to Kinney Lake

The broad trail to Kinney Lake is always within sound of the Robson River. Look for harlequin ducks and dippers in the fast-flowing water. The forest features species normally found in BC's Western Interior Hemlock Forest zone — western redcedar, western hemlock, western white pine, thimbleberry, and devil's club. The trail passes through an old-growth stand of western red-cedars about 2 km from the trailhead. Western redcedar is the provincial tree of British Columbia. Scan the forest for BC's provincial bird — the hooded, blue and black, Steller's jay. At km 3 the trail bisects a mineral lick used by elk, deer, moose, and mountain goats. Look for their tracks.

You reach the outlet of Kinney Lake — some- times referred to as "the mirror of the mount" — 4.2 km from the trailhead. The lake is impounded by the alluvial fan of a creek that drains the basin between Mt. Robson and Mt. Resplendent. One of the better views of the lake is from the viewpoint on its southeast shore, a kilometre beyond the outlet bridge. The blue-green hues of the lake suggest the water's glacial sources, some of which you will have the opportunity to view near Berg Lake. Avalanche slopes on Cinnamon Peak extend to waterline on the opposite shore. The thickets on these slopes typify the dense bush on the BC side of the Continental Divide.

Leaving the Kinney Lake viewpoint, the trail climbs over a rise and descends to the lakeshore. The remaining distance to Kinney Lake camp- ground is across an alluvial fan that contains ma- terial eroded from the southwest face of Mt. Rob- son. Beyond the campground you cross the delta at the inlet to the lake. The seasonal and daily fluctuations of the Robson River create braided streams across the gravels. Some of the bridges that were installed across the braids now stand high and dry, monuments to the temperamental nature of glacial rivers.

### Kinney Lake to Emperor Falls

From the north end of the delta, the trail climbs steeply above the west bank of the Robson River into the Valley of a Thousand Falls. As moun- taineer J.M. Thorington observed in 1925, "If not quite a thousand falls come streaming down from the cliffs on either side, the number is at all events

### The Reverend Mountaineer

**Kinney Lake** was named for Reverend George Kin- ney, who was in the first mountaineering party to attempt Mt. Robson. In 1907, Kinney and A.P. Cole- man approached the mountain on horseback from Lake Louise — a journey that took six weeks. Poor weather and a shortage of food put an end to the exploration before they could set foot on the mountain. Kinney returned in 1908 and again in 1909 when, with outfitter Curly Phillips, he nearly reached the summit by a difficult route on the west face. Given their scant equipment and Phillips' lack of mountaineering experience, it was a bold and remarkable achievement, tainted later by the fact that Kinney claimed to have reached the summit, while Phillips admitted his doubt in the matter.

most satisfactory and surpassed only by the beauty of their height." You will also see three ma- jor waterfalls on the Robson River — White Falls, Falls of the Pool, and Emperor Falls.

The trail descends to a suspension bridge crossing of the Robson River. It is safest to cross the bridge one at a time. Whitehorn campground is on the opposite bank. Emergency assistance may be available at the Whitehorn ranger cabin, on the west bank of the river just north of the bridge. The trail recrosses the Robson River on another suspension bridge 800 m north of the campground. Yellow lady's-slipper orchids bloom on the gravels nearby in early July.

To this point, the elevation gain has been gen- tle compared to what lies ahead. In the next 4.5 km, the trail climbs 503 m. For the 1913 Alpine Club of Canada camp in Robson Pass, outfitter Curly Phillips constructed "The Flying Trestle Bridge" — a decked, log structure that made it possible for pack horses to ascend the first cliff. Viewpoints for the three waterfalls on the Robson River provide scenic distraction from the hard

### Cloud Cap Mountain

**From Emperor Falls** campground, you can often see how Mt. Robson creates its own weather. Pre- vailing winds are from the southwest. When the west side of the mountain is clear, the north and east sides may display a banner cloud. Pluming from the summit, this cloud is created where damp air is forced to rise in order to clear the crest. It does not necessarily presage rain or snow.

However, if clouds begin to mass at mid-height on the western side of the mountain, the weather is likely to deteriorate rapidly. Climbers and hikers on the east and north sides may not see this sure sign of an approaching storm, and are frequently caught in the foul weather that results.

The tendency for weather to change rapidly on Mt. Robson is one of the principal reasons why it is so difficult to climb. Most of the climbing routes require 3 to 5 days for a round trip from the high- way. In some years, when poor climbing conditions and foul weather persist, Mt. Robson may go un- climbed despite dozens of attempts. Between 1939 and 1953, not a single mountaineering party was known to have reached the summit. When The Overlanders passed Mt. Robson in 1862, bound for the Cariboo goldfields, their Native guide in- formed them that he had seen the summit only once in his first 29 visits. Not surprisingly, they called it "Cloud Cap Mountain."

*Western columbine grows alongside the trail to Kinney Lake.*

work. Use caution near the unfenced cliff edges.

As you approach Emperor Falls, note the abandoned river gorge immediately east of the trail. This is a beheaded stream. The Robson River formerly flowed here but the water subsequently eroded a new channel farther east. In places, the new course of the river is above the present level of the trail. At high water, a trickle of the Robson River spills into the abandoned gorge.

Emperor Falls viewpoint is 150 m east on a sidetrail. The drenching spray is a welcome relief on a hot day, but makes the viewpoint a poor location for photographing the falls. The best vantages for photography are on the main trail.

The trail levels and draws alongside the Robson River at Emperor Falls campground. The Emperor Ridge of Mt. Robson rises across the river. The mountaineering route of Kinney and Phillips lay slightly south of this ridge. Today, the Emperor Ridge is considered one of the harder routes on Mt. Robson and in the Rockies. "Emperor" refers to the fact that Mt. Robson is "monarch of the Rockies."

### Emperor Falls to Berg Lake

From Emperor Falls campground, the trail curves east into the upper valley of the Robson River, revealing partial views of Mist Glacier and Berg Glacier on the north side of Mt. Robson. After contouring above the river on a boulderslope, the trail descends to the river flats. Rock-hop as necessary. In the view west, Whitehorn Mountain (3395 m) rises majestically above the Valley of a Thousand Falls. As its name suggests, the

## The Mountain of the Spiral Road

**Mt. Robson (3954 m)** towers more than 3000 m above the trailhead, yet the summit is only 8 km away. This staggering vertical relief is hard to grasp. By way of comparison, Mt. Temple rises slightly more than 2000 m from the floor of the Bow Valley near Lake Louise, and Mt. Stephen rises 1900 m above the Kicking Horse Valley at Field.

Mt. Robson is 207 m higher than Mt. Columbia, the second highest mountain in the Rockies, and 528 m higher than Resplendent Mountain, the next highest peak nearby. Why is Mt. Robson so high? Paradoxically, the mountain is composed of rather easily eroded rock. The secret is that the layers are lying practically flat through the centre of the peak. Flat-lying layers are more difficult for glaciers to erode than tilted layers. (See *Handbook of the Canadian Rockies*, p. 157, for an excellent photographic description.) This rock sandwich — almost 4 km thick — is one of the more complete, unbroken assemblages of Cambrian rock exposed anywhere on Earth.

The strata bend slightly upward from the centre of the mountain toward the east and west, revealing a broad syncline. This creates the illusion of spiral ramps. Shuswap Natives from the interior of BC knew Mt. Robson as *Yuh-hai-has-kun* — "mountain of the spiral road." As impressive as it is, Mt. Robson is not the highest mountain in British Columbia, nor is Mt. Waddington (4042 m), the other popular guess. The honour belongs to Mt. Fairweather (4669 m), on the border of Alaska.

The quest to find the definitive origin of Mt. Robson's name has been a bane for scholars of Rockies' history. You might think that the monarch mountain of the range was named to honour a politician, official, or dignitary. Elsewhere in BC, the name "Robson" appears frequently, commemorating John Robson, provincial premier from 1889–92. However, there is no connection here.

The name "Mt. Robinson" may have been in use for the mountain as early as 1827. Scholars agree that the strongest candidate to lay claim to the name is Colin Robertson, an officer with the North West and Hudson's Bay companies. In 1820, Robertson dispatched a group of Iroquois fur traders to the area immediately west of Mt. Robson. They may have dropped the name, which was subsequently corrupted — twice — through use.

## Snowbird Pass (2425 m), 10.8 km

**The glaciers** you see at Berg Lake only hint at the vast domain of glacial ice concealed on the east slopes of Mt. Robson. You get the full view from the Snowbird Pass trail. This is a strenuous outing that requires a full day.

Head northeast from Berg Lake campground, past the cotton-grass ponds on the Toboggan Creek alluvial fan. Continue through Rearguard campground and onto the glacial flats near Robson Pass. The Snowbird Pass trail branches southeast (right) at km 1.1 just before the pass, and strikes off through the forefield of Robson Glacier. The showy, twisted seedheads of white mountain avens cover the gravels in July and August. Lynx Mountain (3180 m) is directly ahead, between the slopes of Tatei (tat-EH-ee) Ridge (2798 m) on the east (left), and Rearguard Mountain (2720 m) on the west (right). *Tatei* is Stoney for "wind."

The most recent advance of Robson Glacier reached its maximum in 1782. In 1911, A.O. Wheeler marked two large rocks in the forefield, recording the distance from each rock to the toe of Robson Glacier. In 1911, the toe of

*The Snowbird Pass trail parallels Robson Glacier, providing close-up views of this massive river of ice.*

the glacier was 53 m distant from the western rock. By 1989, it had receded 1249 m — an average of 15.3 m per year. Glaciologists have recently discovered the stumps of trees that were overrun by the glacier more than 3000 years ago. The forest was released from its icy tomb as the glacier retreated.

The rocky knoll east of the trail is a nunatak, a bedrock outcrop that protruded through the glacier during its Little Ice Age advance. Robson Glacier splayed around the nunatak early in the 20th century, sending meltwater streams northeast to Adolphus Lake, and southwest to Berg Lake. This was one of a few instances in the world where a single alpine valley glacier fed two oceans. (The Chaba Glacier in the Rockies still does this, as does Two Ocean Glacier in Montana.) Why is this significant? If it were still the case that the BC-Alberta boundary ran along the centreline of Robson Glacier, the provinces would share the summit of Mt. Robson.

If you explore off-trail here, you can trace the ancient meltwater courses, and you will see striations — bedrock scratches caused by stone fragments embedded in the underside of Robson Glacier. The concrete cairns in the vicinity mark the Alberta-BC boundary. They were erected in 1924 by the Interprovincial Boundary Survey.

Meltwater from the terminus of Robson Glacier collects in a marginal lake. The western lobe of the glacier toe exhibits massive horizontal crevasses. As the glacier retreats, huge chunks of ice separate along these fissures, to avalanche into the lake. The dark, lengthwise strips of rubble on the glacier's surface are medial moraines, formed by the merging of tributary glaciers "upstream." On the lower mountainsides either side of the terminus, you can see the trimlines of the Little Ice Age advances. There are two trimlines here, indicating advances of different extent. Vegetation below the trimlines was

## Snowbird Pass (2425 m), 10.8 km

obliterated by the ice.

A rough track angles uphill through moraines east of the marginal lake. Follow cairns where necessary. The graceful horn of Resplendent Mountain (3426 m), one of the more attractive peaks in the Rockies, rises from the head of Robson Glacier. Immediately east of it is Extinguisher Tower (2393 m), a minor summit named for its resemblance to a candle snuffer. Looking back, the summits north of Berg Lake rise in parallel, overthrust ramps. The glaciated peak farthest west is Mt. Phillips (3249 m), named for outfitter Curly Phillips. Farthest east is Mumm Peak (2962 m), named for English mountaineer Arnold Mumm, who was in the party that made its first ascent in 1910.

The track climbs steeply through ice-cored moraines above Robson Glacier. Sections of the cairned route occasionally slump where the ice melts out. The exposed ice appears black. There is some hazard here, especially if you travel off the beaten track.

### Hoary Marmots — Indolent Rodents

*Hoary marmot*

**The hoary marmot** is a large rodent that resembles its relative, the woodchuck. Its preferred habitat is upper subalpine boulderfields and meadows. The marmot eats grasses, leaves, flowers, and berries, never straying too far from its den. Grizzly bears, lynx, hawks, and eagles are its principal predators. Grizzlies will expend considerable time and energy excavating in quest of this apparently delicious rodent.

The shrill whistle of the marmot warns its fellows that a threat is near, and gives rise to its folk name, "whistle-pig." "Hoary" refers to its greyish-tipped coat. The marmot disdains the hardships of winter, autumn, and spring; it hibernates nine months of the year. The Snowbird marmots have little fear of hikers, and a fondness for exploring packs, boots, and lunches without invitation. Please do not feed them.

Look for glacier tables on lower Robson Glacier. These boulders prevent the melting of ice directly beneath, with the result that they become perched on icy pedestals as the glacier surface melts downward. The lower icefalls on Robson Glacier feature myriad free-standing pinnacles of ice, called seracs (sair-RACKS). Seracs form where crevassed glacial ice plunges over irregularities in the bedrock. Slightly east of where Robson Glacier curves to the north, there is a secondary glacier terminus that butts against the lateral moraine. This is a compression lobe of ice — it flows slightly uphill before terminating in seracs that topple onto the moraine.

A steep switchback leads through a cliff to the creek that drains Snowbird Meadows. But, as wonderful as the meadows are, you will probably be looking over your shoulder to where a chaos of cascading ice fills the view west. The icefall at the head of Robson Glacier leads to the rounded summit of The Dome (3090 m). The snow and ice face above is the Kain Face, named for Conrad Kain, who guided the first ascent of Mt. Robson via this route in 1913. At the time, it was the most difficult mountaineering route in North America. Without benefit of the tools and equipment enjoyed by modern mountaineers, Kain chopped more than 600 steps in this icy slope during the ascent. His rope mates, A.H. MacCarthy and W.F. Foster, praised Kain's ability and courage. When he reached the summit, Kain stepped aside and, with customary modesty, announced, "Gentlemen, that's as far as I can take you." The Kain Face is one of two "regular routes" on Mt. Robson today.

The trail climbs eastward through rolling upper subalpine meadows on the north side of the creek toward Snowbird Pass. These meadows are one of two places that could lay claim to being the hoary marmot capital of the Rockies. The other is Maligne Pass. Mountain fireweed and yellow mountain saxifrage grow on the gravels in the creek. The trail becomes vague in the upper meadows, where it fades into two paths. It is easier to approach the pass using the northerly path, which ascends over limestone benches and follows cairns through the final slopes of scree and boulders.

Snowbird Pass is located on the Continental Divide and the boundary between Mt. Robson Provincial Park and Jasper National Park. It commands a lofty view across the 25 km² Reef Icefield and the head of Coleman Glacier to the east. Titkana Peak (2820 m) rises north of Snowbird Pass. *Titkana* is Iroquois for "ptarmigan."

mountain exhibits a classic horn shape, the product of glacial erosion.

The final kilometre to Berg Lake is routed across a large alluvial fan, created by the creek that drains Hargreaves Glacier to the north. From the crest of the fan, Berg Lake comes into view. The trail descends to the northwest shore of the lake at Marmot campground. If you stay here, you will escape the crowds at campgrounds farther along the trail. However, the exposed gravels of the Hargreaves fan can be bleak during poor weather.

## Berg Lake

The trail continues along the northwest shore of Berg Lake, passing the Hargreaves Glacier junction. You can now see the entire north flank of Mt. Robson. Berg Lake is the largest lake in the Rockies into which a glacier flows directly. The remarkable image of ice meeting water is central to the area's scenic charm. Despite the fact Berg Glacier still reaches the lake, it is not advancing. It is considerably smaller than when first photographed in 1908. Two lateral moraines flank the terminus and extend into the lake, giving an indication of the glacier's size during the Little Ice Age.

Berg Lake takes its name from icebergs or "growlers" that calve from the glacier. These ice avalanches provide terrific entertainment for campers. A few hours after an avalanche, the prevailing wind usually will have carried the growlers to the lakeshore near Berg Lake campground. You bring the Scotch; the glacier provides "the rocks."

A.P. Coleman named Berg Lake in 1908. He called the glacier, "Blue Glacier." Subsequently it was called "Tumbling Glacier" — a name already used in Kootenay National Park and so discarded. Berg Glacier is now the official name. Plan on the 2.1 km hike along the shore of Berg Lake taking longer than expected. The incredible north face of Mt. Robson will have you rubbernecking frequently.

Tent sites at Berg Lake campground are on both sides of Toboggan Creek. The Hargreaves shelter is a day-use facility only. The building was constructed as a guest chalet by the Hargreaves family, owners of Mt. Robson Ranch. It was later donated to BC Parks. The shelter is frequently overrun. Store your food in the boxes inside the shelter, along the east wall.

If the crowded environs of Berg Lake campground are not to your liking, continue to Rearguard campground or Robson Pass campground. If you really want to get away from the crowds,

*Hargreaves Glacier and Hargreaves Lake*

Adolphus campground beckons, 4.6 km northeast from Berg Lake in Jasper National Park. You'll need to book the campsite and purchase a wilderness pass from the Jasper visitor information centre.

## The Alpine Club of Canada/ Smithsonian Institution Expedition

**Whitehorn Mountain** was first climbed in 1911 by the Austrian mountain guide Conrad Kain during the Alpine Club of Canada (ACC)/Smithsonian Institution Expedition. A.O. Wheeler, expedition leader and ACC President, was "saving" the ascents of nearby mountains for the glory of a future ACC camp. Kain left camp one afternoon under the pretense of visiting Emperor Falls. When he returned the next morning, it was after having climbed Whitehorn Mountain, solo and in darkness. Wheeler was incensed with Kain's brashness. However, Kain could not tolerate "being among beautiful mountains and not climbing one."

In its outlook, the expedition was a holdover of the Victorian era. Members shot, trapped, and collected almost everything that moved, flew, or grew; and carted the samples back to Washington DC for the glory of science. Future mountaineering routes were planned. Wheeler jealously considered Mt. Robson to be the sole domain of the ACC. Its first ascent was ultimately accomplished from the 1913 ACC camp in Robson Pass, by two ACC members — one of whom was Canadian — led by Conrad Kain. Despite the fact the 1911 expedition walked heavily on the land, the various reports it generated were instrumental in establishing Mt. Robson Provincial Park, the second in British Columbia — an act of considerable foresight.

## Hargreaves Glacier/Mumm Basin, (2103 m) 14.5 km loop

**This strenuous outing** undulates over diverse terrain on the slopes north of Berg Lake, providing incomparable views of Mt. Robson.

From Berg Lake campground, follow the Berg Lake trail southwest for 1.7 km to the Hargreaves Glacier junction. Turn north (right). Ascend a rough, steep track along a dry stream bed, and follow cairns and markers to the east lateral moraine of Hargreaves Glacier. Various routes exist to the crest of the moraine, where the view opens northwest over the rocky basin that contains Hargreaves Glacier and its marginal lake.

*The Hargreaves Glacier-Mumm Basin trail traverses the slopes northwest of Berg Lake and provides stellar views of Mt. Robson.*

As recently as 200 years ago, Hargreaves Glacier filled the basin to the height of this moraine. The glacier is south-facing — not a good thing for ice as the climate warms. The rapid retreat of the glacier has uncovered a fantastically smooth slab of apricot and gray limestone and dolomite of the Tatei Formation. An upturned lip of this rock dams the waters of the lake.

The view south from the moraine provides new detail of Mt. Robson. Mist Glacier terminates in a marginal lake, separated from Berg Lake by a horseshoe-shaped terminal moraine. The cliffs between upper Mist Glacier and the Emperor Ridge are known as the Emperor Face. This face was first climbed in 1978 and has not often been repeated. The ice sheet to the left is the true "north face" of the mountain, first climbed in 1963. A long sought-after prize for extreme skiers, the face was skied in 1996. The two glaciated peaks northeast of Mt. Robson are The Helmet (3420 m), and Mt. Waffl (2890 m), named for Newman Waffl, who died in a 1930 solo attempt on Mt. Robson.

From the Hargreaves moraine, follow the track northeast to treeline. Views ahead include Adolphus Lake in Jasper National Park. The lake was named for Adolphus Moberly, a Métis settler of the Athabasca Valley who guided A.P. Coleman to Mt. Robson in 1908. The lake's dark blue colour indicates that its water is non-glacial.

A steep descent through delightful upper subalpine meadows brings you to a crossing of Toboggan Creek, and a trail junction 150 m beyond. You can exit this hike to Berg Lake campground by following the track 1.2 km downstream (right), past Toboggan Falls — a slab waterfall that resembles a waterslide. Turn northwest (left) at this junction for a sidetrip to "The Cave," a solution cave high on the shoulder of the next ridge. The track climbs steeply through burned forest for approximately 1.5 km to the cave entrance — a horizontal slot in the Eldon Formation limestone.

Bring a headlamp if you'd like to explore, but beware of ice on the floor. The cave itself won't be to everyone's liking, however the panorama of Berg Lake and Mt. Robson from nearby is the climax of this outing. Group of Seven artist Lawren Harris depicted this scene in a work titled *Tumbling Glacier*. Looking south, Resplendent Mountain is in the notch between Mt. Waffl and Rearguard Mountain. If you observe the upper valley of Toboggan Creek carefully, you will see where the creek emerges from underground.

Return to the junction at Toboggan Creek. The Mumm Basin trail continues east (left), ascending steeply through whitebark pine forest to treeline. Follow cairns and markers across boulderfields, screes, and meadows on a vague track that climbs into Mumm Basin. The rocks here are all Middle Cambrian — limestones of the Chetang and Pika formations, and Arctomys (ARK-toe-miss) Formation shale. Wildflower displays include clumps of fringed grass-of-Parnassus, and the showy seedheads of western anemone.

The trail crosses briefly into Alberta, before commencing a steep descent to Robson Pass by contouring southwest along the brink of a high cliff. After re-entering BC at boundary cairn "4U," look carefully for markers, as the trail is easily lost. The steep descent continues on a well-beaten trail to Robson Pass campground. To return to Berg Lake, turn southwest (right) at the junction just beyond.

# Yoho National Park

*Wiwaxy Gap trail on the Lake O'Hara Alpine Circuit*

F ounded in 1886 as Canada's second national park, Yoho includes 1313 km² on the western slopes of the BC

Rockies. "Yoho" is a Cree expression of awe and wonder — sentiments affirmed by many hikers who cherish the park's 350 km of trails. The Classic Hikes in Yoho provide high level views of the park's lake-dotted and glaciated landscape.

The village of Field is in the centre of the park; 85 km west of Banff, 26 km west of Lake Louise, and 57 km east of Golden on the Trans-Canada Highway (Highway 1). Access is by car and by passenger bus. Accommodation and basic supplies are available. The park information centre is on the Trans-Canada Highway at the Field junction. The park has four frontcountry campgrounds with 197 campsites. The Whiskey Jack hostel is near Takakkaw Falls. Yoho is in the Mountain time zone — the same as Banff and Jasper national parks.

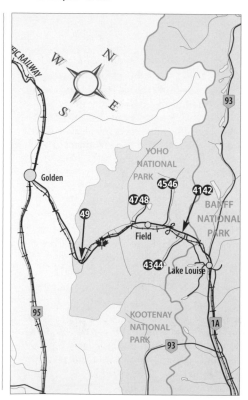

# 41. Paget Lookout

Day-hike

| Route | Elevation (m) | Distance (km) |
|---|---|---|
| Trailhead | 1616 | 0 |
| Paget Lookout jct | 1783 | 1.4 |
| Paget Lookout | 2134 | 3.5 |

**Maps**
NTS: 82 N/8
Gem Trek: Lake Louise and Yoho
Natural Resources Canada: Yoho National Park

## Trailhead

**Wapta Lake** picnic area on the north side of the Trans-Canada Highway, 11 km east of Field, 15 km west of Lake Louise. For safety, eastbound travellers should make a U-turn into West Louise Lodge, 500 m east of the trailhead, and approach westbound. The trailhead is adjacent to the picnic shelter.

In the aftermath of large forest fires in 1936 and 1940, the Dominion Parks Branch surveyed the Rocky Mountain parks to determine suitable sites for fire lookout stations. The sites chosen each possessed unrestricted views of major valleys and were in line of sight with adjacent stations in the lookout system. Paget (PADGE-ett) Lookout was one of three sites chosen in Yoho National Park. It was used until the late 1970s. The access trail is still maintained and the lookout building is open as a day-use shelter. From the lookout you obtain a grand overview of much of eastern Yoho National Park.

### Trailhead to Paget Lookout

Hike northeast from the picnic area for 80 m to a junction. Make a sharp turn west (left). The next 1.3 km of trail ascends through subalpine forest, notable for its inclusion of cottonwood poplar and Douglas-fir, both of which are near their altitudinal limits. In early summer, the undergrowth

## Variation

- Combine this outing with a visit to Sherbrooke Lake, 8.1 km total; or to Sherbrooke Lake and Niles Meadows, 24.9 km total

*The site of Paget Lookout was chosen for its unobstructed view of the upper Kicking Horse Valley and much of southern Yoho.*

is coloured with the blooms of evergreen violets and calypso orchids. You'll see old stumps — evidence of logging during railway construction in the 1880s. Some trees still sport telephone insulators from the days when a line was strung to the lookout.

Turn northeast (right) at the junction at km 1.4. The trail crosses and recrosses an avalanche slope beneath Paget Peak. I've seen spruce grouse here. The cliffs to the north contain a sequence of Cambrian rocks — five formations in all — that dip toward the southwest.

Where the trail begins its switchback ascent through the cliffs of Paget Peak, whitebark pine trees become common. The whitebark pine grows in the upper subalpine ecoregion and prefers windswept locations. On younger trees the bark is smooth and silvery-gray; on older trees it is gray and scaly. The needles are in bunches of five.

The switchbacks provide glimpses of Mt. Niles (2972 m) and Sherbrooke Lake — the third largest lake in Yoho. Mt. Ogden (2695 m) rises from the western shore of the lake. The mountain was named for Isaac Ogden, a vice-president of the CPR. The Lower Spiral Tunnel is in the opposite flank of the mountain. I've often seen boreal toads on these switchbacks, hike-hopping along. At the top of the switchbacks the grade eases, and the trail heads northeast to the lookout. Early season hikers will be treated to displays of glacier lilies.

Paget Lookout commands a 180-degree panorama from Mt. Richardson, the Slate Range,

**175**

and the Bow Valley in the east; to the lofty peaks that surround Lake Louise and Lake O'Hara in the south; and to the Van Horne Range and the middle reach of the Kicking Horse Valley in the southwest. Narao Peak (nah-RAY-owe) (2974 m) peak is across the valley to the southeast. The mountain's name is Stoney for "hit in the stomach," possibly a reference to when James Hector of the Palliser Expedition was kicked by his horse near Wapta Falls in 1858. The forested slopes of Narao Peak show various shades of green, indicating tree stands dominated by different species. Most of the upper Kicking Horse Valley burned in 1889 in fires caused by railway operations. The lighter green canopy indicates stands of lodgepole pine. The darker, taller canopy indicates more ancient stands of Engelmann spruce and subalpine fir.

In the view from the lookout, you can see how the gradient of the Kicking Horse River flowing west from the Continental Divide is much steeper than that of the Bow River, which flows east. River systems on the west slope of the Rockies have only about 525 km straight line distance to flow to the Pacific Ocean. Eastern river systems flow about 1500 km to Hudson's Bay or 2200 km to the Arctic Ocean. A steep gradient gives a river much more energy and enables it to erode a deeper valley. Abrasive sediments in the water also increase a river's erosive power. The town of Field is 16.3 km west of Kicking Horse Pass as the water

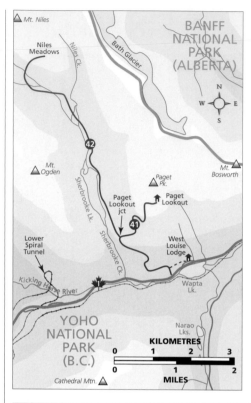

## Waterbars: Going with the Flow

Hiking trails disturb natural drainage patterns. The ideal slope for a hiking trail is 12 degrees. Trails that are less steep may have water collect in low spots. Trails that are steeper often become stream courses. Waterbars are one of several devices that trail crews use to prevent water from collecting underfoot. A waterbar is a log embedded at an angle in the trail, to divert water from the tread surface to an area off-trail where drainage is better. Waterbars are often installed on steep sections of trail that ascend directly upslope or across a sideslope, like those on the upper part of the Paget Lookout trail. Without waterbars, these sections of trail would erode into channels. Waterbars are ideally located where there is a natural dip on the downhill edge of the trail. In the absence of such a dip, trail crews may bevel the trail where they install the waterbar, to increase its effectiveness. Waterbars are often slippery and pose a genuine tripping hazard to hikers. Step over them, not on them.

## Kettles and Sinks

Many of the major east-west passes in the Rockies (Kicking Horse, Vermilion, Yellowhead, and Crowsnest) feature lakes near their summits. These passes were initially scoured by massive ice sheets during the early Pleistocene glaciations, 1.9 million years ago. They have been enlarged by 20 to 30 glaciations since.

Huge blocks of rubble-covered ice detached from retreating ice sheets at the end of the most recent glaciation, the Wisconsin, coming to rest atop mountain passes in the Rockies. As the detached ice blocks melted, the rubble slumped, creating hollows in which water collected. The resulting lakes are known as kettles. Wapta Lake is a kettle, as are Summit Lake and Sink Lake farther east in Kicking Horse Pass. Sink Lake has no visible surface outlet and may drain underground into Wapta Lake. *Wapta* is a Stoney word for "river." It was the original name of the Kicking Horse River.

When the Trans-Canada Highway was constructed through Yoho in 1956, crews excavating a road cut near Wapta Lake found permafrost — evidence of remnant glacial ice from the Wisconsin Glaciation.

*Yoho has an estimated population of 400 mountain goats. Look for them on the slopes of Paget Peak.*

flows, at an elevation of 1242 m. At an equal distance east of Kicking Horse Pass on the Bow River, the valley floor elevation is 1533 m.

Mountain goats frequent Paget Lookout. Yoho has an estimated population of 400 mountain goats. For decades, bighorn sheep were thought to be absent from Yoho. However, since the early 1990s, sheep have made regular appearances at a mineral lick on the lower slopes of Paget Peak, adjacent to the Trans-Canada Highway.

Paget Peak (2591 m) was named for Reverend Dean Paget of Calgary, a founding member of the Alpine Club of Canada who climbed the peak in 1904. Surveyor J.J. McArthur made the first ascent in 1886.

## James Hector

"He was admired and talked about by every man that travelled with him and his fame as a traveller was a wonder and a byword among many a teepee that never saw the man." So wrote Peter Erasmus, James Hector's assistant on the Palliser Expedition of 1857–60. In 1856, Hector was only 22 when he was recommended to the expedition as its doctor and geologist. He had received his medical degree earlier that year, which says something of the medical training of the day, but his real purpose in becoming an MD had been to study the subjects that only enrollment in the medical college at the University of Edinburgh made available — botany, geology, and chemistry. During the expedition's travels, he brought his remarkable powers of observation in these disciplines to bear on the unknown lands of

*James Hector*

western Canada. His journals and official reports are a motherlode of information and detail that paint a lucid picture of the Canadian Rockies just over a decade before the railway surveyors arrived.

In addition to his scholarly work on the Rockies, Hector pounded along his share of tracks and trails — 900 km in one 57-day stint in 1858 alone — and made the first recorded crossings by a European of four passes — Vermilion, Kicking Horse, Pipestone, and Howse. But for all his travels, Hector is best

known for a mishap that took place on August 29, 1858, when he was kicked in the chest by his horse and rendered unconscious. Two days later, his men were calling the river along which they travelled, the "Kicking Horse." Two days after that, they crossed Kicking Horse Pass. Given his injury and the fact that his party was perpetually short of food, it is not surprising that Hector considered the pass a poor choice for a transportation route. The railway builders and politicians of the 1880s should have listened to him.

After surveying Vancouver Island and California at the conclusion of the Palliser Expedition, Hector returned to England to write his contribution to its report. He was off the following year to survey Otago Province in New Zealand, becoming director of that country's Geological Survey in 1865. He was awarded the Lyell Medal in 1875 and was knighted by Queen Victoria in 1886. Hector returned to Canada in 1903, hoping to revisit the site of his mishap near Wapta Falls, and Kicking Horse Pass, where a monument to him had been installed. He was at Glacier House, near Roger's Pass, when his son took ill. Dr. Hector, then 69, did not act soon enough. His son died of appendicitis. Grief-stricken, Hector soon departed for New Zealand, never to return. He died in 1907.

# 42. Sherbrooke Valley

## Route

**Day-hike**

| Route | Elevation (m) | Distance (km) |
|---|---|---|
| Trailhead | 1616 | 0 |
| Paget Lookout jct | 1783 | 1.4 |
| Sherbrooke Lake | 1814 | 3.0 |
| Niles Meadows | 2317 | 9.8 |

**Maps**
NTS: 82 N/8 and 82 N/9
Gem Trek: Lake Louise and Yoho
Natural Resources Canada: Yoho National Park
**See map on p.176**

## Trailhead

**Wapta Lake** picnic area on the north side of the Trans-Canada Highway, 11 km east of Field, 15 km west of Lake Louise. For safety, eastbound travellers should make a U-turn into West Louise Lodge, 500 m east of the trailhead, and approach westbound. The trailhead is adjacent to the picnic shelter.

Although Lake O'Hara and the Yoho Valley attract most of Yoho's hikers, the Sherbrooke Valley has a wilderness quality missing from these other areas. This outing features one of Yoho's larger backcountry lakes, excellent wildlife viewing opportunities, and classic upper subalpine meadows. It's a great pocket of bear habitat. Yoho's first recorded mauling of a person by a grizzly bear took place just beyond the north end of the lake in September 1939.

### Trailhead to Sherbrooke Lake

Hike northeast from the picnic area for 80 m to a junction. Make a sharp turn west (left). The next 1.3 km of trail ascends through subalpine forest, notable for its inclusion of cottonwood poplar and Douglas-fir, both of which are near their altitudinal limits. In early summer, the undergrowth is coloured with the blooms of evergreen violets and calypso orchids. You'll see old stumps — evidence of logging during railway construction in the 1880s. Some trees still sport telephone insulators from the days when a line was strung to Paget lookout. Keep straight ahead at the junction at km 1.4. The right-hand trail leads to Paget Lookout.

*Sherbrooke Lake is Yoho's third largest lake.*

Between the Paget Lookout junction and Sherbrooke Lake, sections of trail have been gravel-capped. Pressure-treated wood decking has been installed to bridge boggy areas. Look for orchid blooms here in early summer, including tall white rein-orchid and hooded ladies'-tresses. You can see Mt. Stephen (3199 m) and Cathedral Crags (3073 m) through the trees to the southwest.

About 60 m beyond the first blowdown, a short sidetrail leads west (left) to the shore of Sherbrooke Lake. Early morning visitors often find the lake a tranquil mirror, reflecting the colourful slabs of Mt. Ogden (2695 m) opposite, and the thumb-like form of Mt. Niles (2972 m) at the north end of the valley. The upthrust sedimentary formations in Mt. Ogden's ridge date to the Cambrian. In the sequence of five formations, the rocks become progressively younger toward the north end of the mountain.

With an area of 35 ha, Sherbrooke is Yoho's third largest lake. It is 12 m deep and is usually frozen until late June. Glacially formed and fed, its waters change colour from clear, to blue-green, to silty gray as the glacial melt season progresses. Lake trout and rainbow trout are present. Surveyor J.J. McArthur named the lake in 1887, after the town of Sherbrooke, Quebec.

The trail follows the east shore. You may see mountain goats high on the cliffs of Paget Peak. Extensive avalanche slopes reach down to the west shore. These slopes are good places to look

## Variation

- Combine this outing with a visit to Paget Lookout, 24.9 km total

*Niles Meadows*

for moose, deer, and elk, that browse on green alder, water birch, and willows. The avalanche slopes are also frequented by grizzly bears in their quest for berries, succulent forbs, and rodents.

At the north end of the lake, the trail passes through another blowdown. There are many dead trees in the lake, with root plates still attached. While the downed trees on shore blew over in a windstorm, those in the lake did not. They were probably uprooted by avalanches from the slope to the west. Deposited on the frozen lake surface, the trees came to rest on the shallow lake bottom when that winter's ice melted.

## Sherbrooke Lake to Niles Meadows

Beyond the lake's inlet, the trail ascends beside a small canyon that contains a waterfall, and then emerges into an extensive subalpine wet meadow dotted with massive boulders. Here Niles Creek, draining the valley to the northeast, converges with upper Sherbrooke Creek.

The trail crosses the two channels of Niles

Creek and then makes several sharp turns as it works its way through willows to the north edge of the meadow. This section is difficult to describe — look for the beaten path. After a gentle switchback ascent into ancient spruce-fir forest — tree ages of 300 years have been recorded here — the grade steepens to crest a rock step alongside a waterfall. About 300 m farther, rock-hop the creek to its west bank, or use a fallen tree if still present.

The upper reach of Sherbrooke Creek is both avalanche slope and creek bed. Snow avalanches from the west sweep directly down the creek, and have severed many tree tops at trailside. Cross a bridge to the east side of the creek.

The mountains along the west side of Sherbrooke Valley feature wildly folded and steeply dipping rock formations. Two waterfalls cascade over the cliff at the head of the creek. The trail angles sharply to the southeast (right) and climbs steeply on an open slope, where clumps of false hellebore grow. A hundred metres after cresting this slope, the trail emerges from the trees and swings north into the meadows beneath Mt. Niles. Take note of where the trail leaves the trees, as it is easy to miss on return.

A rockslide on the west side of the meadow makes a good lunch place. Mt. Niles is the centrepiece in the view north. Its strata show the unmistakable U-shaped fold of a syncline. The mountain was named for William Niles, president of the Appalachian Mountain Club in 1898. For the adventurous, animal trails and mountaineers' paths lead above treeline onto the surrounding benches, where you can enjoy a view of Sherbrooke Lake and the mountains between Lake Louise and Field.

## Blowdown

**Just before Sherbrooke Lake,** the trail passes through the first of the valley's blowdown areas. These Engelmann spruce and subalpine fir trees were uprooted during a violent thunderstorm in August 1984. I was working at Chateau Lake Louise at the time. The storm blew out many of the windows on the ground floor, and flooded the basement. You can still count the tree rings on some of the trees cleared from the trail here. A few of the spruces were roughly 300 years old.

Although it looks like a scene of destruction, this blowdown is one of nature's methods for revitalizing areas of old forest. In the absence of fire, blowdowns create openings in the forest canopy, allowing sunlight to reach the floor. This promotes new growth of the shrubs and wildflowers that provide food for deer, elk, moose, and bears. The fallen trees eventually decompose into soil.

## In the Footsteps of Pioneers

**The first recorded travellers** in this part of the Sherbrooke Valley were mountaineers Charles Fay and party, who, without benefit of a trail, used this approach to attempt Mt. Balfour on the Waputik (WAH-poo-tick) Icefield in 1898. Although unsuccessful on Mt. Balfour, Fay's party made the first ascents of Mt. Niles and the unnamed peak immediately south of Mt. Daly. The trail we now hike originated in 1911, to provide access to the 6th annual Alpine Club of Canada mountaineering camp, which convened at the north edge of the Niles Creek meadow. Here and there you will see rotting corduroy bridges that date to the original trail construction.

# 43. Lake O'Hara Alpine Circuit

## Route

### Day-hike

| Route | Elevation (m) | Distance (km) |
|---|---|---|
| Trailhead | 2015 | 0 |
| Wiwaxy Gap jct | 2018 | 0.3 |
| Wiwaxy Gap | 2538 | 2.2 |
| Lake Oesa jct | 2260 | 4.2 |
| East Opabin jct | 2287 | 6.6 |
| Opabin Lake | 2287 | 7.1 |
| Opabin Prospect jct | 2220 | 8.7 |
| All Souls' jct | 2210 | 8.8 |
| All Souls' Prospect | 2460 | 9.8 |
| Schäffer Lake | 2180 | 11.0 |
| Trailhead | 2015 | 12.4 |

## Maps

NTS: 82 N/8

Gem Trek: Lake Louise and Yoho

Natural Resources Canada: Yoho National Park

The Adventure Map: Lake O'Hara

Lake O'Hara is the most developed and popular hiking destination in Yoho National Park. Within a 5 km radius of the lake, 80 km of hiking trails explore every nook and cranny of an exceptional high country landscape. The Lake O'Hara Alpine Circuit connects sections of seven trails into a rewarding loop, with views of more than a dozen lakes and ponds, and the rugged peaks along the Continental Divide.

Portions of this hike traverse exposed ledges, and about a third of the distance is on rough trails through boulderfields and across scree slopes. In these places, you must pay careful attention to route markers. Avoid this hike during early season, poor weather, electrical storms, and after snowfalls — although for day visitors, the timing of the outing will likely be dictated by your bus reservation, not by the weather. Opabin Plateau is usually closed until the winter snowpack has melted — well into July in most years.

### Trailhead to Wiwaxy Gap

From the interpretive display, follow the lakeshore trail north for 60 m to the outlet bridge. Cross the bridge, turn east (right) and follow the north

## Trailhead

The number of visitors in the Lake O'Hara area is controlled through a complicated quota system administered by Yoho National Park. You can hike the Cataract Brook trail (12.8 km) to Lake O'Hara campground, or walk the fireroad (10.4 km). Most folks fork over the cash and take the bus, which makes four round-trips each day. You don't need a reservation if you are hiking in and out from the parking lot on the same day, but you do need to reserve if you plan on camping or taking the bus. A few seats on the bus and a few tent sites are available each day on a first come, first served basis — for use on the *following* day. As a last gasp, you can show up to meet the bus and hope that someone else is running late. Call 250-343-6433 well in advance for details. Have your credit card information ready.

To reach the staging area, follow the Trans-Canada Highway to the junction with Highway 1A, 12.6 km west of Lake Louise, 13.4 km east of Field. Turn onto Highway 1A, cross the railway tracks and turn west (right) to the Lake O'Hara parking lot. Meet the park attendant at the bus shelter just inside the fireroad gate, or walk the road or the Cataract Brook trail. You can't bike the road. The Alpine Circuit trailhead is next to the warden cabin, 600 m south of the campground.

shore trail 200 m to the Wiwaxy Gap junction. The "north bay" of Lake O'Hara, adjacent to this section of trail, was closed to angling in 1990 to protect trout habitat.

Looking west across the lake, Odaray Mountain (3159 m) may be reflected in the still waters of morning. The southern summit of the mountain (Little Odaray, 2962 m) was first climbed by surveyor J.J. McArthur in 1887. McArthur described the area to Robert O'Hara, a retired British army colonel. O'Hara made at least two visits to the lake, in the 1880s and 1890s. It became known as "O'Hara's Lake."

The climb from the lakeshore to Wiwaxy Gap is the steepest section of trail on any of the Classic

## Variations

- Shorten the outing by exiting from Lake Oesa (7.5 km total), East Opabin (9.7 km total) or West Opabin (10.8 km total)
- Add a visit to Opabin Prospect, 0.8 km return
- Extend the outing by adding Lake McArthur to the end of the circuit, 15.6 km total. See Classic Hike #44.

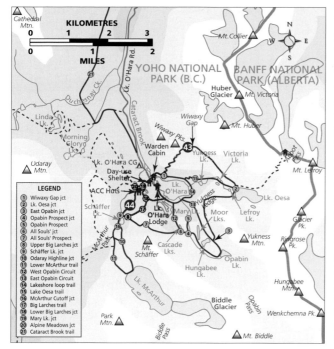

Hikes — a torturous ascent of 503 m in just 1.9 km. The first section switchbacks tightly in a gully that was swept by a debris flow in the summer of 1985. At the top of the gully, you traverse east beneath a 20 m quartzite cliff, and then ascend the cliff on ledges. The steep grade resumes. A remarkable Engelmann spruce tree towers over the trail. Two of its roots have grown laterally out of the steep slope, and then upward to become separate trunks. The diameter of the main trunk is 1.4 m at the base, more than ten times greater than average for a spruce at treeline. Whitebark pine also grows here.

Your rapid ascent soon provides an aerial view of Lake O'Hara. The lake has an area of 34.4 ha, and a maximum depth of 38.1 m. As its vivid colour suggests, the lake is fed by glacial meltwater. If you look southeast into the valley that contains Lake Oesa, you can see that Lake O'Hara is the lowest in a series of five lakes and ponds. Glaciologists call such an arrangement *paternoster lakes,* or a glacial cirque staircase. In past ice ages, glacial ice flowed west and hollowed the basins for each lake at progressively lower elevations. A cascading stream now connects them. As with most lakes created this way, the deepest part of Lake O'Hara is just beneath the headwall, where the glacier plunged into the valley. Across Lake O'Hara to the southeast, Yukness Mountain (2847 m) scrapes the sky. The glacially sculpted horn of Mt. Biddle (3319 m) looms above Opabin Pass to the south. McArthur Pass frames the north glacier of Mt. Owen (3087 m) to the southwest.

The trail traverses more gullies and continues its steep, sidehill ascent. Wherever the trail becomes faint or takes to ledges, the route is indicated with cairns and painted markers — two vertical yellow stripes on a rectangular blue

## Lake O'Hara Lexicon

**Some of the unusual names** at Lake O'Hara come from the Stoney dialect, and were given by American explorer Samuel Allen, who visited the Rockies four times in the early 1890s. He learned the names from William Twin, the Stoney most adept at guiding explorers.

- *Hungabee* (hun-GAH-bee): "chieftain." With an elevation of 3493 m, it is the highest mountain in the area.
- *Oesa* (owe-EE-sah): "ice" (Allen spelled it Oeesa.) The lake is often frozen into July.
- *Opabin* (owe-PAY-bin): "rocky." This name appears often throughout the mountains of western North America.

- *Wiwaxy* (wih-WAX-ee): "windy." Wiwaxy Gap is indeed a windy place. Allen called the valley to the north the "gorge of the winds."
- *Yukness* (YUCK-ness): "sharpened, as with a knife." The mountain's horn shape was "sharpened" by glacial ice.
- Uncertainty surrounds the mountain called *Odaray* (OWE-dah-ray), which was named by surveyor J.J. McArthur. Four meanings have been proposed: "many waterfalls," "very brushy," "windfall" or "cone." As McArthur originally referred to it as "Cone Mountain," the latter was probably the intended meaning.

background. Although you may occasionally have to use your hands on the rock for balance, in no place does the route involve technical climbing. If you lose the way or come face to face with an unscalable cliff, backtrack and look for the route markers.

Above treeline, the trail angles steeply to Wiwaxy Gap, the low point on the ridge that connects the Wiwaxy Peaks (2703 m) to the west, with Mt. Huber (3368 m) to the east. Daisy fleabane, golden fleabane, Drummond's anemone, spotted saxifrage, alpine arnica, moss campion, and white mountain avens are scattered across the screes. Look for the tracks and pellets of mountain goats.

*Lake Oesa*

For those unaccustomed to high places, Wiwaxy Gap may seem more like a mountain summit than a pass. The view north over Cataract Brook includes Cathedral Mountain (3189 m) and the peaks on the Wapta and Waputik icefields in the northern part of Yoho National Park. Two waterfalls on the cliff to the northeast of Wiwaxy Gap are fed by meltwater from Huber Glacier. Above the waterfalls, the keen eye can pick out the rocky summit of Mt. Victoria (3464 m). Its western aspect is entirely unlike the familiar view from Lake Louise. True to its name, Wiwaxy Gap is a windy place, and with the sweat you've worked up during the climb, you are not likely to linger.

## Wiwaxy Gap to Lake Oesa

Head southeast from Wiwaxy Gap on the trail that aims straight for Lake Oesa. Ignore the paths that lead uphill and downhill, left and right respectively. You can see the trail ahead, scratched across the cliff edge. If this does not look to your liking or if snow lingers, turn back here. Also, beware of snow avalanche danger on this next section if you are hiking before mid-July or after a snowfall. The 2.2 km leg to Lake Oesa involves a descending traverse, with fine views to the chain of paternoster lakes. On a calm day, you can hear the cascading water in the cataracts that link the lakes. Across the chasm, Yukness Mountain broods in morning shadow.

The massive mountain wall that backs Lake Oesa is part of the Continental Divide. It extends from Mt. Lefroy (3423 m) on the north, through Glacier Peak (3283 m), to Ringrose Peak (3281 m) on the south. A small drift glacier occupies Lake

Oesa's northeast shore, and a moraine-dammed lake sits above the southeast shore. Lake Oesa is dammed by an upturned, glacier-worn rock slab.

## Lake Oesa to Opabin Plateau

At the first trail junction, turn southwest, downhill to the right. In 150 m you reach the Lake Oesa junction. You want the trail labelled "Opabin Plateau via Yukness Ledge Alpine Route," which angles southeast from the junction. The trail crosses the rock slabs west of the lake and descends toward the outlet. Follow the large cairns and use caution if the rock is wet or icy. At the third cairn, the trail angles off to the south (right) across a small meadow, and then descends a short cliff to the outlet stream. Rock-hop the stream and follow the cairned route west, climbing across slabs and through boulderfields.

## Cairn Building

**The rock piles** you see marking the route and crowning the highpoints of this hike are called cairns. *Carn* is Gaelic for "pile of rocks." Cairns assist hikers and mountaineers when the way is vague or during poor weather when visibility is limited.

The cairns in the Lake O'Hara area have evolved over decades. Many are "overkill" for their intended purpose, cluttering the margin of well-defined routes. Some are no more than landscape graffiti — unnecessary and inappropriate. Please do not add to existing cairns or build new ones. When you move rocks in the alpine ecoregion you alter drainage patterns, overturn lichens, and disrupt the formation of soils. On the small scale, you may be setting back the growth of vegetation by centuries.

## Gog Formation Quartzite: Tough Stuff

*Trilobites made the lumps, and worms made the squiggles, now fossilized in this ripple rock slab of Gog Formation siltstone.*

**The Lake O'Hara** Alpine Circuit is the only Classic Hike that features a single rock formation underfoot for its entire distance. Between lake level and approximately 2750 m, the bedrock is Gog Formation quartzite and siltstone.

Gog quartzite is a very hard, quartz-rich sandstone — the hardest rock in the central Rockies. It is composed of pebble-sized, sand-sized, and silt-sized quartz particles eroded from the Canadian Shield, transported to the southwest by rivers, and deposited in ancient seas during the Early Cambrian, 525 to 545 million years ago. The small spaces between the individual quartz grains are filled with tiny intergrown crystals of quartz, binding the sandstone together very tightly.

Some exposures of Gog quartzite are covered with green and black map lichens (*Rhizocarpon geographicum*). Where protected from weathering, Gog quartzite is often white, pinkish or purplish; where exposed, it may be stained brown and red with iron oxides. Fossil trilobites occur here and there in Gog rocks, but the fossilized burrowings of worms (*Planolites*) and of trilobites (*Rusphycos*) are much more common, as is iron pyrite ("fool's gold") — a source of additional colour. Some quartzite boulders contain a conglomerate of fist-sized pebbles and rocks, bound together with quartz. At the Lake Oesa junction, trail builders have incorporated colourful ripple rock slabs of Gog siltstone into the walking surface.

Beware of rockfall danger here.

The trail descends a natural staircase with some awkward steps, and then switchbacks on the north end of the terrace that overlooks Lake O'Hara. Pay careful attention to the route markers here. At the next junction, turn sharply south (left). If the weather has become foul, you can exit by going straight ahead at this junction. This will bring you to the Lake Oesa trail at Victoria Lake, where you turn west (left) to descend to Lake O'Hara.

For the next kilometre, the trail traverses Yukness Ledge, offering breathtaking views over Lake O'Hara. Move slowly and carefully near the cliff edge, especially if the rock is wet. You may see a sediment plume issuing from "East Opabin Creek" into Lake O'Hara, where the glacial sediment transported by the creek disperses into the lake. The finest particles, called rock flour, are suspended in the lake water. They reflect the blue and green spectra of light, giving the lake its remarkable colour.

Opabin Glacier comes into view straight ahead, tucked beneath the precipitous flank of Mt. Biddle. Samuel Allen named the mountain for A.J. Biddle, a Philadelphia author and publisher. Opabin Plateau is west of the trail, covered with stands of larch and dotted by the Opabin Moor Lakes. When you have travelled slightly more than half of the length above Opabin Plateau, the trail begins a winding and sometimes steep descent through rockslide debris to its junction with the East Opabin Trail. Hungabee Lake is adjacent to the junction.

Turn southeast (left), cross a rock bridge, and ascend the rise to Opabin Lake. Notice the boulders that were inlaid in the walking surface during trail rehabilitation in 1988 and 1989. The thin, clay soils here saturate with water quickly, creating a slippery, poorly drained tread. Undisciplined hikers walk off the trail, damaging the surrounding vegetation. The boulders serve as stepping stones, keeping feet dry and preserving the adjacent upper subalpine meadows.

Hungabee Mountain (3493 m), first climbed in 1903, towers to the southeast of Opabin Lake. The broad, northwest face forms part of the regular mountaineering route from Opabin Pass. Although many mountaineers have this summit on their "wish list," the poor rock on the upper mountain and the frequent presence of snow and ice thwart many attempts to climb it.

The mass of rubble on the south shore of

*Lake O'Hara from Yukness Ledge*

*Opabin Plateau*

Opabin Lake is a terminal moraine, created during the Little Ice Age advance of Opabin Glacier. The moraine has partly filled the lake. Study of lake bottom sediments at Opabin Lake and Lake O'Hara indicates that the Little Ice Age was the most significant glacial advance here in the last 8500 years. Between 3000 and 8500 years ago, glaciers were absent in this area above the elevation of Opabin Lake. The upper Opabin Valley, now a chaos of moraine and ice, supported subalpine forest.

Turn sharply northwest (right) at the junction at Opabin Lake, to follow the West Opabin Circuit. The larch glades here are filled with mountain heather and are frequented by white-tailed ptarmigan. The trail descends rock benches, paralleling West Opabin Creek. You can see where the silty water of Opabin Lake drains beneath a complex of moraines. The moraines record two distinct glacial advances. The lower, older, and larger moraine is covered in lichens. Atop this sits the more colourful rock of the Little Ice Age moraine, approximately 150 years old.

There are fine views ahead of Cathedral Mountain, the Wiwaxy Peaks, and the serried flanks of Mt. Huber (3368 m), reflected here and there in the numerous lakes and ponds on Opabin Plateau. Emil Huber was a Swiss alpinist who, in 1890, made the first ascent of Mt. Sir Donald, near Rogers Pass. Keep to the West Opabin Circuit at all trail junctions, which is always either left or straight ahead. After 1.6 km of delightful hiking, you reach the Opabin Prospect junction. Detour north (right) if you want to make the 0.8 km return trip to this viewpoint. The main trail begins a steep descent with views of Mary Lake and Cathedral Mountain directly ahead. The All

Souls' Prospect junction is 80 m farther. You may exit the Alpine Circuit at this point by continuing straight ahead to descend to Lake O'Hara. Otherwise, turn west (left), and ascend a rock staircase onto the benches beneath Mt. Schäffer (2692 m). The mountain was named for Mary Schäffer, best known for her exploration of Maligne Lake in 1908. Hoary marmots frequent these benches, and you may see mountain goats on the cliffs above.

You climb steeply to the west on scree and then traverse northwest at a more reasonable grade. Beware of rockfall danger here. The ascent brings you to All Souls' Prospect. The peculiar name of this viewpoint was given by Dr. George Link, who cleared many trails in the Lake O'Hara area. All Souls' Day is November 2 — a day of prayer for the souls of the faithful departed.

From All Souls' Prospect, you will enjoy a tremendous and lofty panorama on a clear day. The Cataract Brook Valley is to the north, leading your eye to Mt. Bosworth (2771 m) above Kicking Horse Pass. You can see all of the principal peaks of the Continental Divide in this area, and to the

## Alpine Imagery

**The Lake O'Hara** area has attracted and inspired many artists, among them, J.S. Sargent, W.J. Phillips, Peter and Catherine Whyte, and members of the Group of Seven, including J.E.H. MacDonald. Macdonald in particular was enchanted with Lake O'Hara. He made the first of seven visits in 1924. Several of his works include views of Mt. Biddle, Mt. Owen, and Cathedral Mountain from the trail between Wiwaxy Gap and Lake Oesa, from Opabin Plateau, and from Yukness Ledge.

west and southwest respectively, you have point-blank views of Odaray Mountain and Mt. Owen. Looking southeast, you can see Neptuak Mountain (3237 m) framed through Opabin Pass. From here, Opabin Plateau appears a desolate place, its meadowlands and larch forest dwarfed to insignificance by moraines and rockslides, and by the precipices that ring the valley.

### All Souls' Prospect to Lake O'Hara

Descend north from All Souls' Prospect on a rough path beaten into the screes and boulder-fields. This is a bone-jarring descent, with one 2 m step that requires downclimbing. The proliferation of trails in the Lake O'Hara area has resulted in many redundant and parallel paths. If you look down to the meadows near Schäffer Lake, you can see newly gravelled trails and old trails that have been closed and left to revegetate.

The trail winds through treeline forest and passes the Big Larches junction. Continue straight ahead to the Schäffer Lake junction in 100 m. The lake is a kettle pond fringed with willows. Unless you want to add Lake McArthur to this outing, turn northeast (right) at this junction. As the trail begins its descent to Lake O'Hara, note the gradual transition from larch forest to one dominated by Engelmann spruce and subalpine fir.

The descent brings you to the erroneously named "Alpine Meadow" and the Alpine Club of Canada's Elizabeth Parker Hut. The meadow is below treeline and is "subalpine." The buildings date to 1926 and have been operated by the ACC since 1930. Nine other cabins formerly on this site were moved to the lakeshore and are now the outlying cabins of Lake O'Hara Lodge. Keep straight ahead at the junction adjacent to the hut.

The ACC held the first of six mountaineering camps at Lake O'Hara on this meadow in 1909. Between then and 1974, when random camping and group camping were abolished, the meadows suffered severe impacts from overuse. East of the hut you can see a fenced plot on a closed trail. Look at the subtle difference that more than three decades of natural regeneration has produced in the vegetation — a vivid indication of the harshness of the local climate.

Turn north (left) at the junction 200 m east of the hut. The trail climbs out of the creekbed, swings east, and descends to Le Relais (the day-use shelter), opposite the warden cabin on the fireroad. Outbound buses stop here. If you're staying at the campground, turn north (left) and walk 600 m along the road.

*Even mountains get the blues: Lake McArthur on a perfect summer day.*

# 44. Lake McArthur

## Route

**Day-hike**

| Route | Elevation (m) | Distance (km) |
|---|---|---|
| Trailhead | 2015 | 0 |
| Mary Lake jct | 2030 | 0.3 |
| Big Larches jct | 2050 | 0.6 |
| Schäffer Lake | 2180 | 1.7 |
| McArthur Cutoff jct | 2180 | 1.8 |
| Odaray Highline jct | 2325 | 2.3 |
| High point of trail | 2375 | 2.6 |
| Lake McArthur | 2260 | 3.3 |
| McArthur Cutoff jct | 2180 | 4.8 |
| Schäffer Lake | 2180 | 4.9 |
| Alpine Meadows jct | 2030 | 5.8 |
| Mary Lake jct | 2030 | 6.0 |
| Trailhead | 2015 | 6.3 |

**Maps**
NTS: 82 N/8
Gem Trek: Lake Louise and Yoho
Natural Resources Canada: Yoho National Park
The Adventure Map: Lake O'Hara
**See map on p.181**

**Best lighting:** afternoon

## Trailhead

The number of visitors in the Lake O'Hara area is controlled through a complicated quota system administered by Yoho National Park. You can hike the Cataract Brook trail (12.8 km) to Lake O'Hara campground, or walk the fireroad (10.4 km). Most folks fork over the cash and take the bus, which makes four round-trips each day. You don't need a reservation if you are hiking in and out from the parking lot on the same day, but you do need to reserve if you plan on camping or taking the bus. A few seats on the bus and a few tent sites are available each day on a first come, first served basis — for use on the *following* day. As a last gasp, you can show up to meet the bus and hope that someone else is running late. Call 250-343-6433 well in advance for details. Have your credit card information ready.

To reach the staging area, follow the Trans-Canada Highway to the junction with Highway 1A, 12.6 km west of Lake Louise, 13.4 km east of Field. Turn onto Highway 1A, cross the railway tracks and turn west (right) to the Lake O'Hara parking lot. Meet the park attendant at the bus shelter just inside the fireroad gate, or lace up your boots to walk the road or the Cataract Brook trail. The Lake McArthur trailhead is opposite the warden cabin, 600 m south of the campground.

Lake McArthur is the real jewel of the Lake O'Hara area — a sapphire charm crowned with the diamond snows of Biddle Glacier. The lake may be ice-covered until mid-July. It wasn't for lack of scenery that I omitted Lake McArthur from the first edition of *Classic Hikes*. In 1994, Parks Canada was deliberating closures for the McArthur/Odaray system of trails at Lake O'Hara. The move was prompted by three bear attacks between 1985 and 1992, and by the realization that McArthur Pass is a key wildlife corridor in the most heavily-used piece of backcountry in the Rockies. A decade later at press time, the trail across McArthur Pass to McArthur Creek was closed for part of the summer, with access by permit only for the remainder. The Odaray Highline trail was subject to a "voluntary closure." Please abide by further access restrictions, should they be implemented.

### Trailhead to Lake McArthur

Begin opposite the warden cabin on the north side of Le Relais, the day-use shelter. Head west through ancient forest for 200 m. The trail turns south along the edge of the erroneously named "Alpine Meadow" — it's still well below treeline, here — to reach the Mary Lake junction in another 100 m. Continue straight ahead to the Big Larches junction in 300 m. Turn southwest (right), to begin the ascent to Schäffer Lake.

The aptly named Big Larches trail grinds around the north end of Mt. Schäffer (2692 m), through the jumbled quartzite blocks of a rock-slide known as the "Devil's Rock Pile." The "mountain," which is really the culmination of a ridge of Mt. Biddle, was named for Mary Schäffer, the explorer known best for her trips to Maligne Lake in 1908 and 1911. It's a stiff climb, but the larch forest and the wildflowers offer many incentives to pause. The displays of western anemone are particularly fine. I have seen Columbian ground squirrels here pretending to be porcupines — climbing into the larches to eat the needles.

You pass the junction with the Alpine Circuit just before the trail levels at Schäffer Lake. Walk around the north and west shores of the lake to the McArthur Cutoff junction. Take the left fork, and begin climbing again. The trail crosses a geologic transition during this climb. Most of the bedrock in the Lake O'Hara basin is quartzite, sandstone, and siltstone of the Gog Group of formations. On these slopes you pass through a thin outcrop of Mt. Whyte Formation shale, with the remainder of the ascent being on Cathedral Formation limestone. The rock formations — all of them date to the Cambrian — get younger as you go uphill. Lawrence Grassi, park warden during the 1950s and early 1960s, worked on sections of this trail. The late Jon Whyte wrote of his craft, "The Rockies shall not easily wear away what he built. Centuries from now the pilgrims shall make their way to Lake McArthur along his path, and they shall wonder that one among us had so much art and skill. His name by then may be forgotten, but his art shall not."

Continue straight ahead at the Odaray Highline junction. A short distance later, the trail begins to descend and swings southeast through true alpine meadows to the crags above the north shore of Lake McArthur. I can tell you that the colour of the lake is a marvel, but you must see it

## Variations

- Hike the loop in reverse
- Add a visit to Lake McArthur to the conclusion of the Lake O'Hara Alpine Circuit, 15.6 km total. See Classic Hike #43.

## Canada's First Alpinist

**James Joseph McArthur** was a Dominion land surveyor who worked in the Rockies from 1887 to 1893. His task was to survey the "Railway Belt" — the lands bordering, and given to, the recently constructed Canadian Pacific Railway (CPR). McArthur literally went above the call of duty, occupying scores of summits as survey stations. Because the peaks were often unnamed at the time, some of these ascents have never been credited to him. David Douglas, David Thompson, James Hector, and A.P. Coleman had each made sporadic ascents in the Rockies before 1887. But J.J. McArthur was Canada's first practiced alpinist.

McArthur's work was extremely difficult, accomplished without trails and often without the use of horses to pack gear. His journal entries sum up days of hardship in single sentences, matter-of-factly recording prodigious feats of travel at a time when summers were much more harsh than those of today. Sometimes alone, sometimes with an assistant, he would carry heavy photographic equipment to the summits, some of which were walk-ups, but a few of which — like Mt. Stephen near Field — were not. His ascent of Mt. Stephen — with his assistant, T. Riley — on September 9, 1887, was the first

*Another day at the office; J.J. McArthur and an assistant, ca. 1890*

of any mountain over 10,000 feet in Canada. As the view was marred by clouds and firesmoke, the duo went back in 1892, carrying a length of a tree to the summit, to leave behind as a sighting pole. I have not met too many contemporary mountaineers who, with benefit of guidebooks and an approach trail, and without carrying sections of trees, have cared to climb Mt. Stephen twice.

McArthur's photography was incorporated into the map-making — a process called photogrammetry — yielding extremely beautiful and accurate maps. Many of the elevations we assign to features today have not been changed since those first surveys. McArthur went on to lead the Canadian contingent that surveyed the Alaska-BC boundary, and

later was Canadian representative on the International Boundary Commission. His name adorns four features in Yoho — a pass, a creek, a lake, and a mountain. His remarkable trove of photographs of the Rockies has gone missing. Those of fellow surveyor, M.P. Bridgland, were recently located in a mislabelled stack of boxes at the National Archives in Ottawa. Let's hope that McArthur's images have met no worse a fate.

*"Leaving our alpensticks behind, we stepped across and with face to the wall moved along the ledge to a slanting rift, up which we clambered, our entire weight sometimes dependent on the first joints of our fingers."*

From J.J. McArthur's description of the first ascent of Mt. Stephen in 1887

*Lake McArthur in 1909...*

*...and more recently*

to fully appreciate it. A warm summer afternoon here is backcountry heaven.

## Lake McArthur

With an area of 77 hectares, Lake McArthur is Yoho's second largest lake and, for its altitude, may be the largest backcountry lake in the Rockies. Nestled between two northwest-trending ridges of Mt. Biddle, the lake is a textbook example of a tarn — a lake that occupies a glacially-sculpted basin within a glacial cirque. The maximum depth is 84 m. The lake's size results from two features of the Cathedral Formation limestone bedrock. The rock at the northwest shore dips at an angle of about 24 degrees, effectively damming the water. With its path blocked, the lake water has sought an underground outlet — as water often does in limestone — eroding one or more sinks in the lake bottom. Sinks usually do not drain a lake as fast as an aboveground outlet would, so the water pools before draining. This pooling probably affects the sediment load of the lake, helping to create its spectacular colour. The emergence of the underground outlet has not been determined, but it may be in upper McArthur Creek.

The austere form of Mt. Biddle (3319 m) dominates the head of the cirque. If you think that its dark crest appears formidable, you're right. The upper part of the mountain is Eldon Formation limestone, a cliff-builder just about everywhere in the Rockies, but hereabouts, loose and crumbly. The horseshoe traverse of Mt. Biddle and Park Mountain (2975 m) is a mountaineering test piece, not often accomplished. In 1894, explorer Samuel Allen named Mt. Biddle for his Philadelphia friend, Anthony Biddle. "Park" refers to the park-like vegetation at Park Mountain's base.

Accounts from 1904 and photographs taken in 1909 indicate that in those years, Biddle Glacier extended into the lake. Photographs taken in 1933 show that the ice had receded 300 m from the lakeshore. Today, it is almost a kilometre from the ice to the water.

## Return

In deference to the bears that frequent McArthur Pass, avoid using the Lower McArthur trail when you leave the lake. Retrace your steps to Schäffer Lake, from where you have two options: descend the Big Larches trail, or keep straight ahead at the junction on the north side of the lake, to descend to the Alpine Meadow. Continue straight ahead at the junction at the Elizabeth Parker hut, cross the meadow, turn north (left) at the Mary Lake junction, and walk out to the trailhead.

### Face to Facies

**The saddle** on the ridge that connects Mt. Biddle and Park Mountain is known as Biddle Pass. It has never seen much use as a travel route, but it is a great landmark for spotting the division between the eastern main ranges and the western main ranges. The rock of eastern main range mountains was created from sediments deposited close to shore in relatively shallow seas. Lime-producing algae and cyanobacteria (blue-green algae) lived in these waters. Therefore limestone predominates, along with sandstone and siltstone. Farther offshore, muds sank deep into the relatively lifeless abyss, where they compacted to create shale — the primary rock, or facies, of the western main ranges. You can see the line where the facies change — dark shales to the west, lighter-coloured limestones and quartzite to the east.

# 45. Iceline

## Route

**Day-hike or overnight**

| Route | Elevation (m) | Distance (km) |
|---|---|---|
| Takakkaw Falls parking | 1509 | 0 |
| Iceline/Yoho Pass trailhead | 1501 | 0.6 |
| Hidden Lakes jct | 1638 | 1.8 |
| Yoho Lake/Iceline lower jct | 1646 | 1.9 |
| Yoho Lake-Iceline upper jct | 1860 | 3.0 |
| Celeste Lake upper jct | 2195 | 6.3 |
| Trail summit | 2230 | 6.8 |
| Kiwetinok Pass jct | 2073 | 11.1 |
| Iceline north jct | 2072 | 11.4 |
| Little Yoho CG | 2073 | +0.3 |
| Celeste Lake lower jct | 1768 | 13.9 |
| Whaleback jct | 1768 | 14.0 |
| Marpole Lake/ Twin Falls jct | 1814 | 14.6 |
| Little Yoho jct | 1608 | 16.2 |
| Laughing Falls CG | 1608 | 16.3 |
| Takakkaw Falls parking | 1509 | 21.1 |

**Maps**

NTS: 82 N/7, and 82 N/8, and 82 N/10
Gem Trek: Lake Louise and Yoho
Natural Resources Canada: Yoho National Park

## Trailhead

**Follow the Trans-Canada Highway** to the Yoho Valley Road, 3.7 km east of Field, 22.3 km west of Lake Louise. Turn north and follow this road 14 km to the Takakkaw Falls parking lot. Walk south; continue straight ahead at the junction that leads to the falls. Cross the Yoho Valley Road to the Iceline/Yoho Pass trailhead, just north of Whiskey Jack Hostel. Those travelling without a vehicle can use the hostel or nearby Takakkaw Falls walk-in campground as a base.

Constructed in 1987, the Iceline quickly became one of the premier hikes in the Rockies. Scratched from glacial rubble, the trail follows a sensational line, contouring the edge of Emerald Glacier for 5 km. Spectacular, close-up views of a glacial environment, and panoramic vistas of the Yoho Valley are your rewards for venturing into

*The Iceline traverses an area covered by glacial ice less than a century ago.*

this harsh domain. The rocky benches traversed by the trail are often snowbound until early July.

### Trailhead to the Iceline

The trail ascends the avalanche slope above the hostel and works its way south. Look back to obtain fine views of 254 m Takakkaw (TAH-kuh-kah) Falls and Mt. Balfour (3272 m). At the edge of the avalanche slope, the trail enters old-growth forest. Despite the nearby peril of avalanching snow and the wind blasts it generates, some of the Engelmann spruce trees here have attained diameters of 1.2 m at the base. With ages of 300–400 years, these are among the older trees in Yoho National Park.

The west slope of the Yoho Valley is terraced, with bedrock strata that dip toward the Yoho River. Just before the trail levels out on the first terrace, the sidetrail to Hidden Lakes branches south. It is only 300 m to these unassuming lakelets. Beyond this junction, the main trail returns to the avalanche slope and ascends steeply along its southern edge. You reach the Yoho Pass/Iceline lower junction in 100 m. Turn north (right). (Yoho Lake is straight ahead.)

For the next 1.5 km, the trail climbs across a

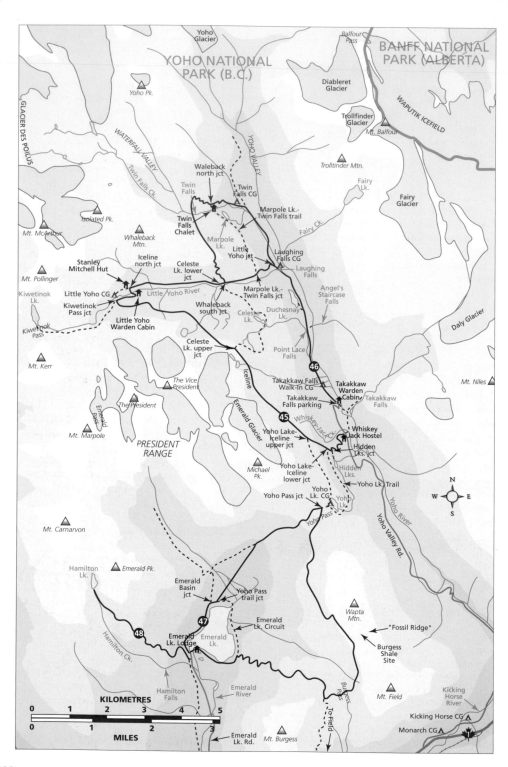

*The bedrock on the Iceline exhibits striations and chatter marks — scratches and pits caused by rocks embedded in the underside of glacial ice.*

second terrace to the Yoho Pass/Iceline upper junction. You will see bedrock in the trail as you gain elevation — limestone of the Eldon Formation. At the junction, turn north (right). Here, you are slightly higher than the brink of Takakkaw Falls across the valley. You can see the waterfall's source in Daly Glacier. *Takakkaw* is Cree for "It is magnificent!"

## The Iceline

To this point, you've been hiking sections of trail that existed before 1987. Just beyond the junction, angle northwest (left) onto the newer trail. The character of the Iceline is soon evident, as the trail ascends a rock staircase. Construction of the Iceline required imaginative trail building techniques. Boulders and rock slabs were used to create bridges, steps, retaining walls, and drainage culverts. Where the trail crosses bedrock slabs, its margin is defined by rows of rubble cleared from the path. These rocks and many artful cairns help guide the way across the bleak, unvegetated forefield of Emerald Glacier. Please refrain from building new cairns.

The Iceline roughly parallels Edward Whymper's route of exploration in 1901, when his party followed the edge of Emerald Glacier from Yoho Pass to the Little Yoho Valley. Whymper, famous for his first ascent of the Matterhorn in 1865, was accompanied by trail guide Bill Peyto, mountaineer James Outram, and four European mountaineering guides. During the trip, party members made first ascents of nine mountains in the Little Yoho, crossed several passes, and named many features.

Emerald Glacier consists of several cirque glaciers tucked under the east flank of The Vice President. During their most recent significant advance — the Little Ice Age — these lobes of ice covered the area now traversed by the trail. Working its way north, the trail climbs and descends a series of lateral moraines. Between the moraines, you cross areas of recently exposed bedrock bisected by meltwater streams. The bedrock displays numerous striations — scratches and grooves etched by stones embedded in the underside of the moving ice.

The vistas from the Iceline improve with each moraine crossed. Just before the Celeste Lake upper junction, the trail draws alongside a marginal lake, fed by meltwater from Emerald Glacier. You may have to rock-hop the outlet of this lake during warm weather, when the glacial runoff peaks. The low ridge of debris north of this lake is a push moraine, created by a minor advance of the closest lobe of ice in the 1970s. Directly north, across the Little Yoho Valley, you can see Mt. McArthur (3015 m) and the rocky prow of Isolated Peak

## Slip Sliding Away

**Whiskey Jack hostel** originated in 1922 as a CPR bungalow camp called Yoho Valley Lodge. The builders chose the avalanche slope because it was close to water and offered a view of Takakkaw Falls. They did not recognize the avalanche hazard. The lodge was damaged by an avalanche in the winter of 1937–38. The surviving buildings were relocated to the south, but not far enough to be out of harm's way. In 1967 another avalanche destroyed the vacant main lodge building. The surviving outbuildings became a hostel in 1969. "Whiskey jack" is a folk name for the gray jay, an inquisitive member of the crow family that is common in the surrounding subalpine forest.

## Variations

- Hike to the trail summit, 13.6 km return
- Exit from the Celeste Lake upper jct via Celeste Lake to the Little Yoho trail, and on to Takakkaw Falls, 17.0 km total
- Add a visit to Marpole Lake and Twin Falls, 25.5 km total. If you camp at Little Yoho and at Twin Falls, you can spend two nights out.
- Approach from Emerald Lake via Yoho Pass to the Yoho Lake-Iceline upper junction in 10.7 km, making the total for the outing 28.8 km. If you camp at Yoho Lake and at Little Yoho, you can spend two nights out.

(2845 m). Mt. McArthur was first climbed by surveyor W.S. Drewry in 1891. He named the peak for fellow surveyor J.J. McArthur.

There is little shelter from either poor weather or intense heat on the Iceline. If you are weary, you may choose to exit at the Celeste Lake upper junction. It is 10.7 km to the Takakkaw Falls parking lot via Celeste Lake and Laughing Falls. Continuing on the Iceline, you contour west into the Little Yoho Valley to reach the apex of the trail on the crest of another moraine. Ahead are the northern aspects of The Vice President (3066 m) and The

*A lateral moraine on the Iceline with Mt. Daly and Daly Glacier beyond*

President (3138 m). These mountains were originally named by members of the 1906 Alpine Club of Canada camp for two officials of the CPR — President Thomas Shaughnessy, and Vice-President David McNicoll. After the camp, it was discovered that the men's personal names had been previously given to two mountains in Glacier National Park, BC. Thus, their titles were applied to these mountains.

Another lobe of Emerald Glacier nestles on the north flank of The Vice President. Its meltwaters feed a lake that is backed by a lofty, 600 m long lateral moraine. The meltwater stream is building a delta into the lake. Another, smaller moraine-dammed lake lies to the north. As you descend

## A Glacial Balancing Act

**The lobes** of Emerald Glacier feature shallow caves, the roofs of which frequently collapse, showering the rock benches below with chunks of dense, blue ice. Situated on the shaded lee side of an 800 m mountain wall, Emerald Glacier receives more nourishment in the form of snowfall and suffers less melting than many other glaciers in the Rockies. When appraising a glacier's well-being, glaciologists talk of "glacial budget." In years of net loss of snow, a glacier goes into debt and recedes. In years where a net gain of snow takes place, a glacier posts a profit and advances. Almost all glaciers in the Canadian Rockies are in retreat. Although Emerald Glacier has receded significantly since the Little Ice Age, one of its lobes advanced briefly in the 1970s. The fact that the glacier can avalanche from a cliff indicates that it is tenuously "holding its own."

toward treeline, Yoho Glacier, Mt. Gordon (3203 m), and Mt. Balfour are to the northeast. The north ridge of The Vice President is unofficially called "Barometer Peak." It features wildly overturned folds. Purple Arctomys (ARK-toe-miss) shale is common at trailside.

### Little Yoho Valley to Takakkaw Falls

The Iceline swings behind the prominent moraine and, 500 m later, begins a steady descent through meadow and subalpine forest to the Little Yoho River and the Kiwetinok Pass junction. Turn east (right) and follow the river 300 m to a bridge. Cross it to the Iceline north junction. The Little Yoho campground is 300 m west (left). This junction is just past the halfway point on the hike. The remainder of the distance is on good trails and can be completed fairly quickly if desired. Head east (right) from the junction on the Little Yoho trail for 3.8 km to Marpole Lake/Twin Falls junction. Turn south (right) and descend to the Little Yoho junction (Laughing Falls) in 1.6 km. Turn south (right) and follow the Yoho Valley trail 4.5 km to the Takakkaw Falls parking lot.

If you feel like marathoning the day, you can add visits to Marpole Lake and Twin Falls — although the falls will be shaded in the afternoon. Keep north (straight ahead) at the Marpole Lake/Twin Falls junction. It's 1.8 km to Marpole Lake and 0.7 km to Twin Falls and the Whaleback north junction. Turn east (right), passing the Yoho Glacier junction in 1.5 km, to reach the Little Yoho junction (Laughing Falls) on the Yoho Valley trail in a further 2.0 km.

# 46. Yoho/Little Yoho

## Route

Overnight, 3–5 days

| Route | Elevation (m) | Distance (km) |
|---|---|---|
| Takakkaw Falls parking | 1509 | 0 |
| Takakkaw Falls CG | 1517 | 0.2 |
| Yoho Valley trailhead | 1520 | 0.4 |
| Angel's Staircase Falls, Point Lace Falls jct | 1540 | 2.3 |
| Duchesnay Lake jct | 1590 | 3.7 |
| Laughing Falls and CG | 1608 | 4.4 |
| Little Yoho jct | 1608 | 4.5 |
| Twin Falls Creek bridge | 1610 | 4.9 |
| Yoho Glacier jct | 1616 | 6.5 |
| Twin Falls CG | 1616 | 6.7 |
| Whaleback north jct | 1768 | 8.0 |
| Twin Falls bridge or ford | 1980 | 10.9 |
| Whaleback trail summit | 2210 | 12.5 |
| Whaleback south jct | 1905 | 14.6 |
| Celeste Lake lower jct | 1905 | 14.7 |
| Iceline north jct | 2072 | 17.5 |
| Little Yoho CG | 2073 | +0.3 |
| Kiwetinok Pass jct | 2073 | 17.8 |
| Iceline trail summit | 2230 | 22.2 |
| Celeste Lake upper jct | 2195 | 22.7 |
| Yoho Lake/Iceline upper jct | 1860 | 26.0 |
| Yoho Lake/Iceline lower jct | 1646 | 27.7 |
| Iceline /Yoho Pass trailhead | 1501 | 28.8 |
| Takakkaw Falls parking | 1509 | 29.4 |

**Maps**

NTS: 82 N/7, and 82 N/8, and 82 N/9, and 82 N/10
Gem Trek: Lake Louise and Yoho
Natural Resources Canada: Yoho National Park
**See map on p.190**

## Trailhead

**Follow the Trans-Canada Highway** to the Yoho Valley Road, 3.7 km east of Field, 22.3 km west of Lake Louise. Turn north and follow this road 14 km to the Takakkaw Falls parking lot. The trailhead is at the north end of the parking lot. Those without a vehicle can use Takakkaw Falls walk-in campground or nearby Whiskey Jack hostel as a base.

*You begin this outing in the thundering presence of Takakkaw Falls.*

Yoho National Park takes its name from a Cree expression of awe and wonder. The Yoho Valley and Little Yoho Valley contain many of the park's wonders — waterfalls, turbulent rivers, glacier-clad peaks, and pockets of alpine meadow. You won't find solitude — except late in the hiking season — but you'll probably fall in love with the place anyway. The close spacing of campgrounds, the well-developed trails, and the convenient access to treeline and glacial environments make the area ideal for novice backpackers.

### Takakkaw Falls to Twin Falls Campground

The outing begins along a gravel road to the Takakkaw Falls walk-in campground. The Yoho Valley trail departs north and heads across alluvial flats into forest. This trail originated after the expansion of the Mt. Stephen Reserve — the forerunner of Yoho National Park — as a corduroy carriage road, constructed between 1903 and 1909. Corduroy is built by laying sections of whole trees side by side across the tread, and covering the bumpy surface that results with dirt. You can still see sections of old corduroy at trailside.

## Variations

- Camp at Laughing Falls (4.4 km), an excellent novice backpack
- Camp at Twin Falls (6.7 km) and day-hike to Yoho Glacier and the Whaleback
- Camp at Little Yoho (10.2 km) and explore

Yoho's interpretive theme of "rockwalls and waterfalls" is exemplified in the Yoho Valley better than anywhere else. The massive U-shaped valley was carved during the Great Glaciation and filled again with ice during the Wisconsin Glaciation. Tributary valleys also filled with ice but were not as deeply eroded. When the ancestral Yoho Glacier receded, the tributary valleys were left hanging above the main valley floor. Their streams now plunge toward the Yoho River as waterfalls. Takakkaw Falls cascades 254 m. The name is a Cree expression that means "It is magnificent!" You may have heard that Takakkaw Falls is the highest waterfall in Canada. It isn't; that honour clearly goes to Della Falls on Vancouver Island. Helmet Falls in Kootenay, Hunlen Falls in Tweedsmuir, and Takakkaw are all in the running as the next highest — depending on whether you measure all the cascades or just the single greatest drop in each waterfall.

At km 2.3, short sidetrails branch east to the bank of the Yoho River and a view of Angel's Staircase Falls, and southwest to Point Lace Falls. The Yoho Valley trail continues north and climbs Hollingsworth Hill, named for a district warden who used dynamite to widen the right of way. The Duchesnay Lake junction is at km 3.7. The sidetrip to the pleasant lake is less than half the 400 m indicated on the park sign. In most years, the lake

## Leaving Well Enough Alone

*Twin Falls cascades over a 180 m cliff at the mouth of a hanging valley.*

**When viewed in context** of the relentless force of flowing water and the shattering effects of frost, the limestone column that divides Twin Falls is a temporary feature. Even more so when you consider that unnatural forces have also been at work. In 1924, trail workers used dynamite in an attempt to make the two falls equal in volume. Debris from the blast blocked the southerly channel and had exactly the opposite effect intended. One can well imagine the panic of the workers as they toiled in that perilous place, in their ultimately successful attempt to set matters right. In hot summers, one of the falls often dwindles by August.

## Quest for Hidden Mountain

*Jean Habel*

**Laughing Falls** was not named because of imaginary voices heard in its cascading waters. The falls brightened up the otherwise glum surroundings during the rain-plagued, first exploration of the Yoho Valley in 1897. The expedition was organized by Jean Habel (AHH-bull), a German mathematics professor and mountaineer. Habel was intent on ascending a mountain that he had seen from the railway the previous year — a peak that he called Hidden Mountain, now named Mont des Poilus.

Habel's party journeyed from Field to Emerald Lake, then over Yoho Pass to the floor of the Yoho Valley at Takakkaw Falls. This 25 km excursion, delayed by the professor's many ramblings, required eight days. Continuing north in the valley, the party was the first to see Laughing Falls and Twin Falls, and the first to set foot on Yoho Glacier. The expedition was curtailed by a shortage of supplies before any serious attempt could be made on Hidden Mountain. However, Habel's report, published the following year in the journal *Appalachia*, stirred up great interest in the Yoho Valley, and was instrumental in the area being added to the national park reserve in 1901. In 1986, a mountain on the Wapta Icefield was named for Jean Habel.

is dry by late summer. Moose frequent this area. Back on the main trail, you draw alongside the Yoho River at a small canyon. The tilted, potholed, rock exposed in the riverbed is Sullivan Formation limestone.

Laughing Falls campground is situated just beyond, on an alluvial fan at the confluence of Twin Falls Creek, Little Yoho River, and Yoho River. For the best views of nearby Laughing Falls, follow beaten paths along the north bank of the Little Yoho River.

Continue north (straight ahead) at the Little Yoho junction just beyond Laughing Falls campground. The trail crosses to the east bank of Twin Falls Creek and follows cobbled flats alongside the Yoho River. I once encountered a herd of 23 elk here. The trail turns sharply south to re-enter the valley of Twin Falls Creek. There are tantalizing views west through the trees to Twin Falls. At the Yoho Glacier junction, the trail to the glacier branches north (right). Turn south (left) for Twin Falls campground in 150 m.

## Twin Falls Campground to the Whaleback

Beyond Twin Falls campground, the trail bypasses a small canyon in the creek and climbs toward the Whaleback junction. Look for a slab of "ripple rock" in the trail. The rock's undulating surface records the action of wavelets on an ancient shoreline. The roar of Twin Falls increases as you approach the Whaleback north junction. Here, several of the Engelmann spruce trees are more than 1 m in diameter and 45 m tall.

Twin Falls Chalet is 80 m south of the Whaleback north junction. The Chalet originated in 1908 as a shelter built by the CPR for its mountaineering guides and clients. It was expanded in 1923. It is now owned by Yoho National Park and has been privately operated under lease since 1962. Out the front door, Twin Falls cascades over a 180 m cliff of Cathedral Formation limestone at the mouth of a hanging valley. Paths along Twin Falls Creek provide uninhibited views of the thundering cascades, which are sunlit until mid-morning.

Turn north (right) at the Whaleback north junction. The trail climbs steadily for the next 1.6 km to the mouth of the Waterfall Valley. You have fine views east to Mt. Balfour (3272 m) — the highest peak in the area — and to the peculiar, castellated summit of Trolltinder Mountain

## Yoho Glacier, 2.3 km

If you arrive early at Twin Falls campground, you may want to hike to Yoho Glacier after setting up camp. Backtrack to the Yoho Glacier junction and head north on a rough trail that rises and falls through an ancient forest of Engelmann spruce and subalpine fir. The trail makes a short switchback descent 2.2 km from the junction

*The upper reach of the Yoho Glacier, as seen from Yoho Peak.*

and emerges abruptly from the forest onto a barren slope that overlooks the forefield of Yoho Glacier. The sudden transition marks the trimline of the glacier. In 1844, the ice stopped here. All forest to the north was obliterated. In this harsh climate with these poor soils, it will take many centuries for forest to become re-established.

Looking north, you can see Yoho Glacier notched between the cliffs of Mt. Gordon (3203 m) to the

east, and the slopes and moraines of Yoho Peak (2760 m) to the west. The glacier has receded almost 3 km. Yoho Glacier is one of eight outlet valley glaciers of the 40 km² Wapta Icefield. Earlier this century, the glacier was the subject of intense scientific study and annual measurement. When glacial retreat made access to the ice difficult for the horses that packed the heavy survey gear, the studies were abandoned.

If you follow a rough track north from the end of maintained trail, you can explore the colourful ice-sculpted and water-worn slabs in the forefield of Yoho Glacier. The rock formations date to the Middle Cambrian. Mountaineers can also follow cairns to the west lateral moraine of Yoho Glacier. This knife-edge ridge of rubble provides a breathtaking panorama of the glacier, the Wapta Icefield, and the Yoho Valley.

(2917 m). The name means "Gnome's Peak." It was given by Jean Habel because of its resemblance to a peak of the same name in Norway. Glaciers that adorn these mountains are part of the 32 km² Waputik Icefield. *Waputik* (WAH-poo-tick) is Stoney for "white goat."

*The Vice President (left) and The President are central in many views from the Little Yoho Valley.*

The trail follows the edge of the cliff south to the former site of Whaleback campground. Camping is no longer allowed. Use caution if you approach the cliff edge. People have died here, from falls into the creek and over the cliff. One hiker fell into the whirlpool at the brink of the falls and survived the chill and the inevitable pull of the current for 45 minutes before being rescued. The area is frequented by mountain goats that are downright aggressive. A goat approached me once, head down, when my back was to the cliff. I ran, he followed.

## The Whaleback

In summer, a decked I-beam bridge spans Twin Falls Creek above the falls. Avalanches from Whaleback Mountain (2633 m) sweep this area. The bridge is installed and dismantled annually to prevent its destruction. If you are hiking when the bridge is out, expect a moderate to difficult ford of Twin Falls Creek, best accomplished about 50 m above the bridge site. The water is silty and extremely cold. Mountaineer Edward Whymper named Whaleback Mountain. When viewed from the south, the shales of its upper slopes suggest a massive whale breaching the ocean's surface. The turreted peak at the northwest end of Whaleback Mountain is Isolated Peak (2845 m). It was first climbed in 1901 by a party that included Whymper and James Outram.

The next 1.6 km is the scenic highlight of the Yoho Valley. The trail makes a steady ascent south from the creek and winds through treeline into delightful upper subalpine meadows. Prominent in the view north from the apex is the pyramidical form of Mont des Poilus (3161 m) — Jean Habel's "Hidden Mountain." The mountain's present name commemorates French foot soldiers of WWI. Group of Seven artist Lawren Harris depicted this scene in a work entitled *Isolation Peak*.

Meltwaters from the glacier in the foreground feed Twin Falls. Mt. Collie (3116 m) and Yoho Peak are to the northeast, separated from Mt. Habel, Mt. Rhondda, and Mt. Gordon by Yoho Glacier. Directly east is Mt. Balfour. To its south are Mt. Daly (3152 m), and Mt. Niles (2972 m) at the head of Daly Glacier. Farther south the view includes Mt. Stephen, Cathedral Mountain, Odaray Mountain, Mt. Victoria, Mt. Huber, and Hungabee Mountain.

A short distance before you reach the south end of Whaleback Mountain, the trail angles sharply right (west). However, continue straight ahead for 80 m to a viewpoint that overlooks the Little Yoho Valley. The glaciated mountains directly across the valley are The Vice President (3066 m) and The President (3138 m), named for executives of the Canadian Pacific Railway. The rocky bench beneath The Vice President is the route of the Iceline trail. A cairn at this viewpoint commemorates a skier who was killed nearby in a

## Next Stop, Little Yoho

**If you don't want** to hump a backpack over the Whaleback trail, turn south (left) at the Whaleback north junction to take the Marpole Connector trail 2.5 km to the Little Yoho trail. You pass Marpole Lake on the way. Richard Marpole was a CPR superintendent of operations in the early 1900s. He distributed lots of free passes to mountaineers, garnering some free publicity for the railway in return, and having a lake and a mountain named for himself when the mountaineers expressed their gratitude. Turn west (right) at the junction on the Little Yoho trail, and follow it 4.1 km to Little Yoho campground. An easy day, as they go.

snow avalanche in 1962. Whitebark pine grows in this windswept location.

The trail switchbacks steeply down an avalanche gully to reach the Little Yoho Valley in 2.1 km. Turn west (right ) onto the Little Yoho trail, and continue straight ahead at the Celeste Lake lower junction just beyond. The trail climbs gradually through subalpine forest for 2.9 km to the Iceline north junction. The Little Yoho campground is 300 m west (straight ahead) of the junction. It makes an excellent base for exploration of the upper valley. Although the only "official" sidetrail is to Kiwetinok Pass, experienced mountaineers may make straightforward ascents of many of the surrounding peaks.

## Loop Hike Options

I recommended that you exit from the Little Yoho Valley by following the Iceline. This 11.4 km route offers spectacular, close-up views of the ice and moraines of Emerald Glacier, and high level views of Takakkaw Falls and the Yoho Valley. (See Classic Hike #45.) A great deal of the Iceline's length is on rubble and rock, and if you have knee, ankle, or back complaints you may find it rough going with a heavy pack. Alternate exits are: follow the Little Yoho Valley trail east to Laughing Falls and then to Takakkaw Falls (9.7 km); follow the Iceline to the Celeste Lake upper junction and take the connector to the Little Yoho trail, then to Laughing Falls and Takakkaw Falls (15.8 km). Those who want to add another night to this outing can follow the Iceline to the Yoho Pass/Iceline upper junction (8.4 km), and take the high trail (straight ahead) for 2 km to Yoho Lake campground. From Yoho Lake it is 4.5 km to the Takakkaw Falls parking lot, via the Yoho Pass trail; or 8.0 km to Emerald Lake.

## Kiwetinok Pass (2454 m), 3.4 km

**From the campground,** backtrack to the Iceline north junction. Cross the Little Yoho River and head west for 300 m to the Kiwetinok Pass junction. Continue straight ahead. After climbing beside a small canyon, the trail drops into the forefield of President Glacier. Rock-hop or ford (straightforward) the meltwater stream and follow cairns west across the rubble. Rock-hop or ford (moderate) the Little Yoho River 500 m later to its north bank. A steep climb on a rough track ensues, leading to the rocky basin that contains Kiwetinok Lake.

*Kiwetinok* is Stoney for "on the north side." At 2454 m, Kiwetinok has been referred to as the highest lake in Canada. It may well be the highest *named* lake, but there is at least one unnamed lake in Banff National Park approximately 50 m higher.

Kiwetinok Lake is often frozen until early August. The lake is partially fed by meltwater from a small glacier on Kiwetinok Peak (2902 m), hence the remarkable colour of the water. You may see white-tailed ptarmigan nearby. Because summer is so brief here, these particular birds never fully develop summer plumage. Feathers on their bellies and legs are white year-round. Looking east down the Little Yoho Valley, you can see a tremendous overturned fold in "Barometer Peak," the ridge that extends north from The Vice President. Beyond are Mt. Daly and Daly Glacier.

From Kiwetinok Lake, you can scramble west over boulders to Kiwetinok Pass. Beyond is the valley of the Amiskwi River, the largest tributary valley of the Kicking Horse River. (*Amiskwi* is a Native word

*The glaciated flanks of the Vice President and the President are close at hand in the view downvalley from Kiwetinok Pass.*

for "beaver." The river was formerly called Beavertail.) Kiwetinok Pass was first crossed in 1901 by the mountaineering party of Edward Whymper. They had a miserable time bushwhacking their way back to Field, as has just about everyone else who has followed since. Whymper named the mountain south of the pass for Robert Kerr of the CPR, the man who had given Whymper free train passage. The mountain north of Kiwetinok Lake was named for Joseph Pollinger, one of Whymper's guides.

# 47. Wapta Highline

## Route

Day-hike or overnight

| Route | Elevation (m) | Distance (km) |
|---|---|---|
| Trailhead | 1302 | 0 |
| Emerald Basin jct | 1308 | 1.3 |
| Yoho Pass jct | 1310 | 1.5 |
| Yoho Pass | 1838 | 7.3 |
| Yoho Lake CG | 1814 | +0.7 |
| Burgess Pass | 2195 | 13.6 |
| Emerald Lake jct | 1300 | 18.8 |
| Trailhead | 1302 | 19.9 |

**Maps**
NTS: 82 N/7 and 82 N/8
Gem Trek: Lake Louise and Yoho
Natural Resources Canada: Yoho National Park
**See map on p.190**

## Trailhead

**Follow the Trans-Canada Highway** to the Emerald lake Road, 2.6 km west of Field. Turn north and follow the road 8 km to its end at the Emerald Lake parking lot. The trailhead is at the north end of the parking lot, next to the bridge.

The Wapta Highline completes an energetic, high-level circuit around Emerald Lake, Yoho's largest and best known body of water. If you day-hike the loop, you'll have a solid workout. As well as great scenery, the hike features interesting geology, human history, and uncommon vegetation. You may see this hike referred to elsewhere as Burgess Highline, Wapta Triangle, or Burgess Triangle.

### Trailhead to Yoho Pass

The first 1.5 km follows the Emerald Lake nature trail. The lush vegetation surrounding the lake is noted for trees uncommon in this part of the Rockies — western redcedar, western hemlock, and western yew. At km 1.3, you reach the Emerald Basin junction. Turn east (right) onto one of the larger alluvial fans in the Rockies. Many alluvial fans were established between 6000 and 7000 years ago by meltwater surges as Earth's climate warmed rapidly after the Wisconsin Glaciation. The Emerald Fan is slowly filling Emerald Lake. Aerial views indicate that 50 percent of the lake's

*Yoho Pass reflected in Emerald Lake*

former area is now rubble.

At the next trail junction in 200 m, branch northeast (left) on the Yoho Pass trail. For the next 2 km, the trail continues across the alluvial fan, offering views north to the impressive peaks that ring Emerald Basin. The centrepiece is a hanging glacier on The President (3138 m). The original road from Field was a log corduroy affair known as the "Tally-Ho Road." It extended across the Emerald Fan. You can see sections beside the trail.

From the east edge of the fan, the trail begins its steady ascent to Yoho Pass. The cliffs of The Vice President dominate the view north, exhibiting a common cliff-building sequence: Cathedral Formation limestone, Stephen Formation shale, and Eldon Formation limestone. All date to the Cambrian. The mountain was named for David McNicoll, a vice-president of the Canadian Pacific Railway. The creek at trailside drains a glacial cirque high above. The Van Horne Range to the southwest and Mt. Vaux (VOX) (3319 m) to the south, ring the horizon. On calm days, you will see these mountains reflected in the lake, even from this distance. Group of Seven artist Lawren Harris painted this scene in 1924, in a work titled *Emerald Lake*. A similar scene graced the Canadian ten dollar bill from 1954 to 1971.

The grade eases as the trail traverses an avalanche slope, and then steepens again where it

## Variation

- If you camp at Yoho Lake, you can make this into a two-day trip, 21.3 km. You can make a three-day trip by adding a day-hike from Yoho Lake campground to the Iceline trail summit, 10.6 km return.

re-enters the forest. Yellow columbine and false hellebore are common at trailside. The entrance to Yoho Pass is marked by a horse-hiker barrier at a trail junction. The dense, ancient forest on the pass does not allow any distant views, but if you want to hike the Iceline or visit Yoho Lake or camp at its campground (1.4 km return), continue straight ahead (east).

Yoho Pass was first crossed in 1897, by the party of Jean Habel. (See sidebar on p.194.) Ralph Edwards was guide on the trip. He called Yoho Lake, "Marina Lake." In 1906, it was known as "Summit Lake" when the inaugural Alpine Club of Canada camp convened on its shores. The tranquil lake is spring fed and contains eastern brook trout. The cliffs of Wapta Mountain (2778 m) loom to the south. The glacial horn of Michael Peak (2696 m), a minor eminence on The Vice President, rises to the northwest.

## Yoho Pass to Burgess Pass

From the Yoho Pass junction, the Wapta Highline turns sharply south (right). After about 500 m, the trail emerges from the forest beneath the gray limestone cliffs of Wapta Mountain. This is a spectacular piece of trail, with a feeling of exposure. The cliff overhangs the path in places. You can see the Van Horne Range again to the west. To the north, "Michael Falls" drops from the cirque on The Vice President in two lofty cascades. You can see the highest mountain in the area, Mt. Balfour (3272 m), to the northeast across Yoho Pass. Pikas live in the rocky debris downslope from the trail.

On August 25, 1988, a tremendous rainstorm struck the vicinity of Field. The west-facing slopes of Wapta Mountain caught the full brunt. The sloping bedrock funnelled the runoff into gullies. Surges of water and debris swept the mountainside below, cutting three swaths through the trail, each 4 m deep. You contour in and out of these flash-flood courses as you approach the avalanche terrain on the western slopes of Wapta Mountain. The view west again includes Emerald Lake — largest of Yoho's 61 mapped lakes and ponds, — now almost 900 m below.

The trail continues south to the avalanche gully beneath Mt. Field (2635 m). This gully is frequently snowbound until early August. Please keep to the trail if snow patches linger. Look for mountain goats on the slopes above. Across the gully, the trail turns west into Burgess Pass. As you traverse an exposed shale slope on the south side of the pass, you have fine views of Mt. Stephen (3199 m) across the Kicking Horse Valley, Mt. Vaux in the distant southwest, and the town of Field.

## The Emerald Fan — A Tough Place to Call Home

**The Emerald Fan** is a harsh home for vegetation. Hardy plants such as common juniper, yellow mountain avens, white camas, and paintbrush are scattered across the gravels. The evergreen leaves of the mountain avens are lightly coloured on the underside to reflect the intense heat that can radiate from the rocks. Yellow lady's-slippers bloom here from mid-June to mid-July. A few lodgepole pines, gnarled white spruce, and white birch comprise the sparse tree cover. Some of the pines have branches on their northeast sides only — they "flag" the prevailing southwest winds. Although the trees look insubstantial, a few of the pines are 150 years old — illustrating the inhospitable growing conditions caused by poor soil, glacial winds, and the fluctuating water table.

You will see various generations of bridges as you cross the Emerald Fan. Glacial melt streams are subject to daily and seasonal fluctuations, and are prone to flash-floods. The I-beam bridges were installed at great expense over streams that promptly changed their courses, leaving the structures high and dry. The "boardwalk bridges" were designed to

*In this view from the north summit of Mt. Burgess, you can see how the aluvial fan is filling the basin occupied by Emerald Lake.*

be portable, allowing trail crews to reposition the bridges as required — a daily ritual during peak run-off in August. In practice, these heavy bridges are not portable. They frequently become buried in the debris of flash-floods. The forces at work here illustrate that nature prevails despite human efforts to gain control. You may get your feet wet.

## Burgess Pass to Emerald Lake

The trail to Emerald Lake plunges north (right) from Burgess Pass. The initial slopes are often snow-covered until mid-July. Most of the descent is in dense forest. The imposing north face of Mt. Burgess (2599 m) towers in profile through a break in the trees. The mountain and pass were named for Alexander Burgess, Canada's Deputy Minister of the Interior in 1886. The last 2 km of this winding and relentless descent features the most extensive western redcedar forest in Yoho. The western redcedar is BC's provincial tree.

Follow the Emerald Lake trail west (left) from the lakeshore junction. Keep right at subsequent junctions. Watch for moose here late in the day. The trail climbs onto the glacial moraine or rock-slide — depending which theory you believe — that dams Emerald Lake, and enters the grounds of Emerald Lake Lodge. Originally constructed by the Canadian Pacific Railway in 1902, the lodge

*The damp, shaded north slopes of Mt. Burgess are home to the largest cedar forest in Yoho.*

was redeveloped in 1986. The main lodge building contains timbers used in the first structure. Complete the loop hike by following the gravel road through the lodge grounds to the parking lot.

## The Burgess Shale

**The west slope** of the ridge connecting Wapta Mountain and Mt. Field is popularly known as the Burgess Shale site. Charles Walcott of the Smithsonian Institution discovered soft-bodied fossils on the slopes above the trail in 1909. During five subsequent summers of collecting, Walcott gathered 65,000 fossil specimens that are now housed at the Smithsonian in Washington, DC. Walcott described the specimens with the knowledge of the day, assigning them to categories known from fossil finds elsewhere in the world. It was 60 years before renewed interpretation of the fossils yielded the significance of this treasure trove of ancient species.

The Burgess Shale contains wonderfully preserved remains of marine animals that lived along the edge of the continental shelf during the Middle Cambrian, approximately 505 million years ago. The edge of the shelf was marked by a submarine cliff, now called the Cathedral Escarpment. Periodic mud flows along the front of the cliff would bury the animals living on the sea floor. As the deaths of the animals were sudden and the remains were entombed, scavenging and decay did

not take place. As a result, the fossils are preserved in exquisite detail as flattened imprints in the shale.

The Burgess Shale fossils preserve 140 species. Paleontologists have painstakingly reconstructed the animals' appearances into three-dimensional figures. Some of the fossils represent the earliest known members of many lifeform groups (phyla) that exist today. Others are unique in the world and represent species that cannot be classified among contemporary phyla. This suggests that the variety of life at "body-plan" level was greater 505 million years ago than it is today. Standard evolutionary theory dictates an increase in diversity as time passes. The Burgess Shale may indicate that mass extinction events and chance have played a greater role in the evolution of life than was previously realized.

Although you may see researchers working at the Burgess Shale site above the trail, the area is closed to public access without a permit from the park superintendent. Guided tours are available. Inquire at the park information centre at Field. Please remember that collection of rocks and fossils is prohibited in national parks.

*Weirder than weird: Hallucigenia was approximately 2 cm long, had seven pairs of unjointed legs, and seven tentacles along its spine.*

# 48. Hamilton Lake

| Route | | |
|---|---|---|
| **Day-hike** | | |
| Route | Elevation (m) | Distance (km) |
| Trailhead | 1302 | 0 |
| Hamilton Falls | 1352 | 0.7 |
| Hamilton Lake | 2149 | 5.3 |

**Maps**
NTS: 82 N/7
Gem Trek: Lake Louise and Yoho
Natural Resources Canada: Yoho National Park
**See map on p.190**

**Best lighting:** mid-morning to mid-afternoon

*Hamilton Lake is a perfect glacial tarn, set in a limestone hollow at the base of Mt. Carnarvon.*

## Trailhead

**Follow Trans-Canada Highway** to the Emerald Lake Road, 2.6 km west of Field. Turn north and follow the road 8 km to its end at the Emerald Lake parking lot. The trailhead is at the southwest corner of the parking lot.

On the Hamilton Lake trail you make an unwavering ascent to a beautiful backcountry lake. The outing features rainforest, whitebark pine trees, and alpine meadows. A waterfall and a mountain display an ancient geological boundary. If you are fortunate, you may see moose, hoary marmots, porcupines, and golden eagles. Grizzly bears and black bears may also be present. This steep trail is a good test of fitness. The final approach to the lake is frequently snowbound until early July, and winter ice may linger on the lake's surface equally as long.

### Trailhead to Hamilton Falls

The trailhead is located in the deep basin that surrounds Emerald Lake. This basin traps storm systems and creates abundant precipitation. Vegetation along the first 700 m contains species typical of the Western Interior Hemlock "rainforest," normally found farther west in BC: western redcedar, western hemlock, western yew, thimbleberry, and devil's club. Queen's cup, western meadowrue, foamflower, and dwarf dogwood are common wildflowers. The white flower of queen's cup yields a striking blue berry in late summer, hence its other folk name — "bluebead." You may

see black bears and moose here.

The trail draws alongside Hamilton Creek and follows it to some large Douglas-fir trees at the shaded base of Hamilton Falls. The damp environment here gives rise to brilliant yellow tree lichens. The features named "Hamilton" honour a prospector who discovered the falls while in quest of more material rewards. Hamilton Creek was formerly the water supply for Emerald Lake Lodge. You may see artifacts associated with the water intake system and pipeline. The falls are at the mouth of a hanging valley and are being eroded into Chancellor Formation limestone.

### Hamilton Falls to Hamilton Lake

You leave the damp forest as the trail switchbacks to a fenced viewpoint at the upper cascades of Hamilton Falls. Here you can see plunge pools, potholes, and evidence of a bedrock fault that has captured Hamilton Creek. Hamilton Falls is the last viewpoint for 2.5 km, during which the grade is often steep. The forest gradually changes from one dominated by lodgepole pine to the combination of subalpine fir and Engelmann spruce typical of subalpine elevations. At km 3.9 there is an opening in the forest that allows a view to Emerald Lake.

Leaving this viewpoint, the trail angles sharply northwest and the grade lessens. The whitebark pine trees at trailside indicate that you have reached the upper subalpine ecoregion. One of these pines has six trunks growing from a single base. The bark of many nearby trees has been damaged by porcupines. These rodents strip the outer bark in culinary quest for the sweet, inner cambium layer. A tree girdled of its bark will usually die.

The trail crosses several avalanche slopes, with views southwest to the Van Horne Range — named for William Cornelius Van Horne, who oversaw construction of the Canadian Pacific Railway from 1881–1885 and later served as its president. The peak with the cleft between its two summits is known locally as "Nimrod Peak," named for the Stoney guide of the Palliser Expedition. (*Nimrod* means "great hunter.") The higher peak to the north, with the prominent niche glacier, is Mt. King (2892 m). Named for a Canadian astronomer and surveyor, the mountain was first climbed in 1892 by J.J. McArthur. The peaks of the Ottertail Range, including glacier capped Mt. Vaux (VOX) (3319 m), stand out to the south. To the southeast (left) of Mt. Vaux, you can see the twin summits of Mt. Goodsir (3562 m, 3525 m), the highest mountains in Yoho National Park, and 9th- and 12th-highest in the Rockies. On the western skyline 90 km distant, you might pick out the granite spires of the Bugaboos in the Purcell Range of the Columbia Mountains.

At a switchback you pass a massive Engelmann spruce, more than a metre thick at the base and 35 m tall — truly a giant for this elevation. In early July, glacier lilies bloom in profusion on the final approach to Hamilton Lake. The protein-rich corm of this plant is a favourite food of grizzly bears. Two other favourite grizzly snacks — hoary marmots and Columbian ground squirrels — live nearby, so approach the lake with caution.

Hamilton Lake is at treeline, a tarn dammed by an upturned lip of Chancellor Formation shale. This rock dam precisely marks the boundary between the eastern main ranges and the western main ranges. Mt. Carnarvon (car-NARR-von) (3340 m) forms the backdrop to the lake. The mountain sits atop a massive anticline — an arch-shaped fold in the bedrock. Mountain goats frequent the grassy areas on the mountain's lower slopes.

While it has been claimed that Hamilton Lake was not "discovered" until 1936, it is in plain view from the south ridge of Mt. Carnarvon, which was first occupied as a survey station in 1887. The mountain was named in 1858 by James Hector for the fourth Earl of Carnarvon, who later was author of the British North America Act. Hector

*Hamilton Falls*

saw the peak from the Kicking Horse Valley. Mt. Carnarvon was first climbed in 1904. The blocky peak north of Hamilton Lake is known unofficially as "Top Hat." Watch for golden eagles soaring on thermals overhead. I've seen them on almost every visit.

## An Ancient Boundary

**The trailhead** is located on the boundary between two geological provinces — the eastern main ranges and the western main ranges. The eastern main ranges are to the northeast. They are typified by the castellated or "layer cake" mountain, whose flanks exhibit resistant cliffs of quartzite, limestone, and dolomite, separated by recessive ledges of shale. For the most part, the rock formations are in horizontal layers. The western main ranges are to the southwest. These mountains contain mostly weak shales and slates, which have been eroded into more rounded shapes that exhibit much folding and faulting — as you can see in the peaks of the Van Horne Range. The sediments of eastern main range mountains were deposited in relatively shallow seas teeming with life, whereas those of western main range mountains collected at the same time in much deeper water, devoid of life. The trail follows the boundary between the two geological provinces all the way to Hamilton Lake, where you can see the transition in the south ridge of Mt. Carnarvon.

# 49. Mt. Hunter

## Route

**Day-hike**

| Route | Elevation (m) | Distance (km) |
|---|---|---|
| Trailhead | 1125 | 0 |
| Lower lookout jct | 1532 | 3.3 |
| Lower lookout | 1532 | 3.5 |
| Lower lookout jct | 1532 | 3.7 |
| Upper lookout | 1966 | 6.6 |

**Maps**
NTS: 82 N/2 and 82 N/7
Gem Trek: Lake Louise and Yoho
Natural Resources Canada: Yoho National Park

## Trailhead

**Follow the Trans-Canada Highway** 24.7 km west of Field to the turnoff for Wapta Falls. There is no sign for westbound travellers. Park in the small lot adjacent to Trans-Canada Highway. The trailhead is across the road on the north side of the highway. Use caution crossing the highway.

The steep trail to Mt. Hunter's two fire lookout sites is usually the first high elevation trail to become snow-free in Yoho. The early season wild-flower displays are exceptional. You may see elk, deer, moose, and mountain goats. The slopes are frequented by grizzly bears. Check yourself carefully for wood ticks if you hike this trail in late May or June. Carry all your drinking water with you.

### Trailhead to Lower Lookout

From the highway, the trail angles east into a forest of lodgepole pine and white spruce. Early in the season, you will be treated to a remarkable display of wildflowers here — western wood lily, yellow lady's slipper, shooting star, prickly wild rose, yellow columbine, dwarf dogwood, wild strawberry, star-flowered Solomon's seal, paintbrush, and blue-eyed grass. Some thoughtless hikers pick the wood lilies and lady's slippers. This illegal practice usually kills the plants, and has led to their disappearance in many areas.

After 225 m, the trail climbs to the CPR main line. Carefully cross the tracks and look for the trail sign 10 m to the west. Ascend a rooted trail into the forest to gain the southeast ridge of Mt.

*Three varieties of juniper grow on Mt. Hunter. Rocky Mountain juniper (photo) is uncommon in Yoho. It has flat scaly leaves that resemble those of western redcedar. It sometimes attains heights of 4–5 m.*

Hunter. I have seen mule deer, a great horned owl, and a grizzly bear here. Some of the white birch and aspens at trailside have been used as "rub trees" by male elk and deer to remove the velvet from their antlers.

The lower slopes of Mt. Hunter are in the montane ecoregion, and are also in the rain shadow of the Columbia Mountains. Vegetation on the lower ridge includes an association of Douglas-fir and Rocky Mountain juniper, more typical of the semi-arid, southern Columbia Valley. At about km 1 there is a Douglas-fir tree that is 0.9 m in diameter. This is a large tree for the Rocky Mountain variety of Douglas-fir. (On the west coast of BC, the coastal variety frequently attains diameters of 4 m.) A standing-dead fir nearby has been drilled full of holes by woodpeckers.

You can see the rain shadow vegetation clearly where the trail draws alongside the cliff edge. Bearberry, shrubby cinquefoil, and creeping juniper are common in the undergrowth. For the next 1.5 km the trail parallels the cliff, offering views of the Kicking Horse Valley and the Beaverfoot Range. These mountains are part of the oldest and smallest geological province in the Rockies — the western ranges. You might see moose and elk in the sloughs near the highway. The many downed trees in the valley resulted from a blowdown in 1993.

The impressive cliff underfoot is Ottertail

*Chancellor Peak towers above the Kicking Horse and Beaverfoot valleys in this view from upper Mt. Hunter lookout.*

Formation limestone. This rock is an anomaly among the weak shales and slates of mountains in the western Rockies. Western main range mountains are typically heavily eroded and gentle in appearance.

A steep climb leads to a junction in a dog-hair forest of lodgepole pine. Turn south (left) to reach the lower lookout. The keeper's cabin has been maintained and is open as a day-use shelter. I once found the paw prints of a grizzly bear on the cabin door and windows. The ladder to the tower is unsafe and should not be used. The huge black panels south of the lookout are part of a microwave communications system.

Across the Kicking Horse Valley, Mt. Vaux (VOX) (3319 m) is the more northerly of the two high mountains. James Hector of the Palliser Expedition named the mountain for William Vaux, a curator at the British Museum. Vaux secured financing so that members of the expedition could write and publish their reports. It is likely that Hector named the mountain after his return to England. The more southerly of the two mountains is Chancellor Peak (3280 m), named for the Chancellor of Ontario, who arbitrated a dispute between the Canadian Pacific Railway and the federal government in 1886. Both mountains were first climbed in 1901.

## Lower Lookout to Upper Lookout

Backtrack to the lower lookout junction and turn left. The trail ascends steadily to the upper lookout through a forest of lodgepole pine and Douglas-fir. Some trees at trailside still contain insulators from the telephone system that connected the upper lookout to the warden station at Leanchoil (lee-ANN-coil), in the valley below. Mt. Hunter is set in an angle of the Kicking Horse River. To the northeast, you can see that the river has the braided character typical of glacially fed streams. To the northwest, the river's course is more confined as it plunges into the V-shaped canyon that leads to its junction with the Columbia River at Golden.

The upper lookout was part of the original

## Hunting through History

**Mt. Hunter (2615 m)** was named by James Hector in 1858. Unfortunately, Hector did not record who he had in mind. Along with several "formal" candidates with the surname Hunter, there are two "informal" ones — Hector's Stoney guide, Nimrod, whose hunting skills Hector praised; and Peter Erasmus, another of Hector's guides. Erasmus made a partial ascent of Mt. Hunter and shot a goat the following day. Given that Hector's party was desperately low on provisions at the time, the importance of the "hunters" to the expedition suggests that they are the best candidates. Peter Erasmus died in 1931 at age 98, the last surviving member of the Palliser Expedition.

## Variations

- Hike to the lower lookout site, 7.0 km return
- Visit both lookout sites, 13.0 km return

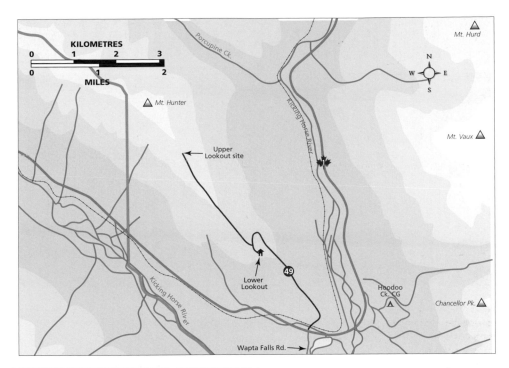

## Snags: Den Trees

*Snag*

**In the past,** foresters regarded standing-dead trees — also called snags — as both a safety hazard and a fire hazard. Now, the emphasis is on preserving snags for their value as nesting and denning sites for many birds and mammals. But with intensive clear-cutting of forests outside protected areas, standing-dead trees are quickly disappearing. Clearcuts remove the shelter provided by adjacent trees, with the result that many of the snags soon succumb to the wind.

system of fire lookouts and was built in 1943. By the 1960s, the facilities were in disrepair. Park managers decided to replace them with a newer structure, lower on the ridge. The tower at the upper lookout was removed in 1992. Although pack rat heaven, the cabin still stands.

The view southwest from Mt. Hunter includes areas outside Yoho National Park. You can see the patchwork of clearcuts. Commercial forestry is rapidly destroying a great deal of habitat adjacent to the Rocky Mountain parks. Logging roads facilitate access to formerly remote park boundaries. This has led to an increase in hunting, poaching, and off-road vehicle use.

## High Cuisine

**In their remote locations,** lookout keepers were often without human contact for several weeks at a time. Their diet was a major concern. The handbook for lookouts continually promoted adequate intake of vitamin C; it recommended that canned tomatoes be added to almost every meal. If the delivery of rations was a week late, innovative use of other canned items was stressed. One recipe describes canned meatloaf glazed with marmalade. Yum.

**205**

# Kootenay National Park

*The summits of Mt. Goodsir are featured in the view from Goodsir Pass.*

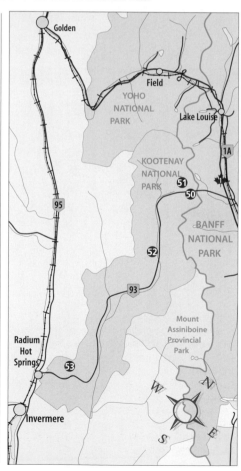

Established in 1920 as Canada's 10th national park, Kootenay includes 1406 km² on the western slopes of the BC Rockies. The park features tremendous geographical and ecological diversity. It is the only national park in Canada in which you may find a cactus and see a glacier. Kootenay offers just under 200 km of hiking trails. The four Classic Hikes in the park immerse you in rolling meadows, alpine ridges, wilderness valleys, and glacial barrens that were covered by ice less than a century ago.

The 104 km Kootenay Parkway (Highway 93) bisects the park. This road connects Castle Junction on the Trans-Canada Highway 34 km west of Banff, with Highway 95 at the town of Radium Hot Springs, 105 km south of Golden. Park information centres are at Vermilion Crossing and at the west park gate. Accommodation and limited services are available at Vermilion Crossing and near the Radium Hot Springs pools, where the warden office is also located. More services are available at the village of Radium Hot Springs, just west of the park; at Invermere, 14 km south of Radium on Highway 95; and at Banff. Kootenay has three frontcountry camp grounds with 340 campsites. There are no hostels. The park is in the Mountain time zone, the same as Banff and Jasper.

# 50. Stanley Glacier

## Route

Day-hike

| Route | Elevation (m) | Distance (km) |
|---|---|---|
| Trailhead | 1593 | 0 |
| Stanley Glacier vpt | 1921 | 4.2 |

**Maps**
NTS: 82 N/1
Gem Trek: Kootenay, or Banff and Mt. Assiniboine

**Best lighting:** mid-morning to mid-afternoon

*Stanley Glacier*

## Trailhead

**South side** of the Kootenay Parkway; 13.4 km west of the Trans-Canada Highway; 91.5 km east of Highway 95.

The Stanley Glacier trail explores a spectacular hanging valley and offers close-up views of three major processes that have shaped the landscape of the Rockies: fire, avalanches, and glaciation. The valley is renowned for its views of glacial ice in summer and frozen waterfalls in winter. You may see moose, mountain goats, white-tailed ptarmigan, and hoary marmots.

## Snow Avalanches

**The slopes on** the east side of the valley feature steep avalanche paths. At trailside, you can see the sun-bleached remains of trees uprooted by sliding snow, and by the wind blasts it generates. Snow avalanches occur when one or more layers within a snowpack release from other layers, or when the entire snowpack separates from the underlying slope. Avalanches are caused by a complex interplay of temperature, humidity, wind, snow depth, slope aspect, and steepness. People and animals travelling on a susceptible slope may trigger an avalanche. Loud noises cannot trigger an avalanche, unless they originate in an explosion that also vibrates the ground.

Although destructive in one sense, avalanches are simply another of nature's tools for ensuring biodiversity. Avalanches remove large vegetation, and create open habitat that supports shrubs and wildflowers. These are important foods for moose, elk, bears, and deer.

### Trailhead to Stanley Glacier Viewpoint

From the parking lot, the trail descends to the Vermilion River and switchbacks up into the Vermilion Pass Burn. This lightning-caused fire consumed 2360 ha of subalpine forest in July 1968. Most of the living trees at trailside are lodgepole pines. The resin-sealed cone of the lodgepole requires a temperature of 45°C to crack open, resulting in a mass seeding after the fire. The subsequent, dense growth of pines is known as a doghair forest.

The trail climbs steadily through the burn, gaining 220 m of elevation in the first 2.4 km. After you crest a small rise, the trail descends slightly to a footbridge across the creek. The entrances to most hanging valleys in the Rockies are blocked by moraines that were pushed up alongside the larger glaciers in the main valleys. The rise just before the footbridge indicates the moraine at this location.

The next 1.8 km of trail is a delight. With the forest canopy removed by the fire, a profusion of sun-loving wildflowers blooms here. Many are pioneering species that grow after fires — camas, common fireweed, fleabane, pink wintergreen, arnica, yellow columbine, groundsel, and vibrantly coloured paintbrush. Damp areas feature rein orchids and gentians.

At one point, the trail separates burned and unburned forest. To the west (right) are mature Engelmann spruce; to the east (left) are blackened timbers and stumps. You will not see as many young lodgepole pines as you did near the trailhead. Trees are regenerating slowly in this part of the burn because of the cold air that drains from Stanley Glacier.

The colossal cliff that flanks the west side of the valley is known as "The Guardwall." The lower 300 m of cliff is Cathedral Formation limestone and dolomite. It contains a number of solution caves — caverns eroded by naturally acidic rainwater. The upper cliff is Eldon Formation limestone. Between the cliffs is a fossil-rich ledge of Stephen Formation shale. These formations date to the Middle Cambrian. The dark streaks on the cliffs are water seeps and rock lichens. In the perpetual shade of winter, the seeps freeze into sheets of ice that become a destination for waterfall ice climbers.

A sign on a knoll marks the end of the maintained trail and is a good vantage from which to study Stanley Glacier. Several lobes of ice terminate on cliffs. Less than two centuries ago, the glacier flowed over these cliffs to reach valley floor. You may hear the creaking and groaning of the ice as it creeps incessantly forward, and possibly see an ice avalanche. Meltwater that cascades over the cliffs is sometimes caught in updrafts, creating waterfalls that seem to disappear in midair.

Toward Stanley Glacier the valley is a barren world of boulders and screes that is home to mountain goats, hoary marmots, pikas, and white-tailed ptarmigan. The summit of Stanley Peak (3155 m) is concealed from view. The mountain was originally named "Mt. Ball" by James Hector in 1858. However, that name subsequently came into use for a higher mountain to the south-

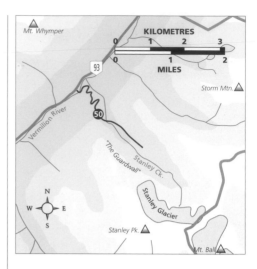

west. The name, Stanley Peak, was given by Edward Whymper in 1901 to honour Frederick Stanley, 6th Governor General of Canada. Lord Stanley's name also adorns the ultimate prize in North American hockey — the Stanley Cup.

Looking north, you can see the U-shape of this hanging valley. Valleys in the Rockies were originally V-shaped, the products of erosion by streams and rivers. As Stanley Glacier advanced the length of this valley — most recently during the Wisconsin Glaciation — it undercut the surrounding mountainsides. When the glacier receded, the mountainsides collapsed, and the valley floor was widened.

## Edward Whymper — Great Expectations

**Mt. Whymper (2845 m)** is framed by the valley walls in the view north from Stanley Glacier viewpoint. The mountain was named for Edward Whymper, who was in the first party to climb the Matterhorn, in 1865. Whymper made five trips to the Rockies in the early 1900s. The first three were under arrangement with the Canadian Pacific Railway. In return for free rail passage and an outfit of mountain guides, Whymper was to pen magazine articles and to make suggestions regarding the location and construction of trails and facilities. The railway hoped to capitalize on Whymper's illustrious reputation, and to make the Rockies into a "new Switzerland."

*Edward Whymper*

Whymper had a dour temperament and a legendary capacity for alcohol. He rapidly alienated his mountaineering guides and packers, and accomplished few of his objectives. Perhaps the greatest disappointment for the railway was that, during his first visit, Whymper did not even attempt to climb Mt. Assiniboine, "the Canadian Matterhorn." The moguls of the railway soon tired of his scheme. Whymper's only significant Canadian mountaineering — accomplished at the prompting of his guides — was completed during the 1901 trip, when Mt. Whymper, Stanley Peak, and a number of mountains in what is now Yoho National Park were first climbed.

# 51. Kaufmann Lake

## Route

Day-hike or overnight

| Route | Elevation (m) | Distance (km) |
|---|---|---|
| Trailhead | 1479 | 0 |
| Upper falls, Marble Canyon | 1494 | 0.7 |
| Fay Hut jct | 1677 | 10.5 |
| Kaufmann Lake jct | 1814 | 13.6 |
| Kaufmann Lake and CG | 2057 | 15.1 |

**Maps**
NTS: 82 N/1 and 82 N/8
Gem Trek: Kootenay

**Best lighting:** afternoon and evening

## Trailhead

**Marble Canyon,** north side of the Kootenay Parkway; 17.2 km west of the Trans-Canada Highway; 88 km east of Highway 95.

While the other Rocky Mountain parks feature lakes aplenty, Kootenay has only 38 mapped lakes and ponds. Of the park's half dozen large lakes, Kaufmann Lake, set in the wilderness heartland of the northern part of the park, is the most remote.

### Trailhead to Fay Hut Junction

From the bustling trailhead at Marble Canyon, follow the interpretive trail for 35 m to a junction where you turn north (right) onto the Tokumm (TOE-kum) Creek trail. *Tokumm* is Stoney for "red fox," an animal that does not occur in Kootenay National Park today. After 200 m, this trail merges with an old cart track that formerly led to mining claims in Prospector's Valley. A short sidetrail at km 0.7 leads west (left) to the 39 m upper waterfall in Marble Canyon. Back on the main trail, continue north through an ancient forest of

## Variations

• Begin the hike along the Marble Canyon interpretive trail. Exit to the Tokumm Creek trail from the upper bridge in the canyon. No significant difference in distance

*Kaufmann Lake is set in a high valley on the south side of the Wenkchemna Peaks.*

Engelmann spruce and subalpine fir, crossing bridges over numerous tributary streams.

At km 3, the trail narrows and descends to the bank of Tokumm Creek, with views of lush avalanche paths across the valley. Stickseed grows here. This metre-tall wildflower has numerous powder-blue flowers, and looks like forget-me-not on steroids. By area, almost half the slopes along Tokumm Creek are avalanche terrain. Many of the avalanche paths extend from ridgetop to valley bottom. The terrific momentum of the avalanches often carries snow and debris across the valley floor and uphill on the opposite slope. These avalanche paths support dense growths of shrubs and forbs, and are important habitat for moose and elk, especially in winter.

For the next 7 km the trail is almost always within sight and sound of Tokumm Creek. The trail is rocky and rooted. You will be constantly adjusting gait, which makes for fatiguing travel. Tokumm Creek has been eroded into a fault that marks the approximate division between the western main ranges and the eastern main ranges. Most rocks in the western main ranges are drab grey shales and limestones formed from sediments deposited in relatively deep water. Rocks of the Chancellor Group of formations are the most common. The eastern main ranges — whose rock formations are generally more colourful — feature limestone, dolomite, and quartzite.

**209**

After passing a massive, limestone boulder — an erratic dropped here by a retreating glacier — you cross the principal meltwater stream from the Wenkchemna Icefield. The Fay Hut junction is just beyond. Fay Hut is 2.3 km to the east along a steep trail. Built in 1927, it was the first climbing hut erected by the Alpine Club of Canada. The hut was named for Professor Charles Fay, an American mountaineer who made a number of pioneering ascents in the Rockies, most during the first five of his 25 visits between 1894 and 1930.

## Fay Hut Junction to Kaufmann Lake

The views north improve beyond the junction. Prominent is Mt. Oke (2920 m), named by explorer Samuel Allen for a prospector he met nearby. You might think this is also the origin of the name "Prospector's Valley." However, this name was applied by Walter Wilcox in 1899 when he found an abandoned prospector's camp near the valley mouth. The old prospectors knew what they were doing. Small-scale commercial mining for lead and zinc took place in this valley just north of Marble Canyon, between 1914 and 1943.

In the last 2 km to the Kaufmann Lake junction, the trail undulates up and down the creek bank. Avalanche snow here often bridges the creek. After you cross the braided outflow of Kaufmann Lake, a sign directs you to the final climb — 243 m in just 1.5 km. This section of trail is old and frustrating — the handiwork of anglers and mountaineers. Initially, the trail works its way south to the outlet stream, rising and falling needlessly. You then ascend mercilessly upslope before the trail levels in a wet meadow near the lake outlet. Please try to keep to the beaten path. You will get your boots wet here.

Your exertions on the final approach are amply rewarded by the view at Kaufmann Lake. The setting features an unfamiliar perspective of familiar mountains. These are the "other sides" of some of the Wenkchemna Peaks, the wall of mountains better known as the backdrop to

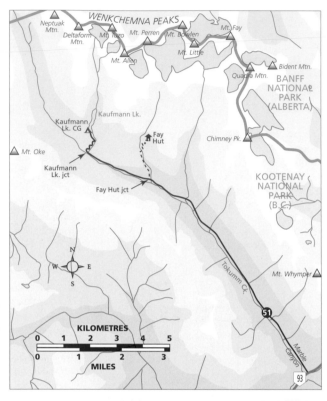

## Icy Headwaters

*Pink mountain heather*

**Most surface water** in the Rockies originates as glacial melt. At km 8.4, the trail to Kaufmann Lake crosses a frigid, silty, meltwater stream that issues from the Wenkchemna Icefield. This stream also channels cold air into the valley bottom. You will see pink mountain heather and white mountain heather here, at an elevation 600 m lower than normal for these plants. Although 6 km distant and 900 m lower than the closest glacier, the banks along this stream bed vividly exhibit the far-reaching effects of glacial ice.

Moraine Lake. Mt. Allen (3301 m) and Mt. Tuzo (3245 m) border the east shore, and Deltaform Mountain (3424 m), the west. The surrounding forest contains scattered Lyall's larch.

Christian and Hans Kaufmann were brothers — Swiss mountaineering guides who worked in Canada between 1900 and 1906. They guided the first ascents of Neptuak Mountain, Deltaform Mountain, Hungabee Mountain, Mt. Biddle, Mt. Tuzo, Mt. Allen, Mt. Bowlen, and Mt. Fay — all mountains nearby. So, you might think that the lake is named for one or the other of them. It isn't. The lake is named for their father, Peter, who guided briefly in Canada in 1903.

# 52. Rockwall

*On a fair day, sunrise at Floe Lake is spectacular.*

## Route

**Overnight 4–6 days**

| Route | Elevation (m) | Distance (km) |
|---|---|---|
| Floe Lake trailhead | 1338 | 0 |
| Floe Lake CG | 2058 | 10.5 |
| Numa Pass | 2370 | 13.2 |
| Numa Creek CG | 1530 | 20.0 |
| Numa Creek jct | 1530 | 20.4 |
| Tumbling Pass | 2256 | 25.3 |
| Tumbling Creek CG | 1890 | 27.9 |
| Wolverine Pass jct | 2188 | 31.0 |
| Rockwall Pass | 2253 | 31.7 |
| South fork of Helmet Creek | 1753 | 39.5 |
| Limestone Summit | 2174 | 36.3 |
| Helmet Creek CG | 1753 | 39.5 |
| Goodsir Pass jct | 1761 | 40.1 |
| Helmet Creek bridge | 1523 | 48.5 |
| Helmet-Ochre CG and Ochre Creek jct | 1520 | 48.7 |
| Tumbling Creek jct | 1470 | 53.0 |
| Paint Pots | 1464 | 54.0 |
| Paint Pots trailhead | 1448 | 55.0 |

**Maps**
NTS: 82 N/1
Gem Trek: Kootenay
The Adventure Map: the Rockwall

## Trailhead

**West side** of the Kootenay Parkway; 32.6 km west of the Trans-Canada Highway; 72.1 km east of Highway 95.

The Rockwall is a remarkable outing that epitomizes the landscape of the Rockies. Peak, pass, and precipice; meadow, forest, and stream; waterfall, glacier, and tarn — the Rockwall weaves these quintessential elements into one of the more rewarding backpacking excursions in the range.

The roller-coaster nature of this outing will make demands on your fitness, but the five campgrounds allow you to break the hard work into short sections. The passes are usually snowbound until early July. Drinking water is scarce. Carry an extra water bottle and top up whenever you draw alongside a clear stream. The hike traverses prime grizzly bear habitat. Travel accordingly.

### Trailhead to Floe Lake

The trail initially descends to cross the Vermilion River at a canyon eroded into Chancellor

## Variations

- Hike the route in reverse
- Day-hike to Floe Lake, 21.0 km return
- Camp at Floe Lake (10.5 km). Day-hike to Numa Pass, 5.4 km return
- Backpack from the Paint Pots to Helmet Creek campground (15.5 km). Day-hike to Wolverine Plateau, 8.5 km. Day-hike to Goodsir Pass, 4.0 km
- By crossing Ball Pass and descending 9.7 km along Hawk Creek, you can add this outing to the Lakes and Larches (Classic Hike #8), making possible a trip of 88.8 km, 6–9 days

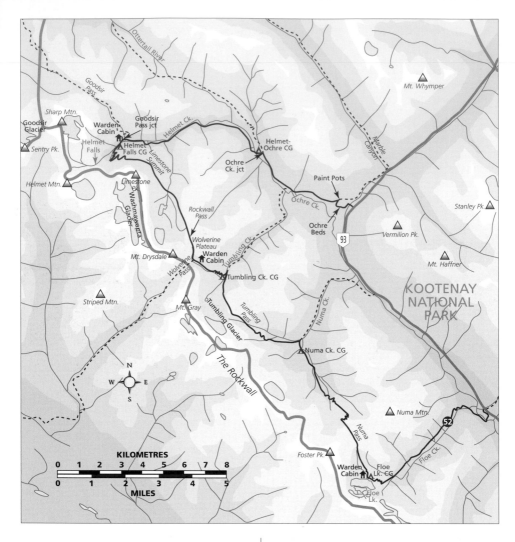

Formation slate. The river's name refers to the red stains of iron oxides found along its banks upstream. Here, the river is often chalky grey, choked with glacial sediment. The trail follows the riverbank northwest to Floe Creek, which you cross on an aluminum bridge.

In the lower valley of Floe Creek, the lush forest includes Douglas-fir and devil's club. Massive Engelmann spruce grow in the upper valley. These trees are more than a metre in diameter and exceed 40 m in height. The dense shrubs and succulent forbs on the many avalanche paths offer food for moose, deer, elk, and bears. Bear cautions are common on this trail. Make lots of noise as you travel along Floe Creek.

At km 8.0 the trail reaches a headwall, where you commence an excruciatingly steep climb — 400 m in the next 2.5 km. The toil ends a few hundred metres before Floe Lake campground, where there is an abrupt transition to an upper subalpine treeline forest dominated by Lyall's larch.

Floe Lake occupies an inspiring setting that embodies all the classic features of the Rockwall. The lake is named for the ice floes or "growlers" that calve from the glacier at the base of the cliff. You may hear the cracking and booming of the glacier as it advances and, with fortune, you may see an iceberg calve into the lake. Sunrise here is one of the more memorable sights in the Rockies.

## Floe Lake to Numa Creek

The trail crosses the campground to the park warden cabin, and then ascends steeply across a series of benches to Numa Pass. The hard work is on a delightful trail that winds through upper subalpine larch forest and glades that feature tremendous displays of wildflowers. Given the high elevation and heavy snows here, the blooms of these flowers are at their peak in early August — a few weeks later than most other locations.

The final kilometre to Numa Pass is across shales and alpine tundra. Repeated freezing and thawing churns the soil into mounds called earth hummocks. A few scraggly larch trees in kruppel-holz form have taken root in the hummocks. The

black-tipped sedge, *Carex nigricans,* is common in the hollows, as are mountain heather, woolly everlasting, and white mountain avens.

Numa Pass is the high point on this outing. Mt. Temple (3543 m) and the "back sides" of the Wenkchemna Peaks are featured in the view north. Foster Peak (3204 m) rises west of the pass. *Numa* is Cree for "thunder." Numa Mountain (2550 m) was originally known as "Roaring Mountain."

The trail traverses west from the pass on a track beaten into the screes and then descends

## The Rockwall: Larger than Life

*The Rockwall*

**This trail** takes its name from the cliff that extends 53 km through western Kootenay and southwestern Yoho national parks and forms the backdrop at Floe Lake. In places, this rampart of Ottertail Formation limestone and dolomite is almost 900 m high. Up close, the rock looks like zebra stripes — alternating layers of darkish limestone and paler dolomite.

Most western main range mountains consist of weak shales and slates. These mountains are more eroded and gentle in appearance than the craggy peaks to the east. The shales and slates were deposited in deep sea water, largely devoid of marine life. But Ottertail Formation sediments were deposited in shallow sea water that probably supported abundant marine life. It seems incredible, but tiny crystals of lime deposited mostly by floating colonies of marine algae and cyanobacteria (blue-green algae) essentially created this monolithic cliff. It didn't happen overnight. The formation was laid down over a period of 10 million years during the Late Cambrian. It's devoid of fossils, so we don't

know the specific creatures responsible — only that there were many of them. They didn't leave an impression, but they left their mark.

### A Natural Snowfence
The cliffs of the Rockwall are oriented southeast-northwest, along the grain or strike of the Rockies. By coincidence, this is at a right angle to the prevailing, southwesterly air flow. The cliffs intercept moisture-laden air from the Pacific. As the air rises, it cools; its moisture condenses into clouds, and precipitation falls.

In the alpine ecoregion, more than 75 percent of the annual precipitation is snow. The prevailing winds scour snow from the southwest slopes of the Rockwall and deposit it into niches and basins on the leeward (northeast) side, where it accumulates to form and sustain drift glaciers, such as the one that feeds Floe Lake. Not only does the cliff create the glacier, but the shade it casts helps to sustain the ice.

north to treeline. The drop to Numa campground is one of the more abrupt on any of the Classic Hikes — 840 m in 6.8 km. The basin north of Foster Peak contains a cirque glacier whose meltwater cascades over cliffs into the upper reaches of Numa Creek. The cliffs rise above avalanche paths that provide excellent habitat for bears. Travel accordingly. The lush vegetation at the edge of the avalanche paths has a rainforest ambiance. Several fallen spruce trees cut from the trail show more than 400 annual rings.

*A wildflower glade on the way to Numa Pass*

Cross the south fork of Numa Creek on the bridge. The red berries of dwarf dogwood, wild strawberry, and dwarf raspberry are common here in late summer. Tent sites at Numa Creek campground are on both sides of the tributary stream. Porcupines frequent this campground. Don't leave your boots or packs unattended.

## Numa Creek to Tumbling Creek

You can make a quick exit from the Rockwall at the junction 400 m beyond Numa Creek campground. The trail straight ahead (northeast) follows Numa Creek 6.4 km to the Kootenay Parkway. Otherwise, turn west (left) to ascend to Tumbling Pass.

Avalanche slopes flank the north fork of Numa Creek. The heavy precipitation in this area supports lush vegetation. In few places in the Rockies will you see shrubs this tall, such a variety of succulent forbs, and such an abundance of berries. Red elderberry is common. In my field notes I called this section of trail "a grizzly grocery store." Visibility is often poor, and the sound of the creek will obscure all but your most vocal noise-making efforts.

The well-conceived trail switchbacks steadily upward through the course of a glacially fed tributary stream. The torrent can be considerable on a hot afternoon. Rock-hop or ford as required. Much of the rubble at trailside is moraine that was pushed over the cliff during Little Ice Age advance of the glacier concealed above. During the climb, you can see Mt. Ball (3311 m) to the east.

## Water Worn and Scoured by Snow

**Floe Creek** occupies a steeply walled, V-shaped valley, typical of the western main ranges, where the valleys owe more to the effects of flowing water than to the direct effects of moving ice. The weak shales and slates of the underlying bedrock erode readily, helping to create the deeply entrenched valley. The steep slopes become natural paths for snow avalanches. Avalanche slopes comprise almost half the area along Floe Creek.

## Pressure-treated Timbers: Designed and Built to Specifications

**Floe Lake campground** has been "hardened" to accommodate heavy use — gravel trails, gravel tent pads, and picnic tables built from "pressure-treated wood." The timber used is treated with the preservative copper-chromium-arsenate, and is advertised to be rot-resistant for 30–50 years. The preservative is a deadly poison, but supposedly becomes inert once applied. However, err on the side of caution. Keep your food and hands from contacting the wood directly.

In the mid to late 1980s, pressure-treated wood was used extensively for trail and campground structures in most of the Rocky Mountain parks. This wood is expensive to purchase, requires transport by helicopter to most sites, and contributes toxins to the environment. Pressure-treated wood structures do not reflect the craft of trail builders. Park managers are re-evaluating the use of pressure-treated wood in the backcountry. Natural timbers, obtained on-site, might once again be used for backcountry bridges, boardwalks, and tables.

*The Rockwall traverses four upper subalpine passes. This is Rockwall Pass.*

dominated by the convoluted, rubble-covered mass of Tumbling Glacier.

The trail descends from Tumbling Pass alongside a lateral moraine that marks the trimline of Tumbling Glacier. To the east of the trail is forest, to the west is a barren of rocks and ice-cored moraine. During the peak of the Little Ice Age, Tumbling Glacier advanced this far east, obliterating the forest.

After you reach the north end of the lateral moraine, angle northeast and descend steeply to Tumbling Creek. You can exit from the Rockwall at this point, 10.3 km along Tumbling Creek and Ochre Creek to the Kootenay Parkway. The Tumbling Creek campground is 300 m west of the bridge. The water in Tumbling Creek is usually too silty to drink. The creek you cross just east of the campground may be dry lower down, however it should be flowing a few hundred metres to the north. It provides clear drinking water. The next water source is in 7.4 km.

After completing the climb, the trail rambles through a kilometre-long boulder meadow — a delightful upper subalpine garden. From the north end of the meadow, you climb steeply over the scree shoulder east of Tumbling Pass. The extra climb detours around a lateral moraine that blocks the true low point of the pass. Ahead is the next installment of spectacular Rockwall scenery,

## Wolverine Pass (2207 m), 225 m

**It is only half** as far to Wolverine Pass as the park trail sign indicates. The short walk takes you to the boundary of Kootenay National Park and to the only significant break in the rampart of the Rockwall. By scrambling a short distance up the scree slopes north of the pass, you are rewarded with a view over Dainard Creek to the Beaverfoot Valley and the distant Purcell Mountains. Extensive clear-cuts scar the valley. This habitat loss affects wildlife within the national park, by disrupting travel routes and by concentrating animals where they compete to mutual detriment. A forestry road leads along Dainard Creek to within 2 km of Wolverine Pass. The easy access granted is at the heart of a chronic poaching problem in this part of the national park.

The peaks flanking Wolverine Pass are Mount Gray (3000 m) to the south and Mount Drysdale (2932 m) to the north. Charles Drysdale was a geologist, and William Gray his assistant. The two drowned on the Kootenay River while conducting fieldwork in 1917. Dainard Creek was named for Manuel Dainard, an outfitter from Golden in the late 1890s.

## Tumbling Creek to Helmet Creek

If you stay at Tumbling Creek campground, the ascent to Wolverine Plateau is a rude awakening, beginning directly from the tenting area. However, now that you are accustomed to the roller-coaster rigors of the Rockwall, this climb will seem short. The trail makes a sharp turn on a slope that overlooks the extensive moraines of Tumbling Glacier. The view northeast includes a surprising landmark — the tower of Castle Mountain in the Bow Valley. The ascent continues through ancient larch forest, leading to the extensive upper subalpine meadows of Wolverine Plateau. The displays of western anemone and paintbrush here are astounding. In 1985, a Lyall's larch with a circumference of 3.86 m was found nearby. This is the thickest Lyall's larch yet recorded in BC.

At the first knoll on the plateau, a sidetrail branches northeast to Wolverine warden cabin. With its idyllic setting, this rustic shelter epitomizes mountain heaven for many a park employee. The Rockwall trail contours the western edge of the plateau, through an outcrop of Chancellor Formation shale. You reach the Wolverine Pass junction in 3.1 km from Tumbling Creek campground. Turn west (left) for the short side-trip to the pass; keep straight ahead to continue on the Rockwall.

Rockwall Pass is the scenic climax of this outing. The 4 km-long precipice of Ottertail Formation limestone between Mt. Drysdale and Limestone Peak (2878 m) dominates the view northwest. This monolithic example of natural architecture is rarely duplicated in form or extent elsewhere in the Canadian Rockies. Another drift glacier lies at the base of the cliff. Its meltwaters drain into a substantial marginal lake. With the alpine meadows of Rockwall Pass as the foreground, the scene is unforgettable.

The surface of the unnamed glacier beneath Mt. Drysdale features alternating dark and light bands called ogives (OWE-jives). These result from different rates of glacial retreat and advance during summer and winter. Black exposures in the extensive moraine system on the near side of the glacier are ice-cored moraines. The melting of these features sustains a number of small ponds.

Five couloirs on the north face of Mt. Drysdale funnel snow, ice, and rock onto the glacier. The ice is dotted with talus (TAY-luss) cones — piles of debris that the moving ice has transported away from the mountain wall. The series of lateral moraines adjacent to the trail records at least five distinct advances of glacial ice during the Little Ice Age. It is not often you will see such a sequence this well preserved. Usually, the largest of the advances obliterated evidence of the lesser ones. In this case, apparently none of the existing moraines was overridden during subsequent advances — in other words, the first advance was the greatest.

The trail descends to cross the outlet of the marginal lake, the headwaters of the south fork of Helmet Creek. There is a waterfall and canyon downstream. The number of animal trails in the area indicates that mountain goats visit the canyon to lick sulphur-bearing minerals from the shales.

The next climb, to Limestone Summit, is

## The Wolverine — A Bad Reputation, a Grim Situation

**Wolverine Pass** is named for the largest terrestrial member of the weasel family. The adult male wolverine is about a metre long and half that high at the midpoint of the back, and weighs 14 to 21 kg. The thick fur is generally dark, with a highlight across the forehead and down each flank. Considerable colour variation occurs. The animal secretes a rank smelling musk,

*Wolverine*

which gives rise to one of its folk names — "skunk bear." Although the animal is seldom seen, the wolverine's range includes the upper subalpine of areas such as Wolverine Plateau. It runs with a lumbering gait, and travels in arrow-straight lines. On a ski mountaineering trip, I topped out on a corniced ridge. A wolverine had come up the valley from the south and — judging from the tracks — without pause, stepped off the cornice. I peeked over. The animal had bum-slid a short distance down a steep slope and then carried on to the north, its tracks fading from sight, perhaps ten kilometres away. There are many stories of wildlife biologists following wolverines that had covered more than 60 km in a day.

The wolverine is an opportunistic scavenger, eating carrion, small birds, and mammals. The animal has a fierce reputation, hence its other folk name — "devil-beast." One wolverine was observed protecting a kill from an approaching grizzly bear. The animal's formidable appearance has contributed to its reputation. It has the typical pointed weasel face, and sharp teeth, which it will bare at any intruder while making an array of intimidating sounds. You can imagine the smell of its breath. You won't soon forget a face to face encounter with a wolverine.

The wolverine is a species of special concern in western Canada because it is particularly sensitive to human activities. The animal requires vast terrain — 2000 km$^2$ is typical for an adult male — and most habitat has been fragmented. Wolverine fur is desired for parka hood trimmings because it resists ice build-up.

*Helmet Falls*

broken in two by a flat meadow. Looking south, you obtain a final, grand, close-up view of the Rockwall. Limestone Summit is not a true mountain pass, but a larch-covered spur of Limestone Peak. The steady descent north brings you to the alluvial flats at Helmet Creek campground. On the way, you have fine views of Helmet Falls. With a total estimated drop of 352 m, Helmet Falls is among the higher waterfalls in Canada. Surveyors argue over whether all the cascades — or just the highest — should be included in a waterfall's height. While Della Falls on Vancouver Island is unquestionably the highest in Canada, Helmet, Hunlen, and Takakkaw each have proponents that claim them to be "second highest."

The headwall that flanks Helmet Falls is a good place to look for mountain goats. This animal is the symbol of Kootenay National Park, which is home to 200 goats. Another 400 goats live in neighbouring Yoho. To the north of Helmet Falls, an underground stream discharges from the cliff in a small waterfall.

## Helmet Creek to the Paint Pots

The Rockwall concludes by following Helmet Creek east to its confluence with Ochre Creek, and then southeast along Ochre Creek to the Paint Pots and the Kootenay Parkway. It's a pleasant hike involving a gradual descent through lush subalpine forest. Red and white baneberry, and the lily, twisted stalk, are common in the undergrowth, along with the wildflowers, dwarf dogwood and queen's cup.

From the bridge crossing on Helmet Creek, you have a last, distant view west to the Rockwall, featuring Helmet Mountain and part of the Washmawapta Icefield. An icefield is a substantial body of ice that sends tributary glaciers into more than one valley. The Washmawapta is the southernmost feature in the Rockies to which the term "icefield" is officially applied. *Washmawapta* is Stoney for "ice river."

Downstream from the bridge, the trail skirts a shale canyon at the mouth of Helmet Creek, then climbs through forest before descending to Ochre Creek. Many of the subalpine fir trees in this vicinity have been stricken with a needle cast that has defoliated them. As you descend to Ochre Creek, notice the V-shape of the Helmet Creek and Ochre Creek valleys.

Cross Ochre Creek to a campground and trail junction. Turn south (right) and follow signs for "Highway 93" at the subsequent junctions. At the far side of the Ochre Beds, the Rockwall trail crosses the Vermilion River on a suspension bridge, to end at the Paint Pots parking lot on the Kootenay Parkway, 12.9 km north of the Floe Lake trailhead.

---

## The Ice River Alkaline Complex: Protected and Exploited

**North of Helmet Falls,** Sharp Mountain (3049 m) contains an outcrop of the Ice River Alkaline Complex. The complex is the largest assemblage of igneous (once molten) rock known in the Canadian Rockies. This blob of magma intruded into older sedimentary formations approximately 245 million years ago. Many rare minerals occur. In total, the complex covers 19 km². The portion within Yoho and Kootenay national parks is a Special Preservation Area. Access and collecting are prohibited.

There have been various attempts to extract the iron-rich mineral magnetite from this complex. All have failed because of the remoteness of the location. In 1991, a mine was proposed for upper Moose Creek, west of the Rockwall, just 300 m outside the boundaries of Yoho and Kootenay national parks. The developers hoped to take advantage of a forestry road scheduled for construction along Moose Creek. So far nothing has come of the proposal, although two slate mines operate farther down the valley.

## Goodsir Pass (2210 m), 4.0–7.6 km

**I omitted Goodsir Pass** from the first edition because Parks Canada was considering closing the trail to protect bear habitat in the nearby McArthur Creek valley. The trail is still open a decade later, so lace up your boots — but do keep a sharp lookout for bears. Strong hikers can quick-trip the pass from Helmet Creek campground and still hike out the same day. But I recommend adding a day to the trip to savour this destination.

Head northeast from Helmet Creek campground for 600 m to the Goodsir Pass junction, where the trail forks. Keep left. You gain a solid piece of elevation on this hike — 445 m in just 4 km — but it's on a well-graded trail. The rambling entry to the pass takes you across an ancient rockslide. You might be expecting the Kootenay/Yoho boundary to be on the crest of the pass. It isn't. Yoho's boundary — set 34 years before Kootenay was established — follows an illogical path (no principal summits) from Neptuak Mountain to Sharp Mountain. The trail rambles for almost 4 km across the pass, through flower-filled meadows and glades of larch. For those adept at off-trail travel, the ridge northeast of the pass beckons.

What you probably came for is the incredible view of the north faces of Mt. Goodsir. The South Tower (3562 m) and the North Tower (3525 m) are the two highest peaks in Yoho and, respectively, are the 9th- and 12th-highest in the Rockies. The South Tower is the highest mountain between Mt. Assiniboine and Columbia Icefield. You might think that

*The Goodsirs from the Yoho side of Goodsir Pass*

these mountains owe their stature to the incorporation of some tough dolomite or quartzite in their flanks — perhaps to a continuation of the Rockwall. Not so. These are truly rotten mountains, assembled from the smashed up shales and slates of the McKay Group of formations with the use of very little glue. The mountains' saving grace is that the rocks lie in horizontal layers that are not readily eroded. James Hector named Mt. Goodsir in 1858 for John Goodsir, an anatomy professor at the University of Edinburgh. The South Tower was first climbed in 1903, and the North Tower in 1909. "The Goodsirs," as they are known, are normally climbed from approaches on their southwest flanks, from the Ice River valley, but both north faces have been climbed. The stupendous elevation gain — more than 2000 m — and the awful rock, combine to turn back many a party. Sentry Peak (3267 m) stands guard to the southeast of the South Tower.

## The Red Earth

**The last points** of interest on the Rockwall trail are the Paint Pots and Ochre Beds. "Ochre" is clay that has been stained yellow and red with iron oxides. This "red earth" was a valuable trading commodity for Ktunaxa (ka-too-NA-hah) Natives from the Columbia Valley in the 1700s. The Ktunaxa collected the ochre, shaped it into cakes and baked it in fire. The resulting compound was mixed with

*Ochre Beds*

fish grease or animal fat to create a body paint used in rituals. The Ktunaxa would stop at the Ochre Beds to gather ochre on their way to Kootenay Plains on the North Saskatchewan River. Their travel route, "The Kutenai Trail," took them north over Goodsir

Pass or Ottertail Pass through what is now Yoho National Park, and across Amiskwi Pass and Howse Pass.

The iron-rich water that stains the clay percolates from three cold mineral springs — the Paint Pots. The ochre has stained rocks downstream in the Vermilion River — the origin of its name. Please do not disturb or remove the ochre.

"Kootenay" or "Kootenai" was the name applied to the Natives by bands east of the Rockies. It means "people from beyond the hills." Anthropologists now use the spelling, Ktunaxa. The Ktunaxa referred to themselves as *Ksanka*, which means "Standing Arrow."

# 53. Kindersley/Sinclair

## Route

**Day-hike**

| Route | Elevation (m) | Distance (km) |
|---|---|---|
| Kindersley trailhead | 1335 | 0 |
| Lookout Point ridge | 1936 | 6.0 |
| Kindersley Pass | 2210 | 8.4 |
| Kindersley Summit | 2393 | 10.1 |
| Sinclair Creek trailhead | 1433 | 16.1 |
| Kindersley trailhead | 1335 | 17.4 |

**Maps**
NTS: 82 J/12 and 82 K/9
Gem Trek: Kootenay

## Trailhead

**Kootenay Parkway,** 10.5 km east of the junction with Highway 95; 94.2 km west of the Trans-Canada Highway. The small parking area is on the south side of the highway. This is a dangerous turnoff for westbound travellers. The trailhead is across the road. Use caution crossing the highway.

The Kindersley/Sinclair trail travels from densely forested valley bottom to barren alpine ridgecrest. The wildflower displays of early summer are superb. Although it gains 875 m in 8.4 km, the trail on the Kindersley side is one of the better constructed in the Rockies, and the grade is seldom steep. Kindersley Pass and Kindersley Summit are usually snowbound until late June.

### Trailhead to Kindersley Pass

From the Kootenay Parkway, the trail initially ascends through a damp forest dominated by Douglas fir. This tree is the climax species of forests in the montane ecoregion of the southern Rockies. Its fire-resistant bark enables it to withstand the periodic ground fires that remove competing vegetation. Western Canada violet, white geranium, western meadowrue, yellow columbine, baneberry, birchleaf spirea, and prickly wild rose

## Variations

- Hike to Kindersley Pass and Kindersley Summit, 20.2 km return
- Cross Kindersley Summit and descend Sinclair Creek, 17.4 km loop

*The Kindersley/Sinclair loop crosses an alpine ridge that is frequented by bighorn sheep.*

are common wildflowers and shrubs in the undergrowth. Where the trail climbs away from the creek onto drier soils, lodgepole pine and massive white spruce grow, with Oregon grape in the undergrowth. This holly-like shrub has yellow flowers that produce blue berries. In autumn, the thick, waxy leaves turn purple and red.

At km 2.8, the view opens to an avalanche path across the valley. The lush vegetation on the slope includes cow parsnip and other succulents that are favourite foods of black bears and grizzly bears. The shrubs offer browse for elk and mule deer. This pocket of habitat is but one in the mosaic that sustains the diversity of wildlife in this valley. You may see mice, voles, squirrels, deer, snowshoe hares, American martens, coyotes, and — if fortunate — a cougar, a lynx, or a wolf. The ancient trees offer good habitat for northern flickers and other woodpeckers.

The trail returns briefly to the valley bottom. Then the switchbacking resumes. During the next 5 km, you may see the blooms of more than 30 species of wildflowers if you are hiking early in the season. Two of these flowers have corms (bulbs) that are favourite foods of grizzly bears — glacier lily and western spring beauty.

At km 6.0, the trail crests the forested ridge west of Lookout Point and contours into an avalanche basin that contains Lyall's larch trees. Look for the tracks and scats of wolves here. The stream at trailside now drains east into upper Sinclair Creek. More switchbacks through avalanche

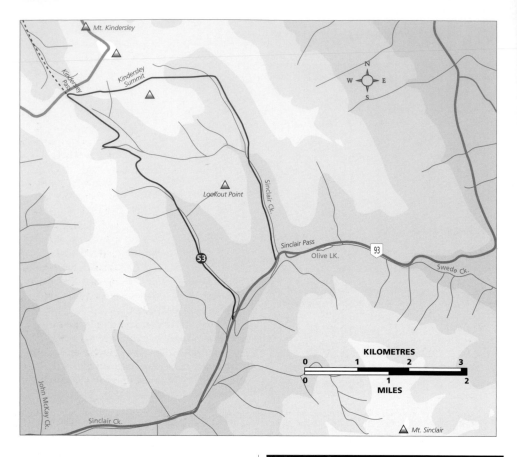

terrain lead to the final approach to Kindersley Pass — a confined, snowmelt stream course, adorned with western anemone. The consolidated avalanche snow here frequently endures the summer.

## Kindersley Pass to Kindersley Summit

Kindersley Pass is on the national park boundary and offers only limited views north into the Brisco Range. Cutblocks scar upper Kindersley Creek — a reminder of the pressures that affect protected areas. Follow a steep track northeast along the park boundary to an errant sign that indicates "Kindersley Pass," perhaps erected here because the view is better than on the true pass below. The trail angles sharply southeast (right) and begins a treeline traverse across avalanche gullies to Kindersley Summit.

Kruppelholz tree islands of Engelmann spruce and subalpine fir dot the mountainside. The firs form twisted mats, from which grow the taller spruce. Bighorn sheep frequent these slopes in summer. Kindersley Summit is the high point on

## The Ice-free Corner of the Rockies

**From a steep sideslope** at km 4.0, you can see the V-shape of this unnamed valley. Southwestern Kootenay is in the western ranges, where many of the smaller valleys are V-shaped. This indicates that they have been eroded principally by water, not by glacial ice — at least not by glaciers of the last big ice age, 25,000 years ago, or perhaps not even by those of the preceding ice age, 75,000 years ago. Earlier glaciations, which were more extensive, certainly helped to produce these valleys. But streams have since taken over the job, cutting deeply into the originally U-shaped troughs. If the bedrock here was resistant limestone or dolomite, the flowing water would have created a slot canyon in this valley. As the bedrock is weak shale and slate principally of the Chancellor Group of formations, the V-shape results. The western ranges between Golden and Invermere do not contain any glaciers today. This part of the Rockies is ice-free.

*Descending the steep and narrow valley of Sinclair Creek*

into the avalanche basin at the head of Sinclair Creek. Follow a steep, sketchy path for 1 km, after which the trail becomes better defined in the vicinity of the creek, which you hop to its east bank. From here on it's smooth sailing on a steep trail that descends through the lush vegetation of this V-shaped valley to the Kootenay Parkway. You cross to the west side of the creek 1.7 km before trail's end. The Kindersley trailhead is 1.3 km southwest (right) along the Kootenay Parkway. Cross the road with caution and walk facing traffic. Sinclair Creek was named for James Sinclair, who in 1841 led a group of 120 settlers from Manitoba through the Rockies to the Oregon country.

this hike. It should probably be called "Sinclair Summit," as it is at the head of the Sinclair Valley, not the Kindersley Valley.

**Kindersley Summit to Kootenay Parkway**

The most straightforward exit from Kindersley Summit is to retrace your route to the trailhead. For the more adventurous, trail markers lead east

## An Eagle-eye View

**Mountaineers may** readily ascend the unnamed peaks southeast (2515 m) and northwest (2683 m) of Kindersley Summit. Both offer detailed views of a tremendous length of the Continental Divide. Mt. Joffre (3449 m) looms in the distant southeast and Mt. Goodsir (3562 m) dominates the skyline in the northeast. Directly east is an unfamiliar view of a well-known mountain — Mt. Assiniboine (3618 m) — highest point in the southern Rockies and sixth highest in the range. The Purcell Range of the Columbia Mountains forms the skyline to the west. Look for golden eagles on the thermals overhead, as well as gliders (sailplanes).

From the northerly summit, the view also includes the Columbia Valley and the complete length of the western ranges, from northeast of Golden to south of Invermere. The western ranges were the first to be thrust above sea level in the Rockies, more

*The shattered peaks of the western ranges with Mt. Goodsir central on the horizon*

than 120 million years ago. Their weak shales and slates exhibit extensive folding and faulting. The northerly summit contains a radio repeater installation, one of eleven in the national park radio system. Its helicopter landing pad makes a great sundeck on a favourable day.

# Peter Lougheed Provincial Park

*Mt. Sir Douglas from "Burstall Bump," Burstall Pass trail*

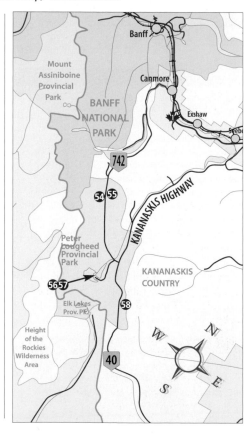

At just 509 km², Peter Lougheed Provincial Park is small in comparison to some of the other parks in this book. But the park's rugged, lake-dotted, front range landscape is packed with more than 100 km of hiking and walking trails. Those embarking from Canmore have two options for approach: the Trans-Canada Highway to Highway 40 (Kananaskis Trail); or the Smith-Dorrien/Spray Trail (Highway 742). (These "trails" are roads.) The latter is the best approach for Chester Lake and Burstall Pass. The park information centre is on the Kananaskis Lakes Trail, 3.5 km south of the junction with Highway 40, 1.2 km south of the junction with the Smith-Dorrien/Spray Lakes Trail. The park's six frontcountry campgrounds are clustered near the Kananaskis Lakes. Random camping is not permitted in the park. There is no hostel in the park; the closest is at Ribbon Creek, north on Highway 40. Peter Lougheed Provincial Park is part of the greater area known as Kananaskis Country. This 4000 km2 reserve includes four wildland provincial parks, five provincial parks, and one recreation area.

# 54. Burstall Pass

## Route

Day-hike

| Route | Elevation (m) | Distance (km) |
|---|---|---|
| Trailhead | 1910 | 0 |
| Robertson Glacier floodplain | 1985 | 3.7 |
| Burstall Pass | 2380 | 7.6 |

**Maps**
NTS: 82 J/14
Gem Trek: Kananaskis Lakes, or Banff and Mt. Assiniboine

## Trailhead

**From the west end** of Main Street in downtown Canmore, follow signs for the Nordic Centre and the Smith-Dorrien/Spray Trail (Route 742). Follow this road 44 km south to the Burstall Day Use area turnoff. Turn west (right). The trailhead is on the west edge of the parking lot.

The lofty break of Burstall Pass provides stunning views that encompass three provincial parks and one national park. The Spray Mountains are close at hand, with distant Mt. Assiniboine a prize for the eye on fair days. Wildflower displays are superb; they peak a bit later than average — early August. The environs of the pass are a wonderful place to ramble. Carry river shoes to use when fording the outflow from Robertson Glacier. Mountain bikes share the first 2.9 km.

### Trailhead to Burstall Pass
You are already on a mountain pass when you begin this hike. Smith-Dorrien Summit separates Smuts Creek to the north, from Smith-Dorrien Creek to the south. All of the waters eventually reach the Bow River, but because of hydro-electric installations on both tributary systems — the Spray and the Kananaskis — Mud Lake, at the trailhead, is dammed to ensure that all of its water

## Variations

- Extend the hike to the Leman Lake viewpoint (1.4 km return)
- Ramble over the intervening ridge to South Burstall Pass to make a 19.0 km loop

*Mt. Birdwood, "The Pig's Tail," and Commonwealth Peak from near Burstall Pass.*

drains north. The lake is frequented by osprey. Jan Smuts was a South African statesman. Horace Smith-Dorrien was a British army commander in WWI.

Walk across the earthen dam. Turn west (right) at the first junction, following the hiker sign. The trail here is an old logging road — you'll see stumps. The logs were hauled to a now-abandoned sawmill site near the lower Burstall Lake. Arnica, buffaloberry, false-azalea, and white rhododendron grow at trailside. The forest here is a good one for birding. I heard boreal chickadees, hermit thrust, warbling vireo, and the drumming of a three-toed woodpecker. In the Rockies, if a woodpecker's drumming speeds up as it trails off, it's probably a three-toed that's making the racket. At about km 1.7 you pass a huge limestone erratic, dropped here when the Burstall valley glacier receded. Sidetrails lead down to each of the three Burstall Lakes, which make nice places to linger if you've packed your bug dope. Henry Burstall was a commander of Canadian forces during and after WWI.

The trail narrows and becomes rocky and rooted beyond the bike lock-up. The surrounding forest is damp, with foamflower, twinflower, wintergreen, bronze bells, cow parsnip, arnica, yellow columbine, and horsetails in the understory. You pass a limestone bluff covered in feathermosses. The trail crosses the forested, less active part of

223

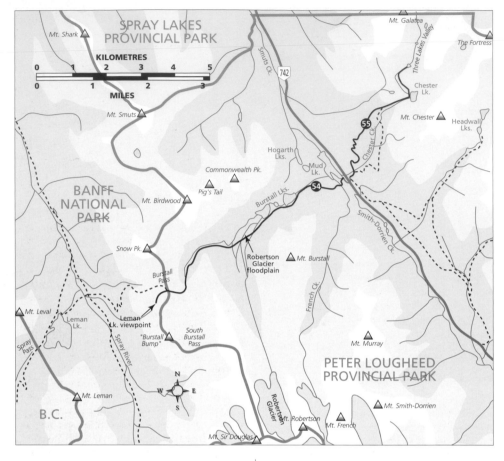

the Robertson Glacier floodplain, where the tributary streams usually behave themselves, flowing in box culverts. You emerge from the forest at km 3.7. Now the fun begins.

It's only about 550 m across the Robertson Glacier floodplain, but, depending on the volume of the numerous streams, it might take you a bit of time. The water level will rise when the snowmelt is on in early summer and when glacial melt is on in August. It will also typically be higher on your return in the afternoon. If you time this hike for low water, you'll get across with the assistance of various logs that have been tossed into the streams, and the odd awkward hop. If the water is high, you'll be putting on river shoes and splashing through ankle-deep to shin-deep channels. Follow the markers across. William Robertson was a British Army general during WWI. You can see his rapidly receding, namesake glacier — responsible for your wet socks — to the south. The horseshoe traverse of Robertson, Haig, and

French glaciers is popular with ski-mountaineers.

Vegetation on the floodplain includes elephant head, yellow hedysarum, yellow

## Dogtooth Mountains

**Banff's Mt. Louis** (see Classic Hike #4) is the most celebrated dogtooth mountain in the Rockies. But at least half a dozen others, including two visible from this hike, rank as equals. Dogtooth mountains were created when their sedimentary formations were thrust up toward the vertical. Mt. Birdwood (3097 m), a classic example, dominates the north side of the Burstall valley. The mountain's resistant slabs are limestone and dolomite of the Palliser Formation. Mountaineers climb routes on the southwest-facing slabs of dogtooth mountains, or, in some cases, on the steep, mini-ridges created by the south-facing edges of the slabs. Mt. Birdwood was first climbed in 1922. It was named for William Birdwood, a military commander in WWI.

*Mt. Sir Douglas*

*The displays of white mountain avens are particularly fine on the benches beneath Burstall Pass.*

paintbrush, yellow mountain saxifrage, yellow mountain avens, and beautiful patches of bog orchids and rein-orchids. Be careful where you step. Downstream, cotton-grass grows profusely near the upper Burstall Lake. White-crowned sparrows sing from within the clumps of willow. These birds, and those I have heard on the west side of Burstall Pass, utter unique variations on the typical song.

Leaving the floodplain, you enter ancient spruce-fir forest and begin a climb of 100 m over the next km. Where the trail draws alongside Burstall Creek, note the transition to upper subalpine groundcover. There is a fine view downvalley, including upper Burstall Lake. The trail levels as it swings southwest into treeline forest. Classic glades of upper subalpine wildflower meadows are dotted with larches. You may detect a reddish tinge on snowpatches in the views ahead to Burstall Pass. This is "watermelon snow," tinged by the pigment of one-celled algae.

The climb resumes over ancient limestone benches — natural terraced gardens where western anemone, yellow mountain heather, white mountain avens, alpine buttercup, cinquefoil,

golden fleabane, dwarf hawksbeard, moss campion, alpine forget-me-not, and glacier lilies grow. Look back during the climb for fine views of the procession of dogtooth mountains on the north side of the valley, and to the limestone slabs of Whistling Ridge to the east. But the vista that tops them all is the bomber view to the south — the glaciated north face of Mt. Sir Douglas (3406 m). The mountain was named for a British army commander in WWI. I've seen wolf scat and bear scat on the trail here. Burstall Pass is a key wildlife corridor in this part of the Rockies. Keep right at the junction where the path to "South Burstall Pass" departs. (You can descend later on that path if you choose to ramble along the ridge from Burstall Pass.)

The trail swings northwest to gain the pass and the Banff National Park boundary, where another spectacular mountain vista is added — the east face of distant Mt. Assiniboine (3618 m), sixth-highest peak in the Rockies. Twice, while on the pass, I have watched a golden eagle soar on thermals overhead.

### Burstall Pass to Leman Lake Viewpoint

The trail crosses the pass and skirts the south edge of a 100 m deep sinkhole — a depression eroded into the underlying Palliser Formation limestone. Mountain sorrel, roseroot, and red-stemmed saxifrage grow on the screes. Were you not in a protected area, you could make a vitamin-rich salad from the leaves of the first two plants. Keep left where the trail forks after 525 m — the right-hand fork descends to the Spray Valley. The left-hand trail climbs gently for 175 m to a knot of spruce and fir on a knoll that overlooks the broad sweep of the upper Spray Valley and the environs of Palliser Pass, with Leman Lake featured in the view. The Interprovincial Boundary Survey of 1923–25 appropriated some of the features in this area originally named by the Palliser Expedition, renaming them for figures connected with WWI. At least the name of Palliser Pass has endured as a tribute to the monumental journeys of that expedition.

*Leman Lake and the upper Spray Valley*

### "Burstall Bump"

Experienced ridge ramblers won't be able to resist the climb onto "Burstall Bump" (2575 m), the minor summit south of Burstall Pass. The views go up a notch or two, particularly that of Mt. Sir Douglas. From the highpoint, you can backtrack, or head south toward South Burstall Pass, from where you descend east over limestone benches (no trail) to pick up the path that rejoins the main trail about 1 km below Burstall Pass. Carry an ice axe if you attempt this route in early summer.

## Captain John and Company

In the 1850s, much of western Canada was unmapped beyond the standard fur trade routes. A young Irishman named John Palliser, stimulated by a hunting trip on the upper Missouri River in 1847–48, was aware of this and dreamed of charting that ground. He took his idea to The Royal Geographical Society as something of a one-man show. The Society liked his idea, but suggested that some men of science accompany him on what they called the "North West America Exploring Expedition." Eugene Bourgeau, the "prince of botanical collectors," was named to the team along with meteorologist Thomas Blakiston, geologist and medical doctor James Hector, and mathematician and secretary John Sullivan. After a frenzied year of preparation, the Palliser Expedition left for Canada in 1857.

*John Palliser and James Hector*

Over the next two years — including forays made in the dead of winter — the Expedition trooped through the southern and central Rockies, assessing passes through the mountains and collecting natural specimens.

The two reports of the Palliser Expedition are matter of fact and make for dry reading — the titles alone occupy half a page each. Stories are told in outline. But if you know something of the country in which the expedition travelled, you soon sense that it is in the unrecorded details that the real adventure is described. We are fortunate that Palliser and his colleagues were such observant people. They left us a legacy of place names and travel routes, some now the paths of highways, others sketchy trails to seldom-seen places in the back of beyond.

# 55. Chester Lake

## Route

Day-hike

| Route | Elevation (m) | Distance (km) |
|---|---|---|
| Trailhead | 1920 | 0 |
| Chester Lake | 2220 | 4.0 |

**Maps**
NTS: 82 J/14
Gem Trek: Kananaskis Lakes
**See map on p.224**

**Best lighting:** afternoon and evening

## Trailhead

**From the west end** of Main Street in downtown Canmore, follow signs for the Nordic Centre and the Smith-Dorrien/Spray Trail (Route 742). Follow this road 44 km south to the Chester Day Use area turnoff. Turn east (left). The trailhead is at the northeast corner of the parking lot.

$S$hort and sweet — and perhaps, crowded — sums up the outing to Chester Lake. The trail to this beautiful tarn is justifiably popular, summer and winter. The meadows near the lake are bedecked with wildflowers, the afternoon light seems to animate the slabby cliffs of Mt. Chester, and the sidetrail to Three Lake Valley provides a delightful ramble through larch forest to lake-dotted, limestone barrens. This is a great hike for birding. Although I don't normally advocate beginning a hike in the evening, when the forecast is fair, experienced hikers might consider packing a dinner instead of a lunch and striking off about 6 pm. I imagine that sunset at Chester Lake would be a magical experience. The first 1.6 km is open to mountain bikes.

### Trailhead to Chester Lake
The trail begins as a gravelled path through spruce-fir forest. Look and listen for gray jays and hermit thrushes. The latter sang from one tree or another throughout my entire time on this trail

## Variation

• Extend the hike to Three Lakes Valley. The first lake is 2.4 km return.

*Chester Lake is ringed by contorted front range peaks, and by subalpine meadows flush with wildflowers.*

and at the lake. In my field notes I called this forest "the hermit thrush capital of the Rockies." One thrush hopped along the trail a few paces ahead of me. The path soon reverts to old logging road. You cross Chester Creek after about 150 m. By keeping left at all the upcoming forks and junctions, you won't end up on a winter ski trail or on an abandoned skidder track. Labrador tea, fireweed, paintbrush, wild strawberry, buffaloberry, and arnica grow in the forest understory. The road makes a series of wide switchbacks with the grade sometimes moderately steep. Views back include the environs of Burstall Pass, Mt. King Albert (2981 m), and directly up French Creek to Mt. Robertson (3194 m) and Mt. Sir Douglas (3406 m).

Beyond the bike lock-up, the trail narrows and becomes rooted. It levels and then descends to a frost meadow whose earth hummocks are topped with yellow mountain heather. The east edge of this clearing features a fantastic larch tree snag — chewed on by porcupines and riddled with woodpecker holes. After a short forested section, you emerge into a second meadow; this one larger, with fine views ahead to Mt. Chester (3054 m). HMS *Chester* was a British battle cruiser, severely damaged in the Battle of Jutland in 1916 but back on station a few months later.

When the trail re-enters the forest, you might notice that the character of the tread is different. The trail here has been capped with gravel. You're right in thinking that it would be a long haul from the trailhead with wheelbarrows. The gravel was delivered in barrel buckets slung under a helicopter, and placed over soil blanket. The blanket prevented the gravel from quickly being punched down into the muck. It's an expensive fix for a trail, but the only worthwhile method on a route this popular. Farther on you'll see where trees have been transplanted into trail braids to encourage you to keep on track.

The last meadow bisected by the trail is the largest of the three. Although the lake is close by, the wildflower displays will probably slow your pace. Western anemone, yellow paintbrush, Sitka valerian, fleabanes, and — in early summer — superb displays of glacier lilies colour the tundra. Just before the lake, you pass an outhouse that appears to be on stilts. The explanation: This is a popular skiing destination; if you elevate the outhouse, you don't have to shovel the door as much.

The trail forks at the lakeshore. The right-hand path crosses the outlet to a grove of spruce, larch, and subalpine fir — a good place to take in the view. Across the lake, a seasonal stream tumbles from a slot canyon. The songbirds I saw and heard here did not surprise me — hermit thrush, pine siskin, Tennessee warbler, boreal chickadee, yellow-rumped warbler, robin, white-winged crossbill, and dipper — but the behaviour of one of the species amazed me. While I waited for the light, I watched two pairs of dippers come and go. They fed at the outlet of the lake, diving underwater and hauling out onto rocks. Two robins joined them, hopped into the stream and foraged underwater. They, too, hauled out on rocks, mid-stream. The robins did everything to emulate the dippers but sing dipper songs and bob their tails.

## Three Lakes Valley (2310 m), 1.2 km

Follow the trail around the west shore of Chester Lake. About 80 m beyond a footbridge over a tributary stream, you come to a small stand of subalpine fir. Turn north (left) onto any of several paths that soon converge. The initial climb away from the lake is steep. The trail swings west to the edge of a sandstone canyon that harbors a pretty stream. I watched the dippers fly through here, too. This canyon marks the seam between the same sandstone and limestone formations that you see in Mt. Chester. The trail soon levels at a meadow that contains the Elephant Rocks — huge, shattered, and beautifully eroded limestone blocks of the Livingstone Formation that have

*The trail to Three Lakes Valley takes you past the Elephant Rocks, where you can let your imagination run wild.*

tumbled from the slopes above. Some of the rocks feature *rillenkarren* — grooves eroded into the limestone by water. The best route is to keep right.

Delightful larch forest borders the trail as it works north, descends slightly, and then angles northeast into the Three Lake Valley. The pond off to the west (left) does not rank as one of the Three Lakes. Alpine speedwell, western anemone, Drummond's anemone, western spring beauty, grouseberry, yellow columbine, alpine

## It's Been a Slice

**The meadow** just before the lake is a good place to appreciate the local and regional geology. The steeply tilted slabs of Mt. Chester are characteristic of overthrust mountains in the front ranges. The formations in the mountain are part of the Sulphur Mountain Thrust Sheet, an assemblage of rocks that was pushed northeastward during mountain building. Between the trailhead and the summit of The Fortress (3002 m) northeast of Chester Lake, the entirety of this thrust sheet — spanning 12 sedimentary formations — is preserved with the formations in sequence. The trailhead is among the shales and siltstones of the 135-million-year-old Fernie Formation. The summit of The Fortress is 366-million-year-old Palliser Formation limestone. It's not often that such a large slice of the crumbly sedimentary sandwich is so well preserved at the surface in the Rockies. You can see the division between two rock types on the scree slopes above the southeast shore of Chester Lake. Tan-coloured sandstone is to the west; gray limestone is to the east. Both rocks belong to the Etherington Formation.

forget-me-not, and Sitka valerian grow at trailside. The outlying slopes of Mt. Galatea (3185 m)
ahead, are a favourite haunt of mountain goats.
HMS *Galatea* was yet another British naval vessel
involved in the Battle of Jutland in 1916.

The trail alternately cuts over and parallels
low, gray bluffs — limestone of the Mount Head
Formation. Finally, it takes one of these mini-
headwalls head on, delivering you in 150 m to the
first of the Three Lakes. Those accustomed to
travelling off-trail can pick their way farther upvalley, beginning with a rough route around the
west shore of the first lake. The second lake is an
attractive spot, the third lake, less so. The views
southwest from any are superb, but I like the first
lake the best for its cotton-grass fringe and
pleasing greenery.

## Earth Hummocks

*Earth Hummocks*

**Hike enough** trails in the Rockies, and certain landscape themes become familiar. One of these is the
subalpine frost meadow. A trail levels at the crest
of a climb, emerging from forest onto the floor of
a tributary valley. A tiny stream meanders through
the valley, bordered by meadow. Willows grow
near the stream. The grassy alp that surrounds the
willows is dotted with small mounds called earth
hummocks. Most people who live in northern
climes know about frost heaves on roadways —
bumps in the pavement that emerge in autumn
and spring. The same sort of process was at work
in frost meadows when they were underlain by
permafrost. The Mazama ash — volcanic fallout
from the eruption of Mt. Mazama 6850 years ago
— is where most earth hummocks in the Rockies
took purchase. Although most earth hummocks
are now relict features, they have been preserved
by the vegetation that grows atop them, where
the soil is marginally warmer than in the
surrounding hollows.

# 56. Mt. Indefatigable

## Route

**Day hike**

| Route | Elevation (m) | Distance (km) |
|---|---|---|
| Trailhead | 1722 | 0 |
| Indefatigable trail jct | 1721 | 0.3 |
| Wendy Elekes viewpoint | 1950 | 1.3 |
| Outlier trail jct | 2222 | 2.3 |
| End of trail | 2225 | 2.5 |
| Mt. Indefatigable Outlier | 2484 | 4.0 |

**Maps**
NTS: 82 J/11
Gem Trek: Kananaskis Lakes

## Trailhead

**From the west end** of Main Street in downtown
Canmore, follow signs for the Nordic Centre and
the Smith-Dorrien/Spray Trail (Route 742). Follow
this road 64 km south to the junction with the
Kananaskis Lakes Trail. Turn south (right), and
drive 13 km to road's end at the North Interlakes
Day Use Area. From the Trans-Canada Highway,
follow Kananaskis Trail (Highway 40) 50 km south
to the Kananaskis Lakes Trail junction. Turn south
(right) and follow the Kananaskis Lakes Trail 15 km
to road's end at the North Interlakes Day Use Area.
The trailhead is at the north end of the parking
lot.

Mt. Indefatigable was named decades before
this tortuous trail was beaten into its slopes.
The mountain may not tire of hikers, but most
hikers tire — perhaps even wilt — at some point
during the head-on climb. But if lofty, panoramic
views are what you seek, the cliff edge of Mt. Indefatigable provides them in short order. When the
forecast is for hot weather, begin early; you'll miss
most of the crowds, too. Much of the trail is rocky
and steep. On my way down, of the 250 people I
met, a few were heading up wearing sandals. I
hope they had duct tape for their feet. Carry your
water as there is no reliable source. Avoid this hike
when electrical storms threaten. Mountain bikes
share the first 300 m of trail.

### Trailhead to Wendy Elekes Viewpoint
The trail begins by crossing the earth-filled Interlakes dam between Upper Kananaskis Lake and

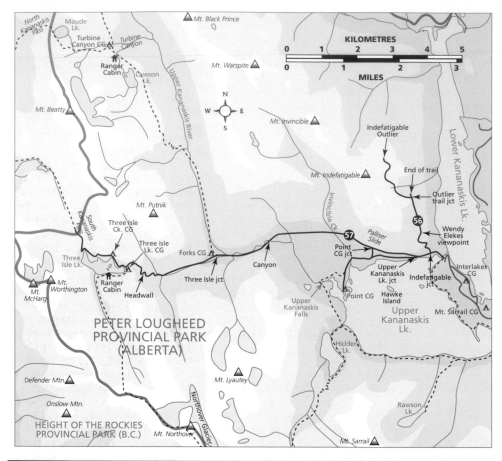

## Drop Those Names

The Alberta-British Columbia Boundary Commission of 1913–25 faced an enormous job. While delineating the boundary between the two provinces, the surveyors trooped up and down the slopes of hundreds of mountains, packing their survey gear and cameras. The enterprise seemed not to exhaust them physically, but when it came to naming features their imaginations became taxed. Rather than appending names that described an aspect of the landscape, in some locations the surveyors — led principally by A.O. Wheeler — resorted to naming groups of mountains after Italian, French, and British politicians, military commanders, and battleships. So prominent was the naval vessel motif in this area that locals knew the peaks as the "Ship Mountains."

HMS *Indefatigable* was a British battle cruiser sunk in the North Sea off Denmark on May 31, 1916, during the largest naval engagement of WWI, the Battle of Jutland. The vessel went down with the loss of 1015 men. Two nearby peaks, Invincible and

Inflexible, were named for sister ships. HMS *Invincible* was hardly that. The ship was broken in two by artillery fire in the same battle, claiming 1025 men, including Admiral Hood. HMS *Inflexible* survived the battle.

Although it is easy to appreciate the patriotism of the era, virtually all of the military names have no legitimate connection with the Rockies. Some, such as Pétain, are now viewed as embarrassments. The sentiment of most contemporary mountain lovers is that the names of mountains — places to which we make peaceful, restorative quests — should not be inspired by acts of war. It is now uncommon for the names of persons, living or dead, to be accepted as place names in Canada. Descriptive words are preferred. New submissions are often rejected with the explanation that the feature might best remain unnamed. The Stoney Nation knew Mt. Indefatigable as *Ubithka mabi* — "nesting of the eagle." Why didn't the surveyors stick with that?

*The Mt. Indefatigable trail parallels the crest of a cliff that grants tremendous views of the Kananaskis Lakes.*

Lower Kananaskis Lake. The structure was completed in 1955 as part of the hydro-electric development on the Kananaskis River. Cliff swallows nest on the spillway gate, and anglers inevitably dot the bouldery shore of Upper Kananaskis Lake. Across the spillway you enter forest and soon reach the Mt. Indefatigable junction. Turn northwest (right) to begin a gentle ascent through open spruce-fir forest, with dwarf dogwood, arnica, twinflower, wild strawberry, and pink wintergreen in the understory. Listen for varied thrushes, red-breasted nuthatches, and Tennessee warblers.

The half kilometre of tranquil forest is a ruse. The true nature of this hike is soon revealed at a sharp westerly turn, with sun-baked, rocky slopes, graced by a Douglas-fir on the right. Say goodbye to the cool of the trees. The switchbacking soon begins as the trail heads north, paralleling a shallow canyon. The climb is on bedrock of the Palliser Formation near the leading edge of the Bourgeau Thrust Sheet. The rocks at the base of this cliff illustrate how thrust sheets "shuffled the deck" of sedimentary formations during mountain building, placing older rocks over younger ones. In this case, 373 million-year-old dolomite of the Cairn Formation lies atop 208 million-year-old shale of the Fernie Formation.

The tread underfoot is solid where the trail cuts over the upturned edges of the limestone,

and loose where it traverses the rubble-covered ground in-between. Pay attention to the beaten path, as you can get off route in a few places. The average grade from the junction to the first viewpoint is 23 percent. It's tough going when dry, worse when wet, and not worth the attempt when snow-covered.

The trail angles southeast (right) at km 1.3 to level ground and a bench known unofficially as the Wendy Elekes viewpoint. (The Friends of K-Country runs a program where patrons can sponsor a bench. The funds raised are used to support park interpretation and research.) Views of Upper Kananaskis Lake and the surrounding peaks are superb. Many of the mountains south of the lake commemorate French figures from WWI. Mt. Sarrail (3174 m) was named for a military commander. Mt. Lyautey (3082 m) was named for the Minister of War. You can pick out the summit of Mt. Joffre (3450 m) — the highest mountain between Mt. Assiniboine and the US border — on the skyline between these two peaks. Joseph Joffre was French Commander-in-Chief in 1916. Mt Foch (3180 m) was named for the man who replaced him by the end of WWI.

## Wendy Elekes Viewpoint to End of Trail

The overall grade moderates beyond the viewpoint. You ascend near the edge of the tremendous limestone cliff that overlooks Lower Kananaskis Lake, with views east across the Kananaskis Valley to the Opal Range and the Elk Range. The Opal Range was named in 1884 when surveyed by G.M. Dawson, who found quartz crystals coated with opal.

Tiny spruce trees grow from within cracks in the bedrock of the trail. Try not to step on them. Many of the older spruce nearby are wind-trained — sculpted by the near constant wind on this ridge. Branches curl from west to east to escape the blast. A few whitebark pines grow here; one overhangs the sheer drop. Other vegetation includes wildflowers that prefer dry soils — the star-like, yellow blooms of stonecrop, yellow hedysarum, arctic aster, yellow locoweed, white moss phlox, nodding onion, mountain death-camas, and common harebell. On a fair day, the sun reflects off the waters of Lower Kananaskis Lake, bathing you in its glare. I heard a common loon as

## Variations

- Hike to the two viewpoints on maintained trail, 5.0 km return
- Extend the hike to the outlier on unmaintained trail, 8.0 km return

*Roseroot grows along the rocky slopes of the outlier.*

*Lower Kananaskis Lake and the Opal Range from the outlier*

I hiked this section, and tracking it by its call, watched it fly from the upper lake, over the dam to the east shore of the lower lake.

About 500 m beyond the viewpoint, the trail passes a lichen-covered quartzite erratic, deposited during the retreat of the glacier that once filled the Kananaskis Valley. Higher along the ridge, grouseberry, buffaloberry, Drummond's anemone, common fireweed, and a few glacier lilies grow at trailside, marking the transition to the upper subalpine ecoregion. You can see the south summit of Mt. Indefatigable, which sports a park radio repeater. The grade eases where the trail re-enters forest. Most of the bushes at trailside here are white rhododendron. In mid-July the blooms saturate the air with their delicate perfume. The leaves and flowers of this shrub are poisonous.

The trail levels at an unmarked junction. Continue north (straight ahead), passing a second junction in 40 m where a hiker sign directs you straight ahead once more. You soon reach the "end of trail" sign and a bench at a viewpoint overlooking Lower Kananaskis Lake.

## Mt. Indefatigable Outlier

Backtrack 200 m to the junction at the hiker sign and turn west (right) onto a well-beaten but unmaintained trail that soon curves north through open larch forest. Continue straight ahead at subsequent junctions, squeezing between the larches as required. You contour along the cliff edge with views down through the trees. Sitka valerian grows profusely here. The trail soon emerges onto avalanche slopes beneath the east face of Mt. Indefatigable. The damp soils are lush with sub-

alpine wildflowers, including white globeflowers.

The trail swings around a forested knoll to the shore of a snowmelt pond, with views ahead to the ultimate destination. Rockhop the pond's outlet as you follow the east shore. You climb through treeline to begin a moderate ascent on grassy slopes that are brightened with the blooms of alpine spring beauty, white mountain avens, alpine smelowskia, blue penstemon, and western forget-me-not. Views improve during the ascent, which culminates as a steep track beaten into the screes followed by a short section of ridge. Keep back from the edge; it's a long way down to the east. Look for mountain goats on the nearby slopes. Roseroot and scorpionweed grow in thin soils on the limestone of the summit.

Mt. Indefatigable (2670 m) makes a fine prospect. The summit area is limestone and dolomite of the Livingstone Formation, which caps dolomite cliffs of the upper Banff Formation. The slopes between the outlier and the main peak feature shales and siltstones of the Exshaw Formation. Mt. Invincible (2730 m) is nearby to the north. The lakes in the basin beneath are known as the Gypsum Tarns. They drain into Gypsum Creek. The features are named for outcrops of the soft, whitish mineral found on the slopes nearby and mined there for a few years in the late 1960s by Alberta Gypsum. The distant view northwest includes the length of the Smith-Dorrien and Spray valleys to the Fairholme Range beyond Canmore. To the southeast, the view takes in Mt. Rae (3218 m), the vicinity of Highwood Pass, and Elk Pass — one of the gentler breaks on the Continental Divide in all the Rockies.

# 57. South Kananaskis Pass

## Route

**Day-hike or overnight**

| Route | Elevation (m) | Distance (km) |
|---|---|---|
| Trailhead | 1722 | 0 |
| Indefatigable trail jct | 1721 | 0.3 |
| Upper Kananaskis Lake jct | 1746 | 0.8 |
| Point CG jct | 1760 | 2.2 |
| Invincible Creek | 1775 | 3.8 |
| Kananaskis River canyon | 1740 | 5.7 |
| Three Isle jct | 1785 | 7.1 |
| Forks CG | 1785 | +0.1 |
| Base of headwall | 1950 | 9.2 |
| Top of headwall | 2190 | 10.6 |
| Three Isle Lake CG | 2180 | 10.8 |
| Three Isle Creek CG | 2185 | 11.2 |
| South Kananaskis Pass | 2285 | 13.5 |

**Maps**

NTS: 82 J/11

Gem Trek: Kananaskis Lakes

**See map on p.230**

## Trailhead

**From the west end** of Main Street in downtown Canmore, follow signs for the Nordic Centre and the Smith-Dorrien/Spray Trail (Route 742). Follow this road 64 km south to the junction with the Kananaskis Lakes Trail. Turn south (right) and drive 13 km to road's end at the North Interlakes Day Use Area. From the Trans-Canada Highway, follow Kananaskis Trail (Highway 40) 50 km south to the Kananaskis Lakes Trail junction. Turn south (right) and follow the Kananaskis Lakes Trail 15 km to road's end at the North Interlakes Day Use Area. The trailhead is at the north end of the parking lot.

The outing to South Kananaskis Pass shares a trait common to only two other Classic Hikes — Fryatt Valley and Berg Lake. For most of the considerable distance to the destination, the grade is relatively gentle. But a headwall intervenes, offering a solid piece of exercise. The climb deters many backpackers from camping at Three

*South Kananaskis Pass is a lofty, windswept alp.*

Isle Lake; they opt instead to base themselves at Forks campground. But this headwall, as with any other steep climb, goes easily enough if you take it one step at a time.

The upper Kananaskis Valley is rich in human history, although details connected with this trail's destination are unclear. Some have argued that South Kananaskis Pass was "first" crossed in 1854 by a party of Red River settlers under the direction of James Sinclair, led by a Cree guide named Mas-ke-pe-toon. The guide had a shortcut across the Rockies in mind, but finally had to admit that he was lost. Accounts of what followed are vague, but it seems unlikely — as you will see — that a hundred people with cattle, kit, and caboodle would have made it up the headwall.

### Trailhead to Invincible Creek

The trail begins by crossing the earth-filled Interlakes dam between Upper Kananaskis Lake and Lower Kananaskis Lake. The structure was completed in 1955 as part of the hydro-electric development on the Kananaskis River. Cliff swallows nest on the spillway gate, and anglers inevitably dot the bouldery shore of Upper Kananaskis Lake. Across the spillway you enter forest and soon reach the Mt. Indefatigable junction. Continue straight ahead on a wide trail — formerly a fireroad — through subalpine forest along the north shore of the lake. Sun-exposed bark on some of the lodgepole pines here is remarkably orange in colour. Red squirrels and dark-eyed juncos are common. I saw a snowshoe hare.

Buffaloberry, dwarf dogwood, wild strawberry, yellow hedysarum, cow parsnip, paintbrush, white geranium, Hooker's thistle, and thimble-berry grow at trailside. You can see Hawke Island and Lower Kananaskis Falls at the west end of the lake. HMS *Hawke* was among the early British naval casualties of WWI. The island is also a casu-alty of sorts, the remains of a much larger land-form, inundated when the hydro-electric reser-voir was created. Three other named islands in the upper lake were completely submerged. Keep right (west) at the next two trail junctions, which provide access, respectively, to the shore of the lake and to Point campground.

Small stands of trembling aspen mark a transi-tion where the trail begins to cross a series of ava-lanche slopes and rocklside paths on the south flank of Mt. Indefatigable (2670 m). The aspens grow near snowmelt streams. The well-drained soils here support common juniper, blue penste-mon, yarrow, stonecrop, fireweed, paintbrush, and a few Douglas-fir trees. Some of the trees have snapped off in avalanches. The standing-dead trees now serve as dens for woodpeckers and squirrels. One Douglas-fir has rocks piled into a split, high up its trunk. The debris probably melted out of avalanche deposit and never made it to the ground. Yellowish-green wolf lichen graces the Douglas-firs.

For almost 1.5 km, the trail cuts across the path of the Palliser Slide — the largest rockslide in Peter Lougheed Provincial Park. Looking south, you can see the runout of the slide and the boul-derfield that resulted. Ponds fill depressions in the debris. Across the lake, the view includes the val-ley of Aster Creek. The prominent mountain with an armchair-like cirque in its north slopes is Mt. Lyautey (3082 m), named for a French Minister of War in WWI. The cirque sits in the base of a U-shaped fold known as the Lyautey Syncline.

The slopes beside the trail have been naturally stabilized by cushions of spotted saxifrage. The centres of the plants have died off as the plants grow outward in mats, in a circular fashion. The low profile allows the mats to survive avalanches. The name "saxifrage" comes from the Latin

words, *saxum* meaning "rock," and *frangere* "to break." The name was given because some sax-ifrages grow from within cracks in rocks. This at-tribute led to belief in a folk medicine cure — sax-ifrage powder was fed to patients suffering from gallstones. A massive Engelmann spruce — al-most a metre thick — stands on the far side of the rockslide where the trail re-enters forest. The trail descends to the flash-flood stream course of In-vincible Creek. Pick your way if the trail has been recently washed out.

**Invincible Creek to Forks Campground**

Across the creek the trail narrows, heralding a marked transition in hiking experience. Gone is the rocky tread underfoot, replaced by soft earth covered with spruce and fir needles. For the next 1.7 km you walk through a quiet, damp forest dominated by subalpine fir. Many of the trees are afflicted with a rust — possibly *Pucciniastrum epilobii*. It's hard on the trees, but is not necessar-ily a fatal affliction. Feathermosses, dwarf

## Dip, Dip, Dipper

*Dipper*

**The dipper** is the only aquatic songbird in North America and is a marvel of adaptation. It is a year-round resident of the mountains, protected from the chill of glacial water and winter by thick, soot-coloured, down that is impregnated with oil. The dipper feeds on insects, snails, and fish fry in tur-bulent streams. It has flaps that cover its nostrils during dives — allowing it to remain submerged for more than a minute — and an extra set of transparent eyelids that allow it to see underwa-ter. Its call is a metallic, staccato trill, made on the wing. Dippers also have a fine repertoire of songs — warbler-like, buzzy, and whistling. K-Country is dipper country. The Christmas bird counts here consistently yield North American highs for the species.

## Variations

- Day-hike to Three Isle Lake, 21.6 km return
- Day-hike to the pass, 27.0 km return
- Backpack to Forks campground (7.2 km). Day-hike to Three Isle Lake and the pass.
- Backpack to Three Isle Lake (10.8 km) or Three Isle Creek (11.2 km)

*Spotted saxifrage forms circular mats on the rocky slopes of the Palliser Slide.*

dogwood, arnica, twinflower, pink wintergreen, yellow columbine, grouseberry, and false-azalea are common at trailside. Although a firestorm of a forest fire affected parts of the Kananaskis Valley in 1936, pockets in the upper valley escaped. There is a stand of Engelmann spruce nearby that dates to 1586.

The trail crests a low, rocky rise and descends to the Upper Kananaskis River at a canyon cut into blocky dolomite of the Banff Formation. It is interesting to contrast the wild nature of the upper river with the tamed nature of the river below the Kananaskis Lakes. Here, the fluctuations are responses to rainfall, runoff, snowmelt, and glacier melt. Down in the main valley, the river's fluctuations are dictated by the manipulations of spillways and the demand for electricity.

Cross the bridge and turn west (right) to head upstream. For the next 1.5 km, the trail follows the river through a narrow breach in the limestone ramparts to Forks campground. Log jams and gravel bars dot the river's meandering course. Moose frequent this area; look for their tracks and droppings. Horsetails grow in wet margins. The trail crosses a talus slope where you can look and listen for pikas. Upvalley, you get your first distant view of the headwall. Mt. Putnik (2940 m) — with graceful limestone slabs — is on the north, named for a Serbian commander in WWI. An unnamed outlier of Mt. Northover is to the south of the headwall. Downvalley, the view includes Mt. Indefatigable. The spar trees from a forest fire cloak its upper slopes.

## Beds and Dips

**The Palliser Slide** from Mt. Indefatigable consists not of Palliser Formation limestone, but mostly of limestone and dolomite of the Rundle Group of formations, which were deposited in ancient seas approximately 350 million years ago. (The name, "Palliser," comes from the site's connection with the Palliser Expedition. John Palliser's party clambered over the rockslide deposits in 1858.) It is true in the Rockies that what went up during mountain building must, eventually, come down. This is accomplished through the chip-chipping of erosion or, more dramatically, through calamitous events such as rockslides.

*The Palliser Slide and Upper Kananaskis Lake*

The front ranges of the Rockies are rockslide country. If you look at the slopes above the trail, you can see why. The rock of Mt. Indefatigable is layered and dips steeply to the southwest — at as much as 50 degrees. The sedimentary layers are known as beds. When deposited they were horizontal; their orientation to each other known as the bedding.

When the ice of the Wisconsin Glaciation flowed through this valley, it widened it, cutting into the lower valley walls and removing the support for the rocks above. Enter gravity. With such a steep dip, it was only a matter of time before rock layers broke free along their beds and slid to the valley floor. The process was expedited by the freezing and thawing of water that percolated into fissures between the beds, pushing them apart and providing lubricant. The volume that let go here is estimated at 90 million cubic metres. Other rockslides will happen in the front ranges, most often on such steeply dipping slopes. Kind of makes you want to pick up the pace, doesn't it?

You cross an alluvial fan and the braids of the tributary stream that drains from the north face of Mt. Lyautey. Use the footbridges or rock-hop, as required. Yellow mountain avens grows on the gravels between the streams. I watched a dipper here, diving into the clear pool of a spring in quest of bugs and invertebrates. Forks campground is located in the angle between the Upper Kananaskis River, which comes in from the north, and Three Isle Creek, which comes in from the west. To carry on for Three Isle Lake, keep left (southwest) at the trail junction just before the campground.

### Forks Campground to Three Isle Lake

The trail skirts the south edge of the campground. Blue clematis, false Solomon's seal, dwarf dogwood, arnica, twisted stalk, fairybells, and foam-flower grow in this tranquil, ancient, tumble-down forest. Listen for the haunting, flute-like songs of hermit thrushes. For about a kilometre, the trail is rough where it is sandwiched between Three Isle Creek and the south slopes of Mt. Putnik. You walk a 40 m section of flash-flood creekbed where you might lose the way. The trail cuts upslope to the northwest (right) and crosses avalanche slopes, where cow parsnip, water hemlock, harebell, yarrow, yellow columbine, groundsel, bracted honeysuckle, and bristly black currant grow. As is often the case, a massive tree stands on the second slope — an Engelmann spruce more than a metre thick at the base. Now standing-dead, it has survived destruction by avalanches for centuries. From the third avalanche slope, you have your first clear view of the headwall.

Many people take a break before the upcoming climb, pausing near a cataract on Three Isle Creek. The waterfall is the emergence of the underground drainage from Three Isle Lake. The resting place is close to the rushing water and is in a pocket of good bear habitat. Make lots of noise. When you leave the stopping place, the trail switchbacks away through lush vegetation. The final leg crosses screes to the base of the headwall.

Although cliffs often surround you as you hike in the Rockies, it is a rare trail that tackles one head-on. The Three Isle Lake headwall features limestone and dolomite of the Palliser Formation, the classic front range cliff-builder. The route ahead appears formidable but is only occasionally steep. The worst is at the corner just above the initial staircase. But for most of the way, the well-conceived trail switchbacks and takes advantage

*The worst of the headwall comes at the beginning. This staircase and handrail help ease the climb.*

## A Rocky Rollercoaster

**If you have hiked** the Mt. Indefatigable trail and read its description, you might be thinking: "You said that Palliser Formation limestone outcropped in Mt. Indefatigable. Here it is again, more than 8 km to the west in the Three Isle Lake headwall. What gives?" The simplest explanation would be that the trail has crossed another thrust fault; the sequence of rock formations has been broken, with older rocks again thrust over younger ones. But the entire assemblage of rocks traversed by this trail belongs to a single thrust sheet — the Bourgeau. What is happening is that, as you hike west from Upper Kananaskis Lake, the trail transects a series of U-shaped and arch-shaped folds in the bedrock — synclines and anticlines — that bring different rock layers to the surface. At roughly the location of Forks campground, the trail crosses the base of the U-shaped Lyautey Syncline. The bedrock here has been bent downward, so that younger rock formations — ones that would have been eroded away if the rock layers had remained level — survive at the surface, while the older rocks are buried. The western arm of the syncline extends up the headwall to Three Isle Lake, so that older rocks — including the limestone of the Palliser Formation — reappear as you hike west. Hello, again.

*The Upper Kananaskis Valley from the crest of the headwall*

ancestral drainage from Three Isle Lake, occupied before the lake's water eroded its subterranean outlet. From the crest of the headwall, you can clearly see the U-shaped form of the valley in the view east. The trail drops into the old streamcourse, where glacier lilies and mountain heather grow. After a gradual descent, you reach Three Isle Lake campground in 200 m. To carry on to South Kananaskis Pass, follow the trail through the campground. To visit the lakeshore, continue straight ahead. Take care with your pack and boots, and don't go barefoot at the campground; it is notorious for its monster porcupines.

of natural contours on the cliff, which is not to say that you won't huff and puff your way up the thing. But if your timing is fortunate, as was mine, you will have plenty of cause to pause and admire the wildflowers. Although many of the indicator subalpine wildflowers are present, the hanging gardens on this cliff are a flower-fest of those that prefer drier soils: showy Jacob's ladder, orange-flowered false dandelion, golden fleabane, scorpionweed, creeping beardtongue, low larkspur, white geranium, and Canada violet. One flower grows with a profusion I haven't seen elsewhere — yellow columbine. Note how it prefers sheltered spots.

I heard red-breasted nuthatches, pine siskins, robins, and Wilson's warblers in the forested draw near the top of the climb. The draw is the

## South Kananaskis Pass

From the east shore, Mt. Worthington (2383 m) — named for a BC soldier who died in WWII — is central in the view across Three Isle Lake. Because it drains underground, the lake's level fluctuates. We don't know who gave the lake its name, but they must have had poor eyesight, been practical jokers, or been visiting when the level was extremely low, for nobody of late seems to have seen the third island. The fluctuating level also affects the trail to South Kananaskis Pass, which skirts the north shore of the lake. When the lake level is high, parts of the trail will be submerged.

You reach Three Isle Creek campground in 400 m. Rather than follow the convoluted lakeshore with its mini-peninsulas, the trail now keeps its distance. You cross a rocky avalanche

## A Lingering Headache

*Kin-e-ah-kis* was a Cree — something of a legend in his time for surviving an axe blow to his head. In 1858, John Palliser gave a corrupted version of the hard-headed warrior's name, Kananaskis, to the river and to the pass that his party crossed in their first traverse of the Rockies. As is often the case, the name Kananaskis, migrated to other features in the vicinity, including the destination of this hike.

But in that migration the name has also created a lingering headache for historians: Which pass did Palliser cross? It has long been assumed that he crossed a nearby pass, now called North Kananaskis Pass. But if you read Palliser's account, it seems likely that he crossed West Elk Pass, south of the Kananaskis Lakes. John Sullivan may have split off

from the main group to cross North Kananaskis Pass, meeting up with the others a few days later. There are numerous clues in the account, but principal is Palliser's claim that the pass he crossed could be made serviceable for horse-drawn carts. The trail from North Kananaskis Pass descends some 600 m in less than 4 km on its way to the Palliser River. That would be some kind of cart ride. South of West Elk Pass, the gradient is one-quarter as steep. We'll never know with certainty which pass Palliser crossed; his journals were destroyed in a fire not long after his return to Ireland. All we have are his official reports, dry and — when compared to those authored by colleagues, Hector and Blakiston — scant on geographical details.

*Three Isle Lake*

# 58. Ptarmigan Cirque

## Route

Day-hike

| Route | Elevation (m) | Distance (km) |
|---|---|---|
| Trailhead | 2200 | 0 |
| Ptarmigan Cirque jct | 2200 | 0.4 |
| Cross Highway 40 | 2206 | 0.4 |
| Loop trail jct | 2347 | 1.2 |
| Trail high point | 2408 | 2.2 |
| Loop trail jct | 2347 | 3.2 |
| Trailhead | 2200 | 4.4 |

Maps
NTS: 82 J/10
Gem Trek: Kananaskis Lakes

Best lighting: afternoon

## Trailhead

**From the Trans-Canada Highway** 31 km east of Canmore, follow Kananaskis Trail (Highway 40) 67 km south to Highwood Pass. The parking area is on the west side of the road, just south of the pass. An interpretive brochure may be available at the kiosk. Highway 40 is closed to motor vehicles south of the Kananaskis Lakes Trail junction, from December 1 to June 15.

path off the westerly outlier of Mt. Putnik before entering cool forest where snow lingers. Arnica, western spring beauty, and a marvelous display of white globeflowers — the match of any in the Rockies — brighten trailside. The trail descends to shoreline near the west end of the lake, with fine views south, including the glaciated, northwest ridge of Mt. Northover (3003 m). The mountain was named posthumously for a Canadian Victoria Cross recipient of WWI. I saw spotted sandpipers here on the shallow beach.

From the west shore of the lake, the trail heads north, winding and climbing steadily through spruce-fir forest. Bedrock here is 378 million-year-old mudstone and siltstone of the Yahatinda Formation, which was deposited on the shore of a bay that formed alongside an ancient reef. The first larches appear near treeline. The trail makes a sharp turn to deliver you suddenly to the crest of South Kananaskis Pass, with its tremendous view north. A narrow alp, dotted with earth hummocks and bordered by larches, stretches away to the slopes of Mt. Beatty (2999 m), named for David Beatty, a British naval commander in WWI. The pass marks the boundary between Alberta's K-Country and BC's Height of the Rockies Provincial Park. For those with the time to explore and who are capable at travelling off-trail, the ridges that flank either side of the pass beckon. Or you could ramble 2 km north across the pass, to where a view of Beatty Lake awaits. But if you've day-hiked from the trailhead, you'll probably want to park it and gawk.

The valley that leads to Ptarmigan Cirque is an alluring landscape — a miniature version of hundreds of other recently deglaciated valleys in the Rockies. Plants and animals cling tenaciously to life; the hallmark of ice is everywhere. The bedrock reveals the fossilized remains of lifeforms that lived in ancient seas. Although the trail is popular — often crowded — grizzly bears frequent the area. The trail is closed from time to time to prevent encounters.

### Trailhead to Loop Junction

Walk north from the parking lot on a wide, gravelled path through the Highwood Meadows. Look for bighorn sheep nearby. The chemistry of bedrock influences the plants that grow on the resulting soils. The bedrock in Highwood Pass is shale, coal, and sandstone. In many places in the Rockies, the bedrock is mostly limestone, which creates alkaline, calcium-rich soils. Calcium limits the growth of many plants. Thus the soils in

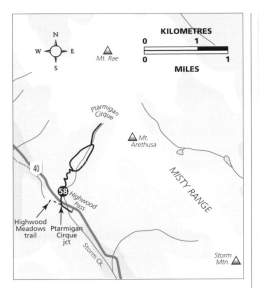

*Treeline is often an imprecise transition. As elevation increases, the forest dwindles to tree islands — clumps of subalpine fir, Engelmann spruce, and larch — that, although small, may be centuries old.*

Highwood Pass are unusual, and foster a relative abundance of plant species. Permafrost in the meadows churns the soil and creates sinkholes. When a series of sinkholes connects over a period of centuries, a new stream is created.

The name Highwood was given in 1858 by Thomas Blakiston of the Palliser Expedition. Members of the expedition were keen observers of the landscape. Blakistion noticed that treeline was higher in this area than in others he had travelled in the Rockies. Indeed, some trees grow at 2400 m — 300 m higher than normal for treeline in this part of the range. The larger trees in the pass are 350 years old; they were mature when Blakiston trooped by. What appear to be sapling trees in the pass and in Ptarmigan Cirque, may be

## Too Cool

**One of the creatures** that lives in the Highwood Meadows is the rock crawler, a slender, wingless insect. The name ice crawler might be more appropriate, for these bugs of the genus, *Grylloblatta*, live in caves, under rocks, or on snow and ice, thriving at temperatures that cause most lifeforms to shut down. Only 10 species are known. They are thought to be related to cockroaches, mantids, and locusts. Rock crawlers eat other insects that become torpid on the snow. Because of where and how they live, rock crawlers probably survived glaciations that killed off many contemporaries. So cold-adapted is this insect, if you were to place one in the palm of your hand, it would die from the effects of your body heat.

as old as a century.

You reach the Ptarmigan Cirque junction in 400 m. Turn northeast (right), and ascend to the west shoulder of Highway 40. Look and listen for traffic; cross the road when it is safe to do so, and pick up the trail on the other side.

The climb begins through an upper subalpine, spruce-fir forest. Yellow hedysarum, blue penstemon, wild strawberry, grouseberry, daisy fleabane, western anemone, paintbrush, common fireweed, alpine spring beauty, bracted lousewort, yellow mountain heather, arnica, glacier lily, low larkspur, and stickseed grow at trailside. The trail switchbacks steeply in a pocket of subalpine fir as it heads southeast toward the drainage from the cirque. You have fine views down to Highwood Pass.

### Loop Trail

The trail angles back to the northwest. The first larches appear at trailside just before the loop trail junction. Trail signs encourage you to keep straight ahead so that your hike will match the numbered stops in the brochure, but feel free to be unfettered in your choice of route. Continuing straight ahead, the trail soon breaks through treeline into a heath meadow. Look for Columbian ground squirrels. You've done most of the climbing now; the trail ahead sidehills and undulates on its approach to the limestone benches at the

**239**

*Ptarmigan Cirque*

apex of the loop.

As elsewhere in the Rockies, snowcover, wind, and temperature groom the vegetation in this valley, dictating what can grow, and where. Gullies offer shelter from the drying effects of wind, promoting growth; depressions collect cold air, stunting growth. Taller, more supple plants — able to withstand moving snow — grow on avalanche paths, offering browse for large mammals. Mat-like plants hug the ground in the open, a survival strategy to thwart the full blast of the wind. Many of the wildflowers have fuzzy stems and leaves — natural insulation to buffet the cold and to reduce moisture loss. Some of the trees flag the wind, others are wind-trained — a few branches curl around the trunk from the windward side to the

## Rock Sandwich

**The southwest ridge** of Mt. Arethusa (2912 m) is a classic signature of front range geology. The Rundle Group of formations that comprise the mountain was tipped nearly vertically during mountain-building, 85 million years ago, when great sheets of rock were being driven northeastward. The rock fractured along thrust faults, the sheet behind the fracture being driven upward and over rocks ahead, to the northeast, creating what are now called overthrust mountains. Mt. Arethusa is part of the Rundle Thrust Sheet. Alternating resistant (limestone-dolomite) and recessive (shale) layers create what appears to be a multi-layered sandwich, dropped on end. The mountain was not named for the nymph of Greek mythology, but for an ill-fated British battle cruiser, sunk in 1916 just two days after it put to sea.

*Mt. Arethusa*

leeward side. Except for the wet meadow in the base of the valley, much of the landscape is virtually desert. Water is frozen for much of the year; the poor, rocky soils drain rapidly. Wind and harsh sunlight quickly evaporate much of what water is available.

The outbound leg of the loop ends where the trail swings southeast (right) at a low headwall. The rock is limestone of the fossil-rich Mt. Head Formation. If you examine the boulders nearby, you may see bumps — the fossilized remains of horn corals that date to 350 million years ago. Looking downvalley, you can see Mt. Tyrwhitt (2874 m) on the west side of Highwood Pass.

## Snow-bird, Rock-bird

*Ptarmigan at Ptarmigan Cirque*

**The white-tailed ptarmigan** (TAR-mih-gan) is a ground-dwelling grouse-like bird that features cryptic plumage. The feathers change colour from white in winter, to a mottled brown, gray, and black in summer. The tail is always white. Males have a reddish-orange comb over each eye during mating season. In winter, feathers grow on all surfaces of the feet, and the toes grow longer, creating natural, insulated snowshoes that decrease the bird's penetration into snow. Ptarmigan are well-camouflaged but unwary, advertising their presence with clucking and soft cooing. The clutch of up to ten chicks typically dwindles drastically through predation. Ptarmigan are non-migratory, foraging for berries, buds, flowers, and bugs. They gather into small flocks in winter. Skiers in the high country occasionally encounter snowbanks with many sets of blinking, black eyes —ptarmigan bedded down. When alarmed, these birds make explosive bursts of flight.

Reginald Tyrwhitt was a British naval commander in WWI.

When the valley is clear of snow, you can follow a rough track northeast from the apex of the loop for 700 m to a second headwall at the mouth of the cirque. But please keep to the trail. The route ascends beside a stream that bisects a meadow. The blooms of moss campion, sawwort, and alpine forget-me-not brighten the rocks. True to the name of the trail, I saw a ptarmigan hen with four chicks here. Seeps on the second headwall feature travertine deposits. Travertine is thin limestone, deposited by algae as a byproduct of photosynthesis. From the top of the headwall, the view north reveals the upper part of the cirque on the slopes of Mt. Rae (3218 m). A cirque is a relatively shallow valley that has been eroded into a mountainside by glacial ice. John Rae was a surgeon with the Hudson's Bay Company, and later participated in the search for John Franklin. James Hector named the peak. The valley contains a rock glacier. Travel beyond this point is on a sketchy trail and exposes you to rockfall — not recommended.

Leaving the loop trail's high point, you rock-hop the stream and descend the south flank of the valley. Travel is along the crest of a ridge of rocks — a combination of glacial moraine, and rockslide from Mt. Arethusa. Pikas and hoary marmots inhabit the boulderfields nearby. Hop the stream again at treeline. A sidetrail leads south (left) to a bench and a viewpoint that overlooks a cascade. The rock exposed is sandy dolomite of the Kananaskis Formation. This waterfall marks the true mouth of the hanging valley that contains Ptarmigan Cirque. It was near here that, during the Wisconsin Glaciation, the Ptarmigan Cirque glacier merged with the main valley glacier that once filled Highwood Pass. This point is known as the "break in slope." The slope beneath — as you know from the approach — is steeper than the slope above.

### Return

After a short descent through forest, you meet the approach trail at the loop junction. Turn southwest (left) to return to the trailhead. If you have the time, detour north (right) at the Highwood Meadows trail junction, 400 m from the parking lot. Interpretive signs along this short trail describe the tough life of plants and animals in the upper subalpine ecoregion.

# Waterton Lakes National Park

*Carthew Lakes from Carthew Summit, Carthew/Alderson trail*

Established in 1895 as Canada's fourth national park, Waterton Lakes includes 525 km² of the front ranges in the extreme southwestern corner of Alberta. The park's theme is "where the mountains meet the prairie." Many viewpoints along the park's 225 km of trails reveal remarkable vistas of the front ranges rising from the plains.

Waterton Lakes National Park is 264 km south of Calgary via highways 22 and 6, and 130 km southwest of Lethbridge via Highway 5. There is passenger bus service to Pincher Creek and Fort Macleod, from where a shuttle service provides access to the park. Otherwise, access is by car. The town of Waterton Park offers supplies, services, and accommodation. The nearby towns of Cardston and Pincher Creek also cater to travellers. The park has three frontcountry campgrounds with 391 sites. The park information centre and warden office are just north of Waterton Park townsite, on Highway 5. There is a hostel on Camas Avenue.

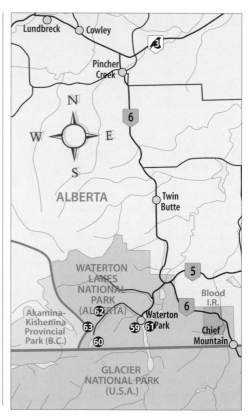

# 59. Bertha Lake

## Route

Day-hike or overnight

| Route | Elevation (m) | Distance (km) |
| --- | --- | --- |
| Trailhead | 1295 | 0 |
| Upper Waterton Lake viewpoint | 1410 | 1.4 |
| Lakeshore jct | 1400 | 1.5 |
| Lower Bertha Falls | 1475 | 2.9 |
| Trail summit | 1767 | 5.4 |
| Bertha Lake CG | 1755 | 5.7 |

**Maps**
NTS: 82 H/4
Environment Canada: Waterton Lakes National Park

**Best lighting:** early morning at the east shore, afternoon at the west shore

## Trailhead

**In Waterton Park** townsite on Evergreen Avenue, 500 m south of Cameron Falls

The Bertha Lake trail climbs steeply to Waterton's most accessible backcountry lake, a charming body of water, surrounded by lush forest. The hike is renowned for its diverse vegetation.

### Trailhead to Lower Bertha Falls

You climb gradually through a mixed montane forest toward Bertha Creek. Fleabane, false hellebore, white geranium, bear grass, harebell, yarrow, paintbrush, fireweed, and pearly everlasting line the trail. Trembling aspen, mountain ash, cottonwood poplar, white birch, Douglas maple, and lodgepole pine are the common trees. Many of the pines are standing-dead. A mountain pine beetle infestation between 1976 and 1983 killed 50 percent of the lodgepole pines in Waterton, and as many as 75 percent of the trees in some stands.

Other trees in this forest have been toppled by

## Variation

- You can add a 3.4 km loop around the lake

*Bertha Lake is situated in a narrow hanging valley. The hike features a tremendous variety of vegetation.*

severe winds. Beetle infestations and blowdowns open the forest canopy and allow new growth. The sunlit areas that result support shrubs and wildflowers, and are important feeding areas for many large mammals. One of the common shrubs here is buffaloberry, whose red and amber berries are a staple food of black bears.

At km 1.4, a short path leads straight ahead to a viewpoint that overlooks Upper Waterton Lake. Across the lake to the southeast is Mt. Cleveland (3190 m), highest mountain in Glacier National Park. It was named in 1898 by conservationist George Bird Grinnell, for Grover Cleveland, US president. Cleveland had established the Lewis and Clark Forest Reserve the year before. The reserve included the area that became Glacier National Park in 1910. Limber pine grows at this viewpoint. It prefers windy locations, so it is well placed here. Its needles are in bunches of five. Showy, brown-eyed Susans also grow here.

In August 1935, a fire consumed the forest between Boundary Creek and Bertha Creek along the west shore of Upper Waterton Lake. The conflagration threatened the townsite. It was extinguished by the efforts of 533 firefighters, aided considerably by wet weather and a change of wind. The young pine forest that you see along the lakeshore is a legacy of this burn.

Backtrack to the main trail and descend to the west. Continue straight ahead at the junction in 40 m. The trail contours around a limestone bluff of the Altyn Formation, whose layers plunge

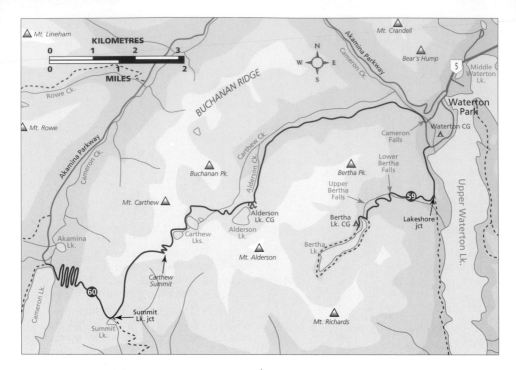

toward the southwest. This is the dip of the underlying rock formations in Waterton. Whether you look at a small cliff or a mountainside, you will see this orientation consistently exposed. Wild bergamont, Jacob's ladder, creeping beardtongue, stonecrop, yellow false dandelion, and bearberry grow on the dry, gritty soils at the base of the bluff.

As you approach Bertha Creek, the vegetation quickly changes to species characteristic of damp subalpine forests. Waterton has the most diverse vegetation of any Rocky Mountain park. It is home to 885 native vascular plant species — 55 percent of the total found in Alberta. Of these, 400 species are mosses and lichens. Of all the species, 179 are rare in Alberta, 22 are unrecorded in the province outside the park, and two are found nowhere else in Canada. A prominent storm track along the 49th parallel brings significant moisture into the southern part of the park, creating damp micro-habitats that support 100 vegetation species normally found in BC. Western yew and devil's club once grew along lower Bertha Creek but have not been seen for many years.

Lower Bertha Falls cascades over another outcrop of the Altyn Formation. At the base of the falls, the water is eroding into the seam between two upturned edges of rock. This creates a natural gutter that captures the flow and channels the water away to the southeast, along a right-angle turn in the stream course. When bedrock dictates the flow of a stream in this fashion, it is said to have structural control. The step-like cascades downstream are also caused by upturned edges of rock in the creek bed.

## Lower Bertha Falls to Bertha Lake

Cross the bridge at the falls and begin a relentless switchback ascent on the lower slopes of Mt. Richards. This is excellent bear habitat, so make lots of noise. After about 2 km, you have views through the trees to Upper Bertha Falls, which are 75 m high. The trail angles away from the falls. From openings in the trees you can look east to Upper Waterton Lake and Vimy Peak (2379 m). The trail makes one final switchback along the base of a cliff before descending to the mouth of the hanging valley that contains Bertha Lake. The campground is 110 m beyond the outlet stream bridge.

With an area of 30.2 ha and a depth of 50.3 m, Bertha Lake is the second-largest and second-deepest of Waterton's high country lakes. The lake is dammed by upturned rock strata and occupies a hollow eroded in the shattered shales of the Greyson Formation. The lake is backed by a 500 m high cliff of Siyeh (SIGH-yuh) Formation

*Lower Bertha Falls*

limestone and dolomite. This cliff extends from Mount Alderson (2692 m) on the northwest, to Mt. Richards (2416 m) on the south. Bertha Peak (2440 m) stands to the north of the outlet. A waterfall tumbles down its south slopes.

It is thought that the name "Bertha" was

## Bear Grass

**The showy, white bloom** of bear grass is the floral emblem of Waterton Lakes National Park — the only national park in Canada in which it is found. Growing from a stem that is 50 to 120 cm tall, the bear grass flower

*Bear grass*

graces meadows throughout Waterton from mid-June to mid-July. Some bear grass plants exhibit a peculiar crook in the upper stem. It is thought these bends occur when the flower head matures during wet periods. Individual bear grass plants bloom sporadically, averaging one to three times in every ten years. Adjacent plants often bloom together, so the local "intensity" of the displays varies greatly from year to year.

Bighorn sheep, deer, and elk eat bear grass flowers. Mountain goats eat the mature leaves, and bears eat the younger leaves in spring. Natives wove the leaves into baskets and items of clothing. Although the leaves appear grass-like, the plant is a member of the lily family. Bear grass does not grow north of Crowsnest Pass.

originally applied to the lake that we know today as Alderson Lake. Bertha Ekelund was an early Waterton resident, reportedly jailed for passing counterfeit money. This made her into a folk hero. She was also a sometime companion of Joe Cosley. A true mountain man, Cosley was, at various times between 1890 and 1930, a prospector, trapper, and Glacier park ranger and guide. He probably knew the landscape of Waterton-Glacier better than anyone else in his day. Cosley named many features for himself, his friends, and — in the case of Bertha and other lakes — for his occasional female companions. The lake had formerly been known as "Spirit Lake."

## Circuit of Bertha Lake, 3.4 km

To fully appreciate Bertha Lake and its valley, allow time to make a circuit of the lake. However, use caution. The upper valley is excellent bear habitat. You may also see a cougar or wolverine. From the outlet bridge, follow a good trail along the north shore of the lake, alternating between meadows and stands of ancient subalpine forest. In early to mid-July, there are tremendous displays of bear grass here.

The trail crosses two red bluffs of Grinnell Formation argillite that dip toward the lake. The bluffs feature mariposa lily, stonecrop, umbrella plant, creeping beardtongue, meadowsweet, and spotted saxifrage. Together with shrubby cinquefoil and juniper, these plants give the illusion of montane meadow at a subalpine elevation. Between the two bluffs, the trail follows the lakeshore with a gravelly beach of red argillite underfoot. In wetter areas, you may see red monkey flowers.

Rock-hop the principal inlet stream. The trail climbs over a bluff, crosses two more inlet streams, and descends to a small pond beyond the western shore of the lake. An abandoned stream course tells of days-gone-by when this pond fed directly into the larger lake. The stupendous cliffs above are home to mountain goats.

The return trail follows the south shore and cuts through several argillite gullies. From the open scree slope near the lake's east end, you obtain fine views of the lake, which is only 50 m wide at this spot. The circuit concludes at the stand of dead trees near the lake's outlet. Climb up to the approach trail to hike out, or cross the outlet bridge to return to the campground.

# 60. Carthew/Alderson

## Route

Day-hike or overnight

| Route | Elevation (m) | Distance (km) |
|---|---|---|
| Trailhead | 1661 | 0 |
| Summit Lake jct | 1931 | 4.3 |
| Carthew Summit | 2311 | 7.9 |
| Upper Carthew Lake | 2195 | 9.3 |
| Lower Carthew Lake | 2159 | 9.9 |
| Alderson Lake jct | 1811 | 13.1 |
| Alderson Lake CG | 1811 | +0.2 |
| Cameron Falls trailhead | 1295 | 19.9 |

### Maps
NTS: 82 G/1 and 82 H/4
Environment Canada: Waterton Lakes National Park

## Trailhead

**Follow the** Akamina Parkway for 16 km from Waterton Park townsite to the parking lot at Cameron Lake. The trailhead is across the footbridge at the outlet of Cameron Lake. Daily shuttle service (fee charged) is available to Cameron Lake. Inquire at the Tamarack Mall in Waterton Park townsite.

The Carthew-Alderson trail traces a spectacular route from Cameron Lake to Waterton Park townsite. It immerses you in ancient forests, takes you across an alpine ridgecrest, and visits five backcountry lakes. The vistas span everything from mountain top to prairie. The trail is usually passable by mid-June, however the slopes north of Carthew Summit can be snowbound into July. Avoid this outing during poor weather and when thunderstorms are forecast. You share the trail with horses.

### Trailhead to Summit Lake

The Carthew-Alderson trail begins at the outlet of Cameron Lake in the heart of a dense subalpine forest. Engelmann spruce, subalpine fir, false hellebore, cow parsnip, foamflower, water birch, bear grass, arnica, queen's cup, thimbleberry,

## Variation

• Day-hike to Carthew Summit, 15.8 km return

*Separated by natural dams of glacier-worn rock, and ringed with red argillite, the Carthew Lakes occupy a series of glacial hollows on the northeast side of Carthew Summit.*

feathermosses, grouseberry, and ferns grow at trailside. In a few places, you may see red monkey flowers, whose attractive blooms are frequented by hummingbirds. As you climb toward Summit Lake, you pass some of the oldest trees in the park, aged 250 to 300 years. As elsewhere in Waterton, there are many standing-dead trees. Tree lichens, notably *Bryoria* species and wolf lichen, cling to their branches.

## Cameron Lake

**Early morning** is a great time to appreciate Cameron Lake. The lake is 39 m deep and has an area of 17.2 ha. It occupies a hollow excavated by glacial ice, and is dammed by a glacial moraine. The lake was named for Donald Cameron, who led the British party that surveyed the international boundary in 1874. The summit of Mt. Custer (2708 m) at the south end of the lake lies entirely within Glacier National Park, Montana. The mountain was not named for the famous general, but for Henry Custer, a topographer with the US Boundary Survey who worked in this area in 1860 or 1861. The avalanche paths at the south end of the lake are frequented by grizzly bears.

The trail to Summit Lake was constructed in 1910. It illustrates how trailbuilders can tackle a formidable slope, yet create a walking surface that is seldom steep. Long switchbacks across this 50-degree sideslope produce a gentle, well-graded ascent. Through breaks in the trees you enjoy views of Cameron Lake, Akamina Lake, and Akamina Pass. *Akamina* (ah-kah-MEE-nuh) is a Ktunaxa (ka-too-NA-hah) word that means "high bench land," "watershed," "mountain pass," or "valley."

At km 3.7 the trail levels and traverses through treeline forest toward the Summit Lake junction. Open meadows here are filled almost entirely with bear grass. The meadows are frost hollows that stunt the growth, hence most plants do not support stalks and blooms. There are some fine examples of ripple rock at trailside.

At km 4.3 you reach the Summit Lake junction. Summit Lake is nearby; a shallow kettle pond, often teeming with bugs. You may see mule deer, licking at the mineral-rich mud. Mt. Custer and Chapman Peak (2867 m) are reflected in the lake on calm days. Robert Chapman was a superintendent of Glacier National Park in 1912. Glaciologists believe that Summit Lake once drained northwest into the Akamina Valley. Glacial overdeepening of the Cameron Lake basin altered drainage patterns. Today, Summit Lake drains south into Boundary Creek in Montana.

## Summit Lake to Carthew Summit

At the Summit Lake junction, turn northeast (left). After a gradual climb of about 500 m, the trail traverses beneath a rock bluff decorated with bear grass, creeping beardtongue, fleabane, and white draba. The surrounding forest contains Lyall's larch trees. The north fork of Boundary Creek drains the basin south of the trail. The surrounding slopes support a ghostly forest of ancient standing-dead trees.

The trail breaks through treeline and contours across a steep, avalanche-swept slope, climbing gradually toward Carthew Summit. From the open scree slopes, you have pleasing views southwest over lush, wet meadows. This foreground contrasts with the forbidding north face of Chapman Peak beyond. Lake Wurdeman — a textbook example of a cirque lake — lies at the base of the peak, fed by meltwater from an apron of glacial ice. The lake's name commemorates yet another topographer with the US Boundary Survey, J.V. Wurdeman. The lake was known to Pikanii (Peigan) Natives as "Bird Rattle Lake," after one of their warriors.

The red rock underfoot is argillite (ARE-jill-ite) of the 1.3 to 1.5 billion-year-old Kintla Formation.

## Mule Deer

**The mule deer** is the more numerous of the two species of deer in the Canadian Rockies, and is abundant in Waterton. To distinguish it from the white-tailed deer, look first at the tail. The mule deer's tail is narrow and white with a black tip. The white-tailed deer's tail is broad; it is the colour of the coat above, and white underneath. The antlers of mule deer bucks are equally branched, whereas those of white-tailed bucks branch upward from a forward reaching beam. The coats of both species are reddish-brown in summer, changing to gray in winter. The rumps are white.

Deer graze on grasses and wildflowers in

*Mule deer*

summer. In autumn and winter, they browse on leaves and buds. In late winter, mule deer may resort to stripping tree bark to get at the sugary cambium layer beneath. The cougar is the principal predator of deer, which is why cougars are common in Waterton.

Waterton's mule deer are not shy. Accustomed to humans and to handouts, many have lost their wildness. But please remember that these animals can inflict serious injury by kicking with their front hooves. Do not approach a doe with fawns, or any deer during the autumn rut. If a deer approaches you, scare it away by shouting and by waving your arms.

Argillite was created from muddy sediments that were deposited on a river delta. The sediments in this rock were exposed to the air after deposition, and the iron "rusted." When the iron did not oxidize, argillite is green. Kintla Formation argillite is thinly layered and easily eroded. It comprises the many colourful scree ridges in the western part of Waterton Lakes National Park.

The final climb to Carthew Summit is on a series of long switchbacks. Scorpionweed, sky pilot, yellow draba, and alpine forget-me-not dot the red screes. Please follow the orange painted markers and keep to the beaten path. You can see Summit Lake and Lake Nooney, to the west and south, respectively.

The scenic climax of this hike bursts into view as you crest Carthew Summit. Framed between the ridges of Mount Carthew (2630 m) and Mount Alderson (2692 m), the Carthew Lakes lead your eye through a rugged hanging valley to the distant prairie. By their arrangement, the Carthew Lakes are known to glaciologists as a glacial cirque staircase, or *paternoster lakes*. This Latin expression means "beads on a rosary." The lakes occupy basins eroded by glacial ice as it flowed down the valley. Each basin is at a progressively lower elevation. Although glaciers are now absent from Waterton, their legacy in creating this exceptional landscape is everywhere.

The screes that flank Carthew Summit feature roseroot, Sandberg's wild parsley, and sky pilot. The pygmy (dwarf) poppy also grows here. This yellow-flowered plant is rare in Canada. Most of the places that it grows are in Waterton. Lt. William Carthew was a Canadian land surveyor who worked with the Interprovincial Boundary Survey that delineated the Alberta-BC boundary between 1913 and 1925. As part of his duties, he climbed Mt. Carthew in 1914. I bet it beat having a desk job.

Many hikers ramble south a short distance from Carthew Summit and scamper onto the bluff that affords views south over Boundary Creek. Avoid this high point if poor weather is approaching.

## Carthew Summit to Alderson Lake

The descent from Carthew Summit to Upper Carthew Lake may be complicated by perennial snow patches on the trail. At first, the trail angles slightly northeast. Then it switchbacks to the southeast to skirt the largest of the snow patches above the west shore of Upper Carthew Lake. Please keep to the beaten path, and for your

*Sky pilot*

safety, stay off large snow patches.

The trail follows the north shore of Upper Carthew Lake to an ancient kruppelholz forest at the lake's outlet. The rock dam that separates the upper and lower lakes is known as a riegel (RYE-gull). Compressive forces during mountain building thrust rock layers upward to the northeast. The resistant leading edges of some thrusts have endured as the natural dams that impound many of Waterton's backcountry lakes.

You switchback down alongside cascades between the upper and lower lakes. Rock-hop the

## Lightning!

**Waterton experiences** more electrical storms than other areas in the Rockies. You should avoid the park's passes and high ridges when thunderstorms approach. Time your outings so that you are on your way down from summits and high points by 1 pm, after which time thunderstorms are more common. However, any time you see a thunderstorm approaching, or hear a buzzing sound emanating from metallic objects or your hair, it is time to descend quickly.

What do you do if you are caught in a high place during a thunderstorm? First, descend at least 100 m vertically from a summit or ridgecrest. Then, avoid open meadows, lakes, glaciers, and snow patches. Do not seek shelter under isolated rock pinnacles or trees. Crouch at the base of a cliff or in a depression that does not have tall trees or large boulders nearby. Keep a metre away from the cliff or depression walls, as these channel the current of a local strike. The metallic objects you carry will not attract a lightning strike. However, they may cause burns if there is a strike within 30 m. Remove these items from your pack and your pockets.

*The Carthew-Alderson trail descends steeply from Carthew Lakes to Alderson Lake.*

soils here — stonecrop, rocky mountain goldenrod, spotted saxifrage, and scorpionweed. From the crest of this short climb, the trail angles north and then east, descending steeply into the basin between Mt. Carthew and Buchanan Peak (2409 m). The cliff is limestone and dolomite of the Siyeh (SIGH-yuh) Formation, which contains an intrusion of igneous rock called the Purcell Sill. You may see eroded fragments of this dark, crystalline lava-like rock on the trail.

The outflow from Carthew Lakes cascades in a fine waterfall to your right. Rock-hop its stream. The adjacent meadows are decorated with wildflowers. Continue the steep descent through a ragged kruppel-holz forest and across scree slopes, with views of Alderson Lake ahead.

If you look carefully at the west shore of Alderson Lake, you will see a series of remnant terminal moraines. These moraines were probably formed during the Little Ice Age, which ended in the mid-1800s. The glaciers responsible have since disappeared. Glaciers in other localities in the Rockies advanced as much as 3 km during the Little Ice Age, and often extended beyond the cirques that housed them. Evidence shows that no glaciers in Waterton advanced beyond their cirque basins in the last 10,000 years. The cliffs above Alderson Lake are a good place to look for mountain goats.

The trail turns northeast above the north shore of Alderson Lake. The slopes below the trail are festooned with bear grass. You might expect that Carthew Creek, flowing through the meadows to the north of the trail, would empty into Alderson Lake, but the lake has been impounded by a moraine. The trail travels along its crest. This moraine keeps Carthew Creek away from the lakeshore.

With a maximum depth of 60 m, Alderson Lake is the deepest of Waterton's high country lakes. It has an area of 10.2 ha. The lake was probably the original "Bertha Lake." Its name was changed in 1915 to honour Lt. General E.A.H. Alderson, who commanded Canadian Forces in France during WWI.

At km 13.1 you reach the Alderson Lake

outlet stream to its south side. As you descend to the west shore of Lower Carthew Lake, you will probably encounter more snow. The trail makes a hairpin turn to the north (left) to follow the west and north shores of the lake. Rock-hop the inlet stream. When the lake level is high, you may have to traverse some rocks just above the water. Two bodies of water comprise Lower Carthew Lake. The largest is 7.3 ha in area and 11 m deep. It is separated from the much smaller Carthew Pond by a dam of rockslide debris.

The trail gains the crest of the cliff that separates Carthew Lakes from Alderson Lake. Wildflowers that prefer dry habitats cling to the thin

## Late-lying Snow

**The novelty** of encountering snow patches in July and August lures many unwary hikers into trouble in places like the basin above Upper Carthew Lake. Because these snow patches have been through many freeze and thaw cycles since the previous winter, they contain a significant amount of ice. This ice sometimes appears snow-like — especially near the edges — where footing can be treacherous.

If you fall on the granular snow and ice, you may cut yourself badly. In addition, you may begin to slide downslope, out of control toward boulder-fields. If you are wearing shorts and short sleeves, you will be, at best a mess, at worst a stretcher case. Unless you have an ice axe in hand, are competent at using it for self-arrest, and are dressed appropriately, stay off late-lying snow. The reddish tinge in these snow patches is called watermelon snow, and is caused by algae with a red pigment.

junction. You have the option of staying overnight at the campground on the lakeshore. However, most hikers do not want to haul a heavy pack over Carthew Summit to camp here, when Waterton Park townsite is only a few hours away. The campground is 250 m east (right) of the junction. It's a buggy place in mid-summer.

## Alderson Lake to Cameron Falls

A few hundred metres beyond the campground junction, an alternate route to the campground branches right. Keep left. The lush upper subalpine forest along Alderson Creek is similar to the one at the trailhead near Cameron Lake, except most of the trees are not as old. The trail bisects numerous avalanche paths that are excellent bear habitat. Make lots of noise here as visibility is limited. If you look up the valley from open slopes, you can see the waterfall on the headwall below the Carthew Lakes. Rock-hop tributary streams as required.

The descent of this valley may seem interminable if you expended all your energy earlier in the day. However, it is hardly a "boring walk in the woods." The subtle transition in the forest is of great interest. As you lose elevation, notice the change from species of the damp subalpine forest, to Douglas-fir and lodgepole pine — dry montane forest species. About halfway along the valley, just to the north of the trail, there is a large Engelmann spruce tree, 1.4 m in diameter at its base.

At long last, the trail switchbacks down and you can see Waterton Park townsite through open forest. The trail parallels a fence at the brink of Cameron Creek canyon. In the creek bed you can see structures built for flood control, and the former water supply for the townsite. The temperamental creek has exhibited a 1000-fold increase in volume of flow between November and the following July. In June 1964, runoff from Cameron Creek and other tributaries raised the level of Upper Waterton Lake 2.8 m above its previous record high, inundating Waterton Park townsite. The most recent serious flood was in 1995. Sediments deposited by Cameron Creek have built the alluvial fan on which the townsite is situated.

At an unmarked junction, turn sharply north (left), and descend into a poplar grove at trail's end, Cameron Falls. The 10 m falls are being eroded into an outcrop of 1.5 billion-year-old Waterton Formation limestone, the oldest rock formation visible in the Canadian Rockies.

# 61. Crypt Lake

## Route

**Day-hike**

| Route | Elevation (m) | Distance (km) |
|---|---|---|
| Crypt Landing | 1279 | 0 |
| Lower Hell Roaring Falls jct | 1350 | 0.4 |
| Upper Hell Roaring Falls jct | 1500 | 3.0 |
| Burnt Rock Falls | 1600 | 5.6 |
| Crypt Lake Headwall | 1925 | 8.1 |
| Crypt Lake | 1945 | 8.7 |

**Maps**
NTS: 82 H/4
Environment Canada: Waterton Lakes National Park

## Trailhead

**Book round-trip** passage on the shuttle boat from the marina at Emerald Bay in Waterton Park townsite (fee charged). There are two departures each morning, and two pick-ups each afternoon — check the times at the marina. The 15-minute boat trip delivers you to the trailhead at Crypt Landing on the east shore of Upper Waterton Lake.

No other outing in the Rockies can top Crypt Lake for its variety of experiences. You begin by crossing Upper Waterton Lake by boat. Then you follow a steep trail from montane shoreline to timberline through a valley of waterfalls. The diversity of the approach culminates with a 25 m crawl through a limestone tunnel and an airy traverse on an imposing cliff. As if all this isn't enough, you can follow a rough track around Crypt Lake and cross the international border into the US.

Do not undertake this outing if you fear heights or enclosed places, or until the headwall below Crypt Lake is free of snow. This is not a hike for those seeking solitude. In peak season, two shuttle boats may deposit more than 100 hikers at the trailhead within a few minutes. The trail passes through prime bear habitat. The valley of

## Variations

- Make a circuit of Crypt Lake, 1.8 km
- Visit Hell Roaring Falls, add 500 m to the outing

# Crypt Lake

*Crypt Lake is concealed in a hanging valley on the Alberta-Montana border.*

Hell Roaring Creek can be torrid in mid-summer, so carry lots of water.

## Crypt Landing to Crypt Lake Campground

From Crypt Landing, head south and begin the switchback ascent toward the drainage of Hell Roaring Creek. The forest near the trailhead is extremely damp and diverse, with a mixture of montane and subalpine tree species — Douglas-fir, white spruce, white birch, Douglas maple, and subalpine fir. Note the large Douglas-firs whose bark is cloaked in tree lichens. You would not normally expect to see this damp a forest at a low elevation in Waterton. However, the bay of Crypt Landing is sheltered from the ever-present winds that would otherwise dry the soils and foliage. Thimbleberry, false Solomon's seal, fairybells, arnica, and western meadowrue are common in the undergrowth.

At km 0.4 you reach the lower Hell Roaring Falls junction. This sidetrip is best left until your return, when the falls and their canyon may be sunlit. At approximately km 1.5, the main trail switchbacks across an open, west-facing slope, surrounded by a more typical low-elevation Waterton forest — one dominated by lodgepole pine with sun-loving flowers in the undergrowth. This slope provides open views of Upper Waterton Lake and the valley of Bertha Creek. Please do not shortcut the switchbacks.

The trail traverses southeast into the drainage of Hell Roaring Creek and contours above the creek through open pine forest. Buffaloberry is common here. This south-facing slope is frequented by black bears and grizzly bears. Use caution. "Hell Roaring" is a most appropriate name for the turbulent creek. The name was probably connected with a mining claim in this

## The Waterton Lakes — Big Water

With a maximum depth of 157 m, Upper Waterton Lake is the deepest lake in the Canadian Rockies. It is 11.1 km long, has an area of 941 ha, and is by far the largest of Waterton's 80 mapped lakes and ponds. It holds approximately 645 million cubic metres of water. The southern reach of the lake extends 4 km into Glacier National Park, Montana.

There are 17 native species of fish in Waterton Lakes National Park, and eight introduced species. Fish were important to Native Peoples in Waterton. They often fished from a camp located on the west shore of The Bosporous between the upper and middle Waterton Lakes. Evidence indicates that it, and other camps nearby, were in use for 8000 years. The largest fish on record in the park is a 23.2 kg lake trout caught in Upper Waterton Lake in July 1920. Reports from the early 1900s describe individuals taking 500 fish from Upper Waterton Lake in a day. Principally as a result of such plunder, fish are not as numerous today.

The Siksika (Blackfoot) Nation knew the Waterton Lakes by several names, one of which meant "big water." Thomas Blakiston of the Palliser Expedition named the lakes in 1858, to commemorate Charles Waterton, an eccentric British naturalist who roamed South America and the Caribbean between 1812 and 1829. Waterton is best known for introducing curare (cure-RAH-ree) to western medicine, and for establishing the world's first bird sanctuary at his home in England. It housed more than 800 species. He never visited the lakes. Blakiston, only 25 at the time he saw the lakes, was a budding naturalist, who thought highly of Charles Waterton.

In the late 19th century the lakes were known locally as the "Kootenai Lakes," after the Kutenai Nation. (This First Nation now prefers to be called Ktunaxa, pronounced, ka-too-NA-hah.) Kootenai Brown, Waterton's most famous resident, settled on the shore of Lower Waterton Lake in 1878. He promoted the establishment of a national park at Waterton and became the first warden in 1895. Later he was its superintendent.

**251**

area in the late 1800s. Keep straight ahead at the upper Hell Roaring Falls junction. The grade eases and the trail contours in and out of drainage gullies. Rock-hop as necessary. Across Hell Roaring Creek, Twin Falls cascades from a hanging valley on the north slope of Mt. Boswell.

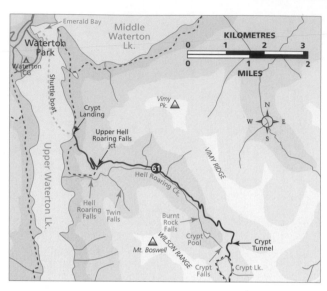

The trail swings south, following Hell Roaring Creek to its sources. You cross more avalanche slopes and pass through another pocket of damp subalpine forest. The shales underfoot have been washed down in flash-floods from the mountainside to the east, creating an alluvial fan that has spread through the forest. When you reach the stream that has created the fan, you get your first view of Burnt Rock Falls.

Now the hard work begins. In the next 3 km the trail climbs approximately 300 m and is often rocky. As you switchback away from the creek, you get several close views of Burnt Rock Falls. The red or "burnt" rock at the base of the falls is iron-rich, Grinnell Formation argillite. Above it is older, pale, Altyn Formation limestone. Why is older rock above younger rock? The two formations are separated by the Mt. Crandell Thrust Fault. During mountain building, the bedrock underlying this area fractured, and the Altyn Formation slid upward and northeastward over younger layers along the fault. Note the massive hollow eroded into the weak Grinnell Formation at the base of the falls. The Altyn Formation resists the flow of water and endures as the brink of the waterfall.

As you draw equal with Burnt Rock Falls, use care as you rock-hop the tributary stream that crosses the trail on a bare rock slab. Now Crypt Falls comes into view, tumbling 175 m down the Crypt Lake headwall. Crypt Pool lies at the base. The remainder of the steep climb to the headwall is across avalanche gullies. Bear grass and cottonwood poplar trees in kruppelholz form, grow at trailside.

## Crypt Lake Headwall to Crypt Lake

Rock-hop or ford (straightforward) the creek below the headwall, and follow the trail that angles southwest through the boulderfield. Look and listen for pikas. You may also hear the shrill whistle of hoary marmots and with luck see these large rodents, the self-appointed guardians of the Crypt Tunnel.

Near the eastern portal of the tunnel is a sign that warns you to stay on the trail — as if you have a choice. The Crypt Tunnel is a natural, water-worn fissure that extends laterally for 25 m

## Windy Waterton

**More often than not,** it is windy on Upper Waterton Lake. The average daily wind speed at Waterton Park townsite is 32.5 km per hour, and gusts of 180 km per hour have been recorded in winter. At such times, spray from the lake collects on the windows of the Prince of Wales Hotel 150 m away, and 40 m above the lakeshore. Many of the windy days in winter and spring are caused by chinooks (shih-NOOKS). A chinook occurs when a Pacific storm system sheds its moisture on the western slopes of the Rockies. The air is forced high to clear the crest of the range. As the dry air sweeps down the eastern slopes and its pressure increases, its temperature rises 1.5°C for each decrease in elevation of 100 m.

Chinook is a Native word that means "snow eater." In nearby Pincher Creek, the warm winds once raised the temperature 21°C in four minutes. Chinooks keep the mountain front snow-free for much of the winter, creating ideal winter habitat for elk, deer, sheep, and goats, which require accessible grasses and browse. The winds also prevent the formation of ice on the Waterton Lakes in some years.

*Crypt Falls*

*The traverse beyond the tunnel*

through the limestone of the Crypt Lake headwall. The tunnel has been slightly enlarged to ease passage. Gain the eastern portal by climbing a 2 m metal ladder. The tunnel narrows and angles down toward the west. When at its narrowest point, you will be obliged to crawl on your hands and knees. Two cautions: watch for ice on the tunnel floor, and do not enter the tunnel wearing a bulky pack — particularly one with an external frame. If your pack gets caught, take it off and push it ahead of you. Exit the western portal over an awkward 1.3 m rock step.

The section just beyond the western portal of the Crypt Tunnel gives this hike its notorious reputation. For 50 m, you traverse and ascend an exposed cliff, which may intimidate those afraid of heights. A steel cable has been installed here. Use

## Sinks and Solutions

**Crypt Lake** is impounded by a series of upturned, glaciated limestone bluffs, called riegels. Limestone is readily eroded by naturally acidic rainwater in a process called solution. Over time, cracks in the surface of limestone bedrock are deepened into fissures by rain and meltwater. The fissures connect into systems that create underground drainage channels called karst. Crypt Lake has no surface outlet. It drains through a karst system, so it is known as a sink lake. The rock at trailside just before the lake contains *rillenkarren*, miniature grooves eroded by water.

it as a handrail. Another caution: take care not to bump your pack against the cable or its anchor posts, especially during descent. This could throw you off balance.

The airy traverse beyond the tunnel delivers you to the crest of the Crypt Lake headwall. Looking north along Hell Roaring Creek, you can see Vimy Ridge and Vimy Peak (2379 m), named for the ridge in France taken by Canadian forces in WWI. The forest on the headwall is upper subalpine. Tufts of pink mountain heather grace the clearings.

The final section of trail traverses beneath a low limestone bluff. At an unmarked junction, you may follow a sidetrail west to the underground outflow of the lake and the brink of Crypt Falls. Use caution. The main trail angles south from the junction, ascending an old watercourse that may have been Crypt Lake's outlet before the karst system developed. Descend gradually to the north shore of the lake.

Crypt Lake has an area of 13.5 ha and a maximum depth of 44 m. It occupies a cirque eroded into shales of the Greyson Formation. Ice lingers on the lake well into summer. The word "crypt" is derived from the Greek *kryptos*, which means "hidden." With its difficult approach, the lake is indeed hidden in its high cirque. The outlet stream is also hidden within the bedrock. The lake is ringed by cliffs and summits of the Wilson Range, including Mount Boswell (2439 m) on the west. W.G. Boswell was a veterinary surgeon with

*Hell Roaring Falls*

the hours at Crypt Lake. But be sure to leave yourself enough time to catch your return boat from Crypt Landing.

## Hell Roaring Falls

On your return to the trailhead you may visit Hell Roaring Falls. From the upper junction, approximately 3 km from Crypt Landing, take the left-hand trail. This descends steeply to the canyon and falls, which have been eroded through colourful, vertically tilted rock. Bears frequent this area. As it angles away from the canyon, the trail offers a view over the alluvial fan at the mouth of Hell Roaring Creek. The trail then contours above the lakeshore through lodgepole pine and Douglas-fir for 1 km, before joining the Crypt Lake trail, 400 m from the trailhead. This sidetrip will add about 500 m to the overall length of the outing.

# 62. Tamarack

| Route | | |
|---|---|---|
| **Overnight, 3–4 days** | | |
| Route | Elevation (m) | Distance (km) |
| Rowe-Tamarack trailhead | 1600 | 0 |
| Lower Rowe Lake jct | 1940 | 3.9 |
| Lower Rowe Lake | 1950 | +0.3 |
| Rowe Meadow | 2010 | 5.2 |
| Upper Rowe Lakes jct | 2015 | 5.5 |
| Lineham Ridge Summit | 2560 | 8.5 |
| South fork of Blakiston Creek | 1870 | 13.6 |
| Lone Lake Summit | 2250 | 15.7 |
| Lone Lake and CG | 1990 | 17.7 |
| South Kootenay Pass jct | 1940 | 21.5 |
| Blakiston Creek jct | 1935 | 21.6 |
| Twin Lake Summit | 2150 | 23.5 |
| Lower Twin Lake jct | 1975 | 24.7 |
| Upper Twin Lake and CG | 1970 | 24.9 |
| Sage Pass jct | 1970 | 25.0 |
| Snowshoe CG, and Lost Lake jct | 1740 | 27.9 |
| Lost Lake | 1875 | +1.9 |
| Goat Lake jct | 1569 | 31.7 |
| Goat Lake and CG | 2025 | +2.6 |
| Red Rock Canyon | 1495 | 36.1 |

**Maps**
NTS: 82 G/1
Environment Canada: Waterton Lakes National Park

the British Boundary Commission of 1872–76. The name was officially applied in 1917. Before that time, the mountain had been called Street Mountain, after Jack Street, a Mountie who died in an avalanche on its slopes. The cliffs of Mount Boswell are a good place to look for mountain goats.

A rough track, about 1.8 km long, leads around Crypt Lake, although during times of high runoff some of the route will be underwater. At its most southerly point, the track takes you into Glacier National Park, Montana, but there is no need to bring your passport. A portion of the circuit crosses the rubble-covered surface of a drift glacier at the water's edge. Use care. The southeast shore of the lake contains an ancient alluvial fan, now partially vegetated. Atop this, an alluvial fan of more recent origin is being deposited by streams and avalanches. The east shore of the lake is bordered by subalpine meadows.

The "undefended border" at the south end of Crypt Lake typifies the spirit of the Waterton-Glacier International Peace Park. Established in 1932 as a gesture of friendship between Canada and the United States, the two existing national parks were combined into the world's first peace park. Today, the parks work together on resource conservation issues.

On a pleasant day, and after the exertions of the approach, you will be tempted to wile away

*The Tamarack trail is an up-and-down affair with tremendous views of the peaks along the Continental Divide.*

## Trailhead

**Follow the** Akamina Parkway for 10.5 km from Waterton Park townsite to the Rowe-Tamarack trailhead.

Although not as strenuous an outing as the Rockwall in Kootenay National Park, the Tamarack trail is cut from the same undulating cloth. This energetic excursion parallels the eastern slope of the Continental Divide, traverses the heads of three valleys, and crosses a mountain ridgecrest that provides a panoramic vista of the southern Rockies. It travels through excellent habitat for mountain goats, bighorn sheep, mule deer, cougars, and grizzly bears. The two campgrounds are located at backcountry lakes, and

## Variations

- Day-hike to the Upper Rowe Lakes, 15.4 km return
- Exit along Blakiston Creek, 2 days, 31.7 km
- Hike the route in reverse
- Backpack the northern leg of the outing, camping at Goat Lake and Upper Twin Lake, 3 days, 27.8 km return
- Make a shorter loop beginning and ending at Red Rock Canyon. Hike the Snowshoe trail to camp at Upper Twin Lake. Follow the Tamarack trail south to Blakiston Creek. Exit to Red Rock Canyon, 2 days, 24.7 km

sidetrails lead to other lakes. You share the Tamarack trail with horses. Lineham Ridge, the apex of the trail, is the fourth-highest point crossed by maintained trail in the Rockies. It will be snow-plugged until mid-July in most years.

### Trailhead to Upper Rowe Lake Junction

The trail begins on the alluvial fan that Rowe Creek has built at its confluence with Cameron Creek. The broad path leads uphill into a dog-hair pine forest. At the prominent corner at 0.3 km, you can see where Rowe Creek is eroding into the red argillite of the Grinnell Formation. The trail climbs away from the creek onto an open slope, where stonecrop, yarrow, umbrella plant, yellow beardtongue, low larkspur, and pearly everlasting grow. You then pass through an older subalpine forest. In the undergrowth you may see bear grass, thimbleberry, cow parsnip, queen's cup, and the delicate mariposa lily.

At approximately km 2.4, the trail emerges from forest onto avalanche slopes beneath the cliffs of Mt. Lineham. These slopes provide excellent food sources for bears and mule deer. Views back down the valley include Buchanan Ridge (2400 m) and Mount Crandell (2378 m). At km 3.9, the sidetrail to Lower Rowe Lake branches south (left). It is 300 m to the lake's outlet. Walled by the east ridge of Mt. Rowe and dammed by a rockslide, the lake beckons as a rest stop. The inlet stream is a waterfall that drains the Upper Rowe Lakes, situated in the hanging valley above. Hoary marmots and pikas whistle and "eeeep" from the talus slopes to the west.

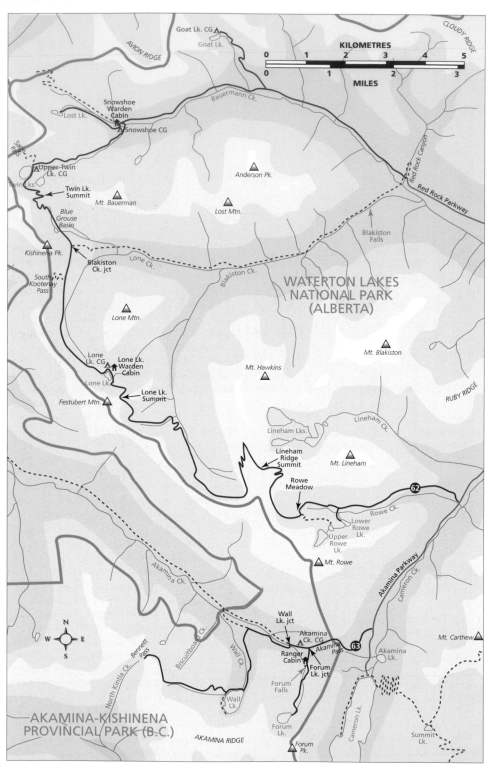

Goat Lk. CG
Goat Lk.

CLOUDY RIDGE

AVION RIDGE

KILOMETRES
0  1  2  3  4  5
0  1  2  3
MILES

Bauermann Ck.

Lost Lk.

Snowshoe
Warden
Cabin
Snowshoe CG

Red Rock Canyon

Red Rock Parkway

Upper Twin
Lk. CG

Twin Lks.

Anderson Pk.

Twin Lk.
Summit

Mt. Bauerman

Lost Mtn.

Blue
Grouse
Basin

Blakiston
Falls

Kishinena Pk.

Lone Ck.

WATERTON LAKES
NATIONAL PARK
(ALBERTA)

Blakiston
Ck. jct

Blakiston Ck.

South
Kootenay
Pass

Lone Mtn.

Mt. Blakiston

RUBY RIDGE

Lone
Lk. CG
Lone Lk.
Warden
Cabin

Lone Lk.

Mt. Hawkins

Festubert Mtn.

Lone Lk.
Summit

Lineham Lks.

Lineham Ck.

Lineham
Ridge
Summit

Mt. Lineham

Rowe
Meadow

62

Rowe Ck.

Lower
Rowe
Lk.

Upper
Rowe
Lk.

Mt. Rowe

Akamina Ck.

Akamina Parkway

Cameron Ck.

N
W    E
S

Bennett
Pass

Biscuitboard Ck.

Wall Ck.

Wall
Lk. jct

Akamina
Ck. CG

Ranger
Cabin

Akamina
Pass

63

Akamina
Lk.

Mt. Carthew

North Kintla Ck.

Forum
Lk. jct

Forum
Falls

Wall
Lk.

AKAMINA-KISHINENA
PROVINCIAL PARK (B.C.)

AKAMINA RIDGE

Forum
Lk.

Forum
Pk.

Cameron Lk.

Summit
Lk.

## Upper Rowe Lakes (2168 m), 1.2 km

*The uppermost Rowe Lake*

**Continue straight** ahead at the junction on the south side of Rowe Meadow. The trail switchbacks on an open slope and then ascends east into a treeline forest of Lyall's larch. After rounding the spur north of the valley that harbors the Upper Rowe Lakes, the trail descends to the southwest and delivers you to the shore of the upper lake. Its east shore features a thick kruppelholz forest that includes Lyall's larch. *Kruppelholz* means "crippled wood" in German.

As with most of Waterton's backcountry lakes, the two Upper Rowe Lakes are situated in a cirque at the head of a hanging valley. They occupy bedrock hollows scooped by a glacier. Although glacial ice is no longer present, perennial snow-drifts cling to shady recesses along the south shores of the lakes. The lakes are separated by a natural dam of resistant rock, and are connected by waterfalls. The outflow of the smaller lake cascades more than 150 m to Lower Rowe Lake. The abundance of larch trees and bear grass, and the opportunity to see bighorn sheep and mountain goats add to the charm of this destination. If you don't want to lug overnight packs here, consider day-hiking on a separate trip.

Beyond this junction, the trail re-enters forest and crosses Rowe Creek several times before Rowe Meadow at km 5.2. The meadow is surrounded by the amphitheatre-like cliffs that connect Mt. Rowe to the south, with outliers of Mt. Lineham to the north. The meadow is home to a boisterous colony of Columbian ground squirrels and swarms of horse flies. The trail leads southwest across the meadow to a bridge over Rowe Creek. The Upper Rowe Lakes junction is 20 m south of the bridge.

### Upper Rowe Lakes Junction to Lone Lake

Rowe Meadow marks the end of smooth sailing for the next day and a half. There are no water sources in the next 8 km. Turn west (right) at the Upper Rowe Lakes junction and begin a torturously steep climb for 500 m onto a bench beneath the cliffs of the Continental Divide. The cliffs contain the two elements of the Siyeh Formation. The lower, more weathered part of the cliff is siltstone and sandstone. The upper, more blocky part is limestone and dolomite. Geologists in the US have subdivided the Siyeh accordingly, calling the lower part the Empire Formation, and the upper part the Helena Formation. The Purcell Lava Sill — an injection of igneous rock — occurs in the Helena Formation as a thin, dark green or black layer. The Siyeh Formation is the backbone of the Continental Divide in Waterton. It flanks the Tamarack trail between here and Twin Lakes.

The grade moderates and the trail undulates needlessly through some depressions. Blazed as a horse route, the Tamarack trail makes many such superfluous climbs and descents in the next 20 km. The hard work created for hikers would be unnoticed by someone on horseback, although probably not by the horse. There are fine examples of ripple rock at trailside. The pockets of avalanche meadow contain glacier lilies and western anemone. From treeline, the trail begins a sweeping rise toward the west ridge of Mount Lineham, on a path beaten into red screes of the Kintla Formation. Use caution if you must cross late-lying snow patches. Scan the slopes above for bighorn sheep.

As you gain elevation, views open to the south, including Mount Custer (2708 m) and Chapman Peak (2867 m) south of Cameron Lake, and Mt. Cleveland (3190 m), the highest mountain in Glacier National Park. Soon the three Rowe Lakes are visible, along with the spectacular peaks in western Glacier. Treeline is high on the northern slopes of Rowe basin, and the trail skirts a kruppelholz forest that features lifeless, silvery spars of wind-blasted, sun-bleached whitebark pine. Centuries old, these skeleton trees serve an important purpose — they anchor the screes, stabilizing thin soils and allowing other vegetation to take root.

Follow the painted orange markers as the trail switchbacks westward to Lineham Ridge Summit — the apex of the Tamarack trail in both elevation and views. A remarkable 360-degree panorama takes in most of Waterton and Glacier national parks, BC's Akamina-Kishinena Provincial Park, and the Rockies north to Crowsnest Pass. The Lineham Lakes lie nestled in the basin directly northeast. The lakes are known individually as Water Cudgel, Hourglass, Ptarmigan, Channel, and Larch. John Lineham was an Alberta businessman of the 1880s, with interests in oil, lumber, and ranching. Mt. Blakiston (2920 m), highest in Waterton, rises northeast of Lineham Basin.

*The argillite of the Grinnel Formation features exposures of ripple rock that record ancient shoreline environments.*

Thomas Blakiston explored here in 1858 with the Palliser Expedition.

After traversing north for a kilometre, the trail switchbacks to the south and begins a mercilessly steep descent on scree into the south fork valley

## Bighorn Sheep

**Rowe Basin** is one of the better places to see bighorn sheep in the backcountry of the Rockies. A sheep's coat is tawny brown with a white rump patch and a dark brown tail. The bighorn ram stands about a metre tall at the shoulder and, when mature, has a set of thick brown horns that spiral forward. These horns are never shed. Together

*Bighorn ram on Lineham Ridge*

with the skull, they can account for 13 percent of the animal's 125 kg weight. It is possible to determine the approximate age of a ram by counting the annuli, or rings, on one of its horns. Each annulus contains a dark and light band, together representing one year of growth. The female sheep (ewe) grows horns too, however these are less spectacular and curve backwards.

The rams flock together in high places during summer and early autumn. The dominant ram must constantly defend his place. Usually, this is done without battle in what is called the "present" (pree-ZENT) — when two rams turn their heads sideways, to allow each to inspect the horns of the other. As the autumn rut approaches and the issue of who will breed with a harem of ewes becomes more

crucial, diplomacy wanes. The rams duel, charging headlong at each other and meeting with a mighty crash. Thick armour bones beneath the horns usually prevent serious injury. However, duels to the death do take place.

Grasses are the most important foods for bighorn sheep. The animal cannot tolerate snow depths of more than 0.3 m that limit its travel and access to food. Hence, wind-scoured slopes in the front ranges offer the best winter habitat for bighorns. Waterton's sheep periodically suffer die-offs caused by parasites or by hard winters. Grizzly bears, wolves, and cougars are the animal's principal predators. They often achieve success by forcing a sheep to run over a cliff. Poaching along the western boundary of Waterton also takes a toll on these animals.

Bighorn sheep are generally accustomed to people, and will often allow hikers to approach closely. This puts you and the sheep in peril. With their horns and sharp hooves, sheep can inflict serious injury. Accustomed to nutrition-poor handouts, sheep may not be able to endure a hard winter. If a sheep approaches you, scare it away.

# Tamarack

*Lone Lake*

of Blakiston Creek. Follow the orange trail markers. The pale mauve blooms of sky pilot dot the slopes. The grade moderates when you reach the larch forest in the valley bottom. The trail curves northwest and parallels the Continental Divide, heading north toward Lone Lake Summit. For the

## The Crown of the Continent

**The phrase,** "Crown of the Continent," was first coined by Charles Bird Grinnell, the conservationist who was the strongest proponent for the establishment of Glacier National Park. He later founded the Audubon Society.

Grinnell envisioned a series of protected areas that would preserve the backbone of the southern Rockies. Today, environmentalists still push for recognition and protection of the Crown of the Continent Ecosystem — extending from central Montana to Crowsnest Pass. In the face of the habitat disruption and fragmentation that has accompanied ranching, logging, mining, and petroleum drilling, protection of this ecosystem has become as crucial as it is elusive. It is now recognized that if wide-ranging carnivores and natural processes are to survive in the southern Rockies and elsewhere, existing national parks must be connected with other reserves, to offer more than small pockets of protected habitat. At press time, the federal government had agreed in principle to expand Waterton Lakes National Park to include lands in BC, but the BC provincial government was thwarting the expansion.

most part, it is pleasant hiking through upper subalpine woods, with a few chronic muddy spots. You will appreciate the shade of the cliff on a hot day, and the fact that your toes are no longer being jammed into the front of your boots. Springs issue from the cliffs and may offer water. Soak your hat here if you need help to cool off.

The next climb is the most trying of this long first day, especially if you expended your reserves crossing Lineham Ridge Summit. The trail climbs 380 m in 2.1 km. This hard work would be more tolerable if the trail didn't ramble and undulate so much, adding elevation. Your first steady descent is *not* to Lone Lake campground. There is still much uphill to come. Rock-hop streams as required. A section of trail is routed directly along a rocky, seasonal stream course. It will be a torrent during heavy rains.

From Lone Lake Summit on the east ridge of Festubert Mountain (2520 m), the nearby campground at Lone Lake beckons. The mountain commemorates a village in France where Canadian troops fought in WWI. The view northeast features the whaleback scree peaks of northern Waterton.

You will probably cross a snow patch as you leave Lone Lake Summit. The descent north switchbacks through a remarkable Lyall's larch forest. It is not often that you see this tree species in such a uniformly aged and widely spaced stand. Lyall's larch grows at high elevation on rocky soils, and consequently is seldom

## Tamaracks or Larches?

**"Tamarack" is a common name** applied throughout North America to three species of coniferous trees that shed their needles annually — tamarack, Lyall's larch, and western larch. The tamarack is the most common of these three trees in Canada, and is found in every province and territory. However, it is not widespread in the Rockies, occurring only in low-elevation wetlands on the eastern slopes, north of the North Saskatchewan River. The western larch is found principally in southeastern BC, with a few stands in southwestern Alberta.

The deciduous conifers along the Tamarack trail are Lyall's larch, also called subalpine larch. This tree species often forms treeline forests. Clearwater Pass in Banff National Park is its northern limit. The tree was catalogued by Eugene Bourgeau of the Palliser Expedition. He named it for David Lyall, a naturalist and surgeon with the Franklin Expedition.

consumed by fire. Several of the trees here are more than a metre in diameter at their bases, indicating ages of perhaps 300 years or more.

The descent ends at an avalanche path that contains a conical mound of landslide debris. As you gain the southeast shore of Lone Lake, pause to admire the view northeast over the U-shaped valley of Blakiston Creek. Rock-hop the outlet of the lake, and follow the trail along the cliff edge, north to the campground.

Lone Lake is 13 m deep and has an area of 2.5 ha. Glaciologists speculate that it once drained entirely north into Lone Creek. A moraine subsequently blocked the drainage, forcing most of the outflow to spill northeast over the cliff into the upper reaches of Blakiston Creek. Don't forget your insect repellent. Lone Lake is bug heaven. The park warden cabin is northeast of the lake.

## Lone Lake to Twin Lake

After the rigors of the first day, your second day on the Tamarack trail brings two options, both of which are much less energetic. You can hike to Twin Lake campground in 7.0 km, or to Snowshoe

*Lower Twin Lake from Twin Lake Summit*

campground in 10.2 km. You can add short side-trails to South Kootenay Pass and Sage Pass.

The trail north from Lone Lake alternates between delightful upper subalpine meadows and ancient forest as it descends gradually to the Blakiston Creek junction. This is excellent habitat for grizzly bears. You cross two wet meadows from which you can study the cliffs of the Siyeh Formation, immediately west.

## South Kootenay Pass (2160 m), 1.7 km

The South Kootenay Pass trail was part of a historic route used by the Ktunaxa (ka-too-NA-hah) Nation and the first European explorers in this region. Known as the Buffalo Trail, this route connected Ktunaxa territory west of the Continental Divide with seasonal hunting and fishing grounds on the prairies. The Ktunaxa had been displaced to the western side of the divide by hostile Stoneys and bands of the Blackfoot Confederacy in the early 1700s. South Kootenay Pass maintained the Ktunaxa access to bison, the animal on which their culture

*Cliffs near South Kootenay Pass*

was based. They used the trail until bison were eliminated from the wild in the 1880s.

The Ktunaxa traded with the Salish, Nez Percé, and Flathead peoples west of the Continental Divide, from whom they obtained obsidian for making arrowheads and tools. This material has been found at some of the 358 known Native archaeological sites in Waterton. The Buffalo Trail followed Blakiston Creek to Lower Waterton Lake. Fifty-six of the park's archaeological sites are in the Blakiston Valley.

The ruts made by travois — sleds that were pulled by dogs, and later by horses — scar the Blakiston Creek alluvial fan. Evidence of five Native camps, along with scattered artifacts and rock cairns, has been found on South Kootenay Pass.

The first crossing of the pass by Europeans was from west to east in 1858, by a group led by Thomas Blakiston, an officer of the Palliser Expedition. Blakiston applied the name Pass Creek to the stream now known as Blakiston Creek. It is not likely that today's trail to the pass follows the precise route of The Buffalo Trail. In places you can see where a much older, windfallen trail cuts across, taking a steeper grade to the pass. Ancient trees in the area carry blazes that mark the original route.

For all its history, South Kootenay Pass is not particularly scenic. The sparsely forested saddle offers limited views west into the logged valleys now included in BC's Akamina-Kishinena Provincial Park, and east over Lone and Blakiston creeks. You will be obliged to carry your packs on this sidetrip, as there is no safe place to cache them.

Fifty metres north of the South Kootenay Pass junction, you reach the Blakiston Creek junction. You may exit the Tamarack trail at this point, by turning east (right), 10.1 km to Red Rock Canyon. Otherwise, continue straight ahead.

Hop the outlet stream of the pond in Blue Grouse Basin. From appearances, the pond formerly occupied a much larger area. Now it is filling with vegetation. The blue grouse is one of three grouse species in the Rockies. It prefers upper subalpine habitats like this, where it feeds on berries and insects. The cliffs of Kishinena Peak (2450 m) are to the west. The mountain's name is a Ktunaxa (ka-too-NA-hah) word that means "balsam fir" or "white fir."

After the tiring climbs on day one, you will hardly notice the modest ascent to Twin Lake Summit. From the crest of the climb, you catch glimpses through larch forest of the Twin Lakes to the north. After a steep descent, the trail contours across a scree slope at the head of the cirque that contains Lower Twin Lake. At the Twin Lakes junction, the sidetrail to the east (right) leads to Lower Twin Lake. The campground at Upper Twin Lake is 200 m straight ahead. The campground is a disappointment, as it is set amid seeps and is out of view of the lake. I had one of my worst backcountry sleeps ever here. Just as we turned in, a fellow camper returned from the lower lake, where he had seen a grizzly bear foraging along the shore.

## Twin Lake to Red Rock Canyon

Hop the outlet stream of Upper Twin Lake. The trail turns east and begins a steady descent along upper Bauerman Creek, named for H.B. Bauerman, a geologist with the British Boundary Commission. After about 1.5 km the trail draws alongside the creek. The meadow here contains many wildflowers and shrubs typical of the montane ecoregion — a strip of prairie in the heart of a subalpine valley.

You cross Bauerman Creek to the Snowshoe campground and warden cabin 3.2 km after leaving Upper Twin Lake. From here, it is an easy 8.2 km walk along the undulating fireroad to Red Rock Canyon. You share the fireroad with mountain bikers. You pass the sidetrail to Goat Lake en route. The steep (455 m in 2.6 km) hike to the lake is not recommended to those with heavy packs unless you plan to spend the night at the campground there.

Some of the rocks along the fireroad feature star-shaped crystals of feldspar, known as phenocrysts. As you approach Red Rock Canyon, note the change in character of the forest. Cottonwood poplar becomes common. The rustle of its leaves on the ever-present wind heralds your arrival at trail's end. Red Rock Canyon is 23 m deep and is being eroded into red and green argillite of the Grinnell Formation. The circuit of the canyon is only 700 m and is highly recommended.

## Lost Lake (1875 m), 1.9 km

*Lost Lake*

**Head north** from Snowshoe campground. At the junction in 0.9 km turn northwest (left). The trail ascends gradually through a damp forest to the lush shore of the jade-coloured lake. Cow parsnip and bear grass grow in abundance along the trail and at the lake. The lake is backed by steep avalanche slopes that are excellent bear habitat. Travel accordingly. Lost Lake was stocked with fish in the past, but avalanche deposits in the lake have killed them.

## Sage Pass (2131 m), 1.4 km

**Head north** from the campground and hop the outlet stream of Upper Twin Lake. The trail turns east. In 100 m, the Sage Pass trail branches north (left) and climbs steadily to the treed pass, from where mountaineers can pick their way northeast or southwest onto ridges for better views. Sagebrush is a shrub of the montane ecoregion. It is common just across the pass, in southeastern BC.

# 63. Forum Lake/ Wall Lake

## Route

Day-hike or overnight

| Route | Elevation (m) | Distance (km) |
|---|---|---|
| Trailhead | 1670 | 0 |
| Akamina Pass | 1783 | 1.5 |
| Forum Lake jct | 1770 | 2.2 |
| Ranger Station | 1775 | 2.4 |
| Forum Falls jct | 1780 | 2.7 |
| Forum Falls | 1785 | +0.1 |
| Forum Lake | 2010 | 4.4 |
| Forum Lake jct | 1770 | 6.6 |
| Akamina Creek CG | 1765 | 6.8 |
| Wall Lake jct | 1755 | 6.9 |
| Wall Lake | 1770 | 9.6 |
| Bennett Pass jct | 1780 | 10.0 |
| Bennett Pass | 2220 | 13.2 |

**Maps**

NTS: 82 G/1 (trail shown incorrectly)
Environment Canada: Waterton Lakes National Park (trail not shown)
**See map on p.256**

**Best lighting:** morning and evening are best at the lakes

## Trailhead

**Follow the Akamina Parkway** 15 km from Waterton Park townsite to the Akamina Pass parking lot on the east side of the road. The trailhead is across the road. Daily shuttle service is available (fee charged). Inquire at the Tamarack Mall in Waterton Park townsite.

The Forum Lake/Wall Lake hike is in Waterton Lakes' neighbouring Akamina-Kishenina Provincial Park, BC. Access is the same as for Waterton. There is one backcountry campground in the park. To reserve a campsite, phone 800-689-9025. The park has no other developed facilities.

*A moody day at Forum Lake, with bear grass in prime*

Long a favourite haunt of backcountry skiers in Waterton, the hike to Forum Lake and Wall Lake became a popular summer outing with the establishment of Akamina-Kishinena Provincial Park in 1995. The lakes — one higher and lesser, one lower and greater — lie buried in glacial cirque pockets beneath stupendous cliffs. If you extend the outing by making the grind to Bennett Pass, you are treated to a wild view south over the headwaters of North Kintla Creek and into Glacier National Park, Montana. In a good year, the bear grass blooms are stunning. You share the trail with horses and mountain bikers.

### Trailhead to Forum Lake Junction

Waterton's Cameron Lake region is the snowfall capital of southern Alberta. The forest at the trailhead is wet in character, more like what you would expect in British Columbia, which is but a 20-minute walk away. As testimony to the wetness, thimbleberry, queen's cup, false hellebore, cow parsnip, western meadowrue, water hemlock, birch-leaved spirea, and bear grass fringe roadside at the trailhead.

The trail to Akamina Pass was cut as an exploratory tote road following the discovery of oil on Cameron Creek in 1901. In 1927, there was a proposal to extend the recently constructed Akamina Parkway over Akamina Pass, to allow a "triangle tour" from Waterton to the Flathead Valley, returning through Glacier National Park, Montana. The BC section of the road was never built, but the tote road into Akamina-Kishinena Provincial Park remains. In places, you'll see sections of corduroy — logs laid across the width of

*Wall Lake: a simple name, well placed*

the tread. *Corduroy* is a French expression that means "road of the king." To keep the king's carriage out of the muck of feudal France, the peasants would lay logs across the tread. A bumpy ride resulted, but at least the king got to his palace without sullying his boots and gown. Hike on; regal wonders await.

You climb steadily through old pine forest, crossing a small stream in 400 m. Note the red rock in the stream bed. This is 1.5 billion-year-old argillite of the Grinnell Formation. You have glimpses of Cameron Lake through the trees. White rein-orchids, hooded ladies'-tresses, meadow parsnip, dwarf false asphodel, groundsel, horsetails, and fleabane line a wet section of trail on the final approach to the treed pass.

There's not much to look at on the pass except a typical installation of signs that welcomes you to BC and the entry to Akamina-Kishinena Provincial Park. Bear warnings will be posted

## A Rhyming Couplet

**The name** of Akamina-Kishinena Provincial Park incorporates two Ktunaxa (ka-too-NA-hah)) words, the precise meanings of which elude toponymers. *Akamina* might mean "high bench land," "mountain pass," "valley," or "watershed." All of these are appropriate for the features so named by the British Boundary Commission. Some people pronounce the name, ah-kah-MY-nah, but most say ah-kah-MEE-nah. The meanings given for *Kishinena* (kish-ih-NEE-nah) that I like best are "balsam" and "white fir." Akamina-Kishinena: It's an exotic sounding couplet, but has a down-to-earth meaning — rocks and trees.

here, and you have the opportunity to sign the register. But please note — this is not a safety register. The information is used for statistics only. The trail descends gradually from the pass to the Forum Lake junction in 700 m. The registration box for the campground is beside the trail. To hike to Forum Lake, turn south (left).

### Forum Lake

Just beyond the park ranger cabin, which is 175 m along the trail, branch left. Just 50 m into the trees you come to a junction. Forum Falls is a short distance to the right — a pleasant sidetrip to the base of a small cascade. Dippers nest here and frequent the stream.

Back on the Forum Lake trail, you alternate between steep grades and level sections, now at creekside, now away. In one section, you hike in an abandoned creek bed. Three shrubs — false-azalea, grouseberry, and blueberry — are common at trailside. Subalpine fir is prevalent in the forest, but more than 30 percent of the trees are standing-dead. As you ascend, the regular complement of subalpine flowers appears. On this north-facing slope and with the heavy snowfall here, they bloom late. I saw shooting stars and glacier lilies freshly in bloom on August 1. The trail crosses a wet meadow on a split log boardwalk. A patch of perennial avalanche snow lies just beyond. You hike through larches. A short distance later you arrive at a bay on the northeast shore of Forum Lake. This spot, in all my experience of the backcountry of the Rockies, was the quietest place I have ever been. It must have been a rare day. Waterton's windiness usually stirs these waters, too.

The colourful cliffs of Akamina Ridge rise

## Variations

- Day-hike to Forum Lake, 8.8 km return
- Day-hike to Wall Lake, 10.4 km return
- Day-hike to Wall Lake and Bennett Pass, 17.6 km return
- Day-hike to both lakes, 20.0 km return
- Day-hike to both lakes and the pass, 26.4 km return
- Camp at Akamina Creek (2.4 km) and explore

almost 500 m above the lake, blocking the sun for much of the day. Look for mountain goats and bears on the terraces. *Forum* comes from the Latin word for "outside." The name was given to the lake by the British Boundary Commission. The forum of Roman times was an outdoor market or meeting place. Perhaps the shape of the lake reminded someone of a Roman market. Forum Peak (2415 m) was named after the lake. It's an appropriate name because the mountain is the meeting place for many borders. Seven jurisdictions crisscross its slopes: two national parks, one provincial park, two provinces, and two countries.

Golden-mantled ground squirrels and Columbian ground squirrels will probably attend your arrival at the lake. Robins, red-breasted nuthatches, and white-winged crossbills are common. A pure stand of larches grows on the steep slope above the rocky east shore.

Forum Lake drains underground (the emergence is just above the wet meadow), so its level fluctuates. If the water level is high, you might be confined to the bay on the northeast shore, from where a shintangle of spruce and fir impedes westerly progress. When the water level is lower, you can follow a path west along the shore. But if the bear grass is in prime, as it was on my visit, you won't feel obliged to go anywhere. You'll probably just gawk in amazement at the blooms and at the tremendous setting of the lake.

## Forum Lake Junction to Wall Lake

It's only 200 m from the Forum Lake junction to Akamina campground, and another 50 m to the three bridges that span the outflow from Forum Creek. Across the creek, turn southwest (left) off the main trail for Wall Lake.

The trail to the lake initially makes a gradual descent through an old forest of lodgepole pine, Engelmann spruce, and subalpine fir. Arnica, queen's cup, and foamflower are among the wildflowers. After about 1.9 km, the trail swings south to enter the Wall Lake valley, where it begins a

## The Siyeh Formation

**The front range** mountains of the Rockies south of Crowsnest Pass lack the massive, blocky, cliff-building limestone and dolomite of the front ranges farther north. Except for one thick limestone layer, the rock is shaly and weak. However, the layers are usually not steeply tilted, which allows them to withstand erosion better than you would expect. They form cliffs as impressive as the sheer walls farther north. The main cliff-builder of Akamina Ridge — as elsewhere in the Waterton area — is the 1.35 billion-year-old Siyeh (SIGH-yuh) Formation. The formation takes its name from *saiyi*, a Siksika (Blackfoot) word that means "mad" or "rabid." The Siyeh has three principal elements, visible at Forum Lake and Wall Lake. The lower two, known to US geologists as the Empire Formation and the Helena Formation, typically form a cliff. The Empire (lower part of the cliff) contains siltstone, sandstone, and greenish argillite

*Akamina Ridge from the Bennett Pass trail*

rocks formed, respectively, from silt, sand, and mud. The argillite is green here rather than the usual red, because the iron in its clays was reduced (lost attached oxygen molecules) after deposition. The Helena Formation (upper part of the cliff) is a thick, pale-weathering limestone layer. Above that is the lower Snowslip Formation, another US name applied to the upper part of the Canadian Siyeh Formation and layers above that. These are reddish argillite and siltstone, the red color coming from rusted iron that has retained its attached oxygen molecules. Forming an obvious dark band in the Helena Formation limestone is the Purcell Sill, an intrusion of igneous (once-molten) rock that squeezed between the layers. The Purcell Lava, which poured out of a volcano, sits atop that. The lava covered the seabed, then was itself buried under younger layers of sediment.

*Kintla Peak and Mt. Kinnerly from Bennett Pass*

visit, the dinner plate, argillite shales nearby showed evidence of being used for exactly that purpose. A bear had recently flipped over a great number, looking for grubs beneath. Arnica and Sitka valerian carpet the peninsula that juts into the lake. Mt. Rowe (2452 m) rises across the Akamina Valley. It was named for V.F. Rowe, a surveyor and officer with the International Boundary Commission of 1872–1876.

### Bennett Pass

It's an honest 3 km to Bennett Pass. The ascent took me an hour and fifteen minutes with a light pack. The Bennett Pass junction is about 400 m west of the outlet of Wall Lake. The trail makes a couple of tight switchbacks away from the lakeshore before rambling through lush forest on the initial ascent, twice drawing alongside the creek that drains the sidevalley. Look for twisted stalk and red monkey flower at trailside. After about a kilometre, you pop out onto an avalanche slope with views ahead to a cliff that spans the valley. I could have raved over the bear grass displays at any number of points on this hike, but I've saved the superlatives for the view west from the top of this cliff. Some locals will tell you that the blooms of bear grass peak every seven years; some say every five. The truth is that each plant blooms every 3 to 10 years. Neighbouring plants often bloom at the same time. So each year, the locations of the blooms and their relative intensity will be different. I hope that, at some point on your travels in the Waterton area, you will see displays to match what I saw in this hanging valley above Wall Lake. The blooms numbered in the tens of thousands, and each, it seemed, was at its peak.

gradual ascent. The trail runs along the base of avalanche slopes off the spur that separates Forum Lake from Wall Lake. Huge spruce grow here — some are more than a metre in diameter at the base and 45 m tall. These avalanche slopes — with their glacier lilies, bear grass, cow parsnip, and berry bushes — are a deluxe piece of bear habitat. Fireweed, ragwort, wild onion, and bracted honeysuckle grow on the trail margins.

### Wall Lake

It's the same setting at Wall Lake as at Forum Lake, but the arrangement of the pieces differs. Wall Lake is two-and-a-half times the size of its neighbour. Akamina Ridge rises half as high again — some 750 m from the south shore of Wall Lake — shutting out the sky. An ancient forest, with a lush understory rings the north shore. Look for red monkey flower at trailside. Cutthroat trout abound in the lake. If you packed a fishing rod, make sure you also packed a BC Fishing Licence.

A good trail leads around the north and west shores of the lake to two bays on the southwest shore, passing the Bennett Pass junction in 400 m. The first of the bays was the former site of a very popular backcountry campground, closed in 1997 on the advice of a bear biologist. Don't camp here, but feel free to use the outhouse. As of 2002, it was being maintained by BC Parks, including the TP. I saw sandpipers and five redhead ducks near shore. The trail ends 150 m later on a scree fan above the second bay. Here, a perennial snow patch — the product of innumerable avalanches — melts into the lake. Keep off the snow. It has been the site of mishaps and close calls over the years. You may see gray-crowned rosy finches feeding on torpid insects on the snow. On my

The trail sidehills along the dry north slope of the valley where sawwort and scorpionweed grow. Look back for views of Wall Lake. Red argillite is common on this slope. Argillite is shale that formed in shallow seas and was subsequently altered by heat or pressure. Look for proof of its marine origin — ripple rock that records the lapping of wavelets on an ancient shore. Just before the second step in the valley, the trail may be buried under avalanche deposit. If the way ahead looks uncertain, aim to ascend the step along the north (right) side of the stream. Stickseed, yellow columbine, and wild chives grow on the outcrop. I saw tiger swallowtail and veined white butterflies on the trail. Nearby, I found the large, delicate bloom of a western wake-robin. This member of the lily family is a rarity on the Classic Hikes.

You get a brief reprieve from the climb where the trail passes through the saddle between Akamina Ridge and its outlier to the north. Many of the trees are now Lyall's larches, some of them half a metre in diameter — big trees for this aspect and elevation. But you'll see something else unusual on the climb ahead — larches in kruppelholz form. Looking north, you can see the Continental Divide ridge, from Mt. Rowe (with the provincial boundary cutline) to Kishinena Peak (2436 m). Biscuitboard Creek rises on the slopes beneath the trail, to drain into Akamina Creek. The origin of the name is unrecorded, but likely had something to do with a sourdough who staked a claim or two nearby.

The last 1.5 km to Bennett Pass is as single-minded a piece of trail as you will find anywhere. It ascends about 240 m, and does this on a sidehill without a hint of a switchback. Fine displays of upper subalpine wildflowers provide distraction from the toil. Golden-crowned kinglets buzzed from tree to tree on my visit, and for a few minutes, a red-tailed hawk soared overhead. You'll be glad when the grade kicks back and the trail begins to turn around the north end of Akamina Ridge, with the true saddle of Bennett Pass about 50 m below and 250 m west of the trail. Watch

*Western wake robin*

your step — the trail is exposed to a tremendous drop for a short section. The trail forks. Straight ahead is the route into North Kintla Creek. Keep left to climb onto the screes of Akamina Ridge. Pick a spot to collapse, catch your breath, and take in the stupendous view into the northwest corner of Glacier National Park, Montana. Kintla Peak (3079 m), Kinnerly Peak (3031 m), and the Agassiz Glacier dominate the view. *Kintla* was a Ktunaxa (Kutenai) personal name. *Kinnerly* may be a misspelling of Dr. C. Kennerly, a surgeon with the US Boundary Survey. Louis Agassiz (ah-GASS-ee) was the Swiss naturalist who first proposed the theory of ice-age glaciations in 1837.

### Return

Retrace your route to Wall Lake. If you've visited all the destinations as a day-hike, don't be ashamed at the pull in your calves on the modest climb back over Akamina Pass.

## Peace Park Plus

**The Akamina-Kishinena** Provincial Recreation Area was established in 1986 when logging threatened to gut the forests along Akamina Creek. Much of the clear-cutting then taking place was "salvage logging" — the cutting of standing-dead trees killed by mountain pine beetles. Provincial park status was conveyed in 1995, and logging stopped in the upper watersheds. More recently, there has been a proposal to add the provincial park — along with 40,500 ha of BC's upper Flathead Valley — to the Waterton-Glacier International Peace Park. The Flathead Valley is crucial to the regional population of grizzly bears. The valley is threatened by an open pit mine and by roads proposed by Fording Coal.

Because the Flathead River flows into the US, the environmental issues of bear habitat and water quality are international ones. In 2002, the Canadian government — responding to public interest in both countries — announced its support for the expansion of the Peace Park. Tembec, the BC forest company that owns the rights to log the area, was willing to modify its activities to protect the Flathead Valley. The Ktunaxa-Kinbasket First Nation had an unresolved land claim in the area. The other stumbling block to the expansion of the park was the BC provincial government. Visit www.peaceparkplus.net for more information.

# Reference

## Equipment

### Boots

Hiking boots are your most important equipment. Your choice in footwear will be influenced by the kinds of trails that you plan to hike. Lightweight hiking boots are suitable for day-hikes on well-maintained trails. Leather boots with a Vibram or similar sole are the best choice when carrying a heavy pack or plowing through horse muck. Most experienced hikers have a selection of footwear and match the boot to the proposed trip and the expected hiking conditions. If you find a pair of boots that you really like and can afford it, buy two pairs. Two or three years from now, you might not be able to find the same model.

Take your hiking socks and orthotics with you when you try on the boots in the store. There should be enough room at the rear of the boot for you to slip your index finger between the boot cuff and your Achilles tendon. Ensure that your toes do not feel crowded, especially while walking down a flight of stairs or a ramp. Bring a loaded backpack with you to see how the boots feel when you are carrying weight. Swap the factory footbeds for a pair of beefier ones. Spend half an hour in the pair of boots that feel best, to be sure that you (and your feet) like them. Because boots are better designed than in years past, breaking them in — around the house or on short walks — is no longer crucial. But if you are blister prone, do try them out before you hit the trail.

### Leather Boots

Most people think of leather boots as Frankensteins for the feet. Collectively, they have a reputation of being stiff, heavy, and expensive. On the last two counts this is generally true when compared to synthetic boots, but in recent years bootmakers have introduced innovations to leather boots — articulated uppers, for instance — that make them more supple, providing support without inhibiting gait. Well-made leather boots last longer than lightweight hikers. They offer better ankle and arch support, are more waterproof and warmer. They have the added advantage of causing less trail damage by allowing you to walk through muck on the trail. Try to buy boots that can be re-soled. Although a boot will tighten-up slightly when resoled, it will provide you more years of use for your investment.

Look for deep lugs on the sole, and for a lacing system that includes locking hooks to allow you to vary the lace tension between the toes and the ankle. A gusseted tongue and a rubber rand that

### Ten Steps to Happy Hiking

**If you've got** these covered, you are well on the way to avoiding problems in the backcountry.

- Strive to carry less than one-quarter of your body weight.
- When hiking in a group, share equipment to collectively reduce pack weights.
- Plan for worst-case scenarios. Carry essential equipment together — stove, fuel, pots, and hot food in the same pack; tent, pegs, tent fly, and cold food in the same pack.
- Never let someone else carry your sleeping bag.
- Carry snacks and water; drink often. On overnight hikes, pack a treat.
- Test all equipment at home; inspect your boots.
- Line the inside of your pack with a durable plastic bag.
- Hike with partners of like mind and similar fitness.
- Keep to your planned route. When the weather is truly foul, turn around and go home.
- Take bear safety seriously.

### Keeping Stride with Change

**No guidebook** can remain up-to-date when it comes to outdoor gear. In a highly competitive market, manufacturers introduce new technology and new equipment each season. It takes several years for a piece of gear to prove itself in the field, so only time will tell if any particular innovation will endure or bomb. Generally, the likelihood of something being useful is inversely proportional to its promotional hype. When choosing between a new and highly touted product, and an old war horse, choose the sure thing — especially when it comes to boots, pack, tent, stove, and sleeping bag. *Outside, Backpacker,* and *Explore* each publish gear guides in the spring. They explain new equipment technologies and give opinions as to their worthiness. Invest a few dollars in one of these magazines before you spend hundreds on new equipment.

encircles the stitching help keep out dirt and water. Fewer seams on the uppers means less likelihood that a boot will blow out. A half-shank of nylon, fiberglass, or steel adds torsional support.

### Lightweight Boots

Lightweight hiking boots are those with hybrid uppers — canvas, leather, and synthetic. Many come with Vibram or similar soles. They are usually cut lower at the ankle. They cost slightly less than good leather boots, cause less damage to dry trails, and require less energy. (Every kg

*All this gear goes into two packs.*

carried on your feet is equivalent to 6 kg carried on your back.) However, lightweight boots have drawbacks:

- They are less durable than leather boots and cannot be resoled.
- They are not as waterproof, so hikers are more likely to step off the trail to avoid wet spots or snow patches, causing more damage off-trail than heavier boots cause on-trail.
- They cannot be edged effectively into the tread when descending steep or slippery trails, scree, or snow slopes.
- They do not offer much ankle or arch support — something you may notice when you carry a heavy pack.
- They are not as warm as leather boots, wet or dry.

### Boot Care

Clean your boots after each use with a stiff brush and warm water. Treat them when they are dry to enhance their ability to repel water, using synthetic or natural compounds. (Don't use leather softeners.) Silicone compounds may attract dirt. Even properly treated boots will eventually soak through. To help dry a pair of waterlogged boots, stuff them with newspaper; changing the newspaper as it becomes wet. Do not attempt to dry boots with direct heat or in an oven. A pair of soggy boots will often dry on their own during a sunny day on the trail. If you can afford it, buy two pairs of boots and alternate their use. This will allow each pair to air dry between trips, and will prolong the life of the stitching.

Dry and treat your boots before storage. When stored, ensure that the boots maintain their proper shape by using a boot tree. Check boots before storage to see if they require resoling,

patching, new laces or stitching in the uppers. These repairs are more convenient during the off-season.

### Socks

Wool or wool blend socks are the warmest and most durable choice for outer socks. Socks that incorporate multiple blends of materials with built-in cushioning feel great the first few times that you use them, but in my experience, they soon wear out. Calf length socks are suitable most of the time. Carry two pairs of socks on overnight trips and wear them on alternate days, or exchange them as they become wet. Thin polypropylene or nylon inner socks help reduce the chance of blisters, and wick moisture away from your feet into the outer sock. A knee-length pair of socks will make camp life more comfortable early and late in the season. Some hikers swear by Gore-Tex socks. If you are having trouble keeping your toes dry, try them.

### Gaiters

Gaiters should cover the lower leg from the boot laces to just below the knee. Try different brands to get the best fit. The most durable gaiters are those made from coated Cordura. Gore-Tex uppers help reduce sweating. To prevent the gaiters from riding too high at the heel, they should have a strap or cable that passes under the sole of the boot.

Besides keeping rain, snow, and mud out of your boots, gaiters also keep out scree. They help keep your feet and legs warm on cold, windy days. When the weather clears, you can tie wet gaiters to the outside of your pack to dry as you hike.

### Blister Prone?

A blister is a painful, localized inflammation of the skin, caused by friction. If left unattended, it may become infected. Blisters are a chronic condition for some backpackers. The cause is almost always poorly fitted boots or boots that fail to provide enough arch support. If you blister at the heel while wearing heavier leather boots, the boots may be too long, causing the heel to lift with each stride. If your boots are too tight across the toes, you can have them treated and stretched at a shoemaker. If the cause of your blisters is boots that are too loose, try thicker socks, but it is likely you will have to purchase a pair of boots that fit better.

With a correctly sized pair of boots on your feet, there is a simple trick to reduce the likelihood of blisters: wear a thin, inner sock, and a thicker outer sock. Much of the friction that could create blisters now takes place between the socks. You can try wearing the inner socks inside out. This places smoother material against your skin, especially across the toes. If your boots are too tight across the toes, skip the front lacing lugs to reduce the tightness in that area.

Stop immediately (that means, right away!) when you detect a hot spot on your feet. Take off your boots and socks. Clean the offending area, dry it, and apply a blister dressing, such as Moleskin or Second Skin. In a pinch, a piece of duct tape will work. (Put a piece of non-adhesive, first-aid dressing over the hot spot first, to prevent the blister dressing from sticking to the blister.) If the cause was a piece of grit or a crumpled sock, your problem is solved. But if your boot is too tight, put on thinner socks or jam a clean rock into the boot for a while to stretch the leather. If your boot is too loose, put on thicker socks, change insoles, or pad the offending part of the boot with a blister

### The Ten (Plus Two) Essentials

**If you don't** have a customized equipment list of your own, take at least this much.

- compass or GPS unit
- extra clothing, including rain gear
- extra food, including purified water
- firestarter
- first-aid kit
- flashlight
- map
- matches
- pocket knife
- rescue whistle
- sunglasses and sunscreen

dressing. The key is prompt action to help prevent many kilometres of misery. Do not burst blisters while out on the trail, as infection may result.

### Packs

Backpacks, like backpackers, come in all shapes and sizes. If you will be hiking a variety of trails, you probably require a day pack and an overnight pack. Pack bodies made from coated ripstop nylon are lightweight and relatively waterproof. Those made from coated Cordura packcloth are more durable. Some packs use both fabrics to create a waterproof body with a durable base. Mesh panels on the back, shoulder, and hips — if well designed — help keep you drier. Whatever pack you select, ensure that it has durable, large-toothed zippers, and buckles that you can operate while wearing mitts or gloves. If you never carry crampons, ice axe, snowboard or skis on your pack, save weight; don't buy one with attachment points for those items. Avoid a pack with multiple pockets (you have to remember what you put in each one), or a zip-off day pack. The zippers, buckles, and stitching add unnecessary weight.

### Overnight Packs

For overnight trips, most people require a pack with a 75 to 80 litre capacity. Although you might think that a large volume pack tempts you to take more gear than you need, a smaller pack with odds and ends strapped all over is the makings of backcountry disaster. You might lose gear or have it soaked by rain, and you will have to unpack and repack every time you want to get inside the main compartment. This kind of pack will also sap your energy as the centre of gravity will shift away from your back, throwing you off-stride.

Most backpackers use internal frame packs. Look for an adjustable shoulder yoke, a comfortable hip belt, compression straps, one or two easily accessible outer compartments, and adequate padding. Some models of overnight packs come in tall, regular, and small sizes. You may be of average height, but what is more important for pack fit is the length of your back. Have the pack fitted to your torso by a knowledgeable salesperson. With the pack fully loaded, the hip belt should take two-thirds to three-quarters of the weight.

If your pack does not have zipper pulls when purchased, add short loops of 3 millimetre cord or bootlace to create your own. Zipper pulls make access to your pack easier while you are wearing gloves or mitts, and also lengthen the life of the zippers. Line the inside of your pack with a durable, light-coloured plastic bag. Besides the additional waterproofing, it will make it easier to find items. Purchase a coated pack cover to use on inclement days.

### Day Packs

A pack with a volume of 35 litres is adequate for day-hikes. A zippered hood compartment and a single storage compartment are all that you need. For the day-hiking options on overnight trips, carry a nylon teardrop pack (15 to 20 litre capacity) to stow in the bottom of your backpack, or condense your main pack using its compression straps.

### Tents

Serious backpackers will have two tents — a three-season model for use at any time, and a summer tent for use during occasional fair weather spells. If most of the body of the tent is mesh and it has only two poles, it is a summer tent, no matter how it may be marketed. Keep the following in mind when you shop for a tent.

- Choose a tent that will comfortably accommodate your party; 3.5–4 m2 of floor space for two people; 4–5.5 m2 of floor space for three people. Consider how much room the door allows for entry and exit beside your slumbering partner(s). Your sleeping bag will brush against the walls of a narrow or short tent. In wet weather, this means a soggy bag.
- Choose a tent that is light enough to carry without complaint.
- Choose a tent with a large fly that comes to the ground. If the fly clips to the poles, it will allow better ventilation beneath, reducing condensation inside. Ensure that the fly has buckles and webbing, so it can be cinched tightly to pegs or anchors.
- Choose a free-standing tent. They are easier to set up, and can be dried quickly by hanging them from a tree on a windy day. Tent pads at some campgrounds on popular trails have been hardened and are almost impossible to peg.
- Choose a light-coloured tent. They are more cheerful when it's pouring outside and you are stuck inside. They dry more quickly and it is easier to read inside them. It is also easier to spot mosquitoes and bugs inside.
- Choose a tent with a vestibule for storing gear, and for putting on and taking off boots, out of the rain.
- If the tent has poles of different lengths, colour-coding helps eliminate confusion during set-up.
- Taped seams are not necessary and make the tent heavier. But you should goop the seams on the fly and the floor before each season.
- A good tent is expensive. Spend as much money as you can afford. The poles and zippers on a cheap tent may last only a season.
- Get inside the tent before you buy it. Most stores have display models set-up.

An overhead tarp is a great addition for camp comfort in inclement or scorching weather. Strung between trees (practice at home!), it can provide additional shelter for cooking and eating. You can buy lightweight backpacking tarps or fashion your own from hardware store poly and a grommet kit. Carry a variety of tent pegs — metal and plastic. Believe it or not, the aluminum noodles provided by tent manufacturers sometimes actually work — such as when you have to force a peg between rocks. If the ground is so hard that you can't peg your tent, weigh down the corners by putting rocks inside, and tie the fly to rocks or nearby trees with cord. Do this anyway if it is windy. I once had a tent blow into a creek, sleeping bags and all.

### Sleeping Bags

Even in mid-summer, most nights in the Rockies are cool. Frost and snow are possible on any night at any location. Most backpackers opt for a three-season, mummy-style, synthetic bag, or a summer-weight, down-filled bag. Early and late in the hiking season, some people will be more comfortable in a winter bag. As a rule, carry a sleeping bag rated 5°C colder than the lowest temperature that you expect. A bag with a durable water repellent (DWR) fabric shell will help keep dampness at bay. Down bags are lighter and more compressible but harder to wash.

In any sleeping bag, a hood with a drawstring, a draft collar, a foot box large enough to allow your feet to stick straight up, and a snag-free, full-length zipper backed by a draft tube are essential features. Carry your sleeping bag inside your backpack. Line the inside of the sleeping bag stuff sack with a large plastic bag for extra protection against rain and sweat. (Some people use a paddling dry bag.) If the morning is fair, air your sleeping bag in the sun while you make breakfast and pack. If you won't be moving camp, leave your sleeping bag unrolled in the tent.

Always air-dry your sleeping bag before storing it after a trip — a blast of full sunshine is best. Don't compress the bag during storage; place it loosely in a cloth bag. Something else to think about: don't store it, your tent, or your backpack where they will be permeated by food odours.

## Sleeping Pads

Whatever sleeping bag you choose, a sleeping pad is essential. The most comfortable and most expensive pads are inflatable. Carry a repair kit. Less expensive and less effective (but lighter) are closed-cell foams. Carry your sleeping pad in a stuff sack to keep it dry and to protect it from scuffing and punctures. If there is room, stow it inside your pack. You don't need to buy a backcountry pillow. Fill a stuff sack with extra clothing. Use an old piece of closed-cell foam as a bum pad to help insulate you from that rock or log that you sit on at camp.

## Clothing

A versatile backcountry clothing system incorporates a series of layers that can be donned or shed quickly as required. There is a backcountry expression: cotton kills. Avoid cotton, denim, and leather, as they soak easily, become clammy, and take a long time to dry. Choose wool, pile, fleece, polypropylene, and other synthetic fabrics.

In the Rockies you will need to beef-up your clothing with more layers to combat the chill of stormy weather and high altitude. Always carry a set of long underwear — tops and bottoms, liner gloves, and a pair of heavier outer gloves or wool mitts. Fingerless wool gloves are useful. A pair of knee length socks and a down vest make camp life more comfortable early and late in the season. Top off your cool weather gear with a warm winter-style hat, such as a toque with ear flaps, or a balaclava. If you lose a glove or mitt, use a spare sock to cover your hand.

Rain in the Rockies can be extremely cold. Although your backpack helps keep you warm and dry, you should invest in a full suit of coated raingear, with adjustable cuffs, and a snug hood. Full or partial zippers on the legs assist ventilation. Choose a rain jacket a size larger than normal to allow extra clothing to be worn underneath, and to compensate for the fact that a full backpack will make your jacket bunch at the shoulders. No fabric is completely waterproof. The purchase of expensive miracle fabrics may not be money well spent. Coated nylons can be re-treated with spray-on waterproofing. Your rainsuit can double as a windsuit when required.

What about the sunny days? Shorts, T-shirts, and a sun hat should be part of your layered system. Skin burns more rapidly at higher elevations. Carry an effective sunscreen (at least SPF 30), and apply it liberally. Zinc ointment is the best for fair-skinned people. Don't forget to apply it to noses, lips, cheek bones, and ear lobes. Light-coloured fabrics have two advantages: they keep you cooler and tend to dry more quickly than darker fabrics. (Royal blue is among the faster drying colours.) You can use a large cotton handkerchief or bandana as a scarf, a head cover, a towel, a sling, and a pressure dressing.

Leave a change of dry clothes, including shoes, in your vehicle at the trailhead. You'll appreciate the comfort if you spent the hike in a monsoon or ended it in a blizzard.

## Accessories

Many hikers like the support of trekking poles or a hiking staff, especially when coming downhill. Walking with one or two poles also helps you keep a rhythmic stride, which can save as much as 20 percent of your energy over the course of a day. The extra support is useful, perhaps crucial, when crossing streams. Collapsible poles made especially for the purpose are popular. Several local craftsmen fashion wooden staffs. Don't trust all your weight to these devices. If they shift when weighted, you could take a nasty tumble.

Your sunglasses should block all but 0.1% of UVA and UVB light, and pass not more than 10% of visible light. Glass lenses are more scratch-resistant than plastic. Don't forget to bring a hard case to protect sunglasses when they are in the hood of your pack.

Compact, lightweight binoculars in the 8 x 20 to 8 x 30 range are the one luxury item I would recommend above any other. They are great for birding and for studying other wildlife from a distance. They can also help you tell if that dark blob on the slidepath ahead is a bear or a tree stump. Many respectable binoculars cost less than a pair of good sunglasses.

Twilight lasts a long time during summer in the Rockies. You won't often need a nightlight but you should have one available for emergencies or for hiking early and late in the season. A headlamp is the best choice as it keeps your hands free. LED bulbs greatly increase battery life, but always carry spare batteries and bulb. Pack your light carefully so that it doesn't shine brightly inside your pack all day, only to fail you when you need it.

## Stoves and the Camp Kitchen

A camp stove is a backcountry necessity in the Rockies. Fires are not allowed at many campgrounds. Even if allowed, cooking with a wood fire can be time-consuming – a fact that you will not appreciate during inclement weather, when a quick, hot cup of tea or soup might save the day.

Carry one stove for every two or three people. Use your stove's windscreen to maximize its efficiency and to minimize cooking times. Take care not to scorch or burn picnic tables at campgrounds. Place your stove on bare ground, on a flat rock, or on top of a metal fire-box.

Liquid-fuel stoves made by MSR, Optimus, and Coleman are the most popular. These stoves are lightweight, dependable, stable, and have built-in pressure pumps that allow for easy priming. This compensates for pressure losses due to cold weather and altitude. The stoves burn white gas (naptha, Coleman fuel) — a fuel that is readily available at hardware stores and most service stations. Stoves with the adjustment knob on the burner, rather than on the fuel bottle, have less lag time for adjustments and generally simmer better.

Buy a field-maintainable stove and carry a repair kit. Test and clean your stove before each trip, and learn how to troubleshoot. The 22 ounce (US) MSR bottle is usually sufficient to cook breakfasts, dinners, and hot drinks for two people during an outing that lasts three days and two nights. You will use more fuel if you treat your drinking water by boiling it. Filter your fuel before you pack it. Carry extra fuel in a combination of one-litre and half-litre bottle sizes to allow you to most efficiently use the space in your pack.

Fuel cartridges are usually available locally for the backpacking versions of butane and propane canister stoves. If you bring a canister stove to the Rockies, be sure that it takes a generic canister, as proprietary canisters might not be available. Test fit each canister to the stove before your trip to make sure that they seal, as manufacturing flaws do happen.

Carry two lighters as well as waterproof, strike-anywhere matches. Seal the matches in doubled plastic bags. Check the lighters before each trip and pack them in different places. A wet lighter can be dried in a pocket. Wet matches may take days to dry, and usually disintegrate. Waterproof your matches by dipping them in melted wax.

Stainless steel cooking pots are more durable than aluminum pots. Carry two cooking pots for every two or three people. Use one pot for boiling water, the other for cooking foods. This simplifies clean-ups and prevents the experience of drinking tea that tastes like spaghetti sauce. Carry your stove and pots in stuff sacks. Hang them with your food at night. A cooking pot that is blackened on the outside absorbs heat faster. Don't forget the potholder.

Each person should carry a pocket knife, a plastic bowl, a spoon — don't bother with a fork — and an insulated travel-mug for hot drinks. Most beverages taste better if made directly in the mug, rather than in a pot. The drinks stay warmer too. If you are hiking solo, skip the bowl and eat out of the pot.

## Food

You can take three approaches to backcountry food: freeze-dried; low budget noodle-ectomy; and dehydrate your own. Each has advantages. The first is the most convenient, but you pay a premium price for it. The second is hit-and-miss but great for trips thrown together at the last minute. For those who backpack often, the investment in a food dehydrator will pay back in a season or two, allowing you to create your own backcountry foods with control over the ingredients.

Use reclosable plastic bags to carry meal-sized portions. Write instructions in ink, directly on the bag. With care, the bags can be washed and reused many times. By using a straw to suck air out of bags as you fill and seal them, your food bags will require much less space.

A consideration that is essential, although not obvious to many, is not to pack foods — such as meat and fish — that are attractive to bears. Cooking food releases odours. Some bear researchers advocate eating only cold foods in the backcountry. It's a nice theory, but one that they probably have not field-tested during a blizzard on the Skyline.

Ensure that your diet includes fresh vegetables and fruits. These will keep for two or three days if you pack them carefully. A daily vitamin-mineral supplement will help compensate for a lack of fresh foods, especially if you are backpacking for an entire summer. Salt tablets are hard on your digestive system. Add extra salt to your food instead, to help maintain your electrolyte balance.

Many people find that while hiking they eat more food and more often than normal. Mixtures of nuts, raisins, seeds, and candies are a standby. You lose time if everyone must stop as each group member becomes hungry. Keep trail snacks at hand and snack on the move. If you feel yourself becoming lethargic or cranky, eat! Low blood sugar is often the culprit. Snacking will usually improve your energy and your outlook. Handy snacks will also allow you to keep moving if foul weather makes stopping at the predetermined lunch spot disagreeable. The snacks may become your survival food in an emergency.

Always pack a few extra soups and hot drink mixes. Use them for a hot lunch during inclement weather or as emergency rations if your trip takes one night longer than planned.

Hang your food, stove and pots at night or when you are away from camp. A see-through dry-bag will weatherproof your grub. It's a bit more of a setback than a nylon stuffsack if it gets chewed on by a critter, but the convenience outweighs that concern. To prevent squirrels and birds from eating your trail mix and cereals (their favourites), store these foods inside your pots.

# Drinking Water

One of the attractive things about the Canadian Rockies is the abundance of water. Backpackers often reach meltwater streams within a stone's throw of their glacial sources. This should be some of the purest water on earth. But is it?

No. If your habit is to drink straight from a stream in the Rockies, you will eventually become sick. The hazards are protozoa, bacteria, and, to a much lesser extent, viruses. The protozoan parasite *Giardia lamblia* gets the most attention. *Giardia* (zjee-ARE-dee-ah) is transmitted to water in contaminated feces. The complaint it produces when ingested by humans, giardiasis, is commonly called beaver fever. But beavers get a bad rap; all mammals can host this parasite. *Giardia lamblia* exemplifies why we must take care of water. Endemic to Siberia, the critter now rules the guts of travellers around the world.

Giardiasis, and the ailment created by its more recently introduced protozoan cousin, *Cryptosporidium parvum,* produce general weakness and gastro-intestinal upset. Diarrhea, abdominal cramps, foul-smelling gas and feces, and lack of appetite are symptoms. Lower abdominal pain while walking downhill is a classic giardiasis indicator. The symptoms occur one to two weeks after ingestion of the cysts, so if you become ill on your first backcountry trip of the season, blame your cooking, not the water. Giardiasis is sometimes — but not always — diagnosed through a stool sample, and is controlled by the drug Flagyl. By the time you are done with the disease and the treatment, your innards will indeed feel flagellated. Untreated, giardiasis runs its course in two to six weeks, but many who have been afflicted say they never again feel right. *Cryptosporidium* runs its course in 2 to 10 days and is untreatable.

Bacteria are the next greatest threat. They may cause gastro-intestinal upset and other illnesses. The most widespread bacteria is *Campylobacter jejuni,* which has on onset of two to five days and a duration of one week. Viral threats in Rockies water are generally not a concern, but may include hepatitis.

Responsible attitudes toward human waste in the backcountry will help reduce the contamination of drinking water. As dogs carry protozoa and may also track the feces of other animals into watercourses, it is a good idea not to take Fido on the trail.

The simplest and safest way to completely purify water is to boil it. The US Centres for Disease Control (CDC) states that, at sea level, three minutes of boiling kills everything. Ninety-eight percent of bacteria are killed as the water is heated to the boiling point, so, at sea level, a rolling boil of

## Comparison of Water Treatment Methods

| | Eliminates *Giardia*? | Eliminates *Crypto*? | Eliminates Bacteria? | Eliminates Viruses? | Environmental Rating |
|---|---|---|---|---|---|
| Boiling | Yes | Yes | Yes | Yes | 2 |
| Iodine* | Yes | No | Yes | Yes | 3 |
| Chlorine* | Yes | No | Yes | Yes | 4 |
| Chlorine Dioxide* | Yes | Yes | Yes | Yes | 4 |
| Filter ≤ 0.3 micron pore size** | Yes | No | Partially | No | 1 |
| Purifier | Yes | No | Yes | Yes | 3 |

* Iodine, chlorine, and chlorine dioxide may be hazardous to your health. All manufacturers of chemical water treatments recommend that you filter the water first. Add lemon juice to chemically treated water to improve the taste.
** A larger pore size is ineffective.

any great duration is literally overkill. However, the boiling point of water decreases 1°C for each 300m above sea level. So you would be wise to stick to the CDC directive at backcountry campgrounds. Carry extra fuel if you will be treating your water by boiling it, and budget time for the process and for the water to cool before you put it into water bottles. When it has cooled, boiled water tastes flat. Add a few drops of lemon juice. The following table compares the various methods of treating drinking water.

### Dehydration

Now that you have treated the water, how much should you drink each day? Dehydration affects your body's ability to digest food, to circulate nutrients, to eliminate toxins, to stay warm in cold weather, and to stay cool in hot weather. A loss of just 5 percent of body fluids may result in a 25 to 30 percent loss of physical energy. Dehydration also contributes to altitude sickness and to the build-up of lactic acid, which causes stiff muscles and fatigue.

The best gauge of adequate hydration is to check how often you pee, and the colour of your urine. You should pee at least three times in a 24-hour period. If your urine is clear or pale yellow, you are drinking enough fluids. If your pee is dark yellow or golden, drink at least a litre of water. Any time that you feel thirsty, you are probably down at least a litre. Avoid beverages that contain alcohol or caffeine, as they contribute to dehydration. For every cup of coffee you drink, you eliminate 1.3 cups of fluid by urine.

The trick is to force yourself to drink. Drink a litre of water in the morning before you break camp. Drink every time you stop. Many backpacks are equipped with a water bottle holster on the waist strap. Use it; you are more likely to drink water from a bottle kept within reach.

Use durable, one-litre plastic water bottles. Those manufactured by Nalgene are the best. Most water filters and purifiers screw onto the Nalgene wide-mouth bottles.

Water sources are not always as close at backcountry campgrounds, especially during hot summers when small streams dry up. Carry a water billy to reduce the number of trips you make to the water source, thereby reducing trampling of vegetation. Commercial water billies range from 2-litre to 10-litre capacities. You can also use a re-fillable liner from a 4-litre wine or juice box.

## Answering Nature's Call

At campgrounds and trailheads, please use the outhouses. Toilet paper is not provided. Put the lid down and secure the outhouse door after use. The facilities you encounter on trails range from fibreglass structures resembling sentry pillboxes, to rustic cedar biffies, to open pits. Some backcountry campgrounds have plastic, open-air thrones that, during inclement weather, guarantee a soaking.

If an outhouse is unusable due to the negligence of those who have gone before you, or damage by animals; or when nature calls while you are on the trail, the following guidelines apply. Urinate well off trail, away from tenting areas, and at least 100 m from all watercourses. Mule deer, bighorn sheep, porcupines, and marmots are attracted by the salt in urine. If you pee near your tent, you may find one of these animals chomping on your front lawn soon after.

When you defecate, dig a small cat hole no more than 10 cm deep, in the dark, biologically active layer of the soil, at least 100 m away from any watercourse. Cover your business, including toilet paper, with the excavations. Alternatively, you may pack your used toilet paper to the next outhouse, or toss it in a burning campfire. Use unscented, undyed, unpatterned toilet paper.

## First-Aid

Your first-aid kit should include blister dressings, adhesive dressings, closure strips, adhesive tape, sterile gauze, pain killers, tensor bandage, triangular bandage, tweezers, disposable medical gloves, pencil, and paper. You can improvise splints from branches, packs or tent poles, or from a rectangular piece of stiff cardboard, but a Sam-Splint is a lightweight and worthwhile investment for that once-in-a-lifetime need. Carry required medications and inform your hiking partners of your allergies and conditions. People with chronic conditions should wear a Medic-Alert bracelet or necklace. Insulin-dependent diabetics should be aware that vigorous exercise may affect their response to medication. Anyone with a pre-existing heart or lung condition should be cautious in their approach to backpacking.

When someone is ill or injured, make a quick assessment to gauge the seriousness. Most cuts, abrasions, bruises, sprains, and minor burns can be treated sufficiently to allow the party to retreat. Usually, simple fractures — those with no bone protrusion — can be field-stabilized, but the patient may be unable to hike. Evacuation may be required. Unresponsiveness, compound (bone protrusion) or multiple fractures, choking, difficulty breathing, non-traumatic abdominal pain or chest pain, vaginal bleeding in pregnancy, diabetic and anaphylactic reactions, hypothermia, heat induced collapse (heat stroke), and severe hemorrhage are the true emergencies of the backcountry and elsewhere. In these cases:

- Do not move the person unless the local environment is life-threatening and shelter is nearby.
- Open the airway and assist with rescue breathing, if required.
- Control all deadly bleeding using direct pressure and sterile dressings.
- Assist with medications, if required.
- Cool the heat stroke patient rapidly and move to the shade.
- Warm the mildly hypothermic patient. Handle all hypothermic patients extremely gently, especially if unconscious.
- Immobilize fractures.
- Treat the person for shock. Most injured patients should be kept on their backs, unless this compromises their breathing. Keep the person warm and comfortable. Be reassuring. For medical complaints or compromised breathing, allow the patient to choose the position of greatest comfort. Most will probably want to be propped up.
- Patients who are semi-conscious or who are otherwise unable to protect their airway should be placed in the recovery position.
- Give no food or drink unless the patient is diabetic or rescue is more than a day away.
- At least one person should stay with the injured.
- If the party is large enough, one or two people should seek help, taking a written description of the injury and the patient's location with them. Take note of possible helicopter landing sites close to the patient. Remember that helicopters can only fly in daylight and in reasonable visibility. If you have a cell phone, now is the time to use it.
- In cases of cardiac arrest, limit cardio-pulmonary resuscitation (CPR) to 30 minutes. The chances of resuscitation in the field beyond that are effectively nil.

# Hazards

## Bugs

Although bugs in the Rockies are not as numerous as in the far north or in the lake country of the Canadian Shield, you will undoubtedly become acquainted with black flies, horse flies, deer flies, no-see-ums, and the 28 species of mosquitoes that call these mountains home. Biting bugs are attracted by body warmth and by exhaled carbon dioxide. From the bugs' points of view, some people are more attractive than others. Certain foods and colours also attract mosquitoes — bananas and dark clothing — as do some cosmetics. Whether bugs find you attractive or not, they will eventually find you, so take along insect repellent.

Biting bugs generally become noticeable in late June or early July, and are usually gone by mid-August. Warm, damp weather helps them proliferate. Cool weather kills them off. Breezes keep them away. Campsites near lakes are often bug heaven. Some of the buggier backcountry campgrounds are Luellen Lake, Baker Lake, Amethyst Lake, Lone Lake, Surprise Point, Three Isle Lake, and Lake Magog.

### Insect Repellents

Controversy over DEET — the principal active ingredient in most synthetic insect repellents — has raged since the substance was introduced in 1957. DEET dissolves plastics and removes paints from metal surfaces. It will foul your film, camera, and Gore-Tex. Nonetheless, as of 2002, the US Food and Drug Administration insists that DEET is safe. But Health Canada has re-evaluated its position and is implementing a ban of products that contain more than 30 percent DEET by volume.

Despite the possible health risk, DEET works — repelling mosquitoes, black flies, fleas, ticks, and no-see-ums. (Horse flies and deer flies will be undeterred. All you can do is swat and hope that you crush them before they chomp you.)

If you are wearing non-synthetic clothing, apply the DEET product to the clothing, not to your skin. Wash your hands after application, but remember, DEET-covered hands dipped into backcountry watercourses introduce pollution. Avoid products that combine DEET with sunscreen as, over the course of a sunny day, you will apply far more DEET than is necessary.

Bug repellents made from natural substances (principally oil of eucalyptus, and oil of citronella) are not as effective, so you need to apply them more often — perhaps as often as every

20 minutes. But they are easier on you, and the environment, too. What about citronella-impregnated wristbands, and Avon Skin-So-Soft bath oil? One study found that the wristbands were effective for 12 to 18 seconds and the bath oil for just under 10 minutes; a DEET formula at 24 percent concentration was effective for 5 hours. Ingesting garlic and Vitamin B — two other methods reported to repel insects — proved to be totally ineffective. If bugs really have it in for you, a head net is an inexpensive, lightweight, and effective means to keep bugs off your face and neck.

## Ticks

Whereas the bites of flying bugs are usually little but a nuisance, the bite of the Rocky Mountain wood tick is potentially more serious. Ticks resemble tiny, flattened spiders. They are usually encountered in the montane ecoregion (low elevation valley bottoms) from early April until mid-June. Areas frequented by bighorn sheep, elk, and deer are havens for these parasites. The tick life cycle has four stages, three of which require the tick to ingest a blood meal. It is the adult stage that preys upon larger mammals.

The dangers to humans from tick bites are Rocky Mountain spotted fever (characterized by a headache and fever that develops 3 to 10 days after the tick bite) and tick paralysis (a reaction to tick-induced toxins that can impair functions of the central nervous system). It develops 5 to 6 days after the tick bite. Both afflictions can kill but, as yet, there has not been a confirmed fatality in the Canadian Rockies. Lyme disease, a multi-system bacterial infection that causes encephalitis, is carried by western black-legged ticks. It has been reported from Waterton and from the Cranbrook area in the southern Rockies.

How can you protect yourself? Wear long pants and long sleeves. Apply insect repellent to socks and pant cuffs. Tuck your pant cuffs into your socks. Tuck your shirt into your pants. Wear light-coloured clothing so that you can spot ticks easily. Avoid grassy meadows during May and June. After any outing in tick terrain, search your clothing, equipment, skin, and hair thoroughly. Have a friend check your scalp, neck, and back, and the places where the elastic straps of underwear press against your skin. A tick will usually roam the skin of a potential host for several hours before biting. Ideally, you are trying to find it before it does.

If you find a tick, grasp it against your skin with a pair of tweezers, or lasso it in an overhand knot tied in a strand of dental floss. Pull gently and lift. If the tick comes away easily, its mouth parts are probably not attached. If there is slight resistance, the tick has bitten. Increase the force of your pull, however try not to break off the mouth parts, which if left imbedded, can still cause problems. Once the tick is removed, wash the bite with soap and water.

If you only get the body of the tick, go after the imbedded mouth parts with a sterile needle, or see a physician as soon as possible. If after removing a tick, you detect a red circle around the bite, or if swelling persists, see a physician promptly. Tell the physician that you suspect a tick bite. The diagnosis is often missed. Do not attempt to squash a removed tick – burn it with a match.

Change your clothes and boots, and empty your pack outside after your hike. Go through all your gear to ensure that you don't inadvertently transport a tick or three into your tent, vehicle, or home.

## Hypothermia

Hypothermia (also called exposure) is the lowering of the body's core temperature. It is one of the principal risks in the backcountry, more so because its onset can be insidious. If allowed to progress from mild (37°C–35°C), to moderate (35°C–30°C), to severe (<29°C), hypothermia can kill.

Hikers lose heat in four ways:
• convection (wind);
• conduction (sitting on a cold rock or a wet stump);
• radiation (ambient heat loss into the air);
• evaporation (sweat, breath vapour).

These natural losses are amplified by cool or cold ambient air, by wind, and by precipitation. Any one of these additional factors can make you hypothermic. Yes, you can get into trouble on a sunny day.

The initial symptom of hypothermia is shivering — the body's attempt to produce heat. Soon, blood is shunted from the extremities toward the vital organs. Pulse and breathing rate increase. This is mild hypothermia, reversible by seeking shelter and putting on warm clothing. If allowed to progress, muscular rigidity develops. The person stumbles and slurs words. Thinking becomes muddled. Pulse and breathing rate decrease. At this point, the moderately hypothermic hiker is unable to salvage the situation without the clear thinking and help of a hiking partner who is not affected. The progression of symptoms can take place over a period of days of inclement weather or in a few hours.

Your ability to resist hypothermia is determined by age, body mass, fitness, underlying medical conditions, diet, and effectiveness of clothing, but most of all by common sense. You are (or should be) carrying extra clothing; so wear it! As much as 55 percent of body heat is lost through the top of your head. Wear a winter hat. Watch your companions carefully for the onset of symptoms. Insist that they wear more clothing if you think they are at risk. Take their advice if they offer the same to you. Eat and drink adequately. Turn back or descend if conditions are truly foul.

## A Family Affair

Children can travel safely in the backcountry, if Mom and Dad — or whoever the backcountry caregivers are — are experienced backpackers, able to take care of themselves. The logistics for overnight trips are huge, but not insurmountable. Our first daughter logged more than 500 km in her child carrier during her first summer. She camped out four nights. She did a six-day trip in her second summer, and a three-day trip in her third. She continues to be an avid hiker. At age five she trooped the Bald Hills, Wilcox Pass, and Bow Glacier Falls on successive days.

Babies are easier to travel with than toddlers, because they weigh less and tend to stay put when you get to camp. We used fold-your-own cheesecloth for diapers. We took along reclosable bags to do the laundry, and air-dried the diapers from our packs as we hiked. We carried dehydrated soup and mush for our daughter to eat. The meals would rehydrate as we hiked. Our daughter slept between us in an inverted down vest, with the armholes sewn shut. Marnie carried our daughter and their clothing. I carried the rest of the gear. We never tried it, but it might help to have had a third, experienced adult come along, to help share the weight.

By the time most children are two-and-a-half, they become quite a load for a child carrier. Much of the time, they would prefer to walk anyway, so you are better off doing day-hikes. Our youngest daughter hiked up Parker Ridge just after her second birthday. When offered the pack, she would say: No! Me! Self!

## Bears

Bears are synonymous with the Canadian Rockies. They are the stuff of fear and fascination, and it seems everyone wants to see one — at least, until a bear walks into their backcountry campground. There are far fewer bears than most people realize. Between 150 and 200 grizzlies range throughout these parks. Even fewer black bears occupy the same area. Most backcountry bears are wary of people. With its keener senses, a bear will usually detect you and leave before you become aware of it. You are more likely to see a bear while you are driving to a trailhead than on a trail.

Bears are both a possible peril to humans and a dwindling promise for the perpetuation of wilderness. In the Rockies, wildlife biologists refer to the grizzly bear as the umbrella species. Because it is near the apex of the food web and has tremendous spatial requirements, if the grizzly bear is protected and stable, so are 90 percent of other species that share its habitat. Lose the grizzly bear from this landscape and wilderness crumbles, figuratively and literally.

### Mom's Point of View

A grizzly bear cub enjoys a lengthy apprenticeship with its mother — two summers, sometimes three. This training enables the cub to become familiar with the diverse and seasonally varied sources of food that comprise bear diet. It is partly because the young are with the mother for so long, that she breeds infrequently. The mother bear (sow) will vigorously protect her young in order to ensure their continuation. Coming between a grizzly sow and her cubs is the ultimate backcountry blunder, and should be avoided at all costs.

### Safety in Numbers?

At time of publication, there was no record of a person hiking in a group of four to six people being killed by a bear, and no record of a bear attacking any person in a group of six or more people. Nonetheless, for aesthetic and logistical reasons, most people prefer to hike in smaller groups, and some prefer to hike alone. I suggest grouping together when you are certain that there is a bear about. If you travel in a large group, remember, you have gained nothing if your group is strung out over a kilometre of trail. You are probably safer travelling smartly alone than with five others who are ignorant of bear safety.

### Banquet Time

Black bears and grizzly bears spend almost every waking moment in quest of food to tide them through their five- to seven-month-long winter dormancy. At the peak of this banquet, in August, an adult Rockies grizzly may feed for 18 hours each day, consuming 36 kg of food, representing 40,000 calories. The bears are omnivores, but 85–90 percent of their diet consists of vegetable matter. They work hard to get most of this food. However, they are also opportunists, and will gladly take a windfall dropped in their lap — a kill left unattended by wolves or coyotes, garbage generated by humans, or improperly stored camping food.

## What to Do During a Bear Encounter

Consider yourself fortunate on three counts if you see a bear from a good distance away. First, you are paying attention. Second, you have seen a bear. Third, you have a chance to leave before things develop into an encounter. Continue on the trail if it means you will not come any closer to the bear, but note the wind direction. Until a bear notices you, you want the wind to be blowing from the bear to you. Don't turn your back on the bear until you are well clear of the area. If continuing on the trail will bring you closer to the bear, choose another route.

If the bear has seen you and is far enough away that you feel you can safely leave, do so by quartering away, either to the left or to the right of the trail, giving the bear a wide berth. Do not run and do not turn your back on the bear.

When you first see a bear, assume that it is a sow with cubs until you know otherwise. If you see a small bear, assume that it is a cub until you know otherwise. Start looking for its mom and its siblings.

In a close encounter on the trail, the bear will probably be as startled seeing you, as you are seeing it. If the bear does not hightail it, what you should do as this, or another kind of close encounter unfolds, is governed by the answers to four questions.

- Is it a black bear or a grizzly bear?
- Can you see cubs?
- Did you see the bear approach; did it charge or was it stalking?
- Is the bear attacking you in your tent?

Four principal rules cover the opening of a close encounter with a non-predatory bear.

- Stand your ground.
- Do not run.
- Do not climb a tree.
- Keep your pack on.

*Grizzly bear*

Running away or climbing a tree may provoke a predatory response. You may need your pack later for protection, and dropping it may entice a bear to hang around to investigate. A close quarters situation may be one in which the bear is not interested in you, but simply wants to continue along the trail in the direction it was going. Form into a group; keep children behind adults. Talk quietly to the bear — let it know that you are not a food source. Look for cubs. Ideally, you want the sow to be between you and her cubs. You also want the wind to be blowing from you to the bear, so that it can smell you.

Climb a tree only as a last resort. If the bear has not made contact, climbing a tree is unnecessary and may provoke the bear to follow you. Black bears can climb up to 30 m and grizzly bears can climb up to 10 m — and they can do this much more quickly than you. If the tree is small, a grizzly bear might be able to just push it over. But if the situation dictates that you must, climb quickly and carefully. Bears have hauled people out of the lower branches of trees by

### Possible Causes for a Bear Attack

- You are between a sow and her cubs or have presented a perceived threat to the cubs.
- You have encroached on a buried kill or are passing through an area that offers a secure food source — a lush berry patch, a field of glacier lilies, a marmot colony.
- You surprise a bear on the trail.
- A heavy snowfall in late summer or early autumn has driven bears to lower elevations, where they are in greater competition for food and are more intolerant of people.
- You have encountered a predatory bear.

## Safety in Bear Country

**Do**

- Learn how to identify the two species of bears in the Rockies.
- Enquire at a park information centre regarding recent bear activity on your chosen hike.
- Travel with a partner or two, and stay together.
- Make noise while hiking. Use your voice.
- Make noise more often when travelling alongside streams, through tall shrubs, and across avalanche slopes.
- Continue to make noise at intervals during rest stops and while fording streams.
- Observe avalanche slopes and berry patches keenly before you cross them — use binoculars. Be cautious on trails lined with buffaloberry bushes in fruit.
- Pay attention to bear sign on the trail. Look for tracks and scrapes in muddy areas. Note the direction of travel. Are they the tracks of a sow and cubs? Learn to recognize bear scat (droppings) and diggings. Make more noise if the sign is fresh.
- Stop every once in a while when hiking through good bear habitat. Look and listen.
- Leave the area immediately if you discover an animal carcass.
- If you see a bear before it sees you, give it a wide berth.
- Be especially observant on trails marked with a bear caution sign.
- Cook at least 50 m downwind of your tentsite. Eat all you cook.
- At night or when away from camp, hang all food, snacks, garbage, pots, stove, and strongly scented non-food items from the food storage cables provided, or by rigging your own food storage system if random camping.
- Pack out all your garbage.
- Report any bear sighting or encounter to a park information centre or park warden, for the safety of those who follow.

**Do not**

- Enter an area that is closed due to bear activity.
- Cook or eat in or near your tent.
- Store food in your tent or at your campsite.
- Leave your pack unattended.
- Stop or camp in areas where there is fresh bear sign.
- Dispose of food or food wastes in tenting areas.
- Take fresh meat, fish, or seafood into the backcountry.
- Catch and retain fish.
- Expect that a bear will hear you coming.
- Hike at night.

grabbing their legs. In other cases people have fallen out of trees to their deaths, only to be left alone by the bears involved. If the bear climbs toward you, climb as high as you can. Kneel or squat on the uppermost sturdy branch. Do not leave your legs dangling.

### What If?

• *The bear appears to be nonchalantly eating, but stops often to raise its head and look at you.*
You are disturbing the bear. Some bears have attacked with no apparent warning other than this simple disruption of the eating routine. If the bear is a good distance away, leave slowly by giving it a wide berth. Don't turn your back on it. If the bear is close, stand your ground. Form into a group. Talk quietly to the bear — let it know that you are not a food source.

• *The bear is standing on its hind legs, looking at you.*
The bear is scenting you. Stand your ground. Form into a group. Talk quietly to the bear — let it know that you are not a food source.

• *The bear does not appear to be agitated but has been hanging around.*
Danger! A bear that hangs around the perimeter of a camp may be predatory, waiting for what it perceives to be an opportunity to attack. Leave if you can. If you cannot, make a stockpile of weapons — rocks and sticks — then set off a bear banger. Get out your bear spray and be prepared to fight.

• *The bear is huffing, woofing, slapping the ground, clacking its teeth, rising and falling.*
Yes, the bear is agitated, but it isn't necessarily going to attack. It doesn't matter if the bear is a black or a grizzly; stand your ground. Keep talking to it. Get out your bear spray.

• *The bear charges and pulls up short.*
This is common. No matter the species, the bear perceives you as a threat and is testing you. It may be trying to run you off. If it succeeds, it may begin to think of you as prey. Stand your ground. Have your bear spray ready. Hold up the other hand to indicate stop. Keep talking to the bear. If the bear does not back off and is within 6 m and conditions are favourable, spray it. If it is farther away, set off a bear banger.

• *Deterrents have not worked or you were unable to use them. The bear charges and makes contact.*
If it is a black bear, fight for your life. People have killed black bears with pocket knives, driven them off with sticks, stones, and hiking boots. If it is a grizzly bear, play dead. Roll face down. Clasp your

hands behind your neck, elbows on the ground, legs together. (If your legs are splayed the bear has more leverage to roll you if it grabs one.) If the bear flips you over, roll back. If a grizzly bear stays over you for more than two minutes, inflicts wounds after the initial contact, or drags you away, you are dealing with a predatory bear. The rules have changed; fight for your life.

• *A bear is approaching closely and you are weaponless — no bear spray, no bear bangers, no rocks, no hiking stick*

At least one bear researcher recommends that, at this point, you should turn the tables — that *you should charge the bear.* Sometimes, apparently, it works. But if it doesn't....

• *The bear is attacking you in your tent.*

No matter the species, it is predatory. Shine a light into its eyes. Shout at it. Fight for your life. Don't use bear spray or launch a bear banger from within a tent.

• *You are helplessly witnessing an attack on your partner or another hiker.*

The usual outcome when someone intervenes in a bear attack is that the bear switches focus and attacks the would-be rescuer. This person is often severely injured or killed. If you dare, set off a bear banger and try stoning the bear. Have your bear spray and other weapons ready.

## Bear Deterrent: Sound

There are three forms of bear deterrent — sound, bear spray, and force. Making noise is your first defense. Your voice — whether a shout as you move along the trail, or a gentle hello at the beginning of a close encounter — is the best sonic deterrent. If you make noise while you hike, there is a better chance that a bear will hear you coming. If it does, it will probably leave before you notice it. If you talk to a bear when it has seen you and you are within earshot, there is a good chance that it will not consider you to be a food source.

Bear bells are ineffective. A cowbell would be a better choice, as would rattling a rock in a pot. But it's not much fun hiking with such clatter going on. Clap your hands now and then as an alternative. I have a friend who blows his rescue whistle as a bear deterrent. A prodigious mountaineer with a quarter century of experience in the Rockies, he has hiked more kilometres of trail and bush than you and I and all our friends put together ever will, and has never (touch wood, Rick) had a serious bear encounter. I used a whistle while hiking trails for this edition, tooting it in a non-marmot-like fashion — a few short blasts in

a row rather than one long, sustained one.

Bear-bangers make the biggest noise. They are miniature fireworks that you launch from a spring-activated, pen-launcher. They typically travel 20 to 30 m in just under a second before exploding. The sound is generally sufficient to startle or scare away a bear, if the bear is unaccustomed to the treatment. If the banger explodes beyond the bear, however, the animal may run toward you. Banger shells are a hazardous material and should be treated with care and kept dry. The shells have a life of two years, so inspect them frequently. Banger shells come as rim-fire or centre-fire. Make sure that your launcher is configured to match the shells that you carry.

## Bear Deterrent: Bear Spray

Bear sprays are pressurized aerosols that contain *Oleoresin capsicum* (capsaisin) — the oil from pulverized hot peppers. The spray comes in a canister about 20 cm tall and 3 cm in diameter, weighing about 225 gm. (Smaller, purse sizes are illegal in Canada.) You activate the spray by removing a safety and depressing a tab near the nozzle. The spray severely irritates the eyes and respiratory tract of any critter that breathes it, and will temporarily incapacitate most threatening bears, allowing you to escape. The spray lasts 3 to 6 seconds and forms a cloud with a maximum initial dispersion of 5–9 m. The truly effective range of the spray is 3–6 m, which is face-to-face with a bear. If you spray into the wind or crosswind, the spray will be less effective and may also affect you or others in your party. In rain or at temperatures less than 5°C, the spray may not disperse well. And although it sounds too stupid to be true, there is another method of application that will render bear spray totally ineffective — some people have intentionally sprayed themselves before heading out on the trail, thinking the potion akin to mosquito repellent. Dial 911.

Aim the spray no more than a metre off the ground, so that if the bear comes closer, it is most likely to get the spray in its face. Hold your breath after spraying. If spraying the bear stops its

## People and Bears: Oil and Water

**Between 1971 and 1998,** 131 grizzly bears were known to have died in Banff and Yoho national parks. Of these, 119 deaths were human-caused. Of the 96 human-caused deaths with precisely known locations, 100 percent were within 500 m of roads or within 200 m of trails.

approach, take your cue and leave. But don't turn your back on the bear.

Do bear sprays work? Yes, used properly under ideal conditions, bear sprays have saved hikers and campers from serious bear-inflicted injury, while not causing lasting harm to the bear. Some bears are only briefly deterred by the first spray; they continue to approach. This seems especially true of black bears. Some bears return after fleeing from the first spray and are not deterred by a subsequent spray. Some bears are attracted to the residue of the spray, hours or days after it was used. So don't camp where you have discharged a spray.

Everyone in your group should carry a spray. Practice using it. Buy two canisters. Discharge one on a calm day in a remote, unpeopled place to see how it works. For half a second each year, test fire the one that you will carry.

Remember, if you choose to carry bear bangers or bear spray, they do not replace the care, common sense, and sound judgement required of you when you travel in bear country. As one researcher has stated, bear spray ain't brains in a can.

### Bear Deterrent: Force

Fight a bear when it is clear that the bear is stalking you, or when a grizzly bear has made contact, is inflicting repeated wounds or has not left after two minutes.

It is illegal for most people to carry handguns in Canada, and it is illegal to carry loaded and assembled firearms in national parks. Anyway, disabling a bear with a firearm — especially a bear on the move — requires firepower and expert marksmanship. But if it comes to the crunch — if all other deterrents have failed or seem about to fail — take the offensive with whatever is at hand. If a bear will not leave or follows you when you attempt to leave, if it has made repeated approaches, behaves aggressively, or comes back after you've sprayed it, you must intimidate it to convince it to leave. Shout, wave your arms, begin throwing things. Get out your knife and your hiking stick. Be prepared to fight tooth and nail.

# Recommended Reading

### Backpacking How-To

Since the first edition of *Classic Hikes* appeared, the market has been deluged with how-to books that describe backcountry travel and camping. The book department at Mountain Equipment Co-op's Calgary store carries an excellent

selection relevant to the Canadian Rockies, as do the Book and Art Den in Banff, Woodruff and Blum Booksellers in Lake Louise, Food for Thought Books in Golden, Jasper Camera and Gift, and the Friends bookstores in the park information centres. For a bewildering sense of all that is available, look on-line at Chessler Books (www.chesslerbooks.com), Alpenbooks (www.alpenbooks.com), Mountain Equipment Co-op (www.mec.ca), and Adventurous Traveler Bookstore (www.adventuroustraveler.com). To see Altitude Publishing's complete line of books on-line, check: www.altitudepublishing.com

### The Essentials

Gadd, Ben. *Handbook of the Canadian Rockies.* Jasper: Corax Press, 1995. If it's not in the *Handbook,* it isn't often in the Rockies.

Griggs, Jack L. *All the Birds of North America.* New York: HarperPerennial, 1997. You might find this wonderful volume too heavy to pack, but not so the companion series of pocket guides:

Griggs, Jack L. *All the Song Birds: Western Trailside.* New York: Harper Resource, 1998.

Griggs, Jack L. and Jerry Ligouri. *All the Birds of Prey.* New York: Harper Resource, 1999.

Griggs, Jack L. and Edward S. Brinkley. *All the Waterbirds: Freshwater.* New York: Harper Resource, 1999.

Kershaw, Linda, Andy MacKinnon and Jim Pojar. *Plants of the Rocky Mountains.* Edmonton: Lone Pine Publishing, 1998. Finally, someone did it — three someones, actually — the best plant book on the Rockies.

### Bears

When it comes to reading about bear behaviour and bear-human encounters, there is a fine line between educating yourself and scaring yourself. Many recent titles tend toward the sensational. These three are the best of those that don't.

Herrero, Stephen. *Bear Attacks: Their Causes and Avoidance.* Toronto: McClelland and Stewart, 2002.

Smith, Dave. *Backcountry Bear Basics.* Seattle: The Mountaineers, 1997.

Van Tighem, Kevin. *Bears.* Canmore: Altitude Publishing, 1997.

Eastern Slopes Grizzly Bear Research Project web site: www.canadianrockies.net/grizzly provides the latest information an the status of grizzly bears and related research.

### General Reference

Anonymous. *Leave No Trace.* Lander: National Outdoor Leadership School, 1992.

# Reference

Berger, Karen. *Everyday Wisdom, 1001 Expert Tips for Hikers.* Emmaus: Backpacker, 1997.

Cameron, Ward. *Canmore and Kananaskis.* Canmore: Altitude Publishing, 2002.

Dunlop, Storm. *Collins Gem: Weather.* Glasgow: HarperCollins, 1996.

Hampton, Bruce and David Cole. *Soft Paths.* Mechanicsburg: Stackpole Books, 1995.

Meyer, Kathleen. *How to Shit in the Woods.*

Berkeley: Ten Speed Press, 1989.

Patton, Brian, ed. *Bear Tales from the Canadian Rockies.* Calgary: Fifth House, 1998.

Pole, Graeme. *Canadian Rockies.* Canmore: Altitude Publishing, 1997.

Pole, Graeme. *Walks and Easy Hikes in the Canadian Rockies.* Canmore: Altitude Publishing, 1996. A companion guide to *Classic Hikes,* packed with frontcountry outings.

## Contacts

**To contact** the Minister responsible for national parks, call Reference Canada, 800-622-6232, or visit www.canada.gc.ca. For assistance contacting Alberta provincial parks while in Alberta, call 310-0000. For assistance contacting BC provincial parks while in BC, call 800-663-7867.

**Banff National Park**
Box 900
Banff, AB, T0L 0C0
Banff.VRC@pc.gc.ca
Switchboard: 403-762-1500
Banff Information Centre: 403-762-1550
Trail conditions: 403-760-1305
Banff Warden Office: 403-762-1470
Lake Louise Information Centre: 403-522-3833
Lake Louise Warden Office: 403-522-1220
Weather: 403-762-2088 (24-hour recording)
Highway conditions (for the four national parks): 403-762-1450
Emergency: 911

**Jasper National Park**
Box 10
Jasper, AB, T0E 1E0
jnp.info@pc.gc.ca
Switchboard: 780-852-6161
Information Centre: 780-852-6176
Trails Office: 780-852-6177
Warden Office: 780-852-6155
Icefield Information Centre: 780-852-6560
Weather: 780-852-3185 (24-hour recording)
Emergency: 911

**Yoho National Park**
Box 99
Field, BC, V0A 1G0
Yoho.info@pc.gc.ca
Switchboard: 250-343-6100
Field Information Centre: 250-343-6783
Warden Office: 250-343-6142
Lake O'Hara Reservations: 250-343-6433
Emergency: 911

**Kootenay National Park**
Box 220
Radium Hot Springs, BC, V0A 2K0
Kootenay.reception@pc.gc.ca
Switchboard: 250-347-9615
Kootenay Information Centre: 250-347-9505
Warden Office: 250-347-9361
Emergency: 911

**Waterton Lakes National Park**
Waterton Park, AB, T0K 2M0
waterton.info@pc.gc.ca
Switchboard and Warden Office: 403-859-2224
Information Centre: 403-859-5133
Emergency: 403-859-2636

**Peter Lougheed Provincial Park**
Suite 201
800 Railway Ave.
Canmore, AB, T1W 1P1
PLH.VisitorInfoCenter@gov.ab.ca
Information Centre: 403-591-6322
Emergency: 911

**Mt. Robson Provincial Park**
Box 579
Valemount, BC, V0E 2Z0
Information Centre: 250-566-4325
Berg Lake trail reservations: 800-689-9025
Emergency: 911

**Mt. Assiniboine Provincial Park**
**Akamina-Kishinena Provincial Park**
Box 118
Wasa, BC, V0B 2S0
250-422-3212
Naiset Hut and Lake Magog campground reservations: 403-678-2883
Akamina Creek campground reservations: 800-689-9025
There is no telephone system in either park.

## Birding

Alsop, Fred J. *The Birds of Canada.* Toronto: Tourmaline Editions, 2002.

Erlich, Paul R., David S. Dobkin and Darryl Wheye. *The Birder's Handbook.* New York: Simon and Schuster, Fireside, 1988.

Sibley, David. *The Sibley Guide to Birds.* New York: Alfred A. Knopf, 2000. Too hefty for the pack but a marvel for the serious birder.

## Geology

Huck, Barbara and Doug Whiteway. *In Search of Ancient Alberta.* Winnipeg: Heartland Publications, 1998.

Ferguson, Sue A. *Glaciers of North America.* Golden, CO: Fulcrum Publishing, 1992.

Ford, Derek, and Dalton Muir. *Castleguard.* Ottawa: Minister of the Environment, 1985.

Trenhaile, Alan S. *The Geomorphology of Canada, An Introduction.* Don Mills: Oxford University Press, 1990.

Yorath, Chris and Ben Gadd. *Of Rocks, Mountains and Jasper.* Toronto: Dundrun Press, 1995.

Yorath, C.J. *How Old Is That Mountain?* Victoria: Orca Book Publishers, 1997.

## Human History

Boles, G., R. Laurilla and W. Putnam. *Place Names of the Canadian Alps.* Revelstoke: Footprint, 1990.

Christensen, Lisa. *A Hiker's Guide to Art of the Canadian Rockies.* Calgary: Glenbow-Alberta Institute, 1996.

Christensen, Lisa. *A Hiker's Guide to the Rocky Mountain Art of Lawren Harris.* Calgary: Fifth House, 2000.

Dempsey, Hugh A. *Indians of the Rocky Mountain Parks.* Calgary: Fifth House, 1998.

Hart, E.J. *Diamond Hitch.* Banff: Summerthought, 1979.

Holterman, Jack. *Place Names of Glacier-Waterton National Parks.* Glacier Natural History Association, 1985.

Marty, Sid. *A Grand and Fabulous Notion.* Toronto: NC Press, 1984.

Marty, Sid. *Switchbacks.* Toronto: McClelland and Stewart, 2000.

Pole, Graeme. *The Canadian Rockies: A History in Photographs.* Canmore: Altitude Publishing, 1991.

Sandford, R.W. *The Canadian Alps, Volume 1.* Banff: Altitude Publishing, 1990.

Schäffer, Mary T.S. *A Hunter of Peace.* Banff: The Whyte Foundation, 1980.

Stutfield, H.E.M. and J.N. Collie. *Climbs and Exploration in the Canadian Rockies.* Calgary: Aquila Books, 1998.

## Vegetation

Arno, Stephen F. and Ramona P. Hammerly. *Timberline: Mountain and Arctic Forest Frontiers.* Seattle: The Mountaineers, 1984.

Potter, Mike. *Central Rockies Wildflowers.* Banff: Luminous Compositions, 1996.

Zwinger, A. and B.E. Willard. *Land Above the Trees: A Guide to American Alpine Tundra.* Tucson: University of Arizona Press, 1989.

## Wildlife

Murie, O.J. *Animal Tracks.* Boston: Hougthon and Mifflin, 1974.

Stelfox, J. Brad, ed. *Hoofed Mammals of Alberta.* Edmonton: Lone Pine, 1993.

Van Tighem, Kevin. *Wild Animals of Western Canada.* Banff: Altitude Publishing, 1992.

## Selected Environmental Organizations

Your experience of the Rockies may prompt you to pen a letter or to send an e-mail in support of preservation. These organizations appreciate copies of correspondence sent to park managers and politicians.

### Alberta Wilderness Association
P.O. Box 6398, Station D
Calgary, AB, T2P 2E1
albertawilderness.ca

### Bow Valley Naturalists
Box 1693
Banff, AB, T1L 1A3

### Jasper Environmental Association
Box 2198
Jasper, AB, T0E 1E0

### Western Canada Wilderness Committee
20 Water St.
Vancouver, BC, V6B 1A4
wildernesscommittee.org

These two web sites provide links to many grassroots environmental organizations:
**www.rockies.ca/y2y**
(Yellowstone to Yukon Network)
**www.WildCanada.net**

# Index

The hikes are in **bold**. The **bold** entries best describe the topic.

## Photography

Colour photography (except p. 216) by **Graeme Pole and Marnie Pole, Mountain Vision**

**Glenbow Archives:** 94 (NA-3544-23), 188 (NA-2622-47), back cover (NA 5566-6)

**Hocken Library, New Zealand:** 177

**Hudson's Bay Archives:** 50

**Jasper-Yellowhead Historical Society:** 161

**B.W. Mitchell, from** *Trail Life in the Canadian Rockies* **(1924): 115**

**National Archives of Canada:** 187 (PA 23141), 226 (C009190)

**Royal Botanical Museum, Kew Gardens:** 59

**Dennis Schmidt:** 216

**James Monroe Thorington, from** *The Glittering Mountains of Canada* **(1923):** 120

**Whyte Museum of the Canadian Rockies:** 23 top right (NA 65-226), 51 left (NA 66-262), 70 bottom left (NA 293-3), 74 (NA 66-2251), 86 left (V554/NA 66-1108), 98 left (V14/AC-OP/772), 127 (V14 AC00P/82), 155 bottom (V439/NA 640), 194 right (V622/NA-3), 208 (NA 345-30)

### The Author

*The author with his field assistants at Bald Hills*

**Graeme Pole** has been writing about the Canadian Rockies since 1984. His books include one novel and five non-fiction works that describe the human history and the natural history of these mountains. His wilderness essays and photography have been widely published. Graeme lives with his family near Hazelton in northwestern BC, where he serves as a paramedic. He would love to hear from you about your experiences in the Rockies. Visit his web site: www.mountainvision.ca

### The Photography

**So many readers** of the first edition, asked: "How did you get that photograph?" Successful backcountry photography incorporates three key ingredients: willingness, readiness, and patience. If you want to photograph Floe Lake at sunrise, you must be willing to camp there the day before and get up before the birds. If you want to take wildlife photos, or catch your hiking partner silhouetted against the sun where the trail cuts over the ridge with the entire valley in view beyond... you must have your camera ready. Carry it, a lens or two, and an extra roll of film in a well-padded shoulder or chest bag. Make a rain cover for it. Sometimes, the weather doesn't co-operate. You must wait, and wait, and wait for the light. Patience, Grasshopper. You may have to go home and come back again. And again. And perhaps again.

All of the colour photographs in this book were taken with one of three Pentax K-1000 camera bodies, and Pentax lenses: 24, 28-50, 28-80, 40-80, and 70-210. The only filters I use are UVB. The K-1000 is strictly manual. Its only battery-powered item is the light meter, so I can still expose photos if the battery fails. Early on in my hiking and mountaineering days, I carried a lightweight tripod, but it was the first thing to go as the years began to add their weight to my pack. I compensate now by carrying labels for film. If I need to shoot in low light, I'll load a new roll and expose it for push-processing, labelling it accordingly. Until 1995, I shot Kodachrome 64 and 200. I now use Provia 100.